Protect Your Information
with Intrusion Detection

PROTECT
YOUR INFORMATION
with Intrusion
Detection

Alex Lukatsky

A-LIST, LLC

295 East Swedesford Rd.

PMB #285

Wayne, PA 19087

702-977-5377 (FAX)

mail@alistpublishing.com

http://www.alistpublishing.com

This book is printed on acid-free paper.

Protect Your Information with Intrusion Detection
By Alex Lukatsky

ISBN: 1-931769-11-7

Printed in the United States of America

03 04 7 6 5 4 3 2 1

A-LIST, LLC titles are distributed by Independent Publishers Group and are available for site license or bulk purchase by institutions, user groups, corporations, etc.

Book Editors: Jessica Mroz, Thomas Rymer, Peter Morly

Contents

Introduction

The topic of this book, intrusion detection, is a relatively new technology, which has recently been attracting more and more attention from security specialists. However, as it usually goes with all new technologies, intrusion detection is surrounded by various myths, conjectures, and fairy tales. Thus, the main goal of this book is to destroy most of these myths and help specialists and other interested individuals to distinguish fairy tales from reality.

Naturally, this book is not the only one on the market. However, other publications on this topic have different aims and solve different tasks. For example, there are books that cover the basics of intrusion detection technologies, methods, algorithms and so on. Other books are dedicated to methods of network traffic analysis aimed at detecting the traces of an attack. As for this book, it covers all of the above-mentioned aspects in brief, but concentrates on the tools that implement these technologies — i.e., intrusion detection systems (IDSs).

One of the main problems that a user choosing an intrusion detection system or security scanner must solve is distinguishing between the truth (i.e., the actual functional capabilities implemented in a specific product) and advertising slogans. Of course, it is no secret that the absolute majority of vendors aim to sell as many of their product as possible. This is obviously why the advertising is so "ambitious" and, what's even more important to realize, sometimes are not even close to the truth. Since intrusion detection technology has not reached maturity yet, it is very important for the customer not to be confused by the large variety of available products, but rather to be able to choose one that actually satisfies his or her needs.

Furthermore, after choosing the correct product, the customer must be able to install, maintain, and support it correctly. These topics do not really get covered in sufficient detail in the available publications. I hope that my book will eliminate this lack, and will be useful to those specialists who intend to introduce this promising technology into their companies.

Since there are a vast amount of attack mechanisms, it is impossible to cover them all within a single book. On the other hand, there is really no need to do so, since there are many books covering this topic. The concepts and principles that serve as a basis for intrusion detection technologies are covered in brief, and when discussing them I tried to avoid using mathematical terminology as much as possible. Rather, I made an attempt to describe intrusion detection basics using simple and understandable language. In this book, special stress is put on the practical usage of intrusion detection technology and security scanning. It is up to you to decide if I have succeeded in achieving this goal. Most examples provided to illustrate the technologies under consideration are taken from real-world practice when working with intrusion detection technologies. The book is structured in such a way as to be useful both to beginners and specialists in the field of information security, so that any reader should be able to find something of interest in it.

This book explains how to use and deploy intrusion detection systems in order to make your network perimeter impenetrable from the outside and protect your network from inside against attacks by both external intruders and insiders. I've tried to describe the advantages and drawbacks of available intrusion detection systems, what they are capable of and what they are not, the possible ways in which the technologies under discussion may develop, etc. Furthermore, this is one of the key differences between this book and similar ones, since it is the first one in which an attempt has been made to summarize all advantages, drawbacks, and problems characteristic to all intrusion detection systems and intrusion detection technology as whole.

In general, this book represents a result of my 6 years of practical experience in the field of intrusion detection technology and security scanning. It is based on the materials used in courses on Internet security, intrusion detection, and security scanning that I have taught, and on my practical experience accumulated while working with the described technology. My work as a trainer/certified security instructor at Internet Security Systems also helped to fill this book with practical recommendations and examples.

I should point out that although this book is oriented towards intrusion detection technology, most of its recommendations are also applicable to other areas, such as firewall technologies or detection of financial or telephone frauds.

Intended Audience

This book is mostly intended for security experts whose main duty is ensuring information security in their organizations. First of all, these are security administrators and system and network administrators. These experts encounter various violations of information security, and they are the ones who must install and configure the tools discussed in the book.

This book will also be helpful for heads of information security departments, who must solve the difficult problem of choosing the security tools that are most suitable for the company's requirements, and take into account the specific features of the information processing technologies adopted in their organizations. Quite a lot of attention is drawn to the evaluation criteria that should be considered when choosing security tools. What's even more important, various aspects of justifying your choice from a financial point of view are also covered.

Content Overview

The book is made up of 14 chapters, each of which considers a specific aspect of intrusion detection. The first chapter is an introductory one. It describes the common drawbacks of traditional information security tools, such as firewalls. It also gives examples of real cases of compromised information systems of various companies and organizations, and describes various methods of bypassing firewalls that can be used by intruders to penetrate corporate networks.

Chapter 2 explains such concepts as "vulnerability", "attack", and "security incident". The classification provided in this chapter will help you understand why contemporary intrusion detection systems (to say nothing about traditional security tools) are not always capable of identifying the actual intruder. In addition, the material in this chapter describes the main steps in the implementation of an attack and the methods used by intruders to conceal traces of unauthorized activities.

Chapter 3 explains why it is necessary to use intrusion detection technologies, all of which are based on the following three principles:

❏ Signs of security policy violations
❏ Information sources in which it is necessary to search for traces of security policy violations
❏ Methods of analyzing the information gathered from the appropriate sources.

Chapter 4 is dedicated to detailed coverage of the three above-mentioned foundations of intrusion detection technology. It contains a large number of facts illustrating various criteria that allow you to draw a conclusion as to the presence of an attack within the controlled space. After studying this chapter, the reader will be able to answer the three major questions: "WHAT", "WHERE", and "HOW" to detect. There are two ways of using this knowledge. The first method implies manual usage of the simplest methods of analyzing the information sources when searching for signs of an attack. This approach will be covered in *Chapter 5*. The second approach requires performing the same tasks in automated mode using specialized intrusion detection tools. These tools will be considered in *Chapter 6*, which provides a classification for them and presents the most typical examples.

Chapter 7 discusses some steps that are absolutely necessary, even if you have deployed the most advanced and efficient intrusion detection system. The list of such actions includes:

- Educating the staff
- Developing the security policy
- Selecting and using the mechanisms of system and network logging
- Creating the network map

Chapter 8 discusses such important aspects as justifying the choice of the intrusion detection system to upper management using a language easily understandable to financial specialists. It covers how to calculate the Total Cost of Ownership (TCO) and Return on Investment (ROI), and also deals with several specific aspects of bringing intrusion detection systems into operation in a large network.

Chapter 9 is particularly important, since it provides many various IDS evaluation criteria. Evaluating and assessing the system according to these criteria will allow specialists to make the correct choice in favor of one of the specific intrusion detection systems available on the market.

Chapter 10 is dedicated to one of the most important aspects of IDS deployment, namely, choosing the right place to install IDS components, especially in contemporary switched networks. This chapter, along with *Chapters 7, 8, 9, 11,* and *12,* are the key chapters of this book.

Chapter 11 considers various aspects of practical use of intrusion detection systems, such as:

- Selection of software and hardware for the intrusion detection system
- Installation and deployment of intrusion detection systems
- Specifying the rules for intrusion detection
- Configuring responses
- Improving the security level of the intrusion detection system

Chapter 12 investigates the most common problems related to intrusion detection technology, and gives examples of things that might complicate intrusion detection technologies, as well as methods of eliminating them.

Chapter 13 is dedicated to standardization in the field of intrusion detection. It provides a list of organizations and standards in the field of intrusion detection technology. *Chapter 14* covers incident response, and attempts to answer the question: "What should you do when you detect an attack?".

The appendixes contain useful materials that might be necessary during the actual operation of the intrusion detection system. They include the following:

- ❐ A list of ports frequently used by Trojan horses
- ❐ A list of the ports that are most frequently scanned
- ❐ A list of address ranges that can be the origin of packets that can arrive to the external interface of the perimeter router or firewall
- ❐ A list of first-level domains
- ❐ A list of identifiers of the IPv4 protocols

The text contains a large number of Internet links, where you can find information on intrusion detection. Certain aspects of this information can only be found there. This information is constantly changing at a rapid rate; therefore, some facts might have lost their importance by the time this book appears. If this is the case, I recommend that you follow these links to find newer or more detailed information.

CHAPTER 1

Introduction to Intrusion Detection

"That general is skillful in attack whose opponent does not know what to defend; and he is skillful in defense whose opponent does not know what to attack."

Sun Tzu, "The Art of War."

The Need for Intrusion Detection Technologies

Writing books on information security with statistical data on computer security incidents has become a good tradition. I will continue this tradition and provide the data obtained by the Computer Security Institute (CSI) and the computer security group of the San Francisco department of the Federal Bureau of Investigation. This information was published in March 2002 in the *"2002 CSI/FBI Computer Crime and Security Survey"* report [CSI1-02]. This information is updated on a regular basis, and the latest version is available at the following address: http://www.gocsi.com.

According to this data:

❏ 90% of respondents (large corporations and governmental organizations) have encountered various attacks on their information resources.

❏ 80% of respondents reported that these attacks have inflicted heavy financial losses on them; however, only 44% of them were able to evaluate it precisely.

During the last few years, the number of losses caused by security policy violations has also grown significantly. In 1997, the total sum of losses was $100 million. In 2000, it grew to $266 million, and in 2002 it reached $456 million. The total sum of losses inflicted by Demial of Service (DoS) attacks has reached $18.4 million. The tables provided below present other interesting information on this topic, such as information on attack sources (Table 1.1), the most common types of attacks (Table 1.2), and total sums of losses inflicted by them (Table 1.3).

Table 1.1. Attack Sources

Attack source (by type)	Attack source (%)
Disgruntled employees	75
Hackers	82
U.S. Competitors	38
Foreign companies	26
Foreign governments	26

What is most characteristic about this data is that hackers and foreign governments implement attacks more and more frequently (this index grows steadily each year), while other indices are slightly decreasing.

Table 1.2. Frequency of Attack Detection

Attack type	Frequency of detection
Viruses	85
Internet abuse by insiders	78
Unauthorized access by insiders	38
Denial of Service	40
System penetration	40
Confidential data theft	20
Sabotage	8
Financial fraud	12
Telecom fraud	9

The data in this category has also changed significantly. Compared to 2000, the number of attacks implemented by insiders has been reduced by fifty percent, while the number of Denial of Service attacks is growing steadily.

Table 1.3. Financial Losses Inflicted by Attacks (Millions of Dollars)

Attack type	1998	1999	2000	2001	2002
Viruses	7.9	5.3	29.2	45.3	50.0
Internet abuse by insiders	3.7	7.6	28.0	35.0	50.1
Unauthorized access by insiders	50.6	3.6	22.6	6.1	4.5
Denial of Service	2.8	3.3	8.2	4.3	18.4
System penetration	1.6	2.9	7.1	19.1	13.1
Confidential data theft	33.6	42.5	66.7	151.1	170.8
Sabotage	2.1	4.4	27.1	5.2	15.1
Financial fraud	11.2	22.5	56.0	93.0	115.8
Telecom fraud	17.3	0.8	4.0	9.0	0.4

It is necessary to interpret such reports critically, since they are usually based on the opinions of a limited group of respondents. However, they do allow us to make quite a plausible assessment of the general situation concerning specific problems. For example, according to the fourth yearly report published by the Information Security Magazine [Infosec1-01], 39% of companies were exposed to Denial of Service attacks (compare this to the result provided by the CSI/FBI report, which says 40%). According to the data provided by the consulting company Ernst & Young [EY1-02], the number of attacks implemented by insiders constitutes 41%, which is rather close to the CSI/FBI data. Only the report provided by KPMG [KPMG1-02] was somewhat different. Early in 2002, KPMG polled large corporations and obtained significantly different results — only 14% of the respondents have encountered DoS attacks in their practice, and only 5% have reported theft of confidential information (in contrast to the CSI/FBI report, where this index equals 20%).

Since attacks are becoming more and more numerous and happening more frequently, the problem of identifying them at the earliest stages and reacting quickly and appropriately is a matter of primary importance. In critical situations, intervention must be implemented much faster than is possible for a human being. Another reason for automating the attack detection process lies in the fact that intruders use automated tools to implement attacks more and more frequently. One example found in the literature noted the fact that intruders made 2,000 attempts to access a server, from 500 locations during eight hours (i.e., four attacks per minute). In that case, the automated intrusion detection system helped to track the source of the attack. Without it, detecting of the attack itself and tracing the intruder implementing it would have simply been impossible.

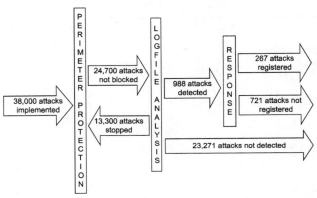

Fig. 1.1. The results of testing the security level of the DoD information system

In 1993, the American Defense Information System Agency (DISA) conducted a rather interesting investigation of the security level of the Department of Defense (DoD) information systems. The invited tiger team (tiger teams are sponsored teams of computer experts that attempt to break down the defenses of computer systems in an effort to uncover, and eventually patch, security holes) proved that in most cases a person was unable to detect attacks implemented during the experiment (Fig. 1.1). The Department of Defense performs such investigations on a regular basis. For example, during 2001, its information security experts investigated about 8,000 computers and detected about 150,000 vulnerabilities.

Information systems must be protected. No one can provide any reasonable argument against this statement. To ensure security, one can choose from the following two ways. The first method of ensuring security is by preventing all attempts of unauthorized access by creating a completely protected system. In practice, however, this can not be accomplished because of the following reasons [Sundaram1-96].

❑ The inevitable presence of software bugs. Bug-free software still remains a dream. Furthermore, few software developers even try to develop it. Most often, a firm's management insists that the product be released as soon as possible, in order to get maximum profit. The most interesting fact is that security tools are not bug-free either. This trend became especially conspicuous in 2000, when reports on vulnerabilities in firewalls, authentication servers, and so on appeared practically each week.

❏ Even a system with the highest level of security is vulnerable, when skilful and knowledgeable users enact the attack. Privileged users can break the security policy requirements, which might result in a weakened level of protection.

❏ The more protected the system is, the more inconvenience one encounters when working with it.

❗ *Potential Attacks on NASA Computers*

• On May 25, 1999, the General Accounting Office (GAO) reported that its specialists were able to intrude upon some NASA systems, including the one responsible for calculating the orbit of one of the space vehicles and the one obtaining scientific data from it. The report states that after a successful attack, it was possible to intercept NASA commands, change the orbit of the space shuttle and so on.

Thus, we can not create a perfectly protected system. Still, it is necessary at least to detect all (or practically all) security policy violations and react appropriately. Intrusion detection technologies, which will be covered in this book, are intended to do just that.

Information System Levels

The Information System (IS) of any company (financial, insurance, trade, etc.) or organization comprises the components intended to solve specific problems. In most cases, a typical IS comprising two or more hosts includes the following four levels (Fig. 1.2):

❏ The application software level. This level is responsible for interface with the user. Examples of IS elements working at this level include Microsoft Word for Windows, Microsoft Excel, Outlook Express, MS Query, and so on.

❏ The Database Management System (DBMS) level. This level is responsible for IS data storage and processing. Examples of the software running at this level include Oracle DBMS Server, MS SQL Server, Sybase and MS Access.

❏ The operating system level. Software at this level serves database management systems and application software. Examples of the elements of this level are Microsoft Windows NT/2000, Sun Solaris, Novell NetWare, and so on.

❏ The network level, responsible for connection between the hosts of the IS. Typical elements of this level are modules interacting according to network protocols such as TCP/IP, IPX/SPX, or SMB/NetBIOS.

Fig. 1.2. Levels of the Information System (IS)

Intruders have the widest range of capabilities at their disposal to violate the security policy at each of the above-listed levels of the IS. For example, to get unauthorized access to financial information stored in one of the MS SQL Server databases, the intruder may try to implement one of the following attacks:

❑ Read database records using SQL queries via MS Query or MS Excel that enable you to access database records (application software level)
❑ Read required data using the DBMS itself (DBMS level)
❑ Read database files using the file system tools (OS level)
❑ Intercept data transmitted via network (network level)

Traditional Security Tools

Statistics are irrefutable, especially when it comes to IS security. According to the FBI data on computer-related crime, from 85% to 97% of attacks on corporate networks are not even detected, to say nothing of blocking them. Experiments conducted in 1995 at the order of the DoD have shown results very similar, those obtained by DISA in 1993. Special groups of experts, also known as "tiger teams," analyzed the security level of 8,932 military objects. In 7,860 cases (i.e., 88%) attacks on DoD objects were successful. The administrators of 390 systems detected attacks, and only 19 of them reported these incidents [Power1-95]. Thus, only 5% of the attacked systems were detected, and only 0.24% of administrators managing successfully attacked systems (or 4.9% of administrators who detected attacks) reported the cases to the appropriate authorities.

Why does this happen? In my opinion, the reason lies not only in the drawbacks of traditional security mechanisms, such as access control, filtering and authentication, among other things. The problem is that most of these mechanisms do not account for many aspects related to modern attacks. Let us discuss these mechanisms, and then, based on this information, consider the existing problems and plan ways to solve them.

Shortcomings of Traditional Security

Let us briefly consider the steps of attack implementation (more detailed information will be provided in the next chapter). First, it is necessary to analyze the prerequisites for successfully accomplishing a specific attack. At this step, one must find vulnerabilities that can be exploited to implement the attack itself (the second step). Finally, at the third step, the intruder completes the attack and removes traces of the illegal activity. Notice that the first and the third steps themselves may represent attacks. For example, a search for vulnerabilities using security scanners such as SATAN or Nmap is an attack in itself.

The existing security mechanisms implemented in firewalls, authentication servers, and access control work only at the second step. In other words, these are tools that may lock an attack, but can not prevent one. In most cases, they protect a network from active attacks already in progress. And even if these mechanisms were able to prevent specific attacks, it would still be much more efficient if they were able to prevent the attacks themselves, i.e., to eliminate the prerequisites of successful attacks. An efficient system of information security must work at all steps of an attack. Adequate protection at the third step of attack is no less important than at the first stages. Only in this case is it possible to evaluate the losses caused by a successful attack realistically and develop measures that would eliminate any further attempts to carry out a similar attack.

However, even if, along with traditional security tools, you are using specialized tools for searching vulnerabilities that detect security holes and provide recommendations on their elimination, your network is not necessarily providing the required security level. There is a wide range of factors that need to be taken into account when using firewalls, authentication, and access control systems. These factors characterize specific features of the technologies mentioned above rather than their points of weakness. Most security systems are based on the classic models of access control developed in the 70s and 80s in military organizations. According to these models, the subject (user, program, process, or network packet) is allowed or denied access to a specific object (such as a file or network host) based on the unique value characteristic for this subject only. In vast majority of cases, this element is a password. In other cases, it may be Touch Memory, iButton, Smart or Proximity Card, user biometrics characteristics, etc. For a network packet, it may be addresses or flags in the packet header, or some other parameters.

One can easily notice that the weakest point of the above-described scheme is the uniqueness of the element. If the intruder has this element, or has somehow managed to replace it, he can provide it to the security system, and the system will take him for an authorized user. Thus, the intruder will be able to act within the range of permissions for the subject whose secret element was stolen. Notice that even top-secret keys are not too difficult to steal, especially when taking into account the rate at which modern technologies are evolving. For example, you can use network sniffers to "eavesdrop" on users entering passwords during transmission via a network. You can crack passwords using specialized tools such as L0phtCrack (the latest version is known as LC3 and can be downloaded from http://www.atstake.com/lc3) or Crack.

Attack on the Network of the National Computer Security Center (NCSC)

Not only normal companies can find their networks under attack, but also specialized organizations professionally studying computer security. For example, in October 1986, the National Computer Security Center's (NCSC) network was successfully attacked. The intruder penetrated its specialized network, Dockmaster, which was intended for exchanging computer security news, including information on its vulnerabilities. By modifying the communication software of one of the European terminals of this network, an unknown intruder managed to intercept user identifiers and passwords. The most interesting fact in this story is that it was not NCSC personnel who detected the intrusion. Rather, it was one of the Dockmaster users [Vacca-96].

Now let us consider yet another example frequently mentioned when discussing this topic. Within each organization, there are users who have practically unlimited network permissions. These are network administrators. They are not controlled by anyone and can do whatever they want within the network. Normally, they use their unlimited rights and permissions to do their jobs. However, imagine what could happen if an administrator were offended by something (for example, disappointed by a low salary, feeling undervalued or anything else). There have been well-known cases in which such employees caused significant losses to their respective companies.

Data Misuse Case

In autumn 1985, the computer security director of the company USPA & IRA attempted to use his position to decrease the sum of taxes that he had to pay, a sum with which he was dissatisfied. However, he was soon fired. Three days later, he went to the office, accessed the company network and deleted 168,000 records from the insurance database. After that, he infected the network with several worms that were intended to delete such records in the future [Vacca-96].

Perhaps you will ask why these problems were not noticed earlier. Actually, the problems were known, they simply were not considered to be particularly important.

This can be attributed to a variety of reasons. First, computer networks have become widespread quite recently — within the last 20 years. Next, the access control models that serve as a basis for contemporary security and data protection systems were developed in military organizations, which have their own specific features — for example, there are practically no users from external organizations. Finally, the number of vulnerabilities of network operating systems and application software and, consequently, the number of possible attacks that can be implemented on their basis is growing at a menacing rate. However preposterous this might sound, the situation is made even worse by the fact that most administrators do not realize the importance of network security problems. Among them, there are few who have time to analyze the latest news about newly discovered vulnerabilities. Those who are able to audit and constantly monitor the network are even less numerous. According to data provided by Jim Harley, the senior analyst of the Aberdeen Group, network administrators have no time to react appropriately and quickly to the growing number of vulnerabilities.

Intrusion detection technologies are intended to eliminate these drawbacks.

Firewall Evasion

If you ask anyone who has at least some experience working with the Internet which tool must be used to protect a computer network from external attack, 99% of the time, you'll get the following answer: "Firewalls." Approximately 68% of respondents consider firewalls "the best solution for ensuring network security" [TechRepublic1-01]. However, although these solutions are rather efficient, they do not provide reliable protection against all types of attacks.

Google versus Firewalls

- As was reported by PCWeek/RE (issue 21, 2001), when Atlanta South Polytechnic University's firewall was temporarily down, the Google search engine indexed the university's internal network and got access to the files containing private information on the students, including street addresses, Social Security numbers, etc.

Why is this so? The reason is, in general, a failure to realize the fact that the firewall system neither detects and nor locks attacks. A firewall is a device that at first prohibits everything, and then permits only those things that must be determined by the administrator. In other words, when you install the firewall, you first prohibit all connections between the network being protected and the external network. After that, the administrator adds specific rules that enable specified traffic to pass through the firewall. A typical firewall configuration prohibits all incoming ICMP traffic, leaving only outgoing traffic enabled, along with some types of incoming traffic based on the UDP and TCP protocols (such as HTTP, DNS, SMTP, etc.). This configuration will allow employees to access the Internet and deny intruders access to internal resources of the network. Do not forget, however, that firewalls are simply systems based on rules that prohibit or allow incoming/outgoing traffic to pass through them. Even firewalls using the "stateful inspection" technology can not state for sure if an attack is present in the traffic. They can only inform the administrator whether or not the traffic satisfies the requirements established by the specific rules.

This fact is best explained by the following analogy. Consider the firewall to be a "fence" around your network, which simply limits access to specific points behind it, but can not detect if someone is trying to dig a tunnel under it. Let us consider some examples that illustrate this concept.

Tunneling Attacks

Tunneling is the method of encapsulating messages of a specific type (which might be locked by the firewall filters) within messages of another type [Bellovin1-94]. Tunneling attacks are possible because most network protocols implement appropriate features. The firewall filters network traffic and decides whether or not to pass or lock packets based on the information on the network protocol being used. Normally, the rules must require that the network be checked to ensure that the specific protocol is enabled. For example, if a firewall enables Ports 25 and 80, it thus allows mail (SMTP) and Web (HTTP) traffic to pass into the internal network. Qualified intruders often exploit this principle of traffic processing. All unauthorized activity is performed within the allowed protocol, thus creating a tunnel through which the intruder can implement an attack. For example, such a security hole in firewalls is exploited when implementing the Loki attack that enables the intruder to tunnel various commands into ICMP Echo requests, and a reaction to these requests in ICMP Echo Reply. Notice that this significantly changes the size of the data field in comparison to the standard one (Listing 1.1).

Listing 1.1. Transmission of the Password File as a Part of LOKI2 Attack

```
luka# loki -d server.test.com
LOKI2   route [© 1997 guild corporation worldwide]
loki> ls /etc/passwd
/etc/passwd
loki> more /etc/passwd
::::::::::::::::
etc/passwd
::::::::::::::::
root:3QZC*SBkLivins:00:0:/root:/bin/bash
```

```
daemon:*1:1:daemon:/usr/sbin:/bin/sh
bin:*2:2:bin:/bin:/bin/sh
sys:*:3:3:sys:/dev:/bin/sh
man:*:6:100:man:/var/catman:/bin/sh
lp:*7:7:lp:/var/spool/lpd:/bin/sh
mail:*8:8:mail:/var/spool/mail:/bin/sh
news:*:9:9:news:/var/spool/news:/bin/sh
uucp:*:10:10:uucp:/var/spool/uucp:/bin/sh
proxy:*:13:13:proxy:bin:/bin/sh
loki>
```

These actions appear to be quite standard for a firewall and for any other traditional network security tool. For example, notice how the TCPdump sniffer logs the transmission of the password file in the ICMP tunnel:

Listing 1.2. Detecting LOKI2 Attack (TCPdump Log-File Fragment)

```
12:58:22.225 client.test.com > server.test.com: icmp: echo request
12:58:22.225 server.test.com > client.test.com: icmp: echo reply
12:58:22.275 server.test.com > client.test.com: icmp: echo reply
12:58:22.285 server.test.com > client.test.com: icmp: echo reply
12:58:28.985 client.test.com > server.test.com: icmp: echo request
12:58:28.985 server.test.com > client.test.com: icmp: echo reply
12:58:28.985 server.test.com > client.test.com: icmp: echo reply
12:58:29.035 server.test.com > client.test.com: icmp: echo reply
12:58:29.055 server.test.com > client.test.com: icmp: echo reply
12:58:29.075 server.test.com > client.test.com: icmp: echo reply
12:58:29.095 server.test.com > client.test.com: icmp: echo reply
12:58:29.115 server.test.com > client.test.com: icmp: echo reply
12:58:29.135 server.test.com > client.test.com: icmp: echo reply
12:58:29.155 server.test.com > client.test.com: icmp: echo reply
12:58:29.175 server.test.com > client.test.com: icmp: echo reply
12:58:29.195 server.test.com > client.test.com: icmp: echo reply
12:58:29.215 server.test.com > client.test.com: icmp: echo reply
12:58:29.235 server.test.com > client.test.com: icmp: echo reply
12:58:29.255 server.test.com > client.test.com: icmp: echo reply
12:58:29.275 server.test.com > client.test.com: icmp: echo reply
```

Another example of a tunneling attack is seen in application-level attacks that search application vulnerabilities by sending packets directly related to these applications

(Fig. 1.3). Internet worms and macro viruses are probably the simplest example to illustrate the use of such tunnels. Usually, worms and viruses infiltrate a corporate network in the form of e-mail attachments. If the firewall allows SMTP traffic to pass into the internal network (and, to tell the truth, I've never seen a firewall that would not allow this), the internal network can be infected by viruses. Let's consider another, more complicated, example. A web server running Microsoft Internet Information Server is protected by a firewall where only Port 80 is enabled. At first glance, this might seem to be an efficient security measure. However, this is not the case. If IIS v. 3.0 is used, then opening the following address: http://www.*domain*.com/default.asp. (notice the terminating dot) allows the intruder to get access to the contents of the ASP file, which might store confidential data (such as access rights to the database). Even if you have installed the latest version of Internet Information Server — IIS 5.0 and applied the Q277873 patch, you still can not consider yourself completely safe. As Georgy Guninsky has said, the request to the address shown below will be passed by the firewall:

```
http://SOMEHOST/scripts/georgi.bat/..%C1%9C..%C1%9C..%C1%9CWinnt/
system32/cmd.exe?/c%20dir%20C:\
```

After passing the firewall, this request will result in running the `dir C:` command.

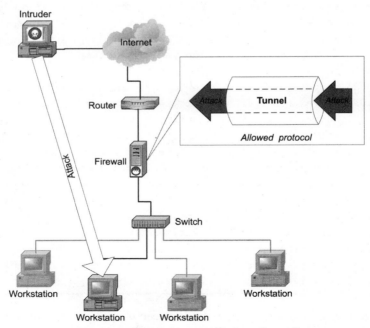

Fig. 1.3. Attack via tunnels in a firewall

Proceeding this way you can run any other command, for example, read the file containing confidential information.

```
http://SOMEHOST/scripts/georgi.bat/..%C1%9C..%C1%9C..%C1%9Ctest.txt
```

Attacks Due to Incorrect Firewall Configuration

As a matter of fact, firewalls and other security tools are installed and configured by humans. And humans tend to make errors. Most intruders are aware of that fact and try to take advantage of it. Just find a security breach in a firewall configuration, and a successful attack becomes possible (Fig. 1.4). This statement can be confirmed by various investigations. For example, statistical data collected in 1999 by ICSA (later renamed TruSecure) (http://www.trusecure.com) shows that up to 70% of all firewalls are vulnerable due to an incorrect configuration. Here I will not even speak about cases where the firewall administrator is not qualified enough (although this is not a rare thing), but rather I will prefer to use another example. Immediately after graduating from college, I got a job in the IT department of a large organization. The Internet connection at that organization was protected by a firewall managed by an administrator from the IS department. Several times, I witnessed situations in which this administrator was visited by friends from other departments, asking him to provide temporary access to certain entertainment servers. Once, I even witnessed a scandalous situation in which a head of department came to this administrator and demanded that he provide him access to an Internet resource. Although this was a blatant security violation, the administrator had to change the firewall settings because he was threatened. This situation is not improving with time. For example, one of the investigations that I performed together with my colleagues revealed the same situation. Firewall settings were providing access to using ICQ, RealAudio, etc. Further investigation showed that the settings were changed because one of the employees from another department, who was on friendly terms with the administrator, asked him to do so.

Listing 1.3. Providing Remote Clients Access to Local Servers by the Telnet Protocol (for IPCHAINS Firewall)

```
Ipchains -A input -i $EXTERNAL_INTERFACE -p tcp \
-s $ANYWHERE $UNPRIVPORTS \
-d $IPADDR 23 -j ACCEPT
ipchains - A output -i $EXTERNAL_INTERFACE - p tcp ! -y \
-s $IPADDR 23 \
-d $ANYWHERE $UNPRIVPORTS -j ACCEPT
```

As a result of these actions, the number of filtering rules increases, and the firewall becomes full of holes, like a sieve. Such a firewall is worth nothing, since it is unable not only to protect the network from the intrusion, but also even to detect it. Furthermore, most filtering rules degrade firewall performance and, consequently, that of communication channels.

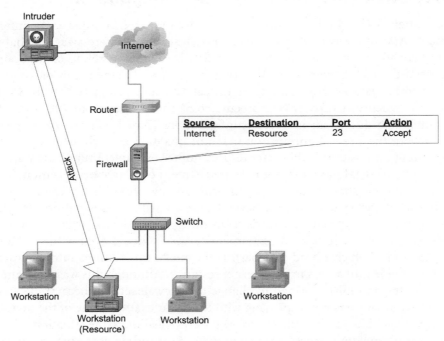

Source	Destination	Port	Action
Internet	Resource	23	Accept

Fig. 1.4. An attack resulting from incorrect firewall configuration

Attacks Based on Bypassing the Firewall

Bypassing security tools is much easier than attempting to implement an attack on them.

❗ *An Example from a Closely Related Area*

- On February 21, 1990, budget analyst Mary Pircham came to work. However, she could not get into the company she worked for, even after entering a four-digit code and saying the pass word into the security system's intercom. Unwilling to be late, she opened the back door entrance with a plastic fork and pocket screwdriver. This security system that Mary so easily bypassed was new and promoted as "reliable and secure," having cost $44,000 [Vacca 1-96].

A similar situation exists with the firewalls. In these cases, a modem can be used as a backdoor entrance. Do you know how many modems are installed in your corporate network and for what purpose are they used? Do not answer "yes" immediately. Consider this situation and carefully think it over. When my organization investigated a corporate network, the head of the IS department stated that he knew precisely all the modems installed in the network. However, after running the Internet Scanner program, we detected all the modems he specified that were used for updating the accounting and legal databases, plus two extra modems. One of these modems was used by an analyst in order to access his directories from home, while the second modem was used for Internet access, bypassing the firewall (Fig. 1.5).

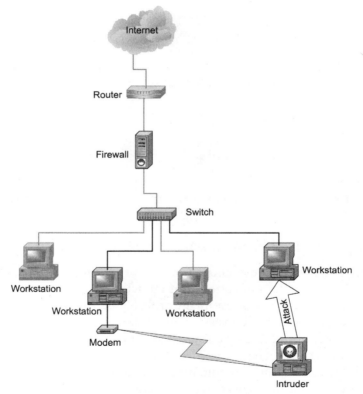

Fig. 1.5. Bypassing a firewall (via a modem)

Not all risks originate on the external side of the firewall. Rather significant losses are caused by security incidents caused by internal users. It is necessary to mention once again that firewalls only filter the traffic at the boundaries between the internal network and the Internet. If the traffic that uses security breaches does not pass via the firewall, then the firewall will never find anything suspicious (Fig. 1.6).

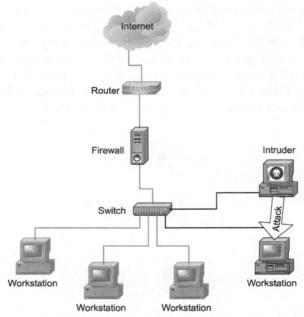

Fig. 1.6. Attacks bypassing the firewall (conducted by employees)

Attacks by Trusted Hosts and Networks

Since most organizations use encryption for protecting files and external network connections, the intruder's interest will be attracted to those locations in the networks where the information of interest might probably be stored and transmitted without protection, i.e., to the trusted hosts or networks. Even if you create a VPN connection between a network protected by a firewall and a trusted network, the intruder will be able to attack efficiently. Furthermore, in this case there is a higher probability of successful attacks, since security requirements for trusted networks and hosts are often lower than similar requirements to other hosts and networks (Fig. 1.7).

▌ WatchGuard Firewall Vulnerability

- In July 2002, a new WatchGuard SOHO Firewall vulnerability was detected. This vulnerability allowed the intruder to be authenticated via the FTP protocol (enabled by default and required for updating the firewall software) without providing a correct username, and then crack the password of the firewall administrator. A specific feature of this vulnerability lies in the fact that such access was allowed only from the internal interface of the firewall (Trusted Network interface).

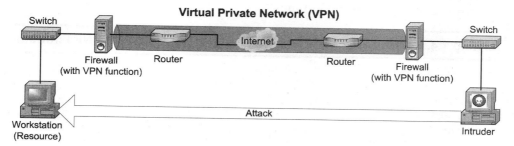

Fig. 1.7. Attack from a trusted network via a VPN connection

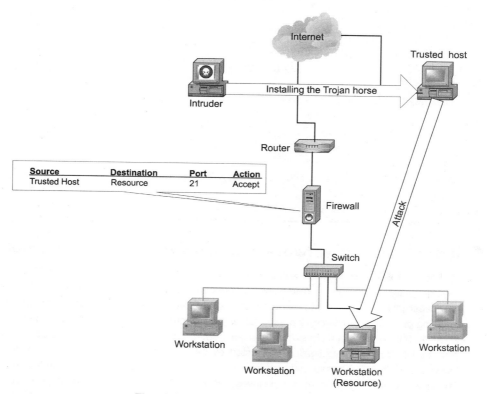

Fig. 1.8. Attack using a Trojan horse

It is possible here to provide an interesting example. Suppose that the administrator is not particularly skilful (or is simply careless). In this case, the intruder can infect the trusted host with a Trojan horse, and then attack the protected network from his own computer. The firewall will interpret all the actions as if they were originating at the trusted host (Fig. 1.8 and Listing 1.4).

Listing 1.4. Remote Attack with the FTP Protocol (for the IPCHAINS Firewall)

```
# incoming and outgoing FTP requests
ipchains -A input -i $EXTERNAL_INTERFACE -p tcp \
-s $ANYWHERE $UNPRIVPORTS \
-d $IPADDR 21 -j ACCEPT
ipchains -A output -i $EXTERNAL_INTERFACE -p tcp ! -y \
-s $IPADDR 21 \
-d $ANYWHERE $UNPRIVPORTS -j ACCEPT
# normal transmission mode
ipchains -A input -i $EXTERNAL_INTERFACE -p tcp \
-s $ANYWHERE $UNPRIVPORTS \
-d $IPADDR 20 -j ACCEPT
ipchains -A output -i $EXTERNAL_INTERFACE -p tcp ! -y \
-s $IPADDR 20 \
-d $ANYWHERE $UNPRIVPORTS -j ACCEPT
# passive transmission mode
ipchains -A input -i $EXTERNAL_INTERFACE -p tcp \
-s $ANYWHERE $UNPRIVPORTS \
-d $IPADDR $UNPRIVPORTS -j ACCEPT
ipchains -A output -i $EXTERNAL_INTERFACE -p tcp ! -y \
-s $IPADDR $UNPRIVPORTS \
-d $ANYWHERE $UNPRIVPORTS -j ACCEPT
```

Attack on the Network of the Johnson Space Center

In March 1995, the security administrator of the Johnson Space Center got a message saying that two computers running Sun OS were under attack by intruders. However, the results of the investigation showed that both computers were compromised earlier (in December 1994) by installing programs for intercepting user IDs and passwords. The logs of these programs contained about 1,300 identifiers and passwords of users from more than 130 systems connected to the compromised hosts. The investigation conducted by experts from JSC and CERT showed that the intruder exploited OS vulnerability, which allowed to log onto the system without a password. The losses were not significant, but the investigation still required months of work. The investigation was performed using the COPS security analysis system [Vacca-96].

Attacks by Source Address Spoofing

Address spoofing is a method of hiding the real address of the intruder. However, it can also be used to bypass a firewall. Notice that the simplest methods, such as replacing the address of the source of network packets with the address of one of the hosts within protected network, can not deceive contemporary firewalls. For the moment, practically all firewalls are protected from this fraud. However, the principle of address substitution in itself still remains an urgent issue. For example, an intruder might substitute his real address with the address of the host having a trusted relationship with the system under attack. This method is different from the above-described one, since, in this case, the intruder only replaces the address by the address of the trusted host (Fig. 1.9).

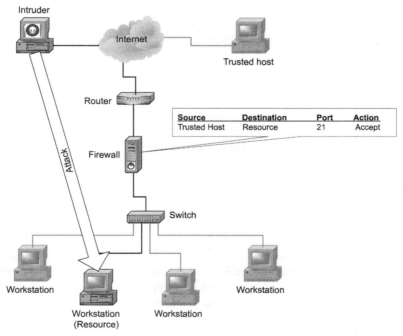

Fig. 1.9. Attack by address spoofing

Attacking the Firewall Itself

Firewalls are themselves often subject to attack. For example, by successfully attacking the firewall, intruders can freely access the resources of the protected network without the risk of being detected and traced (Fig. 1.10).

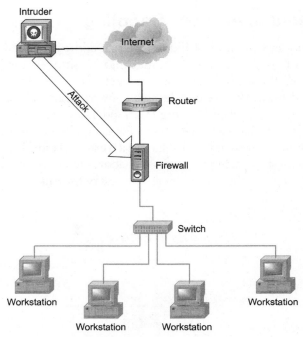

Fig. 1.10. Attack on the firewall

! *Vulnerability of the Raptor, Symantec Enterprise Firewall, VelociRaptor, and Symantec Gateway Security firewalls*

In August 2002, a vulnerability in the IP stack was detected for the following firewalls from Symantec — Raptor, Symantec Enterprise Firewall, VelociRaptor, and Symantec Gateway Security. This vulnerability relates to the fact that the Initial Sequence Number of the TCP packet is not random. This allows you to intercept any connection passing through the firewall.

! *Lucent Brick VPN Firewall Vulnerabilities*

By the end of June 2002, three serious vulnerabilities were simultaneously detected in the Lucent Brick VPN Firewall. These vulnerabilities enabled the intruder to terminate the connection between the firewall and its management console, force the firewall to pass ARP packets regardless of the existing rules, and remotely detect the presence of a firewall in the network.

Attacks on the Firewall Authentication System

As was already mentioned above, even the most powerful and reliable firewall will not protect a corporate network from intrusion if an intruder manages to steal or crack the password of a legitimate user. Furthermore, in this case, the firewall will not even register a security violation, because it will interpret the intruder as an authorized user (Fig. 1.11).

Cisco PIX Firewall Vulnerability

In June 2002, a new vulnerability was detected in the password encryption mechanisms implemented by the `passwd` and `enable` commands of the Cisco PIX Firewall. This vulnerability was due to the fact that, instead of the theoretical limitation (255^{16} possible values of a 16-character password), another number (80^{16} values) was used in practice. This allows the intruder to crack the password within a reasonably short time.

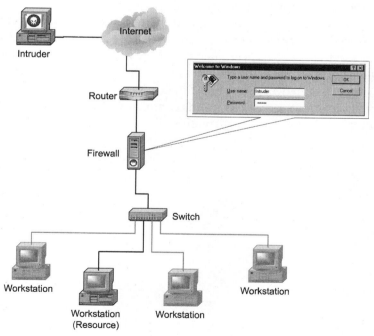

Fig. 1.11. Attack using an intercepted password

Another threat (which was already mentioned) is presented by administrators with unlimited permissions in the managed network.

Community Alert Network Damage

The Risk Digest Bulletin (No. 13.062) describes a security incident that happened at the Chevron oil refinery plant in Richmond (Virginia, USA). This plant was equipped with a Community Alert Network (CAN) system that was intended to inform the local community of any possible danger. A former employee of the New York CAN department, who felt wronged by his termination, introduced malicious changes into the CAN software. Some time later, an emergency situation arose caused by an oil leakage, but the system was not functioning and did not warn the local population of the danger [Vacca1-97].

Summary

Traditional security tools do not provide a high enough level of protection. This, however, does not mean that you need to give up using them. These tools, when correctly confugured, can provide the minimum required level of safety and security for corporate resources. As was already mentioned, traditional security tools were developed when networks were not so common, and methods of attacking these networks were not as advanced as they are today. To take adequate countermeasures for new methods of attacks, it is necessary to understand how these attacks are implemented, what makes them possible and so on. This will enable you not only to take the required steps to protect the network, but also to get a sound understanding of the tools that can detect and prevent such attacks, thus complementing the traditional security tools by extending their functional capabilities. These topics will be covered in the next chapter.

CHAPTER 2

Anatomy of an Attack

"Hence the saying: If you know the enemy and know yourself, you need not fear the result of a hundred battles. If you know yourself but not the enemy, for every victory gained you will also suffer a defeat. If you know neither the enemy nor yourself, you will succumb in every battle."

Sun Tzu, "The Art of War."

In the previous chapter, we considered the drawbacks of traditional security tools (such as firewalls, for example). However, before we proceed any further with a discussion of the mechanisms and tools for detecting intrusions and finding vulnerabilities used to complement traditional mechanisms and improve the safety and security of the corporate network, it would be reasonable to describe what the attacks are, how they are classified and how they are implemented. Without this knowledge, it would be rather difficult efficiently to detect attacks and prevent their negative impact on the resources of a corporate information system (IS). Systematic information on attacks and vulnerabilities helps to explain the drawbacks of traditional security mechanisms and tools described in the previous chapter. Furthermore, to take efficient countermeasures, which can help to prevent attacks on the hosts of a corporate network, administrators must have a sound understanding of the methods used by intruders. This book is not aimed at covering every single vulnerability, attack and method of intrusion in great detail. However, it is necessary to provide general concepts, illustrated by examples. Without at least getting acquainted with them, it would hardly be possible to understand the principles and mechanisms of intrusion detection.

Security Events

As network hosts function, various events take place within them that change their state. In terms of security, these events (Fig. 2.1) can be represented by the following two components — action and target. Actions are steps taken by a specific subject (a user, process, etc.) in order to achieve a specific result. They include the following operations: reading, copying, modifying, deleting, and so on. A target represents a logical (an account, process, or data) or physical (a host, network, or component) system object.

User access to a file is an example of an event. When this event happens in accordance with security rules, it is considered to be a normal event. An event is an elementary unit used in current security tools. Although most security tools include a third parameter, namely, an event source, we will not include it in this description of a security model, because this parameter becomes significant only when a real attack exists.

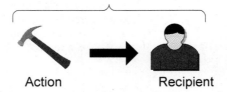

Action   Recipient

Fig. 2.1. A model of a security event

As soon as specific event violates security policy, it must be taken to be a part of an attack.

Vulnerabilities

A vulnerability is any characteristic of an information system that can result in the implementation of a threat if exploited by an intruder. A threat to the information system is any possible event, action, process or phenomenon that can potentially inflict damage on system resources.

! *An Error in Software Code Resulted in a Space Rocket Explosion*

On June 4, 1996 at 9:33:59 a.m., the Ariane 5 rocket attempted its first take-off at a rocket site in French Guiana. The rocket took off and, 40 seconds afterwards, it exploded when it was 50 meters in the air. According to various data sources, the explosion caused $500 million to $6 billion of damages. A month and a half later, on July 19, a committee investigating the cause of this crash published a detailed report stating that the explosion was caused by an overflow error in the software of the on-board computer.

Classification of Vulnerabilities

If you want to devote your efforts to searching and eliminating vulnerabilities, it is necessary to classify them efficiently. If you have no systematic information on either the vulnerabilities or the frequency of their arrival, you can not distribute your limited resources effectively in order to achieve the goal you have set for yourself.

My intentions were not to develop a vulnerability classification and to publish it in this book. Rather, my intentions were more practical. However, it is necessary to characterize the main trends of investigations in this area. This is necessary for IS professionals in order to understand the full importance of this work and its possible complications.

One of the first investigations in this area took place in the mid-70s as a part of the Protection Analysis Project, and was aimed at investigating the vulnerabilities of various operating systems. Within several years, the project participants published articles describing vulnerability categories and vulnerability detection methods. The suggested methods of detection were based on the patterns they had found. The main purpose of the project was to develop ways of searching for vulnerabilities that would not require that personnel be particularly knowledgeable in the field of informational security. However, the methods developed as a result of this investigation could not be easily automated, and the resulting vulnerability database was never published [Aslam1-96].

At approximately the same time, the RISOS project took place. The aims of this project were to classify the vulnerabilities of existing operating systems, and to suggest methods to eliminate them. The operating systems OS/MVT, UNIVAC, and TENEX were studied in the course of this investigation. However, the vulnerability categories developed as a result of this project were too general, which led to ambiguities, such as including the same vulnerability in two different categories.

In 1996, the COAST laboratory at Purdue University developed its own classification [Aslam-96]. Internet Security Systems (ISS) independently developed another one [ISS1-99], which lists the following types of vulnerabilities:

❑ Vulnerabilities implemented or created by a vendor (developer) of software or hardware
❑ Vulnerabilities added by an administrator in the course of the configuration and management of system components
❑ Vulnerabilities introduced by the user in the course of working with the system

Vulnerabilities implemented by the vendor (developer) include the following: errors, OS patches, and hotfixes that were not installed, vulnerable services and configurations that are insecure by default.

Vulnerabilities related to the actions of an administrator include available, but incorrectly used, system settings and parameters, which do not satisfy the requirements of a security policy (for example, the requirements for a minimum password length or unauthorized changes to the system's configuration).

Vulnerabilities related to user activity include non-observance of the rules specified by the security policy, such as neglecting to start anti-virus scanners, using modems to access the Internet bypassing the firewalls, and other, more dangerous actions.

From my own practical experience, I have worked out a somewhat different classification, reflecting the various stages of an information system's life cycle (Table 2.1).

Table 2.1. Vulnerability Categories

Stage of the IS life cycle	Vulnerability category
Design	Design vulnerabilities
Implementation	Implementation vulnerabilities
Operation	Configuration vulnerabilities

A similar classification (however, without explicit linking to the stages of the information system's life cycle) is provided in the section titled *"A Taxonomy of Computer and Network Attacks"* in John Howard's thesis [Howard1-97] and his subsequent publications on the topic [Howard1-98]. The above-mentioned thesis used the term "error" rather than the commonly accepted term "vulnerability." In subsequent work [Howard1-98], this term was replaced by "vulnerability," which is more correct. This classification is used in this book to describe security incidents.

Design Vulnerabilities

This type of vulnerability is the most serious, since such vulnerabilities are hard to detect and eliminate. In this case, the vulnerability is inherent to the project or algorithm and, therefore, even perfect implementation (which is practically impossible) can not eliminate this flaw. A typical example of such a vulnerability is the TCP/IP protocol-stack vulnerability. Since security requirements were underestimated when designing this protocol stack, new vulnerabilities in the TCP/IP protocol stack are detected and reported each month. Even worse, these drawbacks can not be eliminated once and for all — one can only take temporary or limited measures. However, there might be exceptions to this rule. Consider, for example, the project of a corporate network comprising a large number of modems that simplify the lives of employees but, at the same time, make the security personnel's tasks much more difficult. As a result of this flaw in design, several potential ways of bypassing the firewall may appear. If this occurs, such a vulnerability can be easily detected and eliminated.

Implementation Vulnerabilities

The idea of the vulnerabilities included in this category is based on the fact that an error is introduced into the hardware or software at the implementation stage of the project or algorithm, which, in terms of security, is accurate. Buffer overflow errors in implementations of most programs (for example, sendmail or Internet Explorer) represent typical examples of such a vulnerability. According to [Infosec1-01], 32% of all companies experience problems caused by buffer overflow. Vulnerabilities of this type are relatively easy to find and get rid of. If you do not have the source code of a vulnerable application, this vulnerability can be eliminated by upgrading software, or one can stop using it altogether.

Problems with eBay Again

In April 2002, a dangerous vulnerability in the password protection system of the eBay site was reported. As a result, intruders could change the password of any registered eBay user and get full access to their accounts, including information on the bids, items being sold, and credit-card numbers. The most dangerous fact is that, in order to steal a user's account, there is no need to perform any sophisticated manipulations or use complex software tools, since this attack can be done by just a few easy manipulations with two eBay pages. As the eBay representative declared when answering questions for Newsbytes, the company knew about this vulnerability in January 2002 (!), and was considering various methods of eliminating this vulnerability. They promised to take actual measures by the end of summer, when they were due to update the security tools installed on the site. Until then, users had to trace suspicious changes to their accounts on their own.

Configuration Vulnerabilities

The last reason that might cause vulnerabilities to appear involves software or hardware configuration errors. Along with implementation vulnerabilities, this type is the most common. For example, this category includes the Telnet service available, but not used, at the host, security rules that allow one to set "weak" passwords or passwords with less than 6 characters, default passwords left for built-in user accounts (such as SYSADM or DBSNMP for Oracle DBMS) and so on.

Incorrect Configuration of the ICANN Switch

In April 2002, several vulnerabilities were detected in the computer network of the Internet Corporation for Assigned Names and Numbers (ICANN). In the first case, ICANN specialists detected that the switch that serviced the computer networks of the organization could be freely accessed. This vulnerability allowed anyone to change the switch settings using just a Web browser. In the second case, the source code and other information on the system used for processing the results of investigations of disputed domains could also be freely accessed.

These vulnerabilities are the easiest to locate and eliminate (Table 2.2). The main problem in this case is determining if the configuration is vulnerable.

Table 2.2. Capabilities of Locating and Eliminating Vulnerabilities

Vulnerability category	Detection	Elimination
Design vulnerabilities	Time-consuming and difficult	Time-consuming and difficult (sometimes simply impossible)
Implementation vulnerabilities	Relatively time-consuming and difficult	Easy, but might be time-consuming
Configuration vulnerabilities	Quick and easy	Quick and easy

Western Union Database Hacked

On September 8, 2000, Western Union reported that an unknown intruder had copied information from more than 15,700 of their clients' credit cards. According to their statement, it was human error that led to this mishap. Western Union representatives said that the intrusion took place in the course of regular maintenance work. During these operations, system files, which normally could only be accessed by administrators, were accessible to others as well. Western Union insisted that the success of this attack was due to human error rather than to a system security problem. In addition, the FBI states that the information was stolen from the Western Union database by Russian hackers Alexei Ivanov and Vasily Gorshkov, who were arrested in April 2001.

According to statistics published in 1998 by SANS, the five most common vulnerability groups are as follows:

- Network snooping, especially in order to steal passwords or other confidential information
- Buffer overflow, which results in providing a hacker with the capability to run any command remotely
- Security vulnerabilities of specific hosts, for example, CGI scripts vulnerabilities or sendmail errors
- Denial of Service (DoS) attacks
- Vulnerability to loading malicious code, which, besides viruses and Trojan horses, includes some Java applets and ActiveX controls

One can easily notice that the "top five" includes vulnerabilities from all three categories. Password tracking is possible because of the lack of encryption mechanisms in standard Internet protocols (FTP, Telnet, POP3, HTTP, and so on). Buffer overflow, host vulnerabilities and vulnerabilities to DoS attacks can be classified as implementation vulnerabilities and configuration vulnerabilities. Finally, the possibility of loading malignant code falls into the configuration vulnerabilities group.

The most interesting fact is that the list of "top" vulnerabilities changes each year. This proves that the theory on the dynamic evolution of the network technologies is correct, and can be applied to those used in the field of information security [SANS1-01]. There are several reports intended to help security administrators in identifying the most dangerous security holes that must be eliminated first and as soon as possible. Investigations in this area are performed by ISS [ISS2-02], Riptech [Riptech1-02], SecurityTracker [SecurityTracker1-02], SecurityFocus [SecurityFocus1-02], and so on. However, the best-known and most trusted description of common attacks and vulnerabilities is done by the SANS Institute (http://www.sans.org) and the National Infrastructure Protection Center (http://www.nipc.gov), which, before June 25, 2001, published "*The Top 10 Most Critical Internet Security Threats List.*" On October 1, 2001, a new project was launched, based on the Top10 project that was prematurely closed ("*The Twenty Most Critical Internet Security Vulnerabilities*"). In contrast to the Top 10, the Top 20 project was developed by SANS in cooperation with the FBI (http://www.fbi.gov). The steady growth in the number of reported vulnerabilities (especially after the events of September 11 and the epidemics of the Nimda and Red Code viruses) has resulted in doubling the number of vulnerabilities covered by the list. Further, the vulnerabilities listed in the document were subdivided into three classes:

❑ Vulnerabilities common for all platforms
❑ Windows-specific vulnerabilities
❑ Unix-specific vulnerabilities

The Top 20 list is updated on a regular basis. At the time of writing, the latest update — version 2.504, from May 2, 2002 — was available for download at http://www.sans.org/top20.htm. I will not cover all 20 vulnerabilities, but rather will concentrate on the "top seven" security holes, characteristic for absolutely all systems:

❑ "Default" installations of operating systems and applications
❑ Accounts with no passwords or weak passwords
❑ Non-existent or incomplete backups
❑ Large number of open ports
❑ Lack of packet filtering for incoming and outgoing traffic
❑ Non-existent or incomplete logging
❑ Vulnerable CGI scripts

Attacks

Up to now, security specialists have not come to a consensus on the exact definitions of the terms "attack" or "intrusion." Nearly every professional has their own interpretation of these terms. For example: "An intrusion is any action that results in the violation of security policy" or "any action that results in the breach of integrity, confidentiality, and availability of the system and information processed within it." However, I consider the usage of the term described below to be the most correct and closely related to the term "vulnerability." An *attack* on an information system is any action or sequence of interrelated actions by an intruder that results in a threat to the system by exploiting its vulnerabilities. Also, it should be noted that some types of attacks (for example, those based on social engineering) that can also be used for compromising IS are, for the most part, not in the scope of this book. The definition provided here is rather illustrative, and covers practically the whole range of possible attacks, including "social engineering," which primarily uses human weak points. Notice that humans are also part of the information system, just like the computers. Therefore, they also can be considered "weak links."

An attack is different from a security event in that, in the case of an attack, the intruder deliberately tries to get a specific result, which is in direct defiance of the security policy. For example, a user logging in or accessing a file are security events. However, if the user logs in or accesses a file, bypassing files permissions, this event turns into an attack. An analysis of symptoms characterizing an attack will help to determine whether or not this specific case actually represents an attack. These symptoms are described in detail in *Chapter 4*. If we expand the above-described model of a security event, we will get an attack model comprising four elements (Fig. 2.2).

Attack

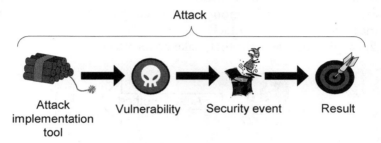

Attack implementation tool   Vulnerability   Security event   Result

Fig. 2.2. Attack model

To implement an attack, the intruder models a specific security event that produces the required result, using some tool exploiting the system's vulnerabilities. The first two elements of this model are used to implement a security event that represents a specific action on the target that violates the security policy.

Before we start to discuss automated tools of intrusion detection, it is necessary to point out that they detect attacks and security events, rather than security incidents. The models shown in Figs. 2.1 and 2.2 do not include such components as "attacker" or "intruder." This component appears only in the description of a security incident. This explains the fact that intrusion detection systems are not always capable of tracing intruders who implement specific attacks.

At the present moment, the actual number of attack methods available is unknown. This is mainly due to the lack of serious mathematical investigations into this area. Among the most important works in a related area, which deserves mention, is the work of Fred Cohen, who made an attempt to describe the mathematical foundations of virus technology. The most interesting result of this work is mathematical proof of the fact that the possible number of viruses is infinite. These results can be extrapolated to attack theory, since viruses are simply a subset of attacks.

In other words, especially when recalling the well-known scientific proverb "a negative result is also a result," we can draw the conclusion that, if an intruder has not achieved the desired result but still exploits some vulnerability, an attack has still taken place.

Informal Model of an Attack

Without going into extensive detail with a mathematical model describing attacks, I would like to provide a brief description of attack mechanisms. It is important that you know how attacks are implemented. Understanding attack mechanisms is one of the keys to success when preventing and detecting intrusions to and taking adequate countermeasures when under attack.

Fig. 2.3 depicts the elements that make up an attack.

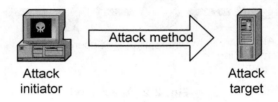

Fig. 2.3. An informal attack model

In some particular cases, the attack initiator (or intruder) and attack target coincide. In these cases, the intruder has already got access (or perhaps has been granted such access within the limits of his permissions) to the host or group of hosts whose resources represent his target. Both the initiator and target of the attack can represent a stand-alone host or group of hosts (for example, a subnet).

It would be logical to assume that the elimination of one of these elements will protect you from an attack. In practice, it is often impossible to remove the attack target; on account of specific features of information-processing technology, though, this would theoretically represent an ideal solution. If the target is missing, an attack becomes impossible. Network-address translation, or locking access to specific hosts within a corporate network using a firewall, represents one of the mechanisms for removal of the attack target.

If an attack target can not be removed, it is necessary to try to eliminate the intruder or attack method. However, this task is something that current security tools can not carry out. Usually, these tools concentrate all their attention on the attack target and some on the attack method. This passive behavior in relation to the attacker results in repeated attacks from the attacker's side (even if they are not successful).

Therefore, a complex approach is required, one that complements traditional mechanisms with additional tools implementing such functions as detection of the intrusion, tracing the attacker and investigation of the incident.

An attack method depends on several parameters:

❑ The type of intruder and the goals of the attack. These determine what method of attack should be expected. For example, if the target of the attack is the MS Exchange mail server, it is improbable that, to attack this server, the intruder would use methods of attacking sendmail or Qmail.

❑ The result of the attack. The method that the attacker would use depends on the result he is expecting from the attack (Denial of Service, compromising the system, etc.). For example, if the intruder plans to get unauthorized access to the password file of your web server, he will mask his actions and search for vulnerabilities in open services, such as HTTP, FTP, IMAP, and so on. If he plans to bring the server down, he can send a storm of requests to it and thus make it unavailable.

❑ The mechanism of attack.

❑ The attack tool.

Model of a Traditional Attack

A traditional model of attack is built according to the "one-to-one" principle (Fig. 2.4) or the "one-to-many" principle (Fig. 2.5), i.e., the attack originates from a single point.

Quite often, intruders use proxy hosts to hide the source of attack or complicate the procedures of tracing it. Using this method, the intruder attacks the selected target via several proxies, rather than directly. As a result, the object under attack interprets the threat as originating from the proxy (Fig. 2.6).

Intruder   Attack target

Fig. 2.4. "One-to-one" relationship

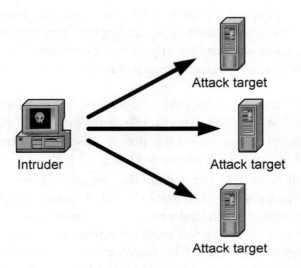

Fig. 2.5. "One-to-many" relationship

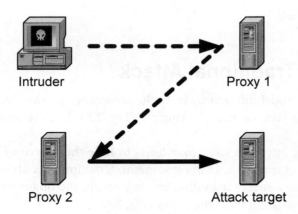

Fig. 2.6. Implementation of the attack via intermediate hosts

Developers of traditional security tools are oriented toward a classical model of attack. In different network locations, several security system agents are installed that transmit information to the central management console. This approach simplifies the system scaling (the increased number of agents does not have a negative impact on the console), simplifies remote control, and so on.

Distributed Attack Model

From 2 till 4 November, 1999, the Coordinate Center of the Computer Emergency Response Team (CERT) (http://www.cert.org) invited 30 leading experts in the field of information security from various organizations, including ISS, NASA, and the NSWC SHADOW Team to participate in a conference dedicated to distributed attacks and tools implementing these attacks. Distributed attacks enable a single intruder or a small group to implement hundreds or even thousands of attacks on a single host or group of hosts simultaneously. Until recently, such a capability was considered to be a myth. It was generally accepted that such an attack would be impossible to implement. The reality, however, is a different story.

One of the first warnings of the possibility of such an attack appeared in September 1998. The Naval Surface Warfare Center (http://mswc.navy.mil) analyzed several cases registered in 1998 and published one of the first reports dedicated to distributed coordinated attacks, based on this analysis. The traditional model usually operates with a single attacking host. This principle serves as a basis for most network security tools. However, the new model for distributed attacks introduces some revisions and encourages developers to design new mechanisms of intrusion detection [Stewart1-99].

Distributed Attacks in February

On Monday, February 7, 2000, at 10:20 a.m. PST, Yahoo users noticed a significant slowdown of the services provided by the portal — e-mail, news and so on. Users accustomed to a Web page taking up to 1.7 seconds to load were annoyed by six-second delays. Later, the situation became even worse. At 10:30 a.m., about a half of all users trying to access Yahoo received only error messages. An analysis of the problem showed that Yahoo servers failed because of an immense number of small packets, which varied from simple diagnostic messages to HTML page requests. This fusillade of packets hit Yahoo servers simultaneously from several Internet hosts. Yahoo specialists counted no less than 50 such points. At 11:00 a.m., less than 10% of all users could access the resources of this portal, and even those who managed to access the server had to wait for at least 20 seconds to get answers to their requests. At 1:15 p.m., all user requests were directed to servers that were not under attacks and, at 3:00 p.m., Yahoo started to function normally.

Yahoo was the first in a series of widely known servers that became targets of a mass attack in the second week of February. The next attack came on Tuesday morning, with the target being the server of Buy.com; and that evening, the servers of eBay, CNN.com, and Amazon.com were attacked. On Wednesday morning, the targets became ZDNet.com, E*Trade, Datek, and Excite. Users were unable to access these servers for 30 minutes to several hours.

The second target, Buy.com, was attacked at 10:50 a.m. on Tuesday. A flood of packets directed to this host exceeded the maximum allowed traffic by eight times and reached 800 Mbit/second. Similar results were reported for the other companies.

The model of a distributed or coordinated attack is based on different principles than those for the classical model. In contrast to the traditional model that uses "one-to-one" or "one-to-many" relationships, the distributed model is based on "many-to-one" and "many-to-many" relationships.

All distributed attacks (Distributed Denial of Service, DDoS) are based on classical DoS attacks or, more precisely, on their subset known as Flood or Storm attacks. They involve sending a large number of packets (a flood or storm) to a specified host within the network (the attack target). The directed storm of packets causes the host to fail, since it will be flooded with a storm of packages and, consequently, will be unable to process requests from authorized users. Various attacks, such as SYN-Flood, Smurf, UDP Flood, Ping Flood, Targa3, and many more, are based on this principle. However, if the bandwidth of the channel to the attack target exceeds the throughput of the attacker, or if the target host has non-standard confuguration, this attack will not normally be successful. In the case of a distributed attack, however, this situation changes. The attack originates simultaneously from several Internet hosts rather than from one, which causes rapid growth of traffic and brings the target server down.

Attack on the White House

On May 4, 2001, the White House server (**http://www.whitehouse.gov**) was blocked for tree hours and, on May 22, the server was unavailable for six hours. Responsibility for these attacks, as well as for attacks on other servers located in the U.S. (for example, the CIA site was unavailable from 10 to 11 a.m. on May 1) was taken by the association of Chinese hackers, who thus celebrated the holidays (May 1 — "International Workers Day," and May 4 — "Youth Day") and the anniversary of the bombing of the Chinese Embassy in Belgrade by American pilots.

This model is illustrated by schemes presented in Figs. 2.7 and 2.8.

A distributed attack is implemented in two steps. At the first stage, attackers search Internet hosts that could possibly be used to implement a distributed attack. The more such hosts are involved, the more efficient the attack will be. As a matter of fact, the most interesting "feature" of this approach is that there are millions of such hosts on the Internet. Regular investigations have shown that most companies are careless enough to pay no attention to the security of their hosts connected to the Internet. Such hosts have become the favorite prey of intruders, who choose them as a "base" for attacks they plan. These hosts may relate not only to university and government organizations' networks, as was the case with the February attacks, but also to networks belonging to ISPs, financial or insurance companies, and so on. Having found vulnerable hosts, the intruder installs special components to implement the attack.

This installation is possible thanks to the points of weakness in the host's security, exploited by the intruder to achieve his aims.

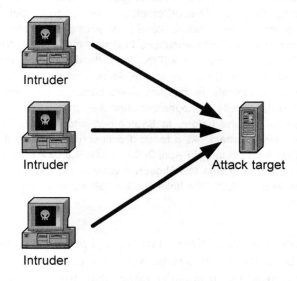

Fig. 2.7. "Many-to-one" relationship

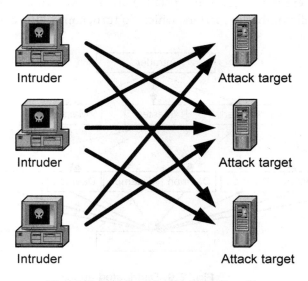

Fig. 2.8. "Many-to-many" relationship

Attacks on Internet Service Providers

The DDoS attacks implemented in February 2002 disrupted the normal operation of many ISPs, including SniffOut, TheDotComplete, The DogmaGroup, Firenet, etc. Actually, these attacks started long before 2002. For example, on December 7 and 14, 1996, the web server of Web Communications LLC was made to fail for nine and 40 hours, respectively. This attack, known as a SYN Flood, disrupted the operation of more than 2,200 corporate clients of Web Communications. As was later stated by Chris Shefler, the president of Web Communications, this happened because the company underestimated this aspect of security, and its management supposed that such a thing could never happen to them. Several months before, in September, another U.S. ISP — Panix — became the target of a similar attack. As a result, Panix servers running the SunOS operating system were down for 12 hours. In April 2000, a DDoS attack paralyzed the operation of another ISP — this time it was the AboveNet company. In August, Eircom, the largest Irish ISP, was attacked. In 2001, the Italia OnLine ISP suffered from an attack by anti-globalist hacker group.

At the second stage of a DDoS attack, several packets are sent to the host being attacked. A specific feature of this stage is that the packets originate from intermediate systems compromised by an intruder rather than from his own computer (Fig. 2.9). There are two types of such agents — masters and daemons, or clients and servers. Computers where these agents are installed are also known as zombies. The intruder manages a small number of masters, which, in turn, control the daemons.

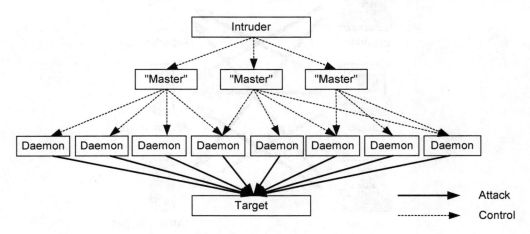

Fig. 2.9. Distributed attack

At first glance, this problem seems relatively simple, because, instead of the normal single-level architecture of a classical attack (intruder → target), a DDoS attack implements three-level architecture (intruder → master → daemon → target). What prevents us from tracing the whole "chain" and from detecting all hosts participating in the attack? This task, in any case, is hardly ever possible.

Detecting and locking one or more "masters" or "daemons" does not result in an attack being finished, since each "daemon" acts independently on the other computers, and, having received specific commands from the "master," does not need a further connection to it. Because "daemons" participating in a DDoS attack function autonomously, detecting and locking them all becomes rather complicated and problematic. Besides, when implementing the attack, it is possible that the originator of malignant packets will have a changed address, which also has a negative impact on the efficiency of the countermeasures. The attacker uses hundreds of unprotected hosts to coordinate the attack. These hosts may belong to various ISPs and be physically located in different countries and even on different continents. Thus, ascertaining the location of the intruder who is coordinating the whole attack is very difficult. Besides, zombie hosts do not contain a complete list of hosts participating in the attack. Therefore, the attack does not stop if a single host is detected and locked.

Distributed Attacks on Pentagon and US Navy Confidential Resources

On September 1998, security specialists of the US Navy reported that DDoS attacks had been performed simultaneously from no less than 15 locations and directed towards confidential resources of the US Navy.

On May 5, 1999, a Pentagon representative stated that, during recent months, most military computers were attacked by intruders, mainly of Russian origin. Approximately 80 to 100 attacks per day were reported, and this number tended to grow. During the investigation, experts discovered the following facts:

❐ Usually, the attacks were implemented from several Internet hosts simultaneously.

❐ Attacks were implemented by knowledgeable hackers who previously undertook a systematic investigation of the vulnerabilities of the presumed attack targets.

❐ Attacks were distributed in time, which prevented security personnel from efficiently detecting them using existing intrusion detection systems [Allen1-99].

This approach provides the following advantages to the attacker:

❐ *Concealment.* Working simultaneously from several addresses significantly complicates the process of tracking down the attackers using standard mechanisms (firewalls, intrusion detection systems, etc.). To thwart such attacks efficiently, it is necessary to apply a data correlation mechanism, which is not provided by most current security tools.

❑ *Power.* Coordinating attacks from several locations enables the organization of a much more powerful attack than would be possible if attacking from a single host. Once again, the existing methods of detecting and stopping attacks are rather inefficient.

❑ *Obtaining various data.* Working from different addresses, including those belonging to different networks, it is possible to get more data on a target in comparison to similar actions conducted from a single host. Proceeding in this way, one can determine the shortest routes to the target, detect trust relationships between network hosts, and so on. For example, this method enables the attacker to discover hosts from which it is possible to access a target using a Trojan horse program (for example, the trick works with host A, and does not work with host B).

❑ *Distributed attacks are hard to stop.* The above-mentioned characteristics make the task of stopping the distributed attack rather difficult.

In documented cases that occurred from 1998 to 1999, distributed attacks used several hundred daemons (for example, according to a report from one of the attacked companies, up to 10,000 daemons took part in the attack). Daemons are installed by exploiting various vulnerabilities at the compromised sites, including those enabling the intruder to get root privileges. After the daemon has been successfully installed, it informs the master (usually from one to four masters). When the master receives specific commands from the intruder, it programs the daemon to accomplish specific actions against the target. Usually, these commands contain the following information:

❑ The target address
❑ The type of attack
❑ The duration of the attack

The intruder can ensure that a large amount of data is sent simultaneously from all hosts participating in the distributed attack. In this case, intense traffic will bring the target host down. As a result, the target host will be unable to process requests from authorized users. This is what happened in early February 2000. To implement a similar attack using a classical paradigm, Internet connection of significant throughput is required in order to organize a storm of packets directed at the attack target. For a distributed attack, this requirement is not absolutely necessary. A normal dial-up Internet connection is sufficient. The flood of packets is only possible when using a large number of relatively slow connections.

It is even possible to evaluate the number of zombies sufficient to cause an Internet server to fail. When using a standard DSL connection (128 Kbit/sec), the number of packets that can be sent per second will not exceed 800 (128,000 divided by average size of an IP packet in Kbits). Since the minimum size of an IP packet is 20 bytes (the header only), a DSL connection allows you to send 128,000/20/8 = 800 packets. Everything else depends on the Internet server's performance. For example, according to tests conducted by TopLayer Networks, a Pentium 400 computer with MS IIS 5.0 installed can process 100 to 120 packets per second. Consequently, a single home PC with a DSL connection can shut down 6 to 7 web servers of poor performance. The number of hosts participating in an attack grows with the performance of the web server.

DDoS Attack Results in ISP Bankruptcy

CloudNine Communications, one of the largest British ISPs, was attacked by intruders in late January, 2002. It became the target of DoS attacks that by that time had become "classics." CloudNine was forced to close the whole business and sell its client database to its competitor — Zetnet. Emeric Miszti, one of CloudNine's founders, declared that the attack against the company was a carefully planned action, which lasted for several months. The intruders spent quite a long time on the key servers and their throughput. They also carefully selected the moment at which to undertake the final strike, after which the company could not continue its business. Emeric Mizty could not explain why his company became the target of this attack and what forces were lurking in the background, noting that both the company and its clients have suffered significant damage.

The intruder uses hundreds of vulnerable hosts to coordinate the attack.

The tools used for implementing distributed attacks are especially dangerous, since they are so easy to use that even unskilled users (known as script kiddies) can use them, and perhaps decide to inflict damage on someone they dislike.

Attacks built according to this scheme are very hard to detect. Network-based intrusion detection systems have serious problems detecting such attacks, especially in cases when connections between agents and servers are encrypted. Hybrid-based intrusion detection systems are more suitable for this purpose. Such attacks can be detected at the agent installation stage. After the agent has been installed, the detection becomes more complicated, since the agent acts as part of the operating system. Agent installation is especially dangerous for open systems, such as Linux and OpenBSD, since the agent can be introduced into the OS kernel, which will make its detection an even more difficult problem. When implementing a "traditional" attack, the intruder visits the compromised host from time to time (for example, using Telnet or using SSH). This can be detected when the administrator views and analyzes logs, or by automated security tools. In the case of a distributed attack, this problem never arises, because it is unnecessary to visit the compromised host. After the agent is installed, it will do everything automatically.

Hybrid Attacks

Technical progress is evolving at a rapid rate, and distributed attacks, which quite recently were considered as the apex of hacker ideas, are also being constantly improved. In particular, there have appeared hybrid attacks, also known as blended threats, by an advanced worm or hydra. Nimda, Code Red, SirCam, and Klez are examples of such attacks [ISS1-02].

Denial of Service attacks (including distributed ones) dominated until summer 2001. Notice that, even now, they have not become less numerous. However, due to the epidemic of hybrid attacks, the percentage of DoS attacks has decreased, down to 9.65%.

The main difference between hybrid attacks and distributed ones (although it would be more correct to define hybrid attacks as an extension of distributed attacks) lies in the fact that they do not use master agents to manage their daemons. This complicates the detection of the source of infection, or makes it practically impossible. Most people often confuse viruses and hybrid attacks. In my opinion, viruses in their traditional form have become outdated. Previously, viruses usually infected files located on a single host. In contrast to this, hybrid attacks infect hosts rather than files. The methods they use for this purpose also differ from traditional virus technologies. For example, previously, the user had to initiate the virus intentionally or accidentally. For hybrid attacks, this condition is no longer mandatory. Advanced worms search for vulnerable hosts, automatically penetrate them, and continue to spread without any intervention from humans.

Nimda is the most famous advanced self-propagating and self-activating worm [ISS1-02]. According to X-Force data, this worm uses a unique algorithm to attack various systems at a rate of approximately 3,500 attacks per hour (the lowest rate is 800 attacks per hour, and the highest 8,000 attacks per hour). During the first quarter of 2001, the number of Nimda attacks reached 7,665,000.

The automated attack technology used in hybrid attacks often allows intruders to bypass security tools, such as antiviral software and firewalls. Older forms of attacks, such as Denial of Service, viruses, and password attacks, could be detected and blocked by one of the existing types of security systems. Hybrid attacks, which use a wide range of attack strategies, can only be thwarted by a multiple-level echelon of security tools.

Some manufacturers of antiviral software try to convince users that their products detect all Internet worms with a 100% probability. Unfortunately, this is not so. Hybrid attacks propagate using various mechanisms, which include sending e-mail as well as penetrating various hosts using different Internet pages (such as ICQ), ShockWave, or Flash technologies, etc. Beside this, such attacks use various hacker methods (such as password attacks), which can not be stopped efficiently by antiviral systems.

Using firewalls also can not be considered an efficient counter-measure against hybrid attacks. As was noted in [ISS2-02], most such attacks are implemented via Port 80, which is practically never blocked by firewalls or filtering routers.

VPN tools also can not provide complete security. Malicious traffic from compromised hosts will be encrypted just the same as from normal hosts that are not infected. Furthermore, traffic from these presumably "protected" VPN hosts will penetrate the internal network, where it will not encounter any counteraction. This is especially true since perimeter protection tools trust traffic from such hosts and never expect any attacks from them.

Intrusion detection systems can identify and block practically all propagation methods used by hybrid attacks. However, even they are not free of shortcomings, the most important among which is their inability to "cure" systems that are already infected.

The only efficient way of protecting against the threat of hybrid attacks is to implement a combined approach, which includes using the products and services outlined in Table 2.3.

Table 2.3. Protective Measures against Hybrid Threats

	Network protection	**OS protection**	**Application protection**
Products	Network scanners Network intrusion detection systems Gateway antiviral software Firewalls	Server and workstation scanners Host-level intrusion detection systems Personal intrusion detection systems Personal antiviral software	Application scanners Database scanners Application-level intrusion detection systems Antiviral software for specific applications (Exchange, Notes, sendmail)

continues

Table 2.3 Continued

	Network protection	OS protection	Application protection
Services	Remote scanning	Remote scanning	Remote scanning
	Remote monitoring and management of intrusion detection systems	Remote management and monitoring of intrusion detection systems	Application security and monitoring
	Remote management of gateway antiviral software	Remote management of antiviral software	
	Remote management of VPN tools		
	Firewall management		
Consulting	Development, maintenance, and support of the security policy	Development, maintenance, and support of the security policy	Development and support of the application security policy
	Security analysis	Security analysis	Analysis of application security
	Tests for system penetration	Tests for system penetration	Tests for system penetration
	Configuration settings	OS customization and configuration	System configuration and customization
	Incident response	Incident response	Incident response
Training	Training course in the field of security standards and policies	Training course in the field of security standards and policies	Training course in the field of security standards and policies
	Training course on hacker methods	Training course on hacker methods	Training course on hacker methods
	Training courses on intrusion detection systems, security scanners, and firewalls	Training courses on intrusion detection systems, security scanners, and firewalls	Training courses on intrusion detection systems, security scanners, and firewalls

Result of an Attack

The results of an attack can be classified as follows:

❏ *Increased access* — any unauthorized action resulting in increasing access rights within the network or specified host (a computer, router, etc.)

❑ *Corruption of information* — any unauthorized change of the information stored within network hosts or transmitted via the network

A Teenage Hacker Attacks the Site of the Goddard Space Flight Center

On February 1, 2002, the U.S. Court convicted the teenage hacker known as Pimpshiz, who, on August 14, 2000, defaced the home page of the Goddard Space Flight center by placing slogans decrying the legal prosecution of Napster there. The verdict of the court was most interesting. Besides the standard measures, such as compensation for the damage, community service, and a period of probation, the court prohibited the hacker from using e-mail and his nickname for two years.

❑ *Disclosure of information* — distribution of information among individuals who have not been granted appropriate access rights

Secret Information Stolen from NASA

As the CNews agency reported, in mid-August 2002, an intruder managed to steal important information on the new generation of space shuttles. The hacker, known by the nickname RaFa, passed on part of the stolen documents to Computerworld journalists in order to prove that the attack was successful. Approximately 43 MB of various documents were disclosed, related to the development of the new generation of space shuttles. Mainly, they all relate to recent developments of the Boeing Corporation, as well as to a joint venture organized by Pratt & Whitney and Aerojet, which develop engines for the new shuttles. RaFa gave Computerworld a PowerPoint presentation containing detailed schemes of the new engines, along with a dozen user accounts for employees working at the White Sands Test Facility. According to statements made by the hacker, in both cases he exploited security holes based on anonymous FTP access. As Computerworld stated, NASA representatives have confirmed the authenticity of the stolen documents. According to them, these documents contain quite a large amount of secret military information. Representatives of the development companies believe that the stolen information would be rather valuable to their competitors.

❑ *Theft of service* — unauthorized usage of the computer or network services without degrading the quality of service provided to other users

Hacker Attacks on Space Flight Centers

On September 6, 2001, the head of the #conflict hacker group, Raymond Torricelli, also known by the nickname Rolex, was given a jail sentence and a fine for penetrating the computers of the Jet Propulsion Laboratory of the NASA branch in Pasadena and infecting them with a Trojan horse program. The job of the infected computers was to perform several important tasks, including the development of automatic space probes and the planning of space expeditions. The laboratory was working on a space expedition to all planets of the solar system, with the exception of Pluto, and a hacker could potentially get access to all this data. According to the statements of Torricelli, the actual penetration had been made in 1998. In February 2002, another hacker also landed in court — 20-year-old Jason Allen Dickman penetrated the JPL NASA network and Stanford University computers used to develop the software responsible for the control over satellites. And it is not only U.S Space Research Agencies that are targets of hacker attacks. In October 2001, the Russian Federal Security Service finished an investigation of a hacker who penetrated the network of the Energia corporation. During the investigation, it was revealed that the hacker used a password attack to access several computers that stored confidential data on communications and cooperation between Energia, the Khrunichev Center, and the Boeing Corporation. All of the above-mentioned attacks were implemented with "plausible" purposes, such as improving Internet access or creating electronic communities.

❑ *Denial of Service* — purposeful degradation of performance of locking access to computer or network resources

Steps in Attack Implementation

One can distinguish the following stages of attack implementation: preliminary actions necessary to prepare the attack (information gathering), attack implementation (exploiting) and attack completion. Usually, when discussing attacks, one talks about the second stage, forgetting the first and the last ones. Gathering of information and completion of the attack (covering the traces) can in turn represent attacks, and as such, also comprise three stages (Fig. 2.10).

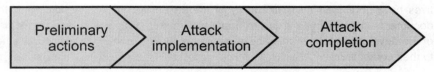

Fig. 2.10. Stages of attack

The main stage of each attack is information gathering. The efficiency of the intruder's work at this stage is the key to a successful attack. First, it is necessary to select the attack target, and all information on it, such as the operating system that it runs, services, configuration and so on. After that, the intruder must identify the vulnerabilities of the system he plans to attack. Exploiting these vulnerabilities leads to the desired result.

At the first stage, the intruder attempts to detect all channels of interaction between the attack target and other network hosts. This allows the intruder to choose the type of attack to be implemented and the tools to implement it efficiently. For example, let us suppose that the host that will be attacked interacts with two servers, one of which runs UNIX, while another runs Windows NT. The attack target has trusted relationships with one of the servers. The attack type and tools used to implement it depend on which server the intruder chooses as an intermediate one. Then, based on the gathered information and the desired result, the intruder selects the attack that will be the most efficient in this particular case. For example, if the intruder wants to bring the server down, he can use SYN Flood, teardrop, UDP Bomb, and so on. On the other hand, to get unauthorized access to the host in order to steal information, he might select PHF script tools for a remote password attack and so on. Having accomplished these tasks, the intruder starts implementing the selected attack.

Traditional security tools come into action at the second stage, leaving the first and the last stages out completely. As a result, it is rather difficult to stop an active attack even provided that you have powerful and efficient security tools at your disposal. Distributed attacks can serve as the best illustration of this statement. It would be logical if security tools started their work at the first stage, i.e., if they prevented the possibility of gathering information on a system planned as an attack target. Even if this did not stop the attack completely, it would significantly complicate the tasks of the intruder.

Traditional tools do not provide the capability of detecting attacks that have already been completed, nor do they enable you to evaluate the damage caused by attack implementation. Consequently, by using these tools, it is impossible to plan the steps required to prevent such attacks in the future.

The intruder focuses his attention on a specific attack stage depending on the result of the previous attack. For example, to inflict a Denial of Service, the intruder performs a detailed analysis of the network planned for attack in order to find backdoor entrances and vulnerabilities to attack the network via these points of weakness. If the intruder wants to steal information, his main attention is drawn to the concealed intrusion of the hosts being analyzed, using vulnerabilities he manage to find.

As was mentioned earlier, a detailed description of all mechanisms used to implement attacks is not the main aim of this book. However, the most common methods are covered in brief. This is necessary in order to understand methods of detecting these attacks. On the other hand, knowing the principles of attacks is the key to successful protection of your network.

Information Gathering

The first stage of attack implementation involves gathering information on the planned target (network or host). It includes various actions, such as determining network topology, type and version of the operating system that the planned target runs, available network and application services, and so on. These actions can be implemented using various methods.

Studying the Environment

When solving this problem, the attacker investigates the environment of the planned attack target. This might include, for example, the host of the target's Internet Service Provider. At this step, the intruder might attempt to determine the addresses of the trusted systems (for example, a partner's network), hosts that have direct connection to the target of the attack (for example, ISP's routers), etc. These actions are rather hard to detect, because they are performed during a significant time period and from outside the area controlled by security tools (firewalls, intrusion detection systems, and so on).

Identifying Network Topology

There are two methods of network topology detection that are used by intruders: TTL modulation and route recording. The first method of network topology detection is implemented by the `traceroute` (UNIX) and `tracert` (Windows) commands. For this purpose, they use the TTL (Time To Live) field in the IP packet header, whose value changes depending on the number of routers that the packet has passed. The ping utility can be used to record the ICMP packet route.

Quite often, it is possible to detect network topology using the SNMP protocol installed on most network devices, where security settings are configured incorrectly. Using the RIP protocol, one can attempt to obtain information on the routing table in the network.

Most of the above-mentioned methods are used by contemporary network management and control systems for creating network maps. Intruders can successfully use the same methods.

Host Detection

As a rule, host detection is done by means of using the ping utility to send the `ECHO_REQUEST` command of the ICMP protocol. Delivery of the `ECHO_REPLY` message serves as evidence of the fact that the host is available. There are several programs that automate and simplify the process of parallel detection of a large number of hosts, for example, such as fping or nmap. This method is potentially dangerous, since the ECHO_REQUEST commands are not registered by standard tools. For this purpose, it is necessary to use specialized tools for traffic analysis, such as firewalls or intrusion detection systems.

This is the simplest method of host identification. However, it is not free of drawbacks. For example, most network devices and programs lock ICMP packets and do not pass them into the internal network (or, in contrast, do not pass the outgoing ICMP packets). For example, Microsoft Proxy Server 2.0 does not allow ICMP packets to pass. As a result, host detection will not be complete. On the other hand, locking of ICMP packets is evidence of the presence of the first line of defense — routers, firewalls, and so on.

Secondly, using ICMP requests allows one easily to detect their source, which, certainly, is undesirable from the intruder's point of view.

There is yet another method of host detection — using the promiscuous mode of the network interface, which allows one to identify a different host in the network segment. However, this method is not applicable to cases in which network-segment traffic is unavailable to the attacker from his own host (i.e., it acts only in local-area networks). Another method of host detection is represented by the so-called DNS discovery, which enables identifying corporate network hosts using a DNS service.

Service Detection or Port Scanning

Service detection is usually achievable by means of detecting open ports (port scanning). Such ports are often related to services based on TCP or UDP protocols. For example, if Port 80 is open, this means that a Web-server service is present; Port 25 means the presence of SMTP server; Port 31337 — the BackOrifice remote administration tool (often considered by administrators to be like a Trojan horse); Port 12345 — the presence of the NetBus server, and so on. To detect services and scan ports it is possible to use various programs such as nmap or netcat.

OS Fingerprinting

The main method used in detecting the operating system remotely is the analysis of the TCP/IP stack. Each OS has its own implementation of the TCP/IP stack, and thanks to this fact, it is possible to determine which OS is installed within the remote host by sending special requests and analyzing the obtained replies.

Another, less efficient and more limited method of remote OS identification is provided by an analysis of network services detected at the previous stage. For example, if Port 139 is open, one can draw the conclusion that a remote host runs an OS from the Windows family. Various programs, such as nmap or Queso, can also help to identify the OS.

Determining the Host Role

The last step in the information gathering stage is determining the host role (for example, a firewall or web server). This step is accomplished based on information already gathered, including information on active services, available hosts, network topology, etc. For example, if port 80 is open, this might be evidence of the presence of the web server. Locking of the ICMP packets can be used as an indirect indication of the presence of a firewall, and names such as proxy.domain.com or fw.domain.com speak for themselves.

Detecting Host Vulnerabilities

The last stage of information gathering deals with searching for vulnerabilities. When performing this step, the intruder (manually or using special automated tools) determines if there are vulnerabilities that can be used to implement an attack. Programs such as ShadowSecurityScanner, nmap, and Retina can play the role of such automated tools.

Implementing an Attack

At this stage, the intruder starts to make attempts to access the host being attacked. Note that this might be direct access (i.e., penetrating to the host) or indirect (for example, implementation of a DoS attack).

In cases where hosts are directly accessed, the implementation of the attack can be divided into the following two stages:

❑ Penetration
❑ Getting control

Penetration

By penetration we mean overcoming perimeter protection tools (such as a firewall). There are different ways to achieve this goal. For example, it is possible to exploit the vulnerability of an "outgoing" service, or by means of passing a macro-virus attached to an e-mail message or via Java applets. Such malicious contents can enable the so-called tunnels in the firewall (do not confuse them with the VPN tunnels), through which the intruder then penetrates his target. Cracking the password of an administrator or other user (by means of the L0phtCrack or Crack utilities, for example) also relates to this step.

Getting Control

After penetration, the intruder gets control over the host being attacked. This can be accomplished by means of installing a Trojan horse program (for example, ALB or SubSeven). Having obtained control over the required host and concealing all traces of his activity, the intruder can perform any unauthorized actions necessary. The intruder can do this remotely, without the authorized user's knowledge. Control over the compromised host must be maintained after rebooting the operating system. To implement this, one can replace one of the boot files or insert a link to the malignant code to the startup files or system registry. The case is reported when the intruder manages to re-program the EEPROM of the network adapter, and can thus repeat his unauthorized actions even after the operating system has been reinstalled. The simpler modification of this example would be to introduce the required code or fragment into the network logon script (for example, the one used to log on to the Novell NetWare network).

Nike.com Lost Control Over Its Own Network

On June 21, 2000, Nike lost control over its own site for 19 hours. During this period of time, all visitors to www.nike.com were redirected to the page of an unknown S-11 organization calling for a protest against the routine meeting of the members of the World Economic Forum that was due to take place from the 11 to the 13 of September in Melbourne, Australia. Thanks to the redirection of the visitors from the Nike site, the number of visitors to the S-11 organization's page grew from 57,000 to 66,000 hits per hour. The total number of hits was 800,000 (only during that 19 hours). The S-11 group, however, did not take responsibility for hacking the Nike site. The administrators of the S-11 site placed a note in which they informed visitors to the site that they had no idea why the visitors of nike.com had been redirected to s11.org, nor did they know who had hacked the site. They also expressed their disapproval of the action, but thanked Nike for the additional hits. As was later reported by the BBC, control over the Nike site was obtained using the Network Solutions automatic registration system. This was not the first instance when hackers managed to change the registration data and redirect visitors to another site on account of the Network Solutions vulnerability. In the past, the internet.com domain was registered to a new owner by sending forged faxes to Network Solutions. Besides nike.com and internet.com, several other sites were "automatically re-registered," including web.net, whoami.com, exodus.net, emory.edu, w3.org and nethead.com. In Nike's case, control over the domain name was transferred to the Frugal Names domain registering company, located in Great Britain, by means of forgery. FirstNET Online Management, the owner of Frugal Names, noticed this and made an attempt to inform the person whose contact information was in the registration database. However, the contact person happened to be an ex-Web master of nike.com who no longer worked for them and did not warn his former employer.

Goals of Attack Implementation

It is necessary to mention that this stage might include two goals. The first goal is to get unauthorized access to the host itself and to the information stored there. Second, unauthorized access to the host might be required for subsequent attacks on other hosts. The first aim is normally achieved after the second one. This means that the intruder must first create a base for further attacks and only after that penetrate other hosts. This is necessary in order to hide the origin of the attack completely or at least to complicate the procedures of searching for it significantly.

There is quite a large variety of attacks, and it is impossible to cover them all in detail within the scope of this book. To anyone interested in more detailed information on this topic, I can recommend various specialized literature, such as the books in the "Hack Proofing" series.

Methods of Attack Implementation

If the intruder has physical access to the computer, they will be able to penetrate it or to execute an attack. The methods they use might vary — from using special privileges granted to the console or terminal to procedures such as the removal of hard drives and reading/writing them on another computer [Graham1-00]. This is known as a physical attack.

A system attack represents unauthorized activity under the assumption that the intruder already has a user account in the system attacked. Usually, it is a normal (unprivileged) user account. If the latest security patches have not been installed in the system, then the intruder has a good chance of carrying out the attack to get additional administrative permissions.

A remote attack presupposes that the intruder attempts to penetrate the target system remotely via the network. In this case, the intruder acts without special privileges. There are several types of such activities [Strebe1-99]:

❐ Local network intrusion, where the intruder attacks the computer or group of computers located in the same network segment as his host.

▼ *Incident in the CIA*

According to Reuters, on December 4, 2000, the Central Intelligence Agency (CIA) fired four employees and penalized 18 more for creating and using a secret chat within the agency's network, in order to chat and flirt during business hours. This chat was discovered in May, and about 160 employees, who were found to have visited this chat regularly, got notifications of the security investigations being conducted at that time. Some of them had even been suspended from their jobs for the entire six months of investigation (though they were still collecting a salary). According to the results announced by the CIA, four employees, one of whom held a high position, were fired. Furthermore, they were claimed to be unreliable, to prevent similar organizations from hiring them. Furthermore, 18 employees had to provide explanations and were fined (from 5 to 45 days' salary). This group also included two high-ranking officers, both of whom were demoted. Officials of the CIA stated that the usage of the agency's network for private, secret chats and databases was a flagrant violation of network integrity. As was revealed by the investigation, the chat used by employees mainly consisted of joking and flirting, and had been created in the CIA network in the mid-80s. There were a total of 160 employees involved, whose communications bypassed the security systems. Seventy-nine employees got off lightly, by simply being reprimanded, and eight people who were accused of having participated were cleared of the charges. The topic of the usage of the CIA's internal network for improper purposes has continued to attract its security department's attention since the end of 1996, when its director, John Deitch, was fired for storing secret files on his home computer, which was connected to the Internet.

❏   Intrusion via public networks, when the intruder attacks a computer or group of computers located in another segment. Usually, such attacks are implemented via the Internet.

❗ *Intrusion upon NASA Computers*

An unknown hacker who penetrated NASA computers in 1997 exposed American astronauts to danger during the docking of the Atlantis space shuttle at the Russian Mir station. On June 3, 2000, General NASA Inspector Roberta Gross gave an interview to the BBC, in which she admitted that the attack overloaded the NASA computer systems to such an extent that the connections between the flight control center, medical systems, and astronauts were terminated. According to Gross' statement, space agencies have several alternatives, and thus this attack did not pose a serious threat to the astronauts. In this case, communications were re-established via the Mir station's systems. However, Gross pointed out that she wanted to draw special attention to the fact, illustrating just how close hackers can get to vitally important systems. Until 2000, information on this 1997 incident had remained closed to the public. Even the astronauts who participated in this flight said, in an interview given to the BBC, that no one had informed them of the threat to their lives that had resulted from the intrusion into the NASA network. According to Gross, from time to time, hackers represent a serious threat to NASA. NASA has even created its own special "cyber-police" department to face this threat.

❏   Intrusion via a dial-up connection, when the intruder attacks a computer or group of computers via a modem.

Accomplishing the Attack

At this stage of the attack, the intruder covers any traces left behind. Usually, this can be done by cleaning the appropriate records from the logs and performing other actions in order to return the attacked system to its initial state.

Hiding the Fact and the Source of the Attack

One of the aims of intrusion detection is identifying the attacker. This problem might be rather complicated, because intruders often use various methods of covering the traces of their unauthorized activity. These methods include [Graham1-00, Daymont1-00]:

- ❏ Attack source address spoofing
- ❏ Creating fake packets
- ❏ Using someone else's computers as a basis for the attack
- ❏ Attack fragmentation
- ❏ Attack encryption
- ❏ Using values different from the default ones
- ❏ Changing the standard attack scenario
- ❏ Attack slow-down
- ❏ Cleaning the logs
- ❏ Hiding files and data
- ❏ Hiding processes

Changing the Address of the Attack Source

Most intruders organize their attacks from intermediate servers that are already cracked, or from proxy servers. Thus, it would be rather difficult to find which one had attacked your server. The more intermediate hosts used by the intruder, the more difficult the task of tracing them will be. Furthermore, if you detect an attack and start trying to lock it with firewalls, filtering at the routers, and other devices, you might lock a real address (possibly even one belonging to one of your clients or partners requiring access to your informational resources) rather than the intruder who is performing the attack.

Creating Fake Packets

The nmap scanner can perform decoy scanning, when real source addresses are substituted by fake addresses. Thus, the administrator of the intrusion detection system must solve quite a difficult problem, namely, selecting the one real IP address from a large number of IP addresses registered in log files from which the scanning was actually performed.

The frequency of changing the source IP address for different types of attacks is outlined in Table 2.4 [SANS1-00].

Table 2.3. Probability of IP-Address Substitution

Attack type	Example	Probability of IP-address substitution
Information gathering	Traceroute, ping	< 1%
Port scanning	Single host or subnet	5%
Multiple-packet attacks (DoS)	Ping Flood, SMURF, Fraggle	Proxy might be used as attack origin
Single-packet DoS attacks (or attacks consisting of several packets)	WinNuke, Ping of Death, SYN Flood	95%
Buffer overflow	Long filenames, long URLs	50%
Commands	Telnet, BackOrifice, Netcat	5%

Attack Fragmentation

Fragmentation is the mechanism of fragmenting an IP packet into a set of smaller ones. When receiving such packets, the TCP/IP device reassembles them and then transmits to the receiving application, or repeatedly fragments them and transmits them further. Most up-to-date intrusion detection systems are not equipped with mechanisms of IP-packet defragmentation. These systems pass such packets (they can possibly send a warning message to the administrator console, with notification of the fragmented packets being detected). Several cases have been registered, in which intrusion detection systems go down because of fragmented attacks. Consequently, current intrusion detection systems may be bypassed using special tools (such as fragrouter, for example).

Changing Default Values

Quite often, intrusion detection systems assume that the port unambiguously identifies the protocol or service. For example, by default, Port 80 relates to HTTP protocol, Port 25 — to SMTP; Port 23 — to Telnet; Port 31337 — to BackOrifice; and so on. Intruders exploit this fact and can use standard protocols on ports different from the default ones. For example, to make the detection of BackOrifice more problematic, the intruder may change the default port (31337) to another value (for example, 31338). Most intrusion detection mechanisms will fail in this case and prove to be unable to process such unusual traffic.

Changing the Standard Attack Scenario

Most intrusion detection mechanisms work according to the principle of comparing the attack to a known template. Databases of well-known attacks enable you to detect attacks with a high level of probability. However, the intruder may slightly change the template and thus easily bypass such systems. The above-described method of changing default values represents one example of such an approach. Another example of such a method is found in replacing a blank character with the Tab character in commands implementing the attack. This problem will be covered in more detail in *Chapter 12*.

Attack Slow-Down

Because of a large amount of registered data, intrusion detection systems are inefficient when it is necessary to trace attacks distributed in time. Thus, it is very difficult to detect a port-scanning procedure if it is distributed in time (ping sweep or port scan), when intruders check one port or address every five minutes (or even every hour). This slow-down significantly complicates attack diagnostics using current intrusion detection systems. Some scanners provide this capability. For example, the third version of the Nmap security scanner has the specialized Idle Scan mode (enabled by the -sI command line options), which is responsible for slowed-down scanning.

Cleaning Logs

Cleaning logs is a rather common method. It requires the removal of all log records that register unauthorized actions. Proceeding in such a way, a skilful intruder can hide all traces of suspicious actions from the administrator of the system being attacked.

Hiding Files or Data

The unauthorized actions of the intruder are often concealed by way of hiding files or data. For this purpose, one can employ various methods, differing by their implementation complexity; for example, setting the Hidden attribute to the file, introducing malignant code into the OS kernel (for UNIX-like operating systems) or attaching such code to an executable file or DLL. For example, Trojan horse programs often propagate using the latter method: The intruder attaches the Trojan code to some executable file (such as game, for example), and the Trojan automatically installs itself in the system, where the changed executable file is then started for execution.

Hiding Processes

This method, similar to the previous one, is often used to conceal the unauthorized activity of the intruder at the attacked host. To achieve this, the intruder might change the kernel of the operating system or modify special utilities responsible for working with processes (such as ps utility in UNIX). Using the rootkit or SunOS represents an example of this method. This kit enables the intruder to intercept various data, substitute the checksums, and so on. It can modify several system utilities (such as `login`, `ls`, `ifconfig`, `ps`, `netstat`, `du`), without allowing one to detect its presence in the system. The simplest method of hiding unauthorized activity of the system process is to change its name to a "standard" one (or very similar to the "standard" one). For example, a malignant process can have names such as in.netd, Winword.exe (at a host without MS Word for Windows) or NDDAGNT.EXE (which is very similar to NDDEAGNT.EXE).

Tools of Attack Implementation

The tools for attack implementation can be classified according to the list provided below [Howard1-98]:

- ❏ *Information exchange* — a tool for obtaining specific information from other sources (such as IRC, FIDO and so on) or from specific individuals (social engineering).
- ❏ *User commands* — a mechanism of exploiting vulnerabilities by means of entering specific commands using the command line interface (CLI) or processes (such as GUI), for example, entering the OS commands via a Telnet or FTP connection.
- ❏ *Script or program* — programs or sequences of commands (described in scripts) can be used by the intruder to exploit a vulnerability. In other words, the script or program represents a shell for one or more user commands. Examples of such programs are Crack or L0phtCrack (programs for password attacks) or NetBus Trojan.
- ❏ *Autonomous agent* — autonomous agents are similar to the previously described tools (scripts and programs). However, in contrast to scripts or special utilities where the intruder selects the target for a manual attack, in this case the target of the attack is selected regardless of the user, according to a special algorithm. Examples of autonomous agents are computer viruses (for example, macro viruses) or worms (such as the Morris worm).
- ❏ *Toolkit* — a toolkit is a set of programs, scripts and autonomous agents used to implement the attack (a rootkit is an example of such a tool).
- ❏ *Distributed tools* — distributed tools are programs, scripts, or autonomous agents distributed by several hosts within a network. Attacks can take place simultaneously from several hosts. These are the most complex type of attack implementation tools (both for implementing and preventing attacks). Typical examples are TFN2K and Stacheldraht.

It is easy to notice that each category of tools (except for information exchange) can contain other categories nested within it. For example, a toolkit always includes several programs and scripts.

According to the assessments of Pentagon specialists, attack-implementation tools are improved approximately once or twice per year. Furthermore, on June 21, 2001, Lawrence Gershwin, one of the CIA's top directors, reported to Congress that his department can not keep pace with the hackers, who improve their technologies much faster than CIA manages to develop appropriate security tools. "All we can do is report the fact of attack," said Gershwin.

Automated Tools for Attack Implementation

The Internet and other public networks provide lots of resources that simplify access to corporate networks for intruders. Information on vulnerabilities is constantly being published in various newslists, bulletins, and so on. Thousands of Internet hosts provide programs implementing attacks that exploit these vulnerabilities for free downloads, thus provoking "crushing" moods. Currently, most attacks are available even for novice users, who can now download an executable file and use it to attack a neighbor just to take "revenge." Several years ago, one had at least to know UNIX and how to compile the source code of an exploit to start such programs. Now the situation has changed dramatically. Most exploits have GUI and run under Windows 95/98, which has significantly simplified things for novice "hackers."

Attack Classification

There are various types of attack classification. For example, attacks can be classified as passive or active, internal or external, intentional or unintentional, and so on. Most of these classifications are rarely used in practice. Therefore, to avoid confusing the reader with a large number of such classifications, I would like to present one that better corresponds to real life [Mell1-99]:

❑ *Remote penetration.* Attacks that enable the intruder to implement remote controlling of the attacked host via the network. Examples of such attacks are NetBus and SubSeven.

❑ *Local penetration.* Attacks that enable the intruder to get unauthorized access to the host where it runs. An example of such an attack is GetAdmin.

❑ *Remote Denial of Service.* Attacks that enable the intruder to interrupt the normal mode of the system functioning or overload the computer via the Internet. Examples of such attacks are Teardrop or trin00.

❏ *Local Denial of Service*. Attacks enabling the intruder to interrupt the normal functioning mode or overload the computer. As an example of such an attack, one can provide a malicious applet that overloads the CPU with an endless loop, thus preventing it from processing queries from other applications.

❏ *Network scanners*. Programs that analyze network topology and detect services available for an attack. The nmap system is an example of such a program.

❏ *Vulnerability scanners*. Special programs that search for vulnerabilities within the hosts in the network and can be used for attack implementation. Examples are systems such as SATAN or ShadowSecurityScanner.

❏ *Password crackers*. Programs that perform password attacks by cracking user passwords, for example, L0phtCrack (Windows) or John the Ripper (Unix).

❏ *Sniffers*. Programs that "sniff" network traffic. Using such programs, one can automatically search for such information as user IDs and passwords, information on credit cards, and so on. Examples of sniffers include such well-known programs as Microsoft Network Monitor, NetXRay from Network Associates or LanExplorer.

Note that this classification does not include the whole class of so-called "passive attacks." Besides traffic "sniffing," this category might include such attacks as a "fake DNS server," "ARP server replacement," and so on. Later in this book, the main focus will be on detecting active attacks.

! *Attacks on the Demos and InfoArt Russian Servers*

In September 1996, one of the first famous attacks on a Russian web server was implemented. The intruders, who were not traced, attacked the InfoArt agency's server, after which visitors were redirected to a server with pornographic content. The most interesting aspect of this attack was that it was not implemented by defacing the site itself, but rather by means of attacking the DNS server and changing the mapping of IP addresses to DNS names. This allowed the intruders to redirect all user requests from the InfoArt server to a pornography server.

Databases of Vulnerabilities and Attacks

The attack classification implemented in most intrusion detection systems should not be too stiff. For example, an attack implementation that might be very dangerous for a UNIX system (say, the `statd` buffer overflow) and result in serious consequences (the highest priority) will hardly be applicable to Windows NT (or present the lowest risk). Furthermore, there is no uniformity or common naming convention for the names of attacks and vulnerabilities. The same attack might have different names in products supplied by different vendors [Tasker1-99] (Table 2.5).

Table 2.5. Different Names for the Same Attack

Organization\company	Attack name
CERT	CA-96.06.cgi_example_code
CyberSafe	Network: HTTP 'phf' Attack
ISS	Http-cgi-phf
AXENT	Phf CGI allows remote command execution
Bugtraq	PHF Attacks — Fun and games for the whole family
BindView	#107 — cgi-phf
Cisco	#3200 — WWW phf attack
IBM ERS	Vulnerability in NCSA/Apache Example Code
CERIAS	Http_escshellcmd
L-3	#180 HTTP Server CGI example code compromises http server

MITRE CVE

To eliminate the above-described chaos with the naming conventions of vulnerabilities and attacks, in 1999, the MITRE Corporation (http://www.mitre.org) suggested an open solution, independent of specific vendors of intrusion detection systems, security tools, and so on [Mann1-99]. This solution was implemented in the form of the Common Vulnerability Enumeration (CVE) database, which was later renamed as the Common Vulnerabilities and Exposures database. This solution allowed all professionals, developers, and vendors to speak the same language. For example, an attack with the different names listed in Table 2.5 obtained the following unified code in this classification: CVE-1999-0067.

Besides MITRE experts, specialists from many well-known companies and organizations participated in the development of the CVE database, including those from ISS, Cisco, BindView, Axent, NFR, L-3, CyberSafe, CERT, Carnegie Mellon University, SANS Institute, UC Davis Computer Security Lab, CERIAS, etc.

ISS became the first company that began to refer the unified CVE codes. This served as an incentive for other vendors. Currently, Cisco, Symantec, BindView, IBM, and other vendors declared that their products supported CVE.

Other Databases

There are other databases of vulnerabilities and attacks, the best among which is SecurityFocus (http://www.securityfocus.com), which contains a vast amount of data on software and hardware vulnerabilities. Hopefully, the new owners (Symantec purchased this resource in July 2002) will keep it just as interesting and informative. The ISS X-Force Threat and Vulnerability Database (http://www.iss.net/security_center/) and ICAT are other examples of vulnerability databases.

Incidents

An incident presents a higher level of the description of security policy violations. An incident is a group of attacks related to each other by several parameters, such as an attack target, an attack purpose and so on. It is this level where the "attack source" concept appears, which is missing in other models (Fig. 2.11).

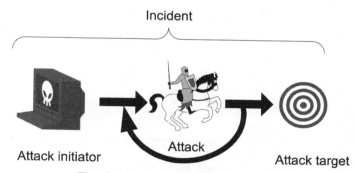

Fig. 2.11. The "Incident" model

An incident can be implemented using a single attack, as well as by using several sequential or parallel attacks. The success of intrusion is determined whether the intruder has achieved the desired result or not. The attack fails if the intruder has not achieved any of his goals. However, the victim remains a victim, and some consequences and losses are possible even in this case.

As statistics have shown, the number of security incidents grows proportionally to the growth of the Internet. Table 2.6, created on the basis of CERT/CC data, illustrates this growth. Notice that the number of processed e-mail messages exceeds these numbers by several times.

Table 2.6. Number of CERT-Registered Security Incidents and Processed E-Mail Messages (from 1998 to the Second Quarter of 2002)

Year	Number of incidents	Number of e-mail messages
1988	6	539
1989	132	2869
1990	252	4448
1991	406	9629
1992	773	14,463
1993	1,334	21,267
1994	2,340	29,580
1995	2,412	32,084
1996	2,573	31,268
1997	2,134	39,626
1998	3,734	41,871
1999	9,859	34,612
2000	21,756	56,365
2001	52,658	118,907
2002	43,136	95,163

An interest in e-commerce will only intensify this growth. Furthermore, another trend has been noticed. During the 80s and early 90s, external intruders attacked Internet hosts just to demonstrate their skills or from mere curiosity. Currently, most attackers want to achieve financial or political goals.

The skills and level of knowledge of the intruders has also changed. In the 80s, these were IT experts (Fig. 2.12) with a sound knowledge of the UNIX operating system, C or Perl programming languages, who created the source code of exploits themselves. More modern intruders, on the contrary, mainly employ ready-to-use GUI tools. According to the latest data, the number of such "hackers," or script kiddies, has reached 95%. Only a limited number of real hackers write exploits themselves. Currently, any user who has a computer with an Internet connection can attack a victim via the Internet and cause that person's hard drive significant damage.

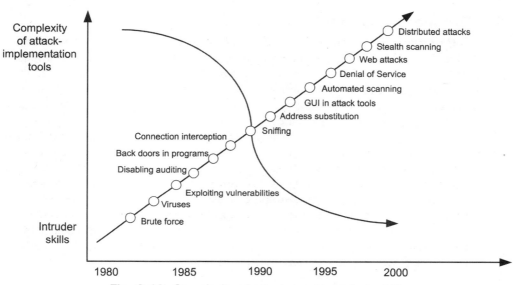

Fig. 2.12. Complexity of attacks and intruder's skills

In the past, an intruder entered commands manually and could not access more than a dozen or hundred remote systems simultaneously. Now, you can attack thousands of remote hosts simply by pressing a key. In contrast to the past, currently it is rather difficult to detect an intruder who has penetrated your system. An intruder can penetrate a network, implement an attack and hide the traces of his or her activity within a few seconds. Denial of Service attacks were not popular in the past, and no one could have predicted that they would become a matter of any importance. Now, the situation has changed (for example, the DDoS attacks on the Amazon, eBay, CNN and other servers).

Intruders

An intruder, i.e., an attack initiator, is the first element in the attack model described earlier in this chapter. This element can be described using the so-called informal model of the intruder, which takes into account their theoretical and practical skills, knowledge, time and place of his actions, level of qualification, and so on. The intruder may act alone, or there might be a group of intruders.

Generally, all intruders can be subdivided into the following six categories.

❑ *Hackers.* They perform attacks to get moral satisfaction, to improve their self-esteem, or to increase their status in others' opinions. This means that they do not get any material benefit from their activities.

The Morris Worm

On November 2, 1988, one of the students of the University of California, at Berkeley, detected a small "alien" program running at the Sun workstation. In the course of investigating this "alien" program, it became clear that the program used small vulnerabilities in the implementations of such common utilities as sendmail, rsh/rexec, and finger. This allowed the program to run on any infected computer, significantly degrading its performance and propagating its copies to any other computers that it could access remotely. Within several hours, hundreds and thousands of computers connected to the Internet went down. During a subsequent investigation of the incident, it became evident that this program was written by 23-year-old Robert Tappan Morris, a student of UC Berkeley. His aim was to create a program that would use the vulnerabilities of the Berkeley UNIX version to check the security level of all computers all over the country. However, the code of his program contained a bug, and what he had meant to be a small, useful program turned out to be a real monster. According to the most optimistic estimations, about 10% of all computers on the Internet were affected, and the total sum of financial losses ranged from $96 million to $300 million. The program is now known as the Morris Worm [Markoff1-95].

❏ *Spies.* They organize attacks in order to gather information that can be used for espionage purposes.

Hackers Recruited by the Argentinian Government

In June 2001, the Argentinian anti-dictatorship group Mothers of Plaza de Mayo (MPM), known to be active defenders of human rights, became a victim of a hack group that destroyed all the information on MPM's computers. According to a statement by the leader of this organization, this attack, along with other actions against the group, was undertaken by the Argentinian government.

❏ *Terrorists.* These are intruders who perform their attacks for blackmailing purposes.

Attack on the Bloomberg Information Agency

In early August 2000, two hackers were arrested in London on charges of cracking the network of the Bloomberg LP agency network and subsequent attempts of blackmail. According to information published by Bloomberg, Oleg Zezov and Igor Yarimaka were arrested during a special FBI operation, in which Bloomberg founder Michael Bloomberg also participated. According to information from police sources, Zezov worked for Kazkommerts Securities, located in Alma-Ata, and a client of the Bloomberg company. He repeatedly e-mailed Michael Bloomberg demanding $200,000 for information on the security hole he had detected in the company's computer system. In March, Zezov showed that he was not joking — Bloomberg received personal files of the company head containing photos of his personal documents, user name and passwords, and other personal information, including credit-card numbers. After that, Bloomberg representatives began to cooperate with the FBI.

❏ *Corporate raiders.* They perform attacks to obtain special information, the theft of which would provide substantial financial benefit for competitors.

❏ *Professional criminals.* These types of intruders mainly act to get personal financial profit.

❏ *Vandals.* The only aim of a vandal attack is to produce as much damage as possible.

The most widely known categories of intruders are hackers and professional criminals. As a matter of fact, hackers become known because they themselves inform the community about successful attacks. Professional criminals are widely known because of the media. In fact, even now, there is no general consensus on the term "hacker." In using this term, the media refers to any specialist who has some criminal agenda, or is looking for profit from their activity. In the professional community, however, the term hacker designates a qualified and skilful professional in the field of information technologies. Therefore, later in this book, I will follow this tradition and designate the criminals by the term "intruder."

In the 60s and 70s, individuals who created programs that made hardware perform undocumented functions were known as hackers. Thus, by the term hackers, one designated programmers who were knowledgeable, and sophisticated in the scope of their knowledge or in their profession. Later on, the term was used for any highly qualified professionals who organized their own community and culture. However, in the 70s and late 80s, this tradition became twisted and distorted, and "hackers" began to intrude upon information systems, leaving their "visiting cards." It was that time when the term "hacker" obtained its negative connotation. Apart from hackers, there are also crackers, phreakers, and so on.

▌ *Cracking Just to Protest*

Sometimes, hacking is simply a way to make a social or political protest. One example of this took place in January 2001 when an unknown hacker intruded upon Bulgarian president Petar Stoyanov's website. He proceeded to delete all information on it and left a message explaining why he did it. The explanation was simple — the young man's parents were poor, himself was unemployed, and lacking any decent job prospects in Bulgaria. Such incidents are part of the new Internet trend, known as hacktivism.

As professionals from the CIA and FBI note, the main threat originates from foreign governments developing technologies of information warfare, rather than from individual hackers. According to data provided by the Defense Information Systems Agency (DISA), besides the U.S., the list of such states includes Russia, Israel, Great Britain, France, China, North Korea, Iraq, Libya, and Cuba. However, it should be noted that commercial companies (even large ones) are unlikely to become the target of attacks implemented by foreign governments. For such companies, individual hackers and hack groups still remain the main threat.

Intruder Goals

It is quite probable that you, upon reading about the hacking of some specific company's site, thought that this could never happen to you. Perhaps you are right. However, it is still necessary to know the reasons why your computer (including your home PC) or your corporate network might become an attack target. There are quite a lot of classifications for intruders developed by various organizations (including the FBI, CIA, Interpol, etc.). Considering them all is a tedious (and practically unnecessary) task. After all, if you suffer from an attack, does it really matter who has hacked you — an amateur or a corporate raider hunting for your secrets? In real-world practice, it would be much better to know the reasons why you might become a target of a hacker attack. To become an attack target, you must attract an intruder's attention. Let us consider what might make you a target, or induce a hacker to choose you or your company. Note that, in this section, we will only consider intentional attacks. Accidental attacks will not be covered here.

Joke

Jokes are rather common, and perhaps one of the first of the motives for hacker attacks. Perhaps nearly everyone has received, for example, anonymous messages containing something like: "Your account will be locked within 5 minutes." Apart from this relatively harmless joke, there are more cruel ones, which can really scare novice users. For example, someone might send you a message inviting you to visit some address on the Internet (for example, http://chatcenter.virtualave.net/delwin). If you do, be prepared to watch how Windows is supposedly being deleted from your computer. Sometimes these jokes can be quite outrageous. One of the latest jokes (at the time of writing) was implemented by a German hack club known as the Chaos Computers Club. On Christmas Eve, the club hacked the system controlling the engineering communications of a building and made various pictures on its façade by switching various lights on and off.

Curiosity

Curiosity comes right after jokes when listing hacking motives. Note that there are two types of curiosity. The first kind is when penetrating the system presents a challenge to the hacker. By bypassing various traps and security tools, the hacker improves skills and self-assurance. The second type of curiosity came into play quite recently, as the Internet plays more and more of a significant role in everyday life. Users surfing the Web find various programs there, and start them out of pure curiosity. Without a proper understanding of the algorithms and working principles of such programs, such "hackers" can inflict serious damage on their friends, colleagues, or other Internet users.

Publicity and Fame

After becoming self-assured enough, some intruders begin to long for fame and publicity. They might search for it among other people of a similar opinion (for example, at hacker conferences and sites) and among other individuals who have at least heard about the Internet. The most common example of such activity is defacing sites, which can be accomplished as self-promotion.

Politics and Ideology

Political motives for hacking activities are also rather common. Practically all more-or-less significant political events are followed by hacker attacks (which they consider a counter-strike).

Ideological motives are also as widespread as political ones. Basic hacker ideology usually disapproves any attempt at restricting access to information. To illustrate this thesis, let us again consider the activities of the above-mentioned Chaos Computer Club, members of which have hacked several government sites and published quite a large amount of confidential information on the Chernobyl catastrophe. Attacks on the IT components of crucial and vitally important infrastructures can also be attempted for ideological reasons. Consider, for example, the second part of the "Die Hard" blockbuster, in which terrorists attack the navigation system of a airport, and cause landing aircraft to crash.

▼ *Anti-Globalists in Cyberspace*

Early in 2002, Italian police traced six members of an anti-globalist hack group suspected of attacking thousands of sites located in 62 countries all over the world. The group started its activities in July 2001 during a summit in Genoa that was accompanied by anti-globalist protests. Among other sites defaced by the group are NASA, Pentagon, Columbia University, Harvard University, Cornell University, etc.

Financial Profit

Financial profit is the most common motive for committing crime, both in the virtual and real worlds. If the attack is successful, the intruder will be able to live comfortably for quite a long time. Financial profit might present a motive both for individual hackers who attack Internet stores in order to steal credit-card numbers, and for companies that recruit hackers in order to attack their competitors. The Western Union site was hacked with especially this purpose in mind.

Revenge and Disappointment

Revenge or disappointment is mainly an internal threat for a company. The motives that might induce employees to implement such an attack include a lack of career prospects, low salary, dissatisfaction with the management policy, etc. Note that practically no one can insure themselves against it, and sometimes this motive even represents the main threat to the company. Furthermore, it is especially dangerous, since knowledgeable insiders can inflict much more serious damage than external intruders.

The Administrator Sets a Logical Bomb

In the autumn of 2001, the Philadelphia courts passed a guilty verdict on Tim Lloyd, ex-administrator of the Omega Engineering network. Lloyd left a logical bomb on one of the corporate servers, which, after a period of time, destroyed the software managing the production processes of the company. The damage reached around $10 million.

Vandalism

Vandalism is relatively rare, although at first glance you might think that this is not the case. DoS attacks represent quite an illustrative example of vandalism. However, things are not as simple as they might seem. In most cases, DoS attacks, destroying information, or other acts of vandalism, are induced by revenge or other motives.

Other Motives

This classification does not come any close to covering all motives, but it does allow us to understand the main motives of the intruders. It should be pointed out that the above-described categories might overlap, and sometimes it is rather difficult to distinguish between them. Apart from this, there are other motives that are rather difficult to identify as falling within a specific category. For example, hacker attacks might be induced by ecological problems, the release of a new version of the Microsoft OS, or anything else. All this might cause dissatisfaction among the hacker community, and thus result in an increase in attacks. Although these reasons are hard to forecast, and can not be applied to most companies, you must keep them in mind.

Why Are *You* Under Attack?

After considering the most common hacker motives, you can now better understand the reasons why you might become a target of their attacks. The main reasons include:

☐ You have openly or implicitly declared that your security system is absolutely unassailable.

▌ Unassailable Oracle Hacked

Any declaration stating that your system contains no vulnerabilities or is absolutely secure will immediately attract thousands of hackers. Be sure that they will, in the end, detect some vulnerabilities, and, in the long run, they will penetrate your unassailable system and cause it to fail. The most illustrative example of this statement was recently confirmed by a successful attack on Oracle9i immediately after release of this version. The PR and marketing specialists of the company characterized the system as "unbreakable." After the ninth version of the Oracle DBMS was announced, hackers all over the world joined efforts to show Larry Ellison that he spoke too hastily. This attempt was successful. Their activity was subdivided into two directions — first, it was necessary to hack the Oracle 9i product, and next the Oracle website. The first direction produced results practically at once — within the last year, quite a lot of vulnerabilities and security holes have been detected in the Oracle 9i software. As for the second type of activity, although hackers did not inflict serious damage, they managed to make the administrators of the Oracle Web site (**http://www.oracle.com**) rather nervous. According to a statement by a representative of Oracle, normally there are about 3,000 attacks on their server per week. After Oracle began its promotion campaign, which included something like "Oracle9i. Unbreakable. Can not break it. Can not break in." into the body of e-mail messages and other material, the number of attacks on its server went up to 30,000 attacks per week. However, this did not teach Oracle marketing experts anything, since they continue to use such terms as "unbreakable" and "unassailable" when naming their new releases (for example, the newest one is similarly toted, developed in cooperation with Dell and based on Linux).

☐ You are the leader in your segment of the market, constantly beating your competitors.

▌ University Battles in Cyberspace

On July 2002, Yale University requested that the FBI verify that its computer network had been penetrated by hackers from Princeton University. In this request, the university stated that its

IS specialists had detected at least 18 attempts to penetrate its internal database from computers belonging to Princeton University. The FBI representative confirmed that this actually took place. According to him, this was done in order to find out who among potential students had submitted applications to both universities. On the other hand, he also pointed out that, although this information was obtained using illegal methods, the data were not used for malicious purpose.

❏   You have made a "strong" statement.

Attack on the RIAA Site

At the end of July 2002, unknown hackers implemented a DoS attack on the Recording Industry Association of America (RIAA) site. According to data published by CNET News.com, the DoS attack started on Friday, July 26, and stopped at about 2 a.m. on Monday, July 29. On Saturday and Sunday, the RIAA site was practically unavailable. RIAA representatives emphasize the fact that the internal network was not penetrated. They also do not know who could have attempted the attack. News.com, on the other hand, supposes that this attack might have been implemented by hackers backing the idea of free music on the Internet. RIAA is famous for its aggressive opposition to numerous file-exchange networks and their users. Furthermore, RIAA quite recently managed to get a bill passed stating that Internet radio stations must pay to broadcast a composition. The amount asked is out of the league of most on-line radio stations, and especially free ones.

❏   Your company is a financial organization or performs on-line payments.

Russian Hacker Arrested

In January 2002, Russian authorities, in cooperation with the FBI, arrested a hacker who blackmailed an American bank in order to get $10,000. Early in 2001, the hacker penetrated one of the servers of the ORCC ASP company and accessed confidential information. When he started to blackmail the bank, its representatives contacted FBI. After a long investigation and communication with the hacker, the FBI found his trail, which led to Russia.

❏   Your company is a well-known brand (for example, Ericsson).
❏   Your main activity lies in the field of communications or security. Hackers enjoy attacking such companies, which they consider their main opponents. This why such companies as Symantec or Network Associates are hacked.

Attack on SecurityFocus

At the end of December 2001, the site of the SecurityFocus company, specializing in information security technologies, was hacked to display the banners of the "Fluffi Bunni" hack group.

Hackers also cracked the server of the Thruport company, whose ads are shown on the SecurityFocus site. Hacker banners appeared for several hours, after which SecurityFocus specialists replaced them with their own. However, the ThruPort site displayed "incorrect" banners for quite a long time. Jay Dyson, an independent security expert, admitted that the "Fluffi Bunni" attack was the most elegant of all the recent attacks, since it was planned down to the smallest detail and perfectly implemented. According to Alfred Huger, SecurityFocus vice president, hackers exploited a newly detected vulnerability of the OpenSSH authorization technology to get control over the ThruPort server. He also stated that the hackers did not attack the security systems of the SecurityFocus site.

❏   You are a governmental organization.
❏   You are supporting a site of some popular or well-known person.
❏   You have a poor employee-relations policy.
❏   You have quarreled with one of your employees.

A Worm in the Pentagon Networks

According to the PCWeek/RE data, in the summer of 2001, Max Butler, an IS specialist collaborating with the FBI, was condemned to 18 years of prison for infecting the Pentagon network with a worm.

❏   You are promoting an idea that has lots of opponents.

Anti-Globalists on the Internet

During the World Economic Forum that took place in New York early in 2002, the site of the forum became unavailable to visitors. The most interesting aspect of this attack was that the technical personnel supporting this site could not answer the simple question of why this happened. According to their opinion, it was unlikely that their site became a target of DoS attack. However, most experts suppose that a DoS attack was the exact reason for this failure. This is especially true since the Electronic Disturbance Theater hack group had been planning to implement just such an attack. However, the World Economic Forum site could never really have been mentioned as among the most secure. For example, in February 2001, 1,400 credit-card numbers of participants were stolen. The list of victims included Bill Gates, Bill Clinton, and Yasser Arafat.

❏   You are using well-known, general-purpose software. For example, hackers never miss an opportunity to demonstrate the vulnerabilities of Microsoft solutions.
❏   You are supporting a hacking resource. In this case, your colleagues or competing groups will also be very glad to hack you, in order to demonstrate their superiority.

Summary

In this chapter, I have attempted to summarize all existing data on attacks and attackers. This should provide a basis for understanding the intrusion detection technologies that will be described in subsequent chapters. As has been shown, most attacks can only be implemented due to vulnerabilities in the components of information systems. If these vulnerabilities were non-existent, most current security tools would be efficient when preventing or stopping all possible attacks. However, programs are written by human beings, and humans tend to make mistakes. Because of this, vulnerabilities appear, which makes attacks possible.

Still, if all attacks were built according to the classical "one-to-many" scheme, firewalls and other contemporary security tools would successfully deter them from preventing and stopping attacks. However, distributed attacks have appeared on the scene, and traditional tools become inefficient when dealing with such an attack. Therefore, new technologies must be developed — namely, intrusion detection technologies, which will be discussed in the next chapter.

CHAPTER 3

Introduction
to Intrusion Detection

*"Plan for what is difficult while it is easy, do what is great
while it is small. The most difficult things in the world must
be done while they are still easy, the greatest things in the
world must be done while they are still small. For this reason, sages never do what is great, and this is why they can
achieve that greatness."*

Tao-te Ching.

Information security is not the only field in which intrusion detection is used. It is also
used in alarm sensors (security alarm systems), financial and wire-fraud detection systems, and homing guidance systems in artillery, among other things. Unfortunately,
the limited scope of this book precludes coverage of all these areas of the application of
intrusion detection technology. Therefore, I will present only information aspects of
this technology, i.e., detecting attacks on hosts within a corporate network.

The main goal of the tools and devices that implement intrusion detection technologies (similarly to other security systems) is the automation of the routine and tedious procedures necessary in managing system security, and to make them understandable for those who are not experts in the field of information security. Generally
speaking, it is not necessary to use automated tools. Practically all attacks can be

detected by means of a "manual" analysis of the logs. In addition, one can use the operating system's built-in tools. Such an approach provides for less expensive deployment of the intrusion detection infrastructure. However, more time is required to accomplish this process. Furthermore, manual analysis or the usage of general-purpose automated tools does not allow the detection and prevention of most attacks in time. For this reason, it is necessary to use specialized, automated tools customized especially for the detection of security policy violations. This book explicitly focuses on such systems. However, universal security tools and manual methods are given brief mention.

It is necessary to take note of the fact that intrusion detection technology is not yet quite established. Nonetheless, it is constantly attracting new vendors and developers that spring up like mushrooms after warm rain. From 1999 to 2002, more than 50 businesses supplying services in this area have appeared. As for commercial, shareware, and freeware tools for intrusion detection, their number has long exceeded 100. On the other hand, firms providing intrusion detection products also quickly disappear, or are taken over by more powerful competitors. Still, despite the lack of a theoretical basis for this particular technology, some rather efficient methods of intrusion detection have already been developed. These methods, along with their advantages and drawbacks, are described in this book.

Like most security mechanisms, intrusion detection technology should solve several important problems. These include:

❑ Simplifying the tasks of security personnel. Automated intrusion detection systems can even totally free up employees' time spent on routine operations related to controlling users, systems, and networks.

❑ The capability to "understand" sources of information on attacks (which might sometimes be encrypted).

❑ The capability to be managed by employees who are not security experts.

❑ Total control over all subjects of the information system (users, programs, processes, and so on, including ones that have been granted administrative privileges).

❑ Detection of known attacks and vulnerabilities, as well as informing IS personnel.

Obviously, some of these tasks can be solved using the mechanisms that have been built into operating systems or application programs. For example, you can audit all actions of all users and programs by means of manually analyzing the log files (AppEvent.evt and SecEvent.evt in Windows NT/2000/XP or syslog in Unix). However, manual analysis of the log is a tedious and time-consuming process, requiring you to perform lots of routine operations. As a result, some violations that deserve the administrator's attention might be overlooked.

According to a public opinion poll conducted in 2002 by the Computer Security Institute (CSI) and the FBI, 60% of respondents use intrusion detection tools in their networks. And, according to the data provided by Ernst & Young, such organizations comprise only 36% [EY1-02], while Symantec reports 41% [TechRepublic1-01]. The vast majority of respondents have detected intruders using these tools (Table 3.1). Hence, the number of companies that use intrusion detection technologies in their work is growing at a rapid rate. Automatic tools for intrusion detection can simplify this process and eliminate the necessity of manual operations, thus enabling security personnel to save time and labor. This is rather important, since, according to the poll, a lack of time is one of the main factors preventing security specialists from improving the security level of corporate resources.

Table 3.1. Sources of Attack Notifications

	1998	1999
Notifications from colleagues	47	48
Analysis of log files on servers and firewalls	41	45
Intrusion detection systems	29	38
Direct damage	41	37
Warnings from partners and clients	14	15

Table 3.2 outlines quite an interesting set of statistics on the percentages of commercial and government organizations using intrusion detection technologies in the United States.

Table 3.2. Percentage of Organizations Using Intrusion Detection Technologies

Market sector	Respondents using intrusion detection technologies (%)
Aerospace agencies and organizations	58
Banks and financial organizations	39
Telecommunications companies	54
Consulting companies	42
Educational institutions	30
Government organizations	42
High-tech companies	48

continues

Table 3.2 Continued

Market sector	Respondents using intrusion detection technologies (%)
Insurance companies	44
Production organizations	42
Medical organizations	27
Military organizations	53
Other	21
Total (average value)	41

About 30% of all 745 respondents plan to use this technology in the future (Table 3.3).

Table 3.3. Percentage of Organizations Planning to Use Intrusion Detection Technologies

Market sector	Percentage of organizations planning to use intrusion detection technologies in the future
Aerospace agencies and organizations	25
Banks and financial organizations	42
Telecommunications companies	32
Consulting companies	19
Educational institutions	25
Government organizations	17
High-tech companies	29
Insurance companies	34
Production organizations	28
Medical organizations	23
Military organizations	41
Other	40
Total (average value)	29

However, if you ask IS specialists what the function of an intrusion detection system is and what problems it can solve, in most cases you'll get the following typical answer: "That's a silly question! It detects attacks like Denial of Service and reacts to them." On the one hand, this is true. On the other hand, however, intrusion detection systems have long ago ceased to be just another security tool. They have become sophisticated sets of tools capable of solving a large variety of problems, some of which I would like briefly to cover.

Backing up Firewalls

Quite often, intruders attack firewalls in order to cause the firewall to fail and penetrate the corporate network. Network-level intrusion detection systems can decrease the risk of such penetration by temporarily backing up firewalls. Systems of this class are capable of filtering network traffic according to various fields of the IP-packet header. This allows the administrator to organize a rather powerful packet filter with functionality comparable to one provided by advanced firewalls. Furthermore, intrusion detection systems can be used as temporary replacement of a firewall during regular maintenance, or, when it is necessary, to update the firewall software or test its settings.

Controlling File Access

Functions of controlling file access are usually delegated to specialized systems intended for protecting network information from unauthorized access, such as Secret Net. However, in some cases, such systems can not be used for controlling access to files containing critically important information (for example, database files or password files). This relates to the fact that most such systems can not run under Unix clones, particularly, Solaris, Linux, HP UX, and AIX. Such systems are ideal for securing Windows, and sometimes, NetWare platforms. However, they are practically useless when it is necessary to protect Unix. In this case, the best thing to do is to use host-based intrusion detection systems. In this situation, it is possible to use both intrusion detection systems based on log-file analysis (for example, RealSecure Server Sensor) and IDSs analyzing system calls (such as Cisco IDS Host Sensor).

Controlling Unreliable Employees and Preventing Information Leaks

It is not rare that employees use a company's Internet connection for their own purposes, such as searching for new jobs, sending CVs, spam, and other unauthorized action. These actions result in a loss of productivity, a useless waste of time, increase the cost of the Internet, etc. Statistical data shows that about 80% of users send private messages using their business workstations. Consequently, companies lose hundreds of thousands of dollars per year as a result of inefficient Internet usage.

It is not superfluous to remind you once more about the possible danger of the leakage of confidential information via the corporate mailing system. During the last year, about 90% of organizations with Internet access have experienced leaks of confidential information, including source codes of software, texts of contracts or financial documents, client information, etc. An information leak can happen not only via e-mail, but also when accessing external web servers.

In order to prevent such activities and to detect unreliable employees, one can use various content-control tools, for example, those of the MIMEsweeper or SurfControl product families. However, if the company can not afford such tools, it is possible to use specially configured network-level intrusion detection systems. The mechanisms of such systems allow the administrator to control network traffic using a set of predefined keywords and key phrases (for example, "company-confidential," "CV," "Jobs," and so on), detect transmission of files with specific names (for example, salary.xls) or filename extensions, and identify requests to specific servers (for example, http://www.playboy.com).

Protection against Viruses

Similar mechanisms allow you to detect some types of viruses and Trojans that have recently captivated the entire Internet. Worm epidemics such as Red Code, Blue Code, Nimda, and so on have once again demonstrated the danger of underestimating the importance of antiviral software. The I Love You virus alone, which appeared in 2000, has inflicted a total of $15 billion dollars worth of damage all over the world. Besides viruses and Internet worms, other dangerous or malicious content can also penetrate a corporate network. Some examples of such content are Java applets and ActiveX controls.

Intrusion detection systems can also be helpful in this case. Although intrusion detection systems can not completely replace classic antiviral software, they can create an additional barrier for viruses and Trojan horses, thus preventing them from infiltrating your corporate network.

Security Service Provider Hacked

On December 3, 2000, Kaspersky Lab reported that hackers had managed to penetrate the Web sites of the Brazilian branch of the Network Associates and McAfee companies. The intruders, who identified themselves as Insanity Zine Corp., defaced the sites by replacing the home pages by the logo of their hack group and texts insulting the Brazilian government and its political leaders. The protests of these Brazilian hackers on the home pages of **http://www.nai.com.br** and **http://www.mcafee.com.br** remained there for approximately 1.5 hours, after which the home pages were restored.

Controlling the Administrator's Activities

IT specialists are often underpaid, and this is a sad and well-known fact. Furthermore, in some organizations, the management adopts a restrictive and unfair policy, attempting to limit the administrator's possibilities of improving their knowledge and skills as much as possible. As a result, these employees become increasingly annoyed and offended. The same might happen if there is a lack of career prospects or insufficient respect. As a result, such disgruntled administrators can cause intentional damage by reconfiguring network equipment or critical servers and other devices in order to take their revenge or blackmail the boss.

Network- and host-level intrusion detection systems can be used to control unauthorized configuration changes of the protected hosts performed by users that have been granted administrative privileges. In this case, such systems can act as an additional control tool. A disgruntled administrator can clear a couple of log files, but the record of his unauthorized activities will remain in another one.

Attack on a Nuclear Power Plant

On January 11, 2001, ZDNet News agency reported an incident concerning a nuclear-power plant in Bradwell, Great Britain. The plant's security specialist attempted to sabotage it by hacking the plant's computer network. However, his attempt to delete some secret information activated the main system for alerting of emergencies. According to data from the Guardian, the intruder was detected by the security service of the nuclear-power plant. He is currently being prosecuted. Representatives of BNFL, the owner of the nuclear-power plant, declared that the incident did not present any risk to the environment, personnel, or citizens living in the surrounding area. The power plant continued to operate in normal mode. However, the management ordered that both overall and computer security be tightened.

Controlling Internet Access

The great majority of companies encounter a loss of productivity and a useless waste of business time caused by employees visiting Internet servers that are unnecessary to their jobs. The statistical information on this topic is rather interesting:

- ❏ 32.6% of users have no particular goal when surfing the Web.
- ❏ 28% of all users go Internet shopping during business hours.
- ❏ The amount of pornographic traffic transmitted during business hours makes up 70% of all such traffic on the Internet.

In order to detect and identify such cases of abuse, one can use content-control tools or firewalls. However, quite often there are no funds to purchase these tools. Because of this, part of the functions for controlling access to Internet resources that are implemented by these tools can be delegated to intrusion detection systems. In these cases, IDS will control network traffic using a set of predefined keywords or requests to specific web servers.

❗ *Vatican Site Hacked*

An hour after the Pope's declaration in which he reminded Catholics around the world about the dangers of using contemporary technologies, particularly electronic mass media, was published, unknown hackers defaced the Vatican site. Reuters reported this case on January 29, 2001. The Pope's declaration was timed to coincide with World Communications Day. The Pope was appealing to all Catholics of the necessity of using current mass media to propagate religious ideas, and paid special attention to the Internet and electronic mass media. In particular, he mentioned the danger of the all-embracing availability of information, which might produce such results as doubts in true belief. The unknown hackers did not hesitate to confirm this. According to the information provided by Il Messaggero, a Brazilian hack group is suspected in this defacement. However, the damage inflicted by the hackers was insignificant, and soon the resource was returned to its normal state.

Detecting Unknown Devices

Cases in which intruders connect their PCs or notebooks to critical network segments in order to access confidential information being transmitted (such as passwords or financial documents) are not particularly uncommon. Network sniffers installed on such computers enable the hacker to intercept all network traffic circulating between the hosts within the critical segment. The danger of such unauthorized connections lies in the fact that they allow the hacker easy access to user passwords (including the administrator's passwords) transmitted as plain text by most protocols based on the TCP/IP stack. For example, the following protocols have no protection against such an attack: HTTP, FTP, Telnet, POP3, IMAP, and so on. Information transmitted between SQL Server and client applications also completely lacks protection.

Quite often, employees of companies where Internet access is controlled and restricted using various security tools (such as firewalls or content-control systems) connect modems to their computer in order to connect to the Internet bypassing the security mechanisms. On the other hand, modems are often used to update various accounting programs or legal information databases. Finally, some users employ modems to access their workstations from home. All this presents a serious threat for most companies, since the computers to which modems are connected are totally unprotected. This means that any intruder who detects such a backdoor entrance can use it for unauthorized access to resources that require protection. In my practice, unfortunately, I have never seen a company in which there was not a modem connected to the Internet in order to bypass the security policy requirements.

Intrusion detection systems allow you to identify the addresses of external hosts within the controlled segments and detect increased traffic from specific workstations that previously were not involved in such activity. All this can serve as evidence of the fact that an intruder has penetrated the corporate network via a modem.

Analyzing the Efficiency of Firewall Settings

Firewalls are required to protect the information resources of a corporate network. However, it can only provide the required security level when it is configured correctly. Installing of a firewall without previously testing its settings and eliminating the existing vulnerabilities in network protocols and services is an open invitation to any qualified hacker.

Installing network sensors with the intrusion detection system before and after the firewall allows you to test the efficiency of its settings by comparing the number of attacks detected before and after the firewall.

Analyzing Information Flows

Also commonplace are situations in which IS and communications specialists have no trustworthy information on the protocols used in protected network segments. Using intrusion detection systems, you can control all the protocols and services used in the corporate network, as well as the frequency of their use. This will enable you to compose a scheme of information flows and create a network map, which is a mandatory requirement for successfully creating an information-security infrastructure.

Analyzing Data from Network Equipment

Log files of routers and other network devices serve as an additional source of information on attacks that target the information resources of a corporate network. However, most organizations do not analyze these log files for traces of unauthorized activities, either because such logs do not exist or because the analysis tools (for example, netForensics) are rather expensive.

The task of collecting log-file information and analyzing logged security events can be delegated to the intrusion detection system, which in this case plays the role of a Syslog server. A Syslog server can centralize the process of collecting log-file information and detect attacks and misuses based on this information. Additionally, this measure protects log files from unauthorized modification, since all events logged by routers are immediately transmitted to the IDS sensor. This prevents the intruder from cleaning up the traces of his or her unauthorized activities.

Collecting Proof and Handling Incidents

Intrusion detection systems can and should be used for collecting proof of unauthorized activity. They provide the following functional capabilities:

- Logging events that take place during an attack, and saving this information for future analysis
- Imitating non-existent applications in order to deceive the intruder (the so-called deception mode)
- Enhanced analysis of the log files created by the system and application software, database servers, web servers, and so on
- The possibility of investigating security events before taking any specific action
- Obtaining information on the intruder, including his DNS, MAC, NetBIOS, and IP addresses

Performing Inventory and Creating a Network Map

Correct and reliable information on the components of a corporate network and vital data structures from the moment of their creation until their deletion is crucial for successful detection of almost any security violations. As I will show later, this data allows you to compare reference information on the status of the information system at the moment of its creation (or at the moment of the last authorized modification) with its current state, and thus detect all unauthorized modification in a timely manner. Approaches used to detect such modifications are usually based on determining the differences between the current state of a controlled object and the previously registered and expected state. Security personnel must always know what resources are present, where they are located, and what the expected states of those resources are. Without this information, it is impossible to determine if something was added, modified, violated, and so on. This is especially important for companies in which there are advanced employees who reconfigure their workstations without informing the IT personnel. A situation in which such employees have been granted administrative privileges is particularly dangerous, since such a user is not limited to his or her own workstation, and can reconfigure the whole network segment.

This step, known as creating the network map, is often underestimated or totally neglected in many organizations. This relates to the fact that the process of collecting the required information on the components of the information system is rather long and tedious. Quite often, the employees of the IS department do not have the necessary skills to obtain all such information. In some situations, they can not even access all the equipment used in the network. Because of this, the task of collecting information for creating a network map must be performed in cooperation with the IT and communications departments. This approach is the only one that will enable you to collect all the required data. Also note that, once it has been created, the network map must be constantly maintained and supported in its most up-to-date state. Only in this case will it serve as a basis for controlling and detecting unauthorized modifications.

To create a network map, it is recommended that you use various network management systems (HP OpenView, SPECTRUM, MS Visio, and so on). Such tools include the AutoDiscovery function, which allows you to maintain the network map in its most up-to-date state automatically and trace all unauthorized changes of the network configuration. However, network-level intrusion detection systems can also be used for this purpose. A network-level intrusion detection system used to create the network map has to allow you to identify the following parameters of the network hosts:

- ❑ The role of the host and its DNS and NetBIOS names
- ❑ Network services
- ❑ Active service headers
- ❑ Types and versions of operating systems and application software
- ❑ NetBIOS Shares
- ❑ User and service accounts
- ❑ General parameters of the security policy (audit policy, user and password policy, and so on)

Detecting Default Configurations

Practice has shown that most system administrators install hardware, operating systems, and application software using the default configurations. This, of course, significantly simplifies their tasks, but, on the other hand, it does the same thing for intruders. A qualified hacker, knowing the default configurations and exploiting their vulnerabilities, can penetrate the hosts of the corporate network. Security scanners can be configured to search the hosts where the software is installed in the default configuration, and to recommend steps needed to eliminate the problems detected. Table 3.4 summarizes the number of vulnerabilities in various default configurations of the Windows family of operating systems detected by the Internet Scanner 6.1.

Table 3.4. Number of Windows Vulnerabilities in Default Configurations

Default configuration	Number of vulnerabilities (by risk levels)		
	High	Average	Low
Windows NT 4.0 Server with SP1 and without IIS	0	7	29
Windows NT 4.0 Server with SP6 and without IIS	0	5	21
Windows 2000 Professional	0	5	18
Windows 2000 Professional with SP2	0	5	18

Security Holes in an Urban Network

On January 25, 2001, Largo, Florida became a victim of a hacker attack. Having exploited the security holes in the urban network, the intruders managed to lock access to e-mail for all local authorities and municipal organizations. According to data reported by E-Commerce Times, an unknown Spanish company had illegally exploited the e-mail service by obtaining an address database and using it for sending spam containing ads for some phone service in Europe. As a consequence, Largo's local authorities and citizens were unable to use e-mail for a week. During this time, several million spam messages were sent from the addresses contained in that database. As a result, many ISPs included the entire city into their lists of spammers, and have refused to forward mail received from addresses containing the "largo.com" string. According to Tim McCormick, an Internet Security Systems analyst, the theft of e-mail address databases from organizations and large companies has recently become very popular among spammers.

Controlling the Efficiency of the IT Department

Quite often, some IT departments or specific employees obtain practically unlimited control over the information system and its components, which results in introducing software and hardware vulnerabilities. These vulnerabilities might exist for quite a long time. Usually this happens because of lack of time, negligence, etc.

Disgruntled administrators of IT departments can also modify the configuration of network equipment, important servers, and other devices in order to do intentional damage. Intrusion detection systems are rather efficient tools (and sometimes the only one) that allow you to ensure control over employees and departments that have unlimited access to the information system of the organization.

Intrusion Detection Systems and Other Security Tools

The first step in ensuring security is different from using intrusion detection systems for overlapping or allied purposes. For example, installing such a system makes no sense if any other security tool (such as a firewall) does not protect access to the corporate network from the Internet, because, in this case, anyone who is willing can enter the network. Intrusion detection is a logical add-on that enhances and broadens the functionality of traditional security tools.

Furthermore, intrusion detection technologies allow one to control the efficiency of other security tools such as firewalls, authentication systems, access control systems, Virtual Private Network (VPN) tools, cryptographic systems, and antiviral systems. They all perform rather important or even business-critical functions related to system security. However, because they play vitally important roles, they often become the intruder's primary target. Of no less importance is the fact that these systems are developed and used by humans and, consequently, are also subject to human errors. In case of incorrect configuration, malfunction or attack, the failure of any element of the security system endangers all components of the protected information system.

Summary

Intrusion detection technologies allow one to solve a whole range of problems in order to improve the security level of the hosts within corporate networks:

❏ Monitoring and analysis of user, network, and system activity
❏ System-configuration audit and intrusion detection
❏ Integrity control of the files and other resources of the corporate network
❏ Detection of patterns reflecting well-known attacks
❏ Statistical analysis of suspicious activity
❏ Automatic installation of vendor-supplied software updates
❏ Installation and support of the trap servers to register information on the intruders

However, do not consider intrusion detection systems to be a universal panacea. Such systems have their own area of use, which happens to be quite broad (but still limited). For example, such systems can be used for controlling specific vulnerabilities that might exist within specific network hosts. Another example is controlling the efficiency of firewalls. However, do not expect wonders from intrusion detection systems.

At the current level of development of information technologies, intrusion detection systems can not do the following:

❐ Compensate for the inefficiency of the identification and authentication mechanisms
❐ Perform a completely automatic analysis of attacks
❐ Eliminate problems of the information system with reliability and integrity
❐ Efficiently analyze traffic in broadband networks

Regardless of the method used for detecting intrusion — manual or automatic — all these methods are based on the following three factors:

❐ Indications describing security policy violations. Types of violations are described in *Chapter 2*.
❐ Sources of information in which to search for indications of security policy violations.
❐ Methods of analysis of the information obtained from appropriate sources in order to find indications of attacks.

A knowledge of these three components enables us efficiently to detect attacks both manually and automatically. These three components will be covered in detail in the next chapter. Universal tools, both manual and automated, will be covered in the next chapters. The remaining part of this book is dedicated to specialized systems of intrusion detection.

CHAPTER 4

The Three Basic Principles of Intrusion Detection

"To secure ourselves against defeat lies in our own hands, but the opportunity of defeating the enemy is provided by the enemy himself. Thus, the good fighter is able to secure himself against defeat, but can not make certain of defeating the enemy."

Sun Tzu, "The Art of War."

For intrusion detection technology to be efficient, you must have answers to the following three questions:

☐ *What to detect?* You must know the signs of security policy violations.

☐ *Where to detect?* You must know sources of information stating where one can search for indications of security policy violations.

☐ *How to detect?* You must know methods of analysis of the information obtained from appropriate sources in order to find indications of attacks.

Attack Indications

To detect security policy violations within a controlled area (network traffic of log file), it is necessary to know how to identify them and how to distinguish them from normal security events. The following events can be considered to be attack indications [Edward1-99]:

- ❏ Repeated occurrence of specific events
- ❏ Incorrect commands or commands that do not correspond to the current situation
- ❏ Exploiting vulnerabilities
- ❏ Inappropriate parameters of the network traffic
- ❏ Unexpected attributes
- ❏ Inexplicable problems
- ❏ Additional information on security violations

Any security tool (firewalls, authentication servers, access control systems, and so on) uses one or two of the above-listed conditions, while intrusion detection systems (depending on the implementation) employ nearly all attack indications.

This chapter will help you understand how intrusion detection systems make decisions. It is also aimed at helping developers create custom systems for detection intrusions or unauthorized activity. This especially relates to those application developers working on financial applications or automated systems for communications. Furthermore, the description of the indications of the unauthorized activity will be useful if you have no automated intrusion detection system at your disposal and therefore need to detect these indications manually.

Repeated Occurrence of Specific Events

Recognizing specific actions or events that take place repeatedly represents one of the best methods of intrusion detection. This mechanism is based on the assumption that, if the first attempt has failed, the intruder repeats his attempts of unauthorized access to a specific resource. For example, port scanning in order to find available network services or any attempts of guessing the password can be considered to be such an attempt. Algorithms used for detecting unauthorized activity must recognize such repeated attempts and decide how many additional attempts are, in fact, indications of an attack. It should be noted that, if the intruder knows for sure how to access the resource (or manages to intercept or guess the ID and password of the authorized user) and does not make any errors, his attempt to gain unauthorized access would be practically impossible to detect. If the intruder manages to create an exact working model of the attack target, and has some practice in how to imitate authorized users, these actions will most probably also go unnoticed. However, creating an entirely identical working model of the attack target is very expensive, and most intruders acting on their own (or even those in organized hacker communities) can not afford it.

Detecting of repeated events represents a powerful approach, since it allows detection even of those attacks about which there is no additional information (in other words, it allows the detection of unknown attacks of a specific type). Either (or both) of the following events can be used as a criterion:

- ❑ The number of repeated events exceeds a specific threshold value (for example, the permitted number of network logons might be exceeded).
- ❑ Events are repeated within a specified time interval (for example, an attempt to connect host ports).

Controlling Threshold Values

In this case, one controls a specific threshold value in order to distinguish authorized repeated events from unauthorized ones. Unauthorized repeated events may correspond both to normal errors and to actual attacks. In any case, the system will detect every situation in which the threshold value has been exceeded. Based on practical experience, one can specify custom threshold values for different system components. Specifying the allowed number of login attempts is a typical example of controlling the threshold value. Setting a maximum number of permitted login attempts in Windows 2000 is a typical example of specifying a threshold value (Fig. 4.1).

Notice that incorrect selection of the threshold value might result in a false negative or a false positive problem. In other words, if the specified threshold value is too low, all control will be reduced to frequent activation of the intrusion detection system, i.e., false detection. On the other hand, if you specify a large value, some attacks will not be detected.

❗ *Attack on the Network of Westminster Bank*

A teller of Westminster Bank in Great Britain established a dial-up connection to the bank network from his home computer. After that, he performed 1,200 transactions, each time transferring £10 to his account. The security service did not notice it, since transfers of small amounts of money were not controlled at all. However, when he wanted to make a larger stake and transferred £984,252 to his friend's account, this event was immediately noticed. The bank fined the teller and demanded compensation in the sum of £15,000. However, the court dismissed this claim and even charged the bank for its inability to protect its own security.

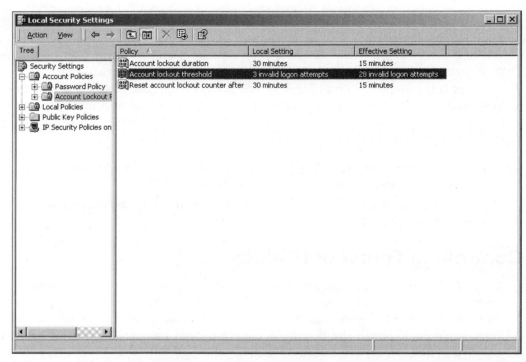

Fig. 4.1. Specifying the maximum number of login attempts permitted in Windows 2000

Controlling Time Intervals

A typical example illustrating this method is the detection of port scanning (Listing 4.1), i.e., detecting the specified number of attempts to access host ports during a specified time interval. From now on, all fragments of listings that deserve special attention appear in bold. Also, I would like to emphasize the fact that most of the listing examples provided in this and subsequent sections were taken from http://www.incidents.org/logs/, or are based on practical exercises performed within the framework of preparing for the Global Information Assurance Certification (GIAC) Certified Intrusion Analyst exam (http://www.giac.org/GCIA.php). Port scanning can be performed using various programs, which differ in the implementation of this mechanism. The simplest programs, such as Haktek, just try all the ports, starting with the first and ending with the user-specified port (Listing 4.1).

Listing 4.1. Port Scanning Implemented Using Haktek (TCPdump Log File)

```
17:17:21.966870 WS_LUKICH.2876 > WS_LUKA.1: S 713310:713310(0) win 8192
<mss 1460> (DF)

17:17:21.967698 WS_LUKICH.2877 > WS_LUKA.2: S 713329:713329(0) win 8192
<mss 1460> (DF)

17:17:21.968612 WS_LUKICH.2878 > WS_LUKA.3: S 713349:713349(0) win 8192
<mss 1460> (DF)

17:17:21.969095 WS_LUKICH.2879 > WS_LUKA.4: S 713364:713364(0) win 8192
<mss 1460> (DF)

17:17:21.969574 WS_LUKICH.2880 > WS_LUKA.5: S 713372:713372(0) win 8192
<mss 1460> (DF)

17:17:21.970041 WS_LUKICH.2881 > WS_LUKA.6: S 713381:713381(0) win 8192
<mss 1460> (DF)

17:17:21.970523 WS_LUKICH.2882 > WS_LUKA.7: S 713391:713391(0) win 8192
<mss 1460> (DF)

17:17:21.971031 WS_LUKICH.2883 > WS_LUKA.8: S 713402:713402(0) win 8192
<mss 1460> (DF)

17:17:21.971539 WS_LUKICH.2884 > WS_LUKA.9: S 713414:713414(0) win 8192
<mss 1460> (DF)

17:17:21.972014 WS_LUKICH.2885 > WS_LUKA.10: S 713427:713427(0) win 8192
<mss 1460> (DF)

17:17:21.973780 WS_LUKICH.2886 > WS_LUKA.11: S 713441:713441(0) win 8192
<mss 1460> (DF)

17:17:21.973814 WS_LUKICH.2887 > WS_LUKA.12: S 713455:713455(0) win 8192
<mss 1460> (DF)

17:17:21.973834 WS_LUKICH.2888 > WS_LUKA.13: S 713469:713469(0) win 8192
<mss 1460> (DF)
```

Note that the incorrect selection of the time interval when controlling the threshold value can also result in false negative and false positive problems described in the previous section.

Recognizing such activities is relatively easy. However, such port scanners are used rarely and only by inexperienced users who do not know that there are more advanced and intelligent utilities. A good example of such a tool is Nmap (http://www.nmap.org), which runs in most Unix clones as well as in Windows. This utility implements a significant number of scanning types — for example, version 3.00 provides more than 10 scanning algorithms, including port scanning (Listings 4.2 to 4.4).

Listing 4.2. Port Scanning (-sT) Using Nmap (a Fragment of the TCPdump Log File)

```
17:26:48.031721 WS_LUKA.2797 > WS_LUKICH.371: S 26274004:26274004(0) win
8192 <mss 1460> (DF)

17:26:48.034533 WS_LUKA.2798 > WS_LUKICH.344: S 26330728:26330728(0) win
8192 <mss 1460> (DF)

17:26:48.035510 WS_LUKA.2799 > WS_LUKICH.919: S 26396113:26396113(0) win
8192 <mss 1460> (DF)

17:26:48.036466 WS_LUKA.2800 > WS_LUKICH.1155: S 26439772:26439772(0) win
8192 <mss 1460> (DF)

17:26:48.037421 WS_LUKA.2801 > WS_LUKICH.117: S 26476417:26476417(0) win
8192 <mss 1460> (DF)

17:26:48.038372 WS_LUKA.2802 > WS_LUKICH.625: S 26518671:26518671(0) win
8192 <mss 1460> (DF)

17:26:48.039338 WS_LUKA.2803 > WS_LUKICH.220: S 26552575:26552575(0) win
8192 <mss 1460> (DF)

17:26:48.040281 WS_LUKA.2804 > WS_LUKICH.770: S 26588454:26588454(0) win
8192 <mss 1460> (DF)

17:26:48.041235 WS_LUKA.2805 > WS_LUKICH.619: S 26633584:26633584(0) win
8192 <mss 1460> (DF)

17:26:48.042170 WS_LUKA.2806 > WS_LUKICH.1652: S 26670889:26670889(0) win
8192 <mss 1460> (DF)

17:26:48.043264 WS_LUKA.2807 > WS_LUKICH.403: S 26734852:26734852(0) win
8192 <mss 1460> (DF)
```

Listing 4.3. Port Scanning (-sS) Using Nmap (a Fragment of the TCPdump Log File)

```
17:22:32.224567 WS_LUKA.52753 > WS_LUKICH.1544: S 866284386:866284386(0) win 1024
17:22:32.225413 WS_LUKA.52753 > WS_LUKICH.427: S 866284386:866284386(0) win 1024
17:22:32.225413 WS_LUKA.52753 > WS_LUKICH.447: S 866284386:866284386(0) win 1024
17:22:32.224845 WS_LUKA.52753 > WS_LUKICH.496: S 866284386:866284386(0) win 1024
17:22:32.225009 WS_LUKA.52753 > WS_LUKICH.597: S 866284386:866284386(0) win 1024
17:22:32.225207 WS_LUKA.52753 > WS_LUKICH.659: S 866284386:866284386(0) win 1024
17:22:32.225413 WS_LUKA.52753 > WS_LUKICH.159: S 866284386:866284386(0) win 1024
17:22:32.225582 WS_LUKA.52753 > WS_LUKICH.529: S 866284386:866284386(0) win 1024
17:22:32.225782 WS_LUKA.52753 > WS_LUKICH.2017: S 866284386:866284386(0) win 1024
17:22:32.225413 WS_LUKA.52753 > WS_LUKICH.427: S 866284386:866284386(0) win 1024
17:22:32.225945 WS_LUKA.52753 > WS_LUKICH.1380: S 866284386:866284386(0) win 1024
```

```
17:22:32.226153 WS_LUKA.52753 > WS_LUKICH.1522: S 866284386:866284386(0) win 1024
17:22:32.226356 WS_LUKA.52753 > WS_LUKICH.1109: S 866284386:866284386(0) win 1024
17:22:32.231078 WS_LUKA.52753 > WS_LUKICH.306: S 866284386:866284386(0) win 1024
17:22:32.233200 WS_LUKA.52753 > WS_LUKICH.274: S 866284386:866284386(0) win 1024
17:22:32.225413 WS_LUKA.52753 > WS_LUKICH.447: S 866284386:866284386(0) win 1024
17:22:32.235295 WS_LUKA.52753 > WS_LUKICH.1663: S 866284386:866284386(0) win 1024
```

Listing 4.4. Port Scanning (-sU) Using Nmap (a Fragment of the TCPdump Log File)

```
17:30:03.034865 WS_LUKA.48796 > WS_LUKICH.670: udp 0
17:30:03.035066 WS_LUKA.48796 > WS_LUKICH.1248: udp 0
17:30:03.035269 WS_LUKA.48796 > WS_LUKICH.25: udp 0
17:30:03.035448 WS_LUKA.48796 > WS_LUKICH.1017: udp 0
17:30:03.035653 WS_LUKA.48796 > WS_LUKICH.1415: udp 0
17:30:03.035815 WS_LUKA.48796 > WS_LUKICH.963: udp 0
17:30:03.036006 WS_LUKA.48796 > WS_LUKICH.11: udp 0
17:30:03.036160 WS_LUKA.48796 > WS_LUKICH.345: udp 0
```

All three fragments of the TCPdump log file presented above are very interesting, since the number of the scanned port is not incremented by 1, which is what happens normally, but rather in a random way. In order to complicate the detection of port scanning, the port number is both increased and decreased. An additional mechanism, concealing the fact of scanning to deceive intrusion detection systems, implies repeat scanning of some ports that were already scanned (for example, 427 and 447).

Besides the classical types of scanning, easily detected by firewalls (Listing 4.5), there are more sophisticated methods of searching for vulnerabilities that can not be detected using traditional network security tools. These include so-called stealth scanning, which uses specific features characteristic for processing network packets that do not correspond to TCP/IP standards. Such methods of scanning will be covered later.

Listing 4.5. Detecting Host Scanning (a Fragment of the Check Point Firewall-1 Log File)

```
"421316"  "29Dec2000"  " 9:32:16"  "daemon"  "localhost"  "alert"  "accept"
""  "x.x.x.x"  "x.x.x.x"  "ip"  ""  ""  ""  ""  ""  ""  ""  ""  ""  ""
"MAD"  "additionals:  attack=blocked_connection_port_scanning"
```

```
"422255"  "29Dec2000"  " 9:33:59"  "daemon"  "localhost"  "alert"  "accept"
""  "x.x.x.x"  "x.x.x.x"  "ip"  ""  ""  ""  ""  ""  ""  ""  ""  ""  ""  ""
"MAD"  " additionals: attack=blocked_connection_port_scanning"
"427220"  "29Dec2000"  " 9:43:26"  "daemon"  "localhost"  "alert"  "accept"
""  "x.x.x.x"  "x.x.x.x"  "ip"  ""  ""  ""  ""  ""  ""  ""  ""  ""  ""  ""
"MAD"  " additionals: attack=blocked_connection_port_scanning"
```

Another sophisticated scanning method that complicates scanning detection implies increasing the time interval during which scanning takes place. Usually, host scanners send requests at a rate of approximately 5 to 10 ports per second. If we change the default time settings (for example, the -sI mode of the Nmap 3.00 scanner, or the -T mode in Nmap 2.xx), most intrusion detection systems will not react to such activities, since they interpret it as normal (Listing 4.6).

Listing 4.6. Host Scanning (a Fragment of the TCPdump Log File)

```
12:01:38.234455 200.0.0.200 > 200.0.0.67: icmp: echo request
12:03:51.543524 200.0.0.200 > 200.0.0.87: icmp: echo request
12:05:04.655342 200.0.0.200 > 200.0.0.134: icmp: echo request
12:07:18.573256 200.0.0.200 > 200.0.0.23: icmp: echo request
12:09:31.676899 200.0.0.200 > 200.0.0.11: icmp: echo request
12:11:44.896754 200.0.0.200 > 200.0.0.104: icmp: echo request
12:13:57.075356 200.0.0.200 > 200.0.0.2: icmp: echo request
```

Controlling time intervals can also be used for detecting Denial of Service attacks. For example, the Smurf attack is characterized by the usage of broadcast packets transmitted for quite a long time interval. There have been some cases in which such packets were sent for several days, thus causing the attacked network to fail, due to its inability to process authorized traffic. Below, I provide a fragment of the Cisco router log file (Listing 4.7), where examples of the Smurf and Fraggle attacks are registered (Fraggle is similar to Smurf, but intended for the UDP protocol). In real-world practice, the number of such records will significantly exceed 100.

Listing 4.7. Detection of the SMURF and Fraggle Attacks (a Fragment of the Cisco Router Log File)

```
Dec 22 16:15:26: %SEC-6-IPACCESSLOGDP: list Internet denied icmp
172.20.20.1 -> 200.0.0.255 (8/0), 1 packet

Dec 22 16:16:26: %SEC-6-IPACCESSLOGDP: list Internet denied icmp
172.20.20.2 -> 200.0.0.255 (8/0), 24 packets
```

```
Dec 22 16:16:56: %SEC-6-IPACCESSLOGP: list Internet denied udp
172.20.20.3(21820) -> 200.0.0.255 (19), 1 packet
Dec 22 16:26:26: %SEC-6-IPACCESSLOGDP: list Internet denied icmp
172.20.20.4 -> 200.0.0.255 (8/0), 3 packets
Dec 22 16:27:26: %SEC-6-IPACCESSLOGDP: list Internet denied icmp
172.20.20.5 -> 200.0.0.255 (8/0), 4 packets
```

Incorrect Commands

Another method of identifying unauthorized activity involves detection of invalid or incorrect requests or responses expected from automated processes or programs. Lack of correspondence to the expected reactions enables us to come to the conclusion that one of the participants of the information exchange — either the one requesting information or the one returning the answer — has been replaced. It is impossible to illustrate the detection of various invalid or incorrect commands within a single book. Therefore, I will concentrate only on the most typical examples of incorrect command usage. As an example, let us consider vulnerable CGI scripts on the web server (as was shown in *Chapter 2*, this is one of the most common vulnerabilities all over the world). In the example provided below, a request for two non-existent CGI scripts — namely, Glimpse cgi-bin and test-cgi — can be detected by analyzing records of the server log file, or by using a network intrusion detection system (Listings 4.8 and 4.9).

Listing 4.8. Detecting Scanning for Vulnerable CGI Scripts (a Fragment of the WWW Server Log File)

```
Mon Dec 27 01:42:58 1999] [error] [client 172.20.20.1] File does not
exist: /web/home/www/www_home/cgi-bin/aglimpse
[Mon Dec 27 01:42:58 1999] [error] [client 172.20.20.1] File does not
exist: /web/home/www/www_home/scripts/iisadmin/bdir.htr
[Mon Dec 27 01:42:58 1999] [error] [client 172.20.20.1] File does not
exist: /web/home/www/www_home/cgi-dos/args.bat
[Mon Dec 27 01:42:58 1999] [error] [client 172.20.20.1] File does not
exist: /web/home/www/www_home/cgi-bin/AnyForm2
[Mon Dec 27 01:42:58 1999] [error] [client 172.20.20.1] File does not
exist: /web/home/www/www_home/cgi-bin/campas
[Mon Dec 27 01:42:58 1999] [error] [client 172.20.20.1] File does not
exist: /web/home/www/www_home/cgi-bin/Count.cgi
[Mon Dec 27 01:42:58 1999] [error] [client 172.20.20.1] File does not
exist: /web/home/www/www_home/carbo.dll
[Mon Dec 27 01:42:58 1999] [error] [client 172.20.20.1] File does not
exist: /web/home/www/www_home/cgi-bin/finger
```

```
[Mon Dec 27 01:42:58 1999] [error] [client 172.20.20.1] File does not
exist: /web/home/www/www_home/cgi-bin/faxsurvey
[Mon Dec 27 01:42:58 1999] [error] [client 172.20.20.1] File does not
exist: /web/home/www/www_home/cgi-bin/htmlscript
[Mon Dec 27 01:42:58 1999] [error] [client 172.20.20.1] File does not
exist: /web/home/www/www_home/cgi-bin/handler
[Mon Dec 27 01:42:58 1999] [error] [client 172.20.20.1] File does not
exist: /web/home/www/www_home/cgi-bin/man.sh
[Mon Dec 27 01:42:59 1999] [error] [client 172.20.20.1] File does not
exist: /web/home/www/www_home/cgi-bin/jj
[Mon Dec 27 01:42:59 1999] [error] [client 172.20.20.1] File does not
exist: /web/home/www/www_home/cgi-bin/pfdispaly.cgi
[Mon Dec 27 01:42:59 1999] [error] [client 172.20.20.1] File does not
exist: /web/home/www/www_home/cgi-bin/nph-test-cgi
[Mon Dec 27 01:42:59 1999] [error] [client 172.20.20.1] File does not
exist: /web/home/www/www_home/cgi-bin/php.cgi
[Mon Dec 27 01:42:59 1999] [error] [client 172.20.20.1] File does not
exist: /web/home/www/www_home/cgi-bin/phf
[Mon Dec 27 01:42:59 1999] [error] [client 172.20.20.1] File does not
exist: /web/home/www/www_home/search97.vts
[Mon Dec 27 01:42:59 1999] [error] [client 172.20.20.1] File does not
exist: /web/home/www/www_home/cgi-bin/test-cgi
[Mon Dec 27 01:42:59 1999] [error] [client 172.20.20.1] File does not
exist: /web/home/www/www_home/cgi-win/uploader.exe
[Mon Dec 27 01:42:59 1999] [error] [client 172.20.20.1] File does not
exist: /web/home/www/www_home/cgi-bin/textcounter.pl
[Mon Dec 27 01:42:59 1999] [error] [client 172.20.20.1] File does not
exist: /web/home/www/www_home/cgi-bin/view-source
[Mon Dec 27 01:43:00 1999] [error] [client 172.20.20.1] File does not
exist: /web/home/www/www_home/cgi-bin/webdist.cgi
[Mon Dec 27 01:43:00 1999] [error] [client 172.20.20.1] File does not
exist: /web/home/www/www_home/cgi-bin/websendmail
[Mon Dec 27 01:43:00 1999] [error] [client 172.20.20.1] File does not
exist: /web/home/www/www_home/cgi-bin/webgais
[Mon Dec 27 01:43:00 1999] [error] [client 172.20.20.1] File does not
exist: /web/home/www/www_home/cgi-bin/www-sql
```

Listing 4.9. Detecting Requests to Vulnerable CGI Scripts Such as Test-cgi and Aglimpse (a Fragment of the Snort Log File)

```
22:00:08.952175 200.0.0.104.53558 > 200.0.0.110.80: P
1677621322:1677621391(69) ack 2335601879 win 8760 (DF) (ttl 242, id 12223)
```

```
0000:  4500 006d 2fbf 4000 f206 0465 80af 0d4a   E..m/.@....e...J
0010:  0a00 0009 d136 0050 63fe 784a 8b36 74d7   .d...6.Pc.xJ.6t.
0020:  5018 2238 4af8 0000 504f 5354 202f 6367   P."8J...POST /cg
0030:  692d 6269 6e2f 7465 7374 2d63 6769 2048   i-bin/test-cgi H
0040:  5454 502f 312e 300a 436f 6e74 656e 742d   TTP/1.0.Content-
0050:  7479 7065 3a20 2a0a 436f 6e74 656e 742d   type: *.Content-
0060:  6c65 6e67 7468 3a20 300a 0a00 19           length: 0....
```

```
01:14:18.042722 200.0.0.104.42930 > 200.0.0.110.80: P
3053993825:3053993920(95) ack 2009011357 win 8760 (DF) (ttl 242, id 57632)
0000:  4500 0087 e120 4000 f206 52e9 80af 0d4a   E.... @...R....J
0010:  0a00 0009 a7b2 0050 b608 3f61 77bf 149d   .d.....P..?aw...
0020:  5018 2238 8704 0000 4745 5420 2f63 6769   P."8....GET /cgi
0030:  2d62 696e 2f61 676c 696d 7073 652f 3830   -bin/aglimpse/80
0040:  7c49 4653 3d5f 3b43 4d44 3d5f 6563 686f   |IFS=_;CMD=_echo
0050:  5c3b 6563 686f 5f69 642d 6167 6c69 6d70   \;echo_id-aglimp
0060:  7365 5c3b 756e 616d 655f 2d61 5c3b 6964   se\;uname_-a\;id
0070:  3b65 7661 6c24 434d 443b 2048 5454 502f   ;eval$CMD; HTTP/
0080:  312e 300a 0a00 20                         1.0...
```

Exploiting Vulnerabilities

According to the above-described definition and classification of vulnerabilities and the definition of the attack, any of the attack indications being considered would also be an indication of vulnerability. For example, unexpected attributes in various requests or packets can be classified as design or implementation vulnerabilities.

However, the process of using automated tools for searching for the most common vulnerabilities (the so-called security scanners) or attack implementation is generally distinguished as a separate category of attack indications. There is a wide range of such tools, from freeware utilities such as X-Spider, or ShadowSecurityScanner, up to commercial products such as the Internet Scanner or Retina. Despite the fact that vulnerability search tools are intended for noble purposes, they are quite often misused. This is especially true for cases when vulnerability searching tools are not protected from such misuse, or are themselves freeware.

There are two aspects of detecting such tools:

☐ *Detection of vulnerability scanners.* Some specialized tools, such as the Courtney system developed in Computer Incident Advisory Capability (CIAC), can detect the fact of the SATAN scanner usage.

☐ *Detection of attack implementation.* The RealSecure Network Sensor system developed by ISS can log that the intruder has imitated the action externally in relation to the host being scanned; this is committed by the intruder using various security scanners such as CyberCop Scanner or Queso.

However, merely using security scanners does not serve as evidence that attacks are in fact taking place. All these tools can also be used for regular authorized checks of the information system. Thus, it is necessary to perform an additional investigation of all registered facts of security scanner usage. For example, if shortly after detecting that some of your hosts are being scanned, the fact that the system's vulnerability is being exploited is registered can itself be considered to be evidence of an attack. Such an analysis and correlation can be performed both manually and using specialized tools such as RealSecure SiteProtector, developed by ISS, or netForensics from the netForensics company.

Inappropriate Parameters of Network Traffic

There are other parameters that can be used as indications of an attack. Certain characteristics of network traffic can be used for this purpose, for example:

☐ External network addresses detected within the internal network that access other external network addresses

☐ Unexpected network traffic (for example, bypassing the firewall or exceeding the amount of transmitted traffic)

☐ Unexpected parameters of network traffic (non-standard flag combinations, etc.)

☐ Detection of scanning attempts (such as identification of network hosts and services)

☐ Repeated half-open connections, which might characterize either DoS attacks or packet spoofing

☐ Successful attempts of connecting to rarely used or unusual services on the network hosts

☐ Sequential connections to network hosts or services running on a specific host

☐ Connections TO and FROM an unexpected location

☐ Repeated failed connection attempts

Parameters of the Inbound Traffic

The most illustrative example of attack indication is represented by incoming network packets arriving to the protected LAN from outside and having a source address corresponding to the address range of the internal network (Fig. 4.2). Most firewalls and other security systems generally register this attack indication.

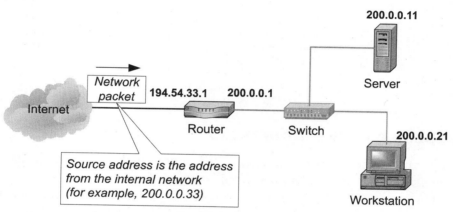

Fig. 4.2. Replacement of the external address

If the intrusion detection system or other access control tool (firewall or router) can not control the traffic's direction, the so-called address-spoofing attack can be implemented. This attack enables the intruder to perform various unauthorized actions in the same way as if they were originating at one of the hosts within the internal network. Normally, security requirements are weaker for such hosts in comparison to those for external hosts.

Parameters of the Outbound Traffic

One example of an attack indication of this sort can be seen with outgoing network packets from the internal LAN that have a source address corresponding to the address range of the external network (Fig. 4.3). In this case, an intruder located within the internal network can attempt to conceal his actions by making them appear as if they have originated from the external network. By doing so, he can draw suspicion away from users within the internal network and mislead investigators.

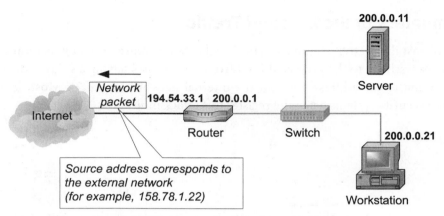

Fig. 4.3. Replacement of the internal address

Unexpected Packet Addresses

In this case, packets with an unexpected source address (or recipient port for TCP/UDP protocols) can be interpreted as an attack indication. The first example is the detection of a packet arriving from an external network with an unavailable IP address (as was the case with the Kevin Mitnick attack) or with an IP address impossible for the external network. For example, there are specific addresses that are not routed on the Internet, for example: 10.*.*.*, 172.16.0.0 through 172.31.255.255, and 192.168.*.* (Listings 4.10 and 4.11). These address ranges are described in RFC 1918 *"Address Allocation for Private Internets."* Besides this category of addresses, there is yet another set of address ranges impossible for packets arriving to your network from outside. These addresses are reserved by IANA. Reserved addresses include: 0.0.0.0/8, 1.0.0.0/8, 2.0.0.0/8, 5.0.0.0/8, 7.0.0.0/8, 23.0.0.0/8, 27.0.0.0/8, 31.0.0.0/8, 36.0.0.0/8, 37.0.0.0/8, 39.0.0.0/8, 41 through 42.0.0.0/8, 58 through 60.0.0.0/8, 67 through 127.0.0.0/8, 219 through 223.0.0.0/8, 240 through 255.0.0.0/8.

**Listing 4.10. Detecting the Usage of Reserved Addresses
(a Fragment of the TCPdump Log File)**

```
03:38:18.285290 10.1.100.23.2483 > 192.168.1.2.21: S 21101636:21101636(0)
win 8192 (DF)
03:38:12.287184 10.1.100.23.2483 > 192.168.1.2.21: S 21101636:21101636(0)
win 8192 (DF)
```

**Listing 4.11. Detecting the Usage of Reserved Addresses
(a Fragment of the Cisco Router Log File)**

```
May 10 09:20:33.328 UTC: %SEC-6-IPACCESSLOGP: list 100 denied tcp
10.1.2.73(0) -> 192.231.90.254(0), 1 packet
May 10 09:26:04.564 UTC: %SEC-6-IPACCESSLOGP: list 100 denied tcp
10.1.2.73(0) -> 192.231.90.254(0), 4 packets
May 10 09:26:34.260 UTC: %SEC-6-IPACCESSLOGP: list 100 denied tcp
10.0.0.57(0) -> 192.231.90.254(0), 1 packet
May 10 09:32:04.708 UTC: %SEC-6-IPACCESSLOGP: list 100 denied tcp
10.0.0.57(0) -> 192.231.90.254(0), 20 packets
```

Another example is represented by the Land attack, in which the address and port of the source coincide with the address and port of the target (Listing 4.12). Processing such packets results in an endless loop.

Listing 4.12. Land Attack (TCPdump Log File Fragment)

```
10:56:32.395383 200.0.0.104.139 > 200.0.0.104.139: S
10:56:35.145383 200.0.0.104.139 > 200.0.0.104.139: S
10:56:36.265383 200.0.0.104.139 > 200.0.0.104.139: S
```

The next example relates to connection requests via Telnet protocol originating from an unknown host or from a host with which you have no trusted relationship. Mismatching MAC and IP addresses of network packets represents just another classical example. The final example of an attack using this feature is the Setiri Trojan, demonstrated at Def Con 10. This Trojan, which exploits Internet Explorer's vulnerabilities, is not detected by firewalls, and, consequently, can not be locked by them. The problem with detection of this Trojan lies in the fact that the Trojan itself does not initiate the Internet connection, like most other Trojans do. Rather, it opens invisible Internet Explorer windows to which the firewall does not react. These invisible windows implement all the unauthorized activities, such as connection to the anonymous proxy server, downloading files from unexpected hosts, and so on.

Unexpected Parameters of Network Packets

One can provide lots of examples of attacks upon unexpected network-packet parameters. These attacks are gradually becoming more and more numerous, since intruders are constantly looking for and finding new vulnerabilities in the TCP/IP stack implementations in practically all operating systems. For example, if you detect a network packet with SYN and ACK bits set (Listing 4.13) (the second stage of establishing a virtual TCP connection), this might conceal unauthorized penetration. The above-mentioned method is widely used in so-called stealth-scanning, which was rather common among intruders [Northcutt1-99].

Listing 4.13. Stealth Scanning Using SYN/ACK (Fragment of the TCPdump Log File)

```
06:41:24.067330 stealth.bad.gay.org.113 > viper.infosec.ru.1004: S
4052190291:4052190291(0) ack 674711610 win 8192

06:42:08.063341 stealth.bad.gay.org.113 > www.infosec.ru.2039: S
2335925210:2335925210(0) ack 674711610 win 8192

06:42:14.582943 stealth.bad.gay.org.113 > un.infosec.ru.2307: S
2718446928:2718446928(0) ack 674711610 win 8192
```

The appearance of a SYN/ACK packet without a previous SYN packet might also serve as evidence of the presence of asymmetric routers within the network. Consequently, if your network supports such routes, you need to do some additional investigation. Besides SYN/ACK bits, it is possible to use the following bits in the TCP packet header: FIN bits — FIN scanning (Listing 4.14), RESET — RESET scanning, and bit combinations — Xmas scanning (Listing 4.15) or a total lack of such bits — Null scanning (Listing 4.16).

Listing 4.14. FIN Scanning (-sF) Using Nmap (a Fragment of the TCPdump Log File)

```
18:18:03.436878 WS_LUKA.57239 > WS_LUKICH.9535: F 0:0(0) win 3072
18:18:03.437131 WS_LUKA.57239 > WS_LUKICH.1482: F 0:0(0) win 3072
18:18:03.437335 WS_LUKA.57239 > WS_LUKICH.617: F 0:0(0) win 3072
18:18:03.437501 WS_LUKA.57239 > WS_LUKICH.148: F 0:0(0) win 3072
18:18:03.437709 WS_LUKA.57239 > WS_LUKICH.638: F 0:0(0) win 3072
18:18:03.437872 WS_LUKA.57239 > WS_LUKICH.1467: F 0:0(0) win 3072
18:18:03.438089 WS_LUKA.57239 > WS_LUKICH.1475: F 0:0(0) win 3072
18:18:03.438286 WS_LUKA.57239 > WS_LUKICH.852: F 0:0(0) win 3072
18:18:03.438446 WS_LUKA.57239 > WS_LUKICH.653: F 0:0(0) win 3072
18:18:03.442145 WS_LUKA.57239 > WS_LUKICH.672: F 0:0(0) win 3072
```

Listing 4.15. Xmas Scanning (-sX) Using Nmap (a Fragment of the TCPdump Log File)

```
18:18:28.038171 WS_LUKA.57407 > WS_LUKICH.1031: FP 0:0(0) win 3072 urg 0
18:18:28.038378 WS_LUKA.57407 > WS_LUKICH.1112: FP 0:0(0) win 3072 urg 0
18:18:28.038643 WS_LUKA.57407 > WS_LUKICH.2048: FP 0:0(0) win 3072 urg 0
18:18:28.038846 WS_LUKA.57407 > WS_LUKICH.6666: FP 0:0(0) win 3072 urg 0
18:18:28.039015 WS_LUKA.57407 > WS_LUKICH.906: FP 0:0(0) win 3072 urg 0
18:18:28.039180 WS_LUKA.57407 > WS_LUKICH.135: FP 0:0(0) win 3072 urg 0
18:18:28.039369 WS_LUKA.57407 > WS_LUKICH.1003: FP 0:0(0) win 3072 urg 0
18:18:28.039575 WS_LUKA.57407 > WS_LUKICH.3141: FP 0:0(0) win 3072 urg 0
18:18:28.039739 WS_LUKA.57407 > WS_LUKICH.1448: FP 0:0(0) win 3072 urg 0
```

Listing 4.16. Null Scanning (-sN) Using Nmap (a Fragment of the TCPdump Log File)

```
18:20:04.466572 WS_LUKA.53497 > WS_LUKICH.2766: . win 1024
18:20:04.466776 WS_LUKA.53497 > WS_LUKICH.534: . win 1024
18:20:04.466995 WS_LUKA.53497 > WS_LUKICH.206: . win 1024
18:20:04.467164 WS_LUKA.53497 > WS_LUKICH.119: . win 1024
18:20:04.467372 WS_LUKA.53497 > WS_LUKICH.636: . win 1024
18:20:04.467575 WS_LUKA.53497 > WS_LUKICH.313: . win 1024
18:20:04.467836 WS_LUKA.53497 > WS_LUKICH.372: . win 1024
18:20:04.468040 WS_LUKA.53497 > WS_LUKICH.378: . win 1024
18:20:04.468204 WS_LUKA.53497 > WS_LUKICH.532: . win 1024
```

Null Scanning can be better illustrated with an example of a log file created by the Snort intrusion detection system (Listing 4.17).

Listing 4.17. Null Scanning Using Nmap (a Fragment of the Snort Log File)

```
[**] NULL Scan [**]
05/28-21:09:23.686988 200.0.0.200:27025 -> 200.0.0.104:1186 TCP TTL:44
TOS:0x0 ID:64660 DF ******* Seq: 0xE4714 Ack: 0xFFFFFFFF Win: 0x0
```

For comparison, we can provide an already-demonstrated example of FIN scanning (Listing 4.18).

Listing 4.18. FIN Scanning Using Nmap (a Fragment of the Snort Log File)

```
[**] SCAN-FIN [**]
02/02-04:49:15.135173 0:D0:58:4A:46:D0 -> 0:10:5A:6C:9A:55 type:0x800
len:0x104 195.11.50.204:2931 -> my-squid:53 TCP TTL:39 TOS:0x0 ID:2037
*F**** Seq: 0x32563E Ack: 0x362C0000 Win: 0x0
```

Any packet that does not conform to the RFC requirements can cause the failure of the communication equipment that processes this packet. Note that this relates not only to routers or switches, but also to firewalls and intrusion detection systems. There are many attacks that use invalid combinations of the TCP flags in network packets. Some combinations cause the hosts processing such packets to fail, while other combinations result in packets not being noticed by some intrusion detection systems or firewalls. RFC 793 describes how various systems must react to normal TCP packets. However, neither this nor other similar documents specify how the system should react to incorrect TCP packets. Consequently, different devices and different operating systems produce different reactions to network packets with invalid combinations of TCP flags. A TCP packet can contain six flags: SYN, ACK, FIN, RST, PSH, URG. Invalid combinations can be detected by at least one of the indications listed below [Frederick1-00]:

❏ SYN+FIN. This combination is invalid because these flags are mutually exclusive. The first flag establishes a connection, while the second one closes it. Various scanners, such as Nmap, use this combination quite frequently. Quite recently, most intrusion detection systems have not been able to detect this kind of scanning. Currently, the situation has changed for the better, and most intrusion detection systems are able to trace such combinations of flags. However, adding at least one extra flag to this combination (for example, SYN+FIN+PSH, SYN+FIN+RST, SYN+FIN+RST+PSH) once again prevents some intrusion detected systems from detecting the modified scanning (Listing 4.19). Some analysts have named such combinations the "Christmas Tree Pattern."

Listing 4.19. The "Christmas Tree Pattern" (Fragment from a Snort Log File)

```
01/23-01:15:22.237103 195.11.212.180:30975 -> 192.0.97.80:49708
TCP TTL:49 TOS:0x0 ID:12207 DF
SFRPAU21 Seq: 0x78FFC22C Ack: 0x78FFC22C Win: 0xC22C
TCP Options => Opt 120 (40): C22C 78FF C22C 78FF C22C 78FF
0000 0000 0000 0000 0000 0000 0000 0000 0000 0000 0000 0000 0000 78 FF C2 2C 78
```

```
FF x..,x.
01/23-01:15:43.538590 195.11.212.180:30975 -> 192.0.97.80:49708
TCP TTL:49 TOS:0x0 ID:13449 DF
SFRPAU21 Seq: 0x78FFC22C Ack: 0x78FFC22C Win: 0xC22C
TCP Options => Opt 120 (40): C22C 78FF C22C 78FF C22C 78FF
0000 0000 0000 0000 0000 0000 0000 0000 0000 0000 0000 0000 0000 78 FF C2
2C 78 FF x..,x.
```

▼ Norton Personal Firewall 2002 Does Not Detect SYN/FIN Scanning

In April, 2002, it was reported that Norton Personal Firewall 2002 running in Windows 2000 does not always detect SYN/FIN scanning when the "detect portscan" option is enabled. What was happening was that, when detecting port scanning, Norton Personal Firewall locks for half an hour on just SYN scanning, and "forgets" about SYN/FIN scanning.

❑ TCP packets must never contain only the FIN flag. Usually, if only the FIN flag is set, this serves as an indication of the stealth FIN scanning.

❑ TCP packets must have at least one flag (except FIN).

❑ If the ACK flag is not set in the TCP packet, and this packet is not the first in the three-way handshake process, this packet is blatantly abnormal, since ACK flag must be present in any TCP packet.

❑ Besides the above-mentioned combinations (Listing 4.20), the following combinations are also suspicious: RST+FIN, SYN+RST.

**Listing 4.20. Detecting a Suspicious Situation
(a Fragment of the Dragon Log File)**

```
20:42:17 [T] 172.20.255.135 10.168.74.96 [TCP-FLAGS] (flags:-1-SR---,
dp=11498,sp=0) (dragon-sensor) [PORT-ZERO] (tcp,dp=11498,sp=0)
```

In the TCP protocol, there are reserved bits intended for future extensions to the protocols. Only a couple of years ago, these bits were not used. Therefore, the arrival of network packets where such bits were used could well indicate unauthorized activity, particularly an attempt of a remote OS identification (OS fingerprinting). Usually, the operating system is identified either by analyzing the packet headers (passive analysis), or by its reaction to packets of a specific format (this case we will cover in detail). At the time of writing, intruders used three utilities for remote OS fingerprinting — QueSO (Listing 4.21), hping, and Nmap.

Listing 4.21. OS Fingerprinting Using QueSO

```
luka# queso -d 200.0.0.253
Starting luka.infosec.com:6363 -> 200.0.0.253:80
IN  #0 : 80->6363 S:1 A:+1 W:7C00 U:0 F: SYN ACK
IN  #1 : 80->6364 S:0 A: 0 W:0000 U:0 F: RST
IN  #3 : 80->6366 S:0 A: 0 W:0000 U:0 F: RST
IN  #4 : 80->6367 S:1 A:+1 W:7C00 U:0 F: SYN FIN ACK
IN  #6 : 80->6369 S:1 A:+1 W:7C00 U:0 F: SYN ACK XXX YYY
200.0.0.253:80        * Linux 1.3.xx, 2.0.0 to 2.0.34

luka# queso -d 200.0.0.200
Starting luka.infosec.ru:15690 -> 200.0.0.200:80
IN  #0 : 80->15690 S:1 A:+1 W:2180 U:0 F: SYN ACK
IN  #1 : 80->15691 S:0 A:+1 W:0000 U:0 F: RST
IN  #2 : 80->15692 S:0 A:+1 W:0000 U:0 F: RST ACK
IN  #3 : 80->15693 S:0 A:+1 W:0000 U:0 F: RST
IN  #4 : 80->15694 S:1 A:+1 W:2180 U:0 F: SYN ACK
IN  #5 : 80->15695 S:0 A:+0 W:0000 U:0 F: RST ACK
IN  #6 : 80->15696 S:1 A:+1 W:2180 U:0 F: SYN ACK
200.0.0.200:80        * Windoze 95/98/NT
```

After starting, QueSO detects an open port on the scanned host and sends several packets that do not meet RFC requirements. The replies to these packets allow you to determine the OS type (Listing 4.22).

Listing 4.22. OS Fingerprinting Using QueSO
(a Fragment of the TCPdump Log File)

```
02:35:10.11 WS_LUKA.29709 > WS_LUKICH.80: S 1173826820:1173826820(0) ack 0
02:35:10.13 WS_LUKA.29710 > WS_LUKICH.80: F 1173826820:1173826820(0)
02:35:10.15 WS_LUKA.29711 > WS_LUKICH.80: F 1173826820:1173826820(0) ack 0
02:35:10.17 WS_LUKA.29712 > WS_LUKICH.80: SF 1173826820:1173826820(0)
02:35:10.19 WS_LUKA.29713 > WS_LUKICH.80: P 1173826820:1173826820(0)
02:35:10.21 WS_LUKA.29714 > WS_LUKICH.80: S 1173826820:1173826820(0)
    4500 0028 ee7b 0000 fc06 2f62 ab45 a42d
    ac15 a569 7412 0017 45f7 2d04 0000 0000
    50c2 1234 14d8 0000 0000 0000 0000
```

The following combinations of flags might appear in sent packets:

- ❐ SYN+ACK with ACK off
- ❐ FIN only
- ❐ FIN+ACK with ACK off
- ❐ SYN+FIN
- ❐ PUSH only
- ❐ SYN+XXX+YYY, where XXX and YYY are reserved flags in the TCP header (two high-order bits in 13th byte of the TCP packet header)

The Nmap scanner uses a similar technique for detecting the OS type. However, its packets use somewhat different flag combinations:

- ❐ SYN only
- ❐ No flags
- ❐ SYN+FIN+URGENT+PUSH
- ❐ ACK only
- ❐ SYN only, sent to closed port
- ❐ ACK only, sent to closed port
- ❐ FIN+URGENT+PUSH, sent to closed port

With the arrival of RFC 2481 [RFC1-99] and 2884 [RFC1-00], the situation became even worse. According to the above-mentioned standards, reserved bits (Explicit Congestion Notification, ECN) can be used for transmitting service information. As shown in [Miller1-00], if the packet corresponding to Listing 4.23 appears in the network, this could serve as an indication that the network is being scanned using Queso, hping, or Nmap).

Listing 4.23. Using Reserved ECN Flags in the TCP Packet Header (a Fragment of the TCPdump Log File)

```
12:25:38.650123 bad.guy.org.1641 > viper.infosec.ru.111: S
1533993767:1533993767(0)
win 512 (ttl 64, id 64461)
4500 0028 fbcd 0000 4006 91f5 xxxx xxxx
xxxx xxxx 0669 006f 5b6e e327 0000 0000
50c2 0200 7b16 0000
```

To understand the meaning of the c2 fragment within the packet (two reserved bits are used), you will need to perform an additional investigation in order to know for sure whether or not this is an attack.

Taking into account the possibility of using ECN flags, the new version of TCPdump — version 3.5 — displays these bits as shown in Listing 4.24.

Listing 4.24. Using Reserved ECN Flags in the TCP Header (a Fragment of the TCPdump Log File)

```
12:25:38.650123 bad.guy.org.1641 > viper.infosec.com.111: S [ECN-Echo,CWR]
380601688:380601688 (0) win 4660 (ttl 244, id 55411)
4500 0028 d873 0000 f406 85b4 xxxx xxxx
xxxx xxxx 0669 006f 16af 8558 0000 0000
50c2 1234 39e5 0000 753a 0000 e3a8
```

Such "intelligent" behavior results in confusing the analysts by the TCPdump system, which will think that the packet corresponds to the RFC 2481 standard, while in reality OS fingerprinting using Nmap is in progress. Thus, we are dealing with a false negative case.

Other indications of the packet "abnormality" are as follows:

❑ Source or recipient port (for TCP and UDP packets) set to 0 (Listing 4.25).

❑ If the ACK flag is set (for TCP packets), the acknowledgement number must never be set to 0.

Listing 4.25. Detecting Suspicious Activity (a Fragment of the TCPdump Log File)

```
21:20:11.084066 172.20.20.1.0 > ftp.infosec.com.1030: F 1310724:1310728(4)
ack 3642168720 win 20496 urg 1250
```

Quite often, a packet that has non-standard size can also be interpreted as an indication of an attack. For example, most ICMP Echo Request packets have an 8-bit header and a 56-bit data field. If packets of a non-standard length are sent to the network, one can draw the conclusion that unauthorized activity is taking place on the network. For example, the Loki attack already considered in *Chapter 1* enables the intruder to tunnel various commands into the ICMP Echo Request and reactions to these commands into the ICMP Echo Reply packets. This significantly changes the size of the data field as compared to the standard one. Another well-known example is the Ping of Death command, during which the attacker creates an ICMP Echo Request packet larger than 65,535 bytes (Listing 4.26).

Listing 4.26. Detecting a Ping of Death attack (a fragment of the TCPdump log file)

```
12:43:58.431 big.pinger.org > 200.0.0.104: icmp: echo request (frag
4321:380@0+)

12:43:58.431 big.pinger.org > 200.0.0.104: icmp: echo request (frag
4321:380@2656+)

12:43:58.431 big.pinger.org > 200.0.0.104: icmp: echo request (frag
4321:380@3040+)

12:43:58.431 big.pinger.org > 200.0.0.104: icmp: echo request (frag
4321:380@3416+)

12:43:58.431 big.pinger.org > 200.0.0.104: icmp: echo request (frag
4321:380@376+)

12:43:58.431 big.pinger.org > 200.0.0.104: icmp: echo request (frag
4321:380@3800+)

12:43:58.431 big.pinger.org > 200.0.0.104: icmp: echo request (frag
4321:380@4176+)

12:43:58.431 big.pinger.org > 200.0.0.104: icmp: echo request (frag
4321:380@760+)

. . .

12:43:58.491 big.pinger.org > 200.0.0.104: icmp: echo request (frag
4321:380@63080+)

12:43:58.491 big.pinger.org > 200.0.0.104: icmp: echo request (frag
4321:380@63456+)

12:43:58.491 big.pinger.org > 200.0.0.104: icmp: echo request (frag
4321:380@63840+)

12:43:58.491 big.pinger.org > 200.0.0.104: icmp: echo request (frag
4321:380@64216+)

12:43:58.491 big.pinger.org > 200.0.0.104: icmp: echo request (frag
4321:380@64600+)

12:43:58.491 big.pinger.org > 200.0.0.104: icmp: echo request (frag
4321:380@64976+)

12:43:58.491 big.pinger.org > 200.0.0.104: icmp: echo request (frag
4321:380@65360)
```

The length of this message, comprising several fragments, is 65,740 (380+65,360) bytes.

If fragmented packets are sent to your network, this is just another classical indication that, in most cases, allows you to detect an attack. Most network security tools can not correctly assemble these fragmented packets. When receiving such packets, these security tools either fail or pass fragmented packets into the protected network. The first of these results (security-tool failure) can be achieved using fragments with an incorrect offset (in the example provided above for the Ping of Death, the transmitted fragment length is not a multiple of 8 — the fragment size is 380 bytes). To produce their second result, intruders use the so-called "Tiny Fragment" attack. In the latter case, one has to create two TCP fragments. The first fragment is so small that it does not even include the complete TCP header and — even more important — the recipient port. The second fragment contains the remaining part of the header. Most firewalls allow the first fragment (or even both fragments) to pass into the corporate network (Listing 4.27).

**Listing 4.27. The Tiny Fragment Attack
(a Fragment of the TCPdump Log File)**

```
06:25:55.315 [|tcp] (frag 38783:16@0+)
06:25:55.315 bad.guy.org > viper.infosec.ru: (frag 38783:4@16)
06:25:55.315 [|tcp] (frag 16422:16@0+)
06:25:55.315 bad.guy.org > viper.infosec.ru: (frag 16422:4@16)
06:25:55.315 [|tcp] (frag 43143:16@0+)
06:25:55.315 bad.guy.org > viper.infosec.ru: (frag 43143:4@16)
06:25:55.315 [|tcp] (frag 18544:16@0+)
06:25:55.315 bad.guy.org > viper.infosec.ru: (frag 18544:4@16)
06:25:55.315 [|tcp] (frag 8231:16@0+)
06:25:55.315 bad.guy.org > viper.infosec.ru: (frag 8231:4@16)
06:25:55.315 [|tcp] (frag 45846:16@0+)
06:25:55.315 bad.guy.org > viper.infosec.ru: (frag 45846:4@16)
06:25:55.315 [|tcp] (frag 6245:16@0+)
06:25:55.315 bad.guy.org > viper.infosec.ru: (frag 6245:4@16)
```

The `[|tcp]` label specifies that TCPdump could neither grab the whole TCP header nor interpret packet destination.

Network Traffic Anomalies

Anomalies of network traffic are any deviations that network parameters may possess. These parameters include the workload factor, typical packet size, average number of fragmented packets, and so on. Deviations from the standard parameters can be an indication of an attack, as well as an indication of network problems caused by network equipment malfunctions.

Suspicious Characteristics of Network Traffic

Suspicious characteristics identifying attacks include the following:

❑ *Suspicious traffic from a specific sender or to a specific recipient.* In some cases, specific types of traffic or its contents can raise suspicion. For example, this might be an e-mail message containing specific keywords, access to certain servers, such as http://www.playboy.com, http://www.recruitment.com, http://www.vacation.com, or work by the protocol that is not expected from the specified address (for example, Telnet requests from a bank's operations department).

❑ *Suspicious traffic (independent of the sender or recipient).* Some kinds of traffic are suspicious in themselves, regardless of the recipient, such as traffic using unexpected protocols or traffic from addresses that do not belong to the internal network. For example, a security specialist in one of the banks using the RealSecure Network Sensor system detected unauthorized modem usage by one of their employees, who connected his office workstation from home and thus surfed the Internet using a faster connection. Another example of suspicious traffic involves sending confidential documents from a company to some address outside the company network. Such traffic can be detected by means of monitoring and tracing with appropriate keywords (such as "company confidential," "top secret" etc.).

Default Values

The default values of the attributes are just another common indication of an attack. Such attributes might include names of files or resident processes (for example, Trojans), used ports, etc. Let us take a look at this indication in more detail using the example of Trojan Horses.

Since most Trojans have predefined names of files or processes, their appearance on your computer might be considered unauthorized activity. For example, if you notice a file named Patch.exe, this might be interpreted as the presence of the NetBus, Digital RootBeer, Krenx, or Solid Gold Trojans on the host. A list of filenames of known Trojans can be downloaded from: http://www.simovits.com/trojans/trojans_files.html. Apart from this, there you can find information on the ports that are most frequently used by the Trojans. The list of active processes also can be used for detecting Trojans. In Unix, you can obtain this list using the ps utility, while in Windows NT/2000, you can get it by starting the Task Manager utility (Fig. 4.4). Naturally, you must be sure that the intruder has not installed rootkit on your computer.

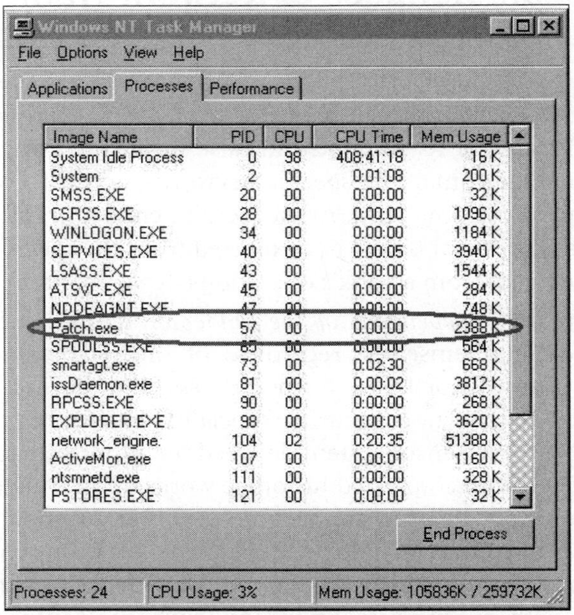

Fig. 4.4. The Patch.exe process starting the NetBus Trojan

Another method of detecting Trojans implies the analysis of specific ports (control of requests or detection of an open port). According to this principle, it is possible to detect most Trojans, which are bound to specific port numbers. If the Trojan uses non-standard ports, it can be detected using specific keywords in network traffic, for example, by the commands received and sent, or by the password used for communication between its client and server parts. Provided below are several examples illustrating detection of the well-known SubSeven Trojan (Listings 4.28 through 4.34), which usually communicates via Port 1243 or 27374 (version 2.1).

**Listing 4.28. Detecting the SubSeven Trojan
(a Fragment of the Snort Log File)**

```
[**] BACKDOOR Attempt- Subseven [**]
12/26-23:09:42.219109 0:90:27:F:22:A2 -> 0:40:5:F6:34:51 type:0x800
len:0x4E
```

```
216.192.29.30:3216 -> 206.18.108.130:1243 TCP TTL:64 TOS:0xD0 ID:11841
S***** Seq: 0x4908C6 Ack: 0x0 Win: 0x2000
TCP Options => MSS: 536 NOP WS: 0 NOP NOP TS: 0 0 Opt 9 (40): 0000 0000
0000 0000 0000 0000 0000 0000 0000 0000 0000 0000 0000 0000 0000 0000
0000 0000
```

**Listing 4.29. Detecting the SubSeven Trojan
(a Fragment of the IPCHAINS Log File)**

```
Jan 5 02:56:39 input REJECT eth1 PROTO=TCP 152.166.212.218:2102
192.168.1.1:1243 L=48 S=0x00 I=38494 F=0x4000 T=108 SYN (#13)
```

**Listing 4.30. Detecting the SubSeven Trojan
(a Fragment of the Ascend SecureConnect 3.03 Log File)**

```
Mar 30 19:44:02 209-30-73-81.flash.net ASCEND: wan5 tcp 209.30.73.80;27374
<- 24.29.78.48;1493 58 syn !pass (totcp-1)
Mar 30 19:44:02 209-30-73-81.flash.net ASCEND: wan6 tcp 209.30.73.81;27374
<- 24.29.78.48;1494 58 syn !pass (totcp-1)
Mar 30 19:44:02 209-30-73-81.flash.net ASCEND: wan5 tcp 209.30.73.82;27374
<- 24.29.78.48;1495 58 syn !pass (totcp-1)
Mar 30 19:44:02 209-30-73-81.flash.net ASCEND: wan6 tcp 209.30.73.83;27374
<- 24.29.78.48;1496 58 syn !pass (totcp-1)
Mar 30 19:44:02 209-30-73-81.flash.net ASCEND: wan5 tcp 209.30.73.95;27374
<- 24.29.78.48;1508 58 syn !pass (totcp-1)
```

**Listing 4.31. Detecting the SubSeven Trojan
(a Fragment of the ZoneAlarm Log File)**

```
Name Packet sent from 24.226.103.143 (TCP Port 3387)
to x.x.x.x (TCP Port 27374) was blocked
    Status Dropped
    Source IP Address 24.226.103.143
    Destination IP Address x.x.x.x
    Source Port 3387
    Destination Port 27374
    Link Layer Protocol 1
    Network Layer Protocol 1
    Transport Layer Protocol 2
    Count 1
```

```
Status Code 100002
Lock Level 0
Security Information 0,1,0,2
Operating System Windows 98-4.10.1998- -SP
Product ZoneAlarm
ProductVersion 2.0.26
Language 0409
State Find Code 13
```

Listing 4.32. Detecting the SubSeven Trojan
(a Fragment of the NFR Back Officer Log File)

```
17:54:19.596269 ip 60: 24-216-141-52.hsacorp.net .1566 > my.box.1243:
  S 12759610:12759610(0) win 8192 <mss 1460> (DF) (ttl 19 , id 61249)
17:54:19.624034 ip 54: my.box.1243 > 24-216-141-52.hsacorp.net.1566:
  R 0:0(0) ack 12759611 win 0 (ttl 128, id 4263)
```

Listing 4.33. Detecting the SubSeven Trojan
(a Fragment of the BlackICE Defender Log File)

```
59  2000-05-04 19:35:31  2003105  SubSeven port probe  172.142.109.211
  AC8E6DD3.ipt.aol.com  152.207.70.106  port=1243&name=Sub_7  8
```

Listing 4.34. Detecting of the SubSeven Trojan
(a fragment of the Pix firewall log file)

```
Jun 03 00:06:26 [FW1] Jun 03 2000 00:08:00: %PIX-2-106001:
  Inbound TCP connection denied from 216.58.19.218/3483
  to server1/27374 flags SYN
Jun 03 00:06:26 [FW1] Jun 03 2000 00:08:00: %PIX-7-106011:
  Deny inbound (No xlate) tcp src outside:216.58.19.218/3487
  dst outside:global/27374
```

The Satans Trojan uses the number 666 for connection (the same port number is used also by the BackConstruction Trojan). Note that the Satans Trojan can also be detected by the presence of a running program named WinVMM32 (Listing 4.35).

Listing 4.35. Detecting the Satans Trojan (a Fragment of the Snort Log File)

```
[**] BACKDOOR Attempt- Attack FTP / Satans Backdoor [**]
12/26-23:09:51.159109 0:0:0:0:0:0 -> 0:0:0:0:0:0 type:0x800 len:0x4E
216.192.29.30:3215 -> 206.18.108.130:666 TCP TTL:65 TOS:0xC8 ID:25409
S**** Seq: 0x4907EF Ack: 0x0 Win: 0x2000
TCP Options => MSS: 536 NOP WS: 0 NOP NOP TS: 0 0 Opt 9 (40): 0000 0000
0000 0000 0000 0000 0000 0000 0000 0000 0000 0000 0000 0000 0000 0000 0000
0000 0000
```

The BackOrifice Trojan communicates to the master via port 31337. Furthermore, it leaves traces of its activity in the Windows registry under HKLM\Software\ Microsoft\Windows\CurrentVersion\RunServices (Listings 4.36, 4.37).

Listing 4.36. Detecting the BackOrifice Trojan (a Fragment of the SHADOW Log File)

```
15:20:48.698626 172.20.20.1.31338 > 192.168.1.1.31337: udp 19
```

Listing 4.37. Detecting the BackOrifice Trojan (a Fragment of the IPCHAINS Log File)

```
Jan 4 20:59:40 input REJECT eth1 PROTO=UDP 24.114.172.74:3764
192.168.1.1:31337 L=47 S=0x00 I=65460 F=0x0000 T=123 (#16)
```

As I mentioned above, Trojans can be detected not only by analyzing requests to specific ports, but also by tracing specific keywords in network traffic (this is especially useful if the Trojan does not use the default port). For example, BackOrifice can be detected by the following password signature: "ce 63 d1 d2 16 e7 13 cf," present in the first 8 bytes of the data field in the UDP packet (Listing 4.38).

Listing 4.38. Detecting the BackOrifice Trojan (a fragment of the TCPdump log file)

```
09:39:36.695 200.0.0.104.1613 > 200.0.0.200.31337: udp 19
          4500 002f cea7 0000 7d11 cd56 ab45 a49b
          ac15 a5c9 064d 7a69 001b 30e7 ce63 d1d2
          16e7 13cf 38a5 a586 b275 4b99 ad32 58
09:39:36.695 200.0.0.200.31337 > 200.0.0.104.1613: udp 53
```

```
        4500 0051 b408 0000 2011 44d4 ac15 a5c9
        ab45 a49b 7a69 064d 003d bc7b ce63 d1d2
        16e7 13cf 1ea5 a586 7a75 4b99 2d61 2196
        c7fc 8502 192a
09:39:36.695 200.0.0.200.31337 > 200.0.0.104.1613: udp 48
        4500 004c b508 0000 2011 43d9 ac15 a5c9
        ab45 a49b 7a69 064d 0038 bb34 ce63 d1d2
        16e7 13cf 1ba5 a586 7b75 4b99 6d71 2d97
        c1fc 8656 5031 ...
```

In *Chapter 2*, I mentioned that, apart from classical attacks based on the "one-to-one" or "one-to-many" models, there are the so-called distributed attacks, which correspond to "many-to-one" and "many-to-many" models. Some Trojans are based on this principle, such as WinTrin00 (Listing 4.39), TFN2K, Stacheldraht, mstream (Listing 4.40), etc. These Trojans can also be detected by the port numbers used.

Listing 4.39. Detecting the WinTrin00 Trojan (a Fragment of the Cisco Router Log File)

```
Feb 25 21:14:38 134.161.1.101 21043: %SEC-6-IPACCESSLOGP:
list ingress denied udp 38.29.63.57(4419) -> 134.161.67.71(34555), 1 packet
Feb 25 21:14:51 134.161.1.101 21044: %SEC-6-IPACCESSLOGP:
list ingress denied udp 38.29.63.57(4420) -> 134.161.67.71(34555), 1 packet
Feb 25 21:14:57 134.161.1.101 21045: %SEC-6-IPACCESSLOGP:
list ingress denied udp 38.29.63.57(4421) -> 134.161.67.71(34555), 1 packet
Feb 25 21:15:00 134.161.1.101 21046: %SEC-6-IPACCESSLOGP:
list ingress denied udp 38.29.63.57(4422) -> 134.161.67.71(34555), 1 packet
Feb 26 00:35:40 134.161.1.101 22024: %SEC-6-IPACCESSLOGP:
list ingress denied udp 38.29.63.57(4523) -> 134.161.67.71(34555), 1 packet
Feb 26 11:01:56 134.161.1.101 24967: %SEC-6-IPACCESSLOGP:
list ingress denied udp 38.29.63.170(4531) -> 134.161.67.71(34555), 1 packet
Feb 26 11:09:24 134.161.1.101 25007: %SEC-6-IPACCESSLOGP:
list ingress denied udp 38.29.63.170(4541) -> 134.161.67.71(34555), 1 packet
Feb 26 11:09:26 134.161.1.101 25008: %SEC-6-IPACCESSLOGP:
list ingress denied udp 38.29.63.170(4542) -> 134.161.67.71(34555), 1 packet
```

**Listing 4.40. Detecting the mstream Trojan
(a Fragment of the TCPdump Log File)**

```
00:04:38.530000 192.168.0.20.1081 > 192.168.0.100.6838: udp 9
          4500 0025 ef75 0000 4011 098a c0a8 0014   E..%.u..@.......
          c0a8 0064 0439 1ab6 0011 2b63 6e65 7773   ...d.9....+cnews
          6572 7665 7200 0000 0000 0000 0000        erver........
```

To detect Trojans, it is not necessary to control all of the network traffic — it is sufficient to just analyze the open ports. Using this approach, you can identify most Trojans that are bound to specific port numbers. You can find open ports both locally and remotely. Locally, you can view the list of all open ports by running netstat or a similar utility with the −a parameter (Listing 4.41).

**Listing 4.41. Detecting the NetBus Trojan
(the Output Produced by the Netstat −a Command)**

```
Active Connections

  Proto   Local Address             Foreign Address        State
  TCP     ws_lukich:135             0.0.0.0:0              LISTENING
  TCP     ws_lukich:901             0.0.0.0:0              LISTENING
  TCP     ws_lukich:2998            0.0.0.0:0              LISTENING
  TCP     ws_lukich:9991            0.0.0.0:0              LISTENING
  TCP     ws_lukich:12345           0.0.0.0:0              LISTENING
  TCP     ws_lukich:12346           0.0.0.0:0              LISTENING
  TCP     ws_lukich:1026            0.0.0.0:0              LISTENING
  TCP     ws_lukich:1026            localhost:1027         ESTABLISHED
  TCP     ws_lukich:1027            localhost:1026         ESTABLISHED
  TCP     ws_lukich:137             0.0.0.0:0              LISTENING
  TCP     ws_lukich:138             0.0.0.0:0              LISTENING
  TCP     ws_lukich:nbsession       0.0.0.0:0              LISTENING
  TCP     ws_lukich:nbsession       ws_luka:3055           ESTABLISHED
  UDP     ws_lukich:135             *:*
  UDP     ws_lukich:nbname          *:*
  UDP     ws_lukich:nbdatagram      *:*
```

In this case, we detected that the NetBus Trojan is present on the WS_LUKICH local host. This Trojan works on Ports 12345 or 12346. A list of ports used by Trojans can be found at http://www.simovits.com/trojans/trojans_files.html.

Remote detection of Trojans by analyzing open ports requires that you use the methods used by intruders — any port scanner, such as Nmap, which can run in most Unix clones and in Windows NT (Listing 4.42).

**Listing 4.42. Detecting the NetBus Trojan
(the Output Produced by the nmapnt –sS 200.0.0.200 Command)**

```
Starting nmapNT V. 2.53 by ryan@eEye.com
eEye Digital Security ( http://www.eEye.com )
based on nmap by fyodor@insecure.org  ( www.insecure.org/nmap/ )

We skillfully deduced that your address is 0.0.0.0
Interesting ports on WS_LUKICH (200.0.0.200):
(The 1518 ports scanned but not shown below are in state: closed)
Port        State       Service
135/tcp     open        unknown
139/tcp     open        unknown
901/tcp     open        unknown
12345/tcp   open        NetBus
12346/tcp   open        NetBus

Nmap run completed -- 1 IP address (1 host up) scanned in 1 second
```

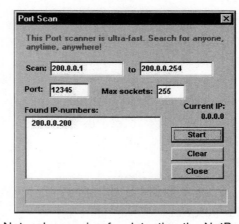

Fig. 4.5. Network scanning for detecting the NetBus Trojan

Remote scanning of the WS_LUKICH host additionally detected that Ports 12345 and 12346 were open, leading to the conclusion that the NetBus Trojan is present on that host. Finally, you can also use a non-traditional method. For example, some programs intended to manage Trojans provide the capability of scanning the specified address ranges and detecting the installed components. The NetBus Trojan also provides this function (Fig. 4.5).

Unexpected Attributes

Requests from any system, network or user are characterized by certain attributes that describe the so-called system, network, or user profile. These profiles are used for monitoring and analyzing the controlled object. The most frequently used parameters that provide the capability of detecting a potential attack are considered below.

Date and Time

Date and time represent the most characteristic attributes that are used when detecting security policy violations. Let us suppose, for example, that a system logon that happened after 18 : 30 was registered in the log. If the user who logged on was one of the system administrators, this might be an authorized logon by a user who is working overtime. However, if an intrusion detection system registers a system logon by an employee working in the financial department, this fact might be a reason for additional investigations (whether that user was authorized to log on in order to do their job or whether some intruder attempted to implement the attack by guessing the user's login name and password). Similar situations might arise if an intrusion detection system registers a logon attempt during weekends and holidays. Let's look at a more specific example related to banking. In most banks, all payments made after a specific hour are suspended until the next business day. For example, if a payment is made on Friday, activity on the concerned accounts will be delayed till the following Monday. If a transaction is accomplished after a specific period of time, this might be a signal indicating that an attempt of fraud has been detected. Let us consider yet another example which uses time as the attack indicator: If the time interval between data input and payment confirmation is too small (insufficient for normal procedure of review of the transaction), one can suppose that the payment is incorrect or fraudulent.

Location

Normally, the user logs onto the system from the same computer or connects to the Internet via a dial-up connection using the same phone number. Consequently, a logon from another computer or another phone number can be considered to be an abnormal event that needs to be investigated. In a large corporate network whose departments are distributed all over the country (or the world), intrusion detection systems often monitor the geographical location from where the logon is performed. Thus, a change of the typical location from where the user logs on can also be an attack indication. Let us consider another example, typical for financial applications. Operations such as data input for payment transaction and confirmation of that payment must be performed from different sites. These procedures are separated in order to prevent employees from abusing their work permissions. Thus, time is a rather important criterion, allowing you to determine if specific actions are authorized. In particular, control over the date and time allows you to detect an untimely launch of processes and programs, and unexpected reboots, startups, and shutdowns.

System Resources

Characteristics of most system resources can also serve as attack indicators. For example, a processor workload that differs significantly from the average can indicate various abnormal activities. For example, this might happen if the operating system or specific application works incorrectly, or if someone attempts a brute-force attack. Other resources that can indicate an active attack include intense memory or disk activities, requests to communication ports, etc. If you unexpectedly experience a shortage of hard disk space, this might serve as evidence of the appearance of a "bomb" in your system. The "bomb" is a packed file of small size, which, when expanded, will consume several dozens gigabytes (such "jokes" were rather common in FIDO in the early 1990s).

User and System Profiles

Using profiles represents a more general approach than does analysis of requests to services or system resources. User and system profiles include such requests. However, they are complemented by additional parameters that take into account specific characteristics of the user, process, or host. These parameters include, for example, the time of maximum and minimum workloads, duration of a typical session, normal logon and logoff time, and so on. Deviations of these parameters from typical values may serve as evidence of abnormal behavior.

A particular case of this attack indication might be control of the services that are most frequently requested by the subject (user, process, and so on) in its day-to-day activity. For example, if employees need to access the Internet in order to do their jobs, you can generate a list of the most frequently used web servers and trace requests to servers not included into this list. Such requests might be interpreted as security policy violations. Requests of specific files, sending or receiving e-mail to or from specific addresses, using specific services (such as FTP or Telnet), and other types of activities can also be classified as indications of security policy violations.

Other Parameters

There are other indicators that allow one to detect security policy violations. These include, for example, the above-mentioned procedure with input and authorization of the payment. Suppose, however, that an employee abusing his position performs this operation from different workstations in order to transfer money to fraudulent accounts. In reality, such a situation would not arise. The function of entering and authorizing a transaction must be distributed between different computers and different users.

▼ Polling System Hacked

In May 2002, the French corporation Vivendi Universal suspected that its wireless system of electronic polling used for shareholder meetings had been hacked. An abnormally high number of abstentions during one of the polls related to the payment of interest was interpreted as an indication of an attack.

The detection of a specific action performed on the account of an ex-employee (whose user account was not deleted from the controlled system for some reason) or an employee who is on vacation must also be considered to be a security policy violation.

Unexpected Problems

Any problem that arises in the corporate network must give occasion for additional investigations. Even if, in the course of this investigation, you find out that the problem does not relate to security, the fact of its detection will have a positive influence on system performance and reliability. Problems of this type include the following:

- ❑ *Problems with software and hardware.* Router failure, server reboots, or inability to start one of the system services might indicate an attempt to implement a Denial of Service attack.
- ❑ *Unexpected user behavior.* An unexpected request to a resource, which the user has never tried to access before, might well mean that the intruder has intercepted or cracked the password of the legitimate user and is now attempting to access important data on behalf of that user.

▼ Cuckoo's Egg

A classical example of intrusion detection is described in [Stoll1-96] by Clifford Stoll, a computer specialist and professional astronomer who accidentally detected a small discrepancy in the system's accounting machine time. After careful investigation, security specialists discovered that some unknown user had "borrowed" several seconds of machine time without paying (the sum was rather small, something like ¢0.75). As a result, the intruder was detected and turned out to have intruded upon dozens of top secret Pentagon systems.

Banners

This indicator is used only in security analyzers that will be covered later. Most network services generate responses to the requests they receive. This response is known as a "banner." Analysis of banner information (such as version number, for example) enables security specialists to determine whether or not the service is vulnerable.

Such an analysis often allows you to detect the version of the scanned service, the type of operating system, and so on, which enables you to investigate potential vulnerabilities in this component of the information system. For example, an attempt to establish a Telnet connection to Port 143 (IMAP service) will display a standard message containing information on the version and developer of the IMAP service (Listing 4.43).

Listing 4.43. Analysis of the Header Returned by the IMAP Service

```
Trying x.x.x.x...
Connected to bank.ru
* OK bank IMAP4rev1 Service 9.0(157) at Wed, 14 Oct 1998 11:51:50 -0400
(EDT)
(Report problems in this server to MRC@CAC.Washington.EDU)
. logout
* BYE bank IMAP4rev1 server terminating connection
. OK LOGOUT completed
Connection closed by foreign host.
```

This information, which at first might seem insignificant, enables the security administrator performing the security scan to find on hacker servers all information on the presence of vulnerabilities in the current IMAP version (Fig. 4.6).

Proceeding in a similar way, it is possible to analyze other software, such as web servers (Fig. 4.7).

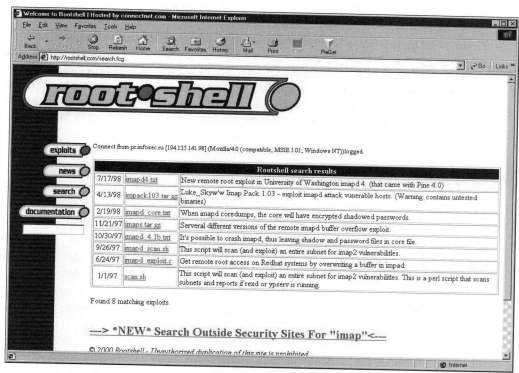

Fig. 4.6. Searching for information on IMAP service vulnerabilities
at the rootshell.com server

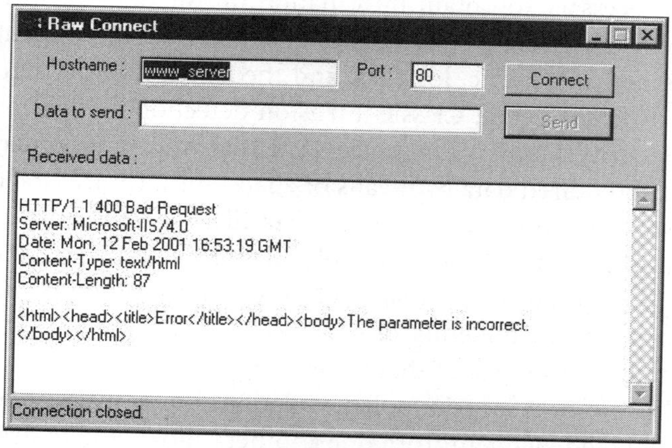

Fig. 4.7. Analysis of the header returned by a web server

A Practical Example

Once, I had to deal with a unique Trojan (which could not be detected by antiviral software). According to the idea of its authors, this Trojan was to steal my Internet password imperceptibly. However, when implementing the Trojan, its authors did not take into account that the victim might connect to the Internet via a LAN, rather than a dial-up connection. Being launched on computer specially dedicated for this purpose, the Trojan tried to find the RAS service in vain. Since there was no RAS service installed, the Trojan finally failed and displayed an error message (through which it was detected).

Digital "Fingerprint"

This indicator also finds application in security analyzers and is based on a comparison of the software fragment's digital "fingerprint" and the "fingerprint" of a well-known vulnerability. Antiviral software products also use a similar method by comparing the fragments of software being scanned for viruses with virus signatures stored in a special database. Control sums or dates of the software being analyzed represent a variation of this indicator. If the current value does not match the standard one, this means that the object being controlled was changed (this change might have occurred as a result of the attack).

Sources of Information on Attacks

Before we can come to a conclusion about an attack based on the above-described principles, it is necessary to obtain information on the basis of which one can draw such a conclusion. There are two categories of such sources: main and auxiliary. Main sources include network traffic, log files, and the system objects' current activity (users, programs, processes, etc.). Classic intrusion detection systems make active use of these sources. Security scanners that detect potential attacks use other sources. In most cases, they get the required data by means of analyzing software (including implementations of network services), processes, or data files. Usually, security analyzers look there for various attack indications (as a rule, digital "fingerprints" and headers). Additional sources of information on attacks represent information obtained from system users, messages in security bulletins, etc.

It is important to understand that information from a single source can not serve as unequivocal proof of a security policy violation. Using information from different sources (preferably independent from one another) allows you to draw conclusions on the presence and type of attack more reliably.

Log Files

This method was the first one to be used for detecting security policy violations. Even today, it still remains one of the most efficient methods. A specific feature of this method is that it is indispensable in cases in which there are no other intrusion detection methods available for use. The necessity of registering system and security events in log files is stated in most security documents and requirements, including the famous "Orange Book," ISO 17799, etc. I will not concentrate on the formats of the log files produced by different types of software and hardware, since this task can not be practically implemented. Each system has its own, unique format of log file. Furthermore, even different versions of the same product might use different log file formats. Therefore, I will limit myself to providing several examples of log files — Cisco IOS (Listing 4.44), Windows 2000 (Fig. 4.8), CheckPoint Firewall-1 (Listing 4.45), and Apache (Listings 4.46 and 4.47).

Listing 4.44. Examples of Security Messages Produced by Cisco Equipment (for IOS 12.0 T)

```
Feb 25 21:14:38 134.161.1.101 21043: %SEC-6-IPACCESSLOGP: list ingress
denied udp 38.29.63.57(4419) -> 134.161.67.71(34555), 1 packet
Dec 22 16:15:26: %SEC-6-IPACCESSLOGDP: list Internet denied icmp
172.20.20.1 -> 255.255.255.255 (8/0), 1 packet
May 10 09:26:34.260 UTC: %SEC-6-IPACCESSLOGP: list 100 denied tcp
10.0.0.57(0) -> 192.231.90.254(0), 1 packet
```

Listing 4.45. A Fragment of the Check Point Firewall-1 Log File

```
"421316"  "29Dec2000"  " 9:32:16"  "daemon"  "localhost"  "alert"  "accept"
""    "x.x.x.x"  "x.x.x.x"  "ip"  ""   ""   ""   ""   ""   ""   ""   ""   ""   ""   ""
"MAD"  " additionals:

attack=blocked_connection_port_scanning"
"422255"  "29Dec2000"  " 9:33:59"  "daemon"  "localhost"  "alert"  "accept"
""    "x.x.x.x"  "x.x.x.x"  "ip"  ""   ""   ""   ""   ""   ""   ""   ""   ""   ""   ""
"MAD"  " additionals:  attack=blocked_connection_port_scanning"
"427220"  "29Dec2000"  " 9:43:26"  "daemon"  "localhost"  "alert"  "accept"
""    "x.x.x.x"  "x.x.x.x"  "ip"  ""   ""   ""   ""   ""   ""   ""   ""   ""   ""   ""
"MAD"  " additionals:  attack=blocked_connection_port_scanning"
```

Listing 4.46. A Fragment of the Apache Log File (access_log)

```
193.56.123.47 - - [04/Apr/1997:16:39:06 -0500] "GET /etc/passwd HTTP/1.0" 404 139
```

Listing 4.47. A Fragment of the Apache Log File (error_log)

[Fri Apr 4 16:37:39 1997] HTTPd: access to /export/home/httpd_root/
cgi-bin/phf failed for 193.56.123.47, reason: script does not exist from –

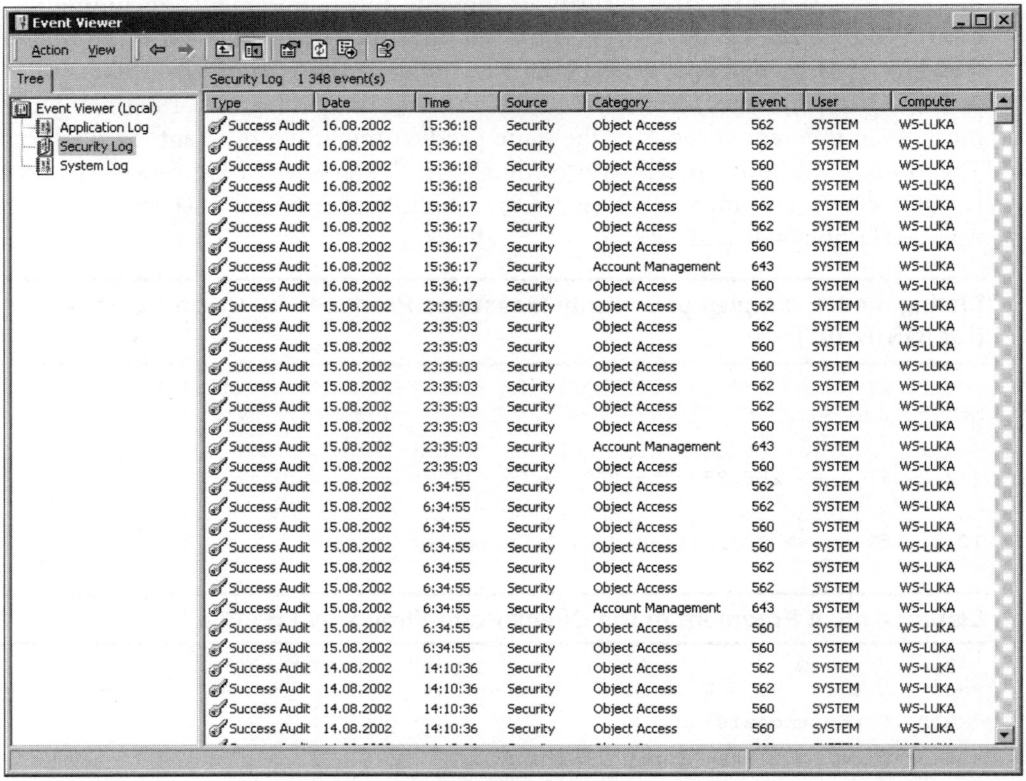

Fig. 4.8. A Windows 2000 Security Log file

I would just like to make one small comment. You need to study the formats and specific features of the log files used in your systems carefully. Otherwise, a situation similar to something that happened to me once might occur. A security administrator sent me a message asking me to help him resolve a conflict with his IT department. Along with this, he sent me a fragment of a log that, he suspected, had been tweaked by the network administrator.

Network Traffic

Network traffic is one of the most basic sources of information used by intrusion detection systems. Network traffic consists of network packets being transferred (also known as frames). Without diving into details of implementation of different network architectures, let us take the *packet* as the basic unit of network traffic, which in general cases comprises the following three parts:

❑ Packet header (service information, source address, destination address and other fields)

❑ Data field of the packet

❑ Packet trailer(control sums, delimiter and so on)

Depending on the network architecture, some parts might be missing. Based on an analysis of the above-listed parts of the network packet, the intrusion detection system decides if security policy violations really took place. In early 2000, 70% of all networks were TCP/IP networks, and this number is gradually increasing. On the other hand, percentages taken by other protocol stacks (IPX/SPX, SMB/NetBIOS etc.) do not exceed 20%. This explains why intrusion detection systems using network traffic as the source of information usually function only in TCP/IP networks.

Activity of System Subjects

This source reflects all actions performed by the objects within a controlled system (users, processes, etc.) in real-time mode. These actions can also be analyzed on the basis of log files. However, not all events that take place in the system being controlled are registered in log files. Therefore, it is much more efficient (but at the same time much harder) to analyze all system activity in real time. Looking somewhat ahead, I would like to mention that only a small number of the systems intended for detection of abnormal activity work according to this principle. The complications related to implementation of this mechanism prevent developers from using it in intrusion detection systems, because it requires them to build the interception system into all requests. Intrusion detection systems work according to another principle — they never lock specific activity immediately. Rather, they first analyze it, and then react appropriately. The more complicated the analysis algorithm is, the more resources it requires for implementation and, consequently, the more it degrades the performance of the system it controls.

Additional Sources

Information on an attack can be obtained not only from various software tools, but also from additional indicators. Most intruders, especially the ones who attack networks in order to improve their self-esteem, boast of their deeds to their colleagues. Quite often, whole Web sites or sections of Web sites are dedicated to these achievements (for example, you can find such a topic at http://www.alldas.org). You can use this information to get additional knowledge and find out additional attack indicators. Here are some sources where you might be able to find some useful information:

- ❒ Hacker magazines (including e-zines)
- ❒ Mailing lists (such as the one from SecurityFocus)
- ❒ Books (such as "Maximum Security" or "Counter Hack")
- ❒ Hacking resources on the Internet (such as http://www.securityfocus.com or http://packetstormsecurity.nl)
- ❒ USENET and FIDONET conferences
- ❒ IRC channels
- ❒ Conferences and seminars (such as DEFCON).

Notifications from the Users

Notifications from the users represent an additional source of information that must not be neglected. Although these notifications often are only figments of the imagination of unskilled users, sometimes they can help to reveal problems that can not be detected using other methods. Notification of the appearance of a duplicate IP address can serve as an example of such a message. If you are not able to react in a timely manner to the notifications from the users of your informational system, it is necessary at least to register them. If a problem arises, these records can be used for further investigation.

Mail Lists

Mail lists are rather popular all over the world. Except for the cost of an Internet connection, this additional source of information does not require any additional expenses, since notifications on new vulnerabilities found and new attack methods are distributed for free to all interested persons.

Such bulletins are composed by so-called Response Teams as a reaction to security incidents. The most famous among such teams are the Computer Emergency Response Team (CERT/CC), SecurityFocus, X-Force, and SecuriTeam.

The above-mentioned groups collect statistics on the attacks and vulnerabilities found in software and hardware, develop efficient countermeasures against these attacks, and publish this information for all interested individuals via mail lists and/or web servers. All response teams and developers of intrusion detection systems work in contact with software and hardware developers in order to provide efficient methods of counteracting attacks. However, information on a newly found vulnerability is not officially published before the team develops efficient countermeasures. This is the main drawback of all methods used for searching for vulnerabilities, because intruders can use the available information before anyone finds a method to eliminate the security breach.

Web Servers

web servers are among the most common additional information sources from which specialists can get information on attacks and vulnerabilities. Such sources can be classified into the following three categories:

- ❑ *Servers supported by software and hardware manufacturers and vendors.* This list includes the above-mentioned technical-support sites of such companies as Microsoft, Novell, Sun, Hewlett-Packard, Cisco, and so on. These servers mainly contain information on security holes detected in solutions provided by these companies.
- ❑ *Servers of specialized organizations and companies.* This resource list includes web servers supported by ISS, Symantec, MITRE, along with servers of such organizations as NASA, Purdue University, etc.
- ❑ *Independent servers*, such as Insecure (http://www.insecure.org). You can find such servers using various search engines, such as http://neworder.box.sk.

Internet and FIDONET Conferences

With the development and growth of messaging technologies, which allow one to distribute information via web servers and mail lists, USENET conferences and FIDONET echo conferences are gradually losing their popularity. Still, several years ago, the FIDO network was nearly as popular as the Internet. Recently, as Internet connections become less expensive, its popularity is constantly growing, while the number of FIDO participants has significantly decreased. However, even now, FIDO members are still quite numerous.

Intrusion Detection Technologies

Intrusion detection requires one of the following two conditions to be satisfied: You either need to understand the expected behavior of the controlled system object or know all possible attacks and their modifications. In the first case, the anomaly detection technology is employed, while, in the second case, the misuse detection technology is applicable. Usually, commercial systems combine both approaches, trying to get the most out of both technologies and eliminate the drawbacks characteristic of each of them.

Anomaly Detection

This technology is based on the assumption that attacks or any other malignant actions often manifest themselves as unusual or anomalous behavior of the system, application program, or user. For example, a large number of connections during a short time interval, a high processor or network workload, attempts to access peripherals that are not normally used can all be considered to be anomalous behavior. Supposing that we can describe the profile of normal object behavior, any deviation from this profile can be interpreted as anomalous behavior. However, anomalous behavior does not necessary indicate an attack. For example, this relates to the case of a large number of responses to the requests on the workstation activity from the network management system. Many intrusion detection systems would identify this case as a Denial of Service attack. Taking this factor into account, one can notice that two extremities are possible when using such systems:

❑ *False positive* — a case when intrusion detection system detects and classifies some anomaly as an attack when it is not a real attack.
❑ *False negative* — a situation in which the intrusion detection system does not detect the situation that does not satisfy the definition of anomalous behavior. This case is much more dangerous than a false positive.

Therefore, when customizing and using the systems of such a category, the administrator must work on:

❑ *Creating the behavior profile of an object.* This problem is rather complicated, hard to formulate, and time-consuming. Also, it requires a large amount of preparatory steps from the administrator.
❑ *Determining boundary values of the object behavior characteristics.* This is required to decrease the probability of false positive and false negative situations.

This technology is rather expensive, and the results are hard to achieve when employing it, because logging of all activities of the controlled object required for this kind of detection significantly degrades the performance of the protected host. Usually, such systems are characterized by heavy loads on the CPU and require large amounts of disk space to store the collected data. In general, such systems are not suitable for real-time systems where performance and response time are or critical importance.

For example, operators in banks perform the same actions in their day-to-day activities. For such deterministic systems, one can easily develop anomaly detection methods that, strictly speaking, are implemented in fraud detection systems. However, for many environments, these methods and approaches are inapplicable. Such environments include, for example, university networks or web servers accessed by thousands of users via a single user account.

The scheme of a typical intrusion detection system based on anomaly detection is shown in Fig. 4.9.

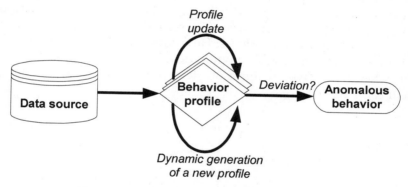

Fig. 4.9. A typical anomaly detection system

Usually, anomaly detection systems use log files and current user activity as their main information sources. However, there are examples of systems detecting anomalies in network traffic (such as the Traffic Signature technology, implemented in the *n*Genius Performance Management System from the NetScout) company [NetScout1-02].

It is important to understand that this approach is becoming more and more widely used in contemporary intrusion detection systems. Most developers of security tools implement this mechanism. In particular, control over network workload fluctuations is especially useful for detecting DoS and DDoS attacks.

The Department of Defense Detects Anomalies

In April 2001, the US Department of Defense signed a contract for $20 million with the American Institute for Research to develop an Advanced Intrusion Prevention System (AIPS) based on the anomaly detection mechanisms. Currently, the system is under construction and is to be released in December 2004.

Detecting Malicious Activity

Another approach to intrusion detection is based on misuse detection. This approach implies describing an attack as a pattern or signature and searching for a specific pattern within the controlled area (for example, in network traffic or in log files). This technology is very much like non-heuristic scanning for viruses (most antiviral scanners represent examples of intrusion detection systems). This means that the system is capable of detecting all known attacks, but it is hardly equipped to detect new attacks that are not already included in the database.

The approach implemented in such systems is rather simple. It is this principle upon which most contemporary intrusion detection systems available on the market are implemented. However, administrators often encounter problems when working with such systems. The first problem lies in creating a signature description mechanism, i.e., attack description language. The second problem is the consequence of the first one, and is formulated as follows: How does one describe a known attack in such a way as to register all its possible modifications?

The scheme of a typical intrusion detection system based on this principle is shown in Fig. 4.10.

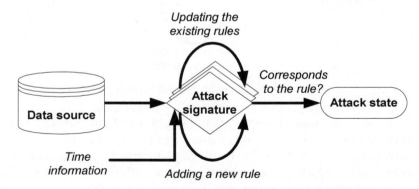

Fig. 4.10. A typical misuse detection system

Normally, misuse detection systems employ log files and network traffic as their basic information sources.

Approaches to Intrusion Detection

In the following few sections, we will concentrate on a description of the two main approaches used for intrusion detection — statistical and expert approaches. However, I will also provide useful references on the new and prospective directions of the development of intrusion detection technologies, such as those implementing artificial neural networks, genetic algorithms, etc.

Statistical Analysis

This approach is widely used in anomaly detection. Deviation from the mean value (i.e., dispersion) of the normal behavior profile notifies the administrator of the fact that attack has been detected. Average frequencies and variable values are calculated for each type of normal behavior (such as, for example, number of logons, number of access-denial events, time, and so on). The system reports a probable attack when these values do not fit within the range of normal values, i.e., exceed the specified threshold. For example, statistical analysis can help to detect an abnormal event such as a logon of the authorized user in unusual time (for example, from 6 a.m. to 8 p.m.).

Parameters included in the behavior pattern can be classified into the following groups:

❒ Numeric parameters (amount of data transferred using different protocols, processor workload, number of accessed files, etc.)

❒ Category parameters (file names, user commands, opened ports, etc.).

❒ Activity parameters (number of attempts to access files or number of connections per specified time period)

When using this approach, it is important to make a correct selection of controlled parameters for the intrusion detection system. A small number or incorrect selection of these parameters will result in an incomplete model of system-object behavior. Thus, many attacks will not be covered by such a system. On the other hand, an excessive number of monitoring parameters will significantly degrade the host performance at the expense of increasing system-resource requirements (RAM, disk space, processor workload, and so on).

Although statistical methods are rather efficient and can reliably detect some types of attacks, they are not widely used at the moment because of the above-mentioned drawbacks. One of the most significant drawbacks of statistical methods lies in the difficulties of specifying the correct threshold values. If the threshold value is set too high, many attacks will not be detected. On the other hand, if this value is too small, many false attack signals will result. Note that some intrusion detection systems, such as the RealSecure Network Sensor, allow users to customize threshold values for some kinds of attacks. However, selection of correct values for these parameters is a nontrivial task that requires a solid knowledge of the controlled system. Other drawbacks of the statistical approach are listed in Table 4.8.

Table 4.8. Advantages and Drawbacks of Statistical Methods for Intrusion Detection

Advantages	Drawbacks
Statistical systems can detect new and unknown attacks.	Intruders can mislead the intrusion detection system, which will interpret the activity indicative of the attacks as a normal activity due to gradual changes of the working mode and "adaptation" of the system to anomalous behavior.
Statistical methods allow the detection of more complex attacks than other methods.	When using statistical methods, the probability of false positive events (false attack notifications) is significantly higher than when using any other method.
Statistical systems can be adapted to changes in user behavior.	Statistical methods are not the most correct ones when it is necessary to process changes in user activities (for example, when a manager performs the duties of his subordinates in critical situations). This drawback can cause serious problems in organizations where such changes are frequent. As a result, false attack notifications might appear, as well as false negative events (attacks that remained unnoticed).
	Statistical methods are not capable of detecting attacks performed by subjects whose pattern of typical behavior is impossible to describe.
	Statistical methods prove to be inadequate when detecting attacks on the part of subjects, which initially perform unauthorized actions. Thus, the typical behavior pattern will initially include attacks.
	These methods require preliminary customization (including correct threshold values for each parameter for each user).
	These methods are not sensible to the event order.

Expert Systems

In contrast to anomaly detection, which is usually oriented towards monitoring of the threshold values, misuse detection methods are based on rules that describe an attack scenario. The misuse detection mechanism identifies potential attacks if user activity coincides with the rules specified for a certain attack. The most important aspect of intrusion detection systems based on this principle is the availability of complete databases of known attacks. An expert system is a system that makes a decision to classify a specific event as an attack on the basis of existing rules. These rules are created on the basis of practical experience of security professionals and stored in a special database, known as a knowledge base. In most cases, the expert system rules use so-called signatures, for which the system searches the controlled area.

Signatures are patterns matched to find attacks or cases of misuse. They can be rather simple (a string of characters for searching for a specific condition or command) or very complex (for example, a change of security status in the form of mathematical expressions, predefined sequences of actions, or a set of log-file records).

Signature analysis involves controlling the matching between system settings and activities of the user (or other system object), and comparing network traffic to the database of known attacks and vulnerabilities. Most commercial intrusion detection products perform signature analysis in comparison to the database of known attacks, which is supplied by the product vendor. Additional signatures installed by the client can also be added in the course of the system installation and configuration process.

Despite the fact that, in most cases, expert systems are employed for misuse detection, there are also methods for anomaly detection. For example, the method of predictive pattern generation assumes that future events will be predicted on the basis of an event that has already occurred. This rule can be written as follows:

$$\Pi_1 - \Pi_2 \Rightarrow (\Pi_3 = 75\%, \Pi_4 = 20\%, \Pi_5 = 5\%).$$

This means that, if the event Π_2 occurs after the event Π_1, then the event Π_3 will occur with a probability of 75%; the probability for the event Π_4 is 20%, and the probability that the event Π_5 will take place is 5%. However, you can see that this method is not free from the common drawbacks of all expert systems. For example, if a specific attack scenario is not registered in the knowledge base, this attack will be impossible to detect. Despite the fact that it is possible to overcome this drawback by defining all unknown events as attacks (this will produce a negative effect resulting in a false positive problem) or as normal events (in contrast to the previous case, this will result in a false negative problem), the problem as a whole will not be eliminated by this approach.

Seventy percent of contemporary commercial intrusion detection systems are based on methods devised by experts, while approximately 30% are statistical. Unfortunately, expert systems require constant upgrading in order to remain up-to-date. The required updates may be either ignored or applied manually (by the administrator). This, at least, will result in an expert system with reduced functionality [Cannady1-98]. In the worst-case scenario, lack of maintenance reduces the security level of the whole network and misleads users by producing a false impression of safety and security.

Systems based upon misuse detection rules are unable to detect scenarios of attacks that are take place over a long period of time. Any attack distribution (either in time or between several intruders apparently not related to one another) also complicates intrusion detection using these methods. Advantages and drawbacks of expert systems for intrusion detection are outlined in Table 4.9.

Table 4.9. Advantages and Drawbacks of Expert Systems for Intrusion Detection

Advantages	Drawbacks
Simplicity of implementation.	Inability to detect unknown attacks.
Intrusion detection systems based upon the misuse detection rules are fast.	Small modifications of the same attack make it undetectable.
Elimination of false positive alarms.	The system depends on the skills and qualifications of the specialists who support its knowledge base.

Neural Networks

This method is relatively new, and has not yet been widely adopted in intrusion detection technologies. However, some specialists and even manufacturers do use neural networks in their solutions.

There are some research works investigating the usage of neural networks in the field of intrusion detection. Artificial neural networks are potentially very useful for solving a wide range of problems covered by other contemporary approaches to intrusion detection. Artificial neural networks were declared to be alternatives to the statistical analysis components of anomaly detection systems.

Neural networks were specifically proposed for identifying typical characteristics of system users and statistically meaningful deviations from the standard working mode of the user.

Artificial neural networks are also supposed to be used when detecting computer viruses. In some works, the authors have even suggested neural networks as an approach for statistical analysis when detecting viruses in computer networks. The architecture of the neural network selected for this purpose is represented in the Self-Organizing Map ("Cohonen networks") using a single layer (level) of neurons for representing the information from a single domain in the form of a geometrically organized map. The suggested network was intended for the study of the characteristics of normal system activity, and to identify statistical deviations from normal values, which could indicate the presence of a virus.

The constantly changing nature of network attacks requires flexible protection and a security system that would be able to analyze an enormous amount of network traffic using methods that are less structured than those used in systems based on misuse detection rules. Intrusion detection systems on the basis of neural networks might solve many serious problems that exist in systems based on the rules. One of such examples is the AUBAD (Automated User Behavior Anomaly Detection) system, developed at Melbourne University in Australia, that represents an example of a system created on the basis of this principle.

The most significant disadvantage of using neural networks for intrusion detection lies in the fact that such networks, by their nature, are similar to "black boxes." In contrast to expert systems, which have predefined strict rules for event analysis, neural networks adapt this analysis in response to the "teaching" procedures performed in the network. The weight of connections and transmission functions of different network nodes does not usually play any significant role after the network achieves an acceptable level of success in event identification. Although network analysis achieves a significant probability of success, the basis of this level of precision often remains unknown. The "black box" problem is the most serious vexation in neural-network usage [Cannady1-98]. This area of the neural networks' practical usage is open for further investigation. The advantages and drawbacks of neural networks currently used in practice are outlined in Table 4.10.

Table 4.10. Advantages and Drawbacks of Neural Networks for Intrusion Detection

Advantages	Drawbacks
Capable of detecting unknown attacks.	Results often lack explanations.
Able to function in environments with a large amount of noise.	Lack of learning materials.
System retains usability when data are incomplete or corrupt.	Lack of commercial intrusion detection systems based on neural networks.
Able to predict user behavior and new attacks.	

Combined Approaches

There are systems combining several approaches to the problem of intrusion detection. Furthermore, as well as the three main approaches discussed above, there are other approaches and methods, which will be briefly outlined in the next few sections.

The NIDES System

The NIDES system, representing the further development of the IDES system, is one of the first examples of a combined approach. This system, which was developed between 1992 and 1994 in Stanford Rescarch Institute (SRI), combines anomaly and misuse detection. As its anomaly detection component, the NIDES system uses a statistical approach determining deviation from the normal user-behavior profile, composed on the basis of more than 30 various parameters (processor workload, Input/Output operations, system errors, user commands, and so on). These profiles are periodically adapted to user behavior. The "expert" component stores scenarios of already known attacks described using the P-BEST attack-description language. The advantage of this solution includes the fact that attacks missed by the first component are detected by the second one, and vice versa. An analysis is performed in real-time mode. The NIDES system differs from the IDES by the presence of special RESOLVER component, which is responsible for joining data obtained from statistical and expert components of the system.

The EMERALD System

The EMERALD system (Event Monitoring Enabling Responses to Anomalous Live Disturbances) was also developed in SRI. However, it appeared later than the NIDES system. In contrast to NIDES, EMERALD also combines both approaches to intrusion detection and is oriented towards large, distributed corporate networks. A specific feature of this system is its capability to perform data analysis from each sensor, both separately and in any combination. It is also possible to integrate third-party tools into this system.

Other Solutions

James Kennedy from the School of Computer and Information Sciences, at Nova Southeastern University, Fort Lauderdale, Florida, proposed an interesting solution combining all three of the above-described approaches. He joined neural network technologies and the RealSecure Network Sensor from ISS. The results of these combinations were overwhelming. The intrusion detection probability reached 98%, while the probability of errors decreased to 5%.

While the solution discovered at Nova Southeastern University was used to detect intrusions in network traffic, a solution proposed at Texas University, in Austin, was used to detect attacks on the basis of analyzing commands issued by the user. This intrusion detection mechanism, based on the learning mechanism with reverse propagation, was named NNID — Neural Network Intrusion Detector. This algorithm was studied when solving the attack identification problem, and was tested experimentally in a system comprising 10 users.

The GASSATA (Genetic Algorithm for Simplified Security Audit Trail Analysis) misuse detection system was developed at the University of Rennes in France. This system is intended for analysis of events obtained from the AIX operating system log file. As a registration data mechanism, this system uses a genetic algorithm.

The AID (Adaptive Intrusion Detection) system appeared as a result of a research project conducted at Brandenburg University of Technology in Germany. This project was sponsored by the German Department of Science, Education, and Culture from 1994 to 1996. The AID system is built on client/server architecture. It is intended for the detection of suspicious activities in local area networks. The AID system obtained its input data from the operating system, translated these data into an OS-independent format and transmitted them to the management console, which then processed these data. The analysis was performed using the real-time expert system RTworks (http://www.talarian.com/rtworks.html). This analysis used the deterministic finite automates mathematical method. The first version of the AID system ran under the Solaris operating system on the Sun SPARC platform. In the course of system investigation, the researchers aimed to achieve the following:

❐ Develop agents for the analysis of activities not only on the network, but also at the host level

❐ Implement Windows NT support

❐ Integrate the neural networks mechanism (Cohonen networks)

The NetSTAT intrusion detection system is the newest product from the STAT family developed at the University of California, Santa Barbara. This product, which was started in the early 1990s, was oriented towards the creation of real-time intrusion detection systems using the so-called transition state control. The idea of this approach was as follows. To implement the attack, the intruder had to achieve the transition of the controlled system from one state (the initial state) to another state (the compromised state). In contrast to most other host-level intrusion detection systems that analyze log files directly, systems from the STAT family have an intermediate component, known as the audit trail analyzer. This component processes log-file records and transforms them into so-called abstracts (also known as signatures). The resulting signatures determine transitions of the controlled system from one state to another. The intrusion detection system then analyzes these transitions. From this point of view, attacks are also transitions from one state to another, and, therefore, the system can compare them to the information retrieved from the log file. The main advantage of this approach is of its ability to detect an attack before the system reaches a compromised state.

The first system from the STAT family was named USTAT. It was intended for the detection of intrusions upon UNIX hosts. Its successor, the NSTAT system, was aimed at protecting a range of networked hosts rather than stand-alone hosts. The NetSTAT system is currently under development and, and in contrast to USTAT and NSTAT, is oriented towards network-level intrusion detection.

Some developers use different approaches. For example, the British company ProCheckUp (http://www.procheckup.com) provides the ProCheckNet penetration testing service, which uses Artificial Intelligence algorithms to imitate intruders. According to the manufacturer, the AI of this system is capable of bypassing a large variety of security tools. The PROMIA company (http://www.promia.com/) has chosen a different approach. After studying and analyzing the problems characteristic of most contemporary intrusion detection systems (including a large number of false positives and the inability to detect unknown attacks), the company has developed the Intelligent Agent Security Module (IASM), which uses both traditional mechanisms (comparing to a predefined pattern) and new anomaly detection technologies (neural networks and fuzzy logic). In September 2001, the Space and Naval Warfare Systems Command (SPAWAR) decided to deploy this system.

Summary

A lack of a mathematical basis of intrusion detection systems prevents researchers from developing efficient intrusion detection methods. All existing methods are based either on the developer's individual preferences or on scientific achievements in related areas. The existing tools and mechanisms currently have no solid scientific basis, which does not allow the user to confirm or rule out the proposed solutions. Currently, there are some positive trends in this area; however, all research works are very far from being accomplished.

Thus, in this chapter we have described three basic principles representing the foundation for all intrusion detection technologies. Now we know *what*, *where* and *how* to detect. There are two methods of using this knowledge in practice. First, you can manually apply the simplest methods of analysis to find the known attack indications. This approach will be covered in *Chapter 5*. The second approach requires the same actions to be performed in automatic mode. This approach will be covered in *Chapters 6* through *12*.

CHAPTER 5

Detecting Attack Traces

"By discovering the enemy's dispositions and remaining invisible ourselves, we can keep our forces concentrated, while the enemy's must be divided."

Sun Tzu, "The Art of War."

We already know how to detect attack indications within the controlled resources. We also know what methods can be used to detect security policy violations within the controlled area. These topics were covered in *Chapter 4*. Now we will look at how to detect these violations.

When detecting attack traces, it is necessary to take into account the following aspects [Firth1-97]:

❑ Integrity control for programs, data files and other information resources to be protected
❑ An analysis of user and process activity, along with a network-traffic analysis within the controlled system
❑ Control over physical attacks on the information-system elements, including mobile storage media (such as a mobile rack)

❏ Suspicious activity investigation performed by administrators or other reliable sources (CIRT, for example)

According to this classification, actions related to intrusion detection described in Table 5.1 can be performed in both the automatic and manual modes (Fig. 5.1).

Table 5.1. Factors Related to Intrusion Detection

Factor	Actions
Data-integrity control	Viewing unexpected changes to files and folders
Control over user and process activity, including control over network traffic	Analysis of log files, including those of operating systems, DBMS, user programs and network applications
	Analysis of alerts and system messages from network-monitoring systems and system-monitoring tools (including OS built-in monitoring tools)
	Analysis of suspicious behavior of the active processes
Control over physical forms of intrusion	Detecting unknown or unauthorized devices (modems, for example) connected to the controlled system
	Detecting traces of unauthorized access to physical resources
Investigating incidents	Analysis of the user reports and data from external sources on the behavior of the system, processes, programs and network events.

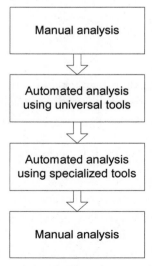

Fig. 5.1. Methods of analyzing attack information

However, I should mention that the last two rows of Table 5.1 go beyond the scope of this book.

Automatic analysis can also be classified into two categories — universal and specialized. Universal analysis is performed using the built-in tools supplied with the software. This group of tools includes, for example, Network Monitor or Event Viewer, used to view Windows NT/2000/XP log files. Specialized analysis is carried out using special tools intended for detecting security policy violations. This group of tools includes, for example, Snort, Tripwire, System Scanner and others.

Manual methods are free, if you do not consider the salary of the specialist performing the analysis and other parameters comprising the Total Cost of Ownership (TCO). However, they can not guarantee rapid detection of intrusions, to say nothing of taking appropriate counter-measures. Furthermore, these methods are not effective when dealing with networks that are distributed over a large area. Nonetheless, the use of these methods is sometimes justified. This is the case, for example, when performing an analysis of remote affiliates, network segments and hosts that are not of critical importance, or when purchasing an automated intrusion detection system is within the means of your budget. These methods are also of value after an automated analysis has already been run since, despite all of the provided by these methods, some attacks are very difficult to detect without manual analysis and human intuition. In this case, however, the amount of data that needs to be processed manually is significantly smaller than the initial data amount. As stated in [Allen1-99], the complete automation of the intrusion detection process still remains an unattainable dream. In practically all known incidents that have been reported and in which the intruder was traced, security specialists used manual methods, based on the high level of care and concentration that are characteristic of the IDS operators, or on additional custom software that enhances the security system's functionality. Finally, manual analysis is to be preferred for security professionals, since it allows them to improve their skills and knowledge.

The universal automated methods used in the initial stages are more efficient than manual methods. However, even these methods are not capable of detecting security policy violations within a reasonable time. Instead, these methods can simplify the processing of large amounts of information, perform filtering, and select data sets for subsequent manual analysis. But manual processing is still necessary.

The final option for performing the actions described in Table 5.1 is applying specialized systems that differ from the universal ones in the use of logic. Usually, these systems have quite a large database of security policy violations (attack indications or vulnerabilities) that can be detected within the information sources using specific methods (systems detecting abuses or abnormalities).

However, you must not draw the conclusion that only specialized systems are capable of performing the task and, therefore, are the best choice. Based on the messages generated by these tools, one can overlook or misinterpret some events. Therefore, you should not limit yourself solely to the messages generated by even the most advance intrusion detection system. You still have to perform manual analyses of data gathered not only by intrusion detection system, but also by other tools (network sniffers, for example).

Control of File and Folder Integrity

To conceal their presence in the affected system, intruders often change or substitute various programs in such a way that the replacement programs perform the same functions, except those that would reveal the intruder's presence. After such changes, some programs can perform other specific actions than those ones designed by the developer.

Quite often, intruders modify log files in order to delete the records containing information on unauthorized activity.

Furthermore, intruders can write new files to your disk — executable files, for example — that allow them to bypass existing access-control mechanisms. Besides programs, user files also often become the targets of attack targets. Unauthorized access to user files can result in the exposure of confidential information or, for example, the alteration of recipient data in a user-generated invoice.

Sometimes intruders are also interested in public information, such as Internet servers. The example illustrated in Fig. 5.2 is rather interesting. Take a look at the banner in the upper part of the window, which is the evidence that the site has been hacked. But wait … it was not the SecurityFocus site that was hacked, but rather the site of the Thruport company that places its advertising materials on the SecurityFocus site.

Of course, you can go further than simply controlling changes to files and directories. Sometimes it is useful to control specific fields within a file, such as database fields or system-registry keys. Most unauthorized programs (especially "Trojan horses") use various components of the system registry to start automatically during booting of the operating system. These keys include:

- ❏   HKEY_LOCAL_MACHINE\SOFTWARE\Microsoft\Windows\CurrentVersion\Run
- ❏   HKEY_LOCAL_MACHINE\SOFTWARE\Microsoft\Windows\CurrentVersion\RunServices
- ❏   HKEY_LOCAL_MACHINE\SOFTWARE\Microsoft\Windows\CurrentVersion\RunOnce
- ❏   HKEY_LOCAL_MACHINE\SOFTWARE\Microsoft\Windows\CurrentVersion\RunServicesOnce

- ❏ HKEY_USERS\DEFAULT\SOFTWARE\Microsoft\Windows\CurrentVersion\Run
- ❏ HKEY_CURRENT_USER\SOFTWARE\Microsoft\Windows\CurrentVersion\Run
- ❏ HKEY_CURRENT_USER\SOFTWARE\Microsoft\Windows\CurrentVersion\RunServices
- ❏ HKEY_CURRENT_USER\SOFTWARE\Microsoft\Windows\CurrentVersion\RunOnce
- ❏ HKEY_CURRENT_USER\SOFTWARE\Microsoft\Windows\CurrentVersion\RunServicesOnce
- ❏ HKEY_LOCAL_MACHINE\SOFTWARE\Microsoft\Windows\CurrentVersion\RunOnceEx

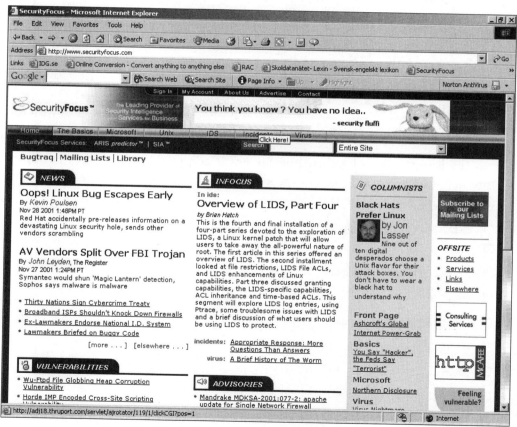

Fig. 5.2. The hacked www.securityfocus.com server

For example, the Donald Dick Trojan can be identified by the presence of the HKLM\System\CurrentControlSet\Service\VxD\VMLDR registry key (for Windows 9*x*), or the HKLM\SYSTEM\CurrentControlSet\Control\SessionManager registry key (for Windows NT). The BackOrifice Trojan can leave traces of its activity in

`HKLM\Software\Microsoft\Windows\CurrentVersion\RunServices`. This registry key, along with other keys, such as `Run`, `RunOnce`, `RunServicesOnce`, and `RunOnceEx`, is frequently used by various Trojans that need to load automatically at the system startup. For example, the NetBus Trojan can be detected by the presence of a key named after the Patch.exe file (Fig. 5.3).

Fig. 5.3. Control over the Windows registry

The list of registry keys used by Trojans is constantly growing. For example, the Internet Scanner system, besides the keys that were already mentioned above, checks the following registry branches:

☐ `HKLM\Software\Microsoft\Windows\CurrentVersion\App Paths`

☐ `HKLM\Software\Microsoft\Windows\CurrentVersion\Controls Folder`

☐ `HKLM\Software\Microsoft\Windows\CurrentVersion\DeleteFiles`

☐ `HKLM\Software\Microsoft\Windows\CurrentVersion\Explorer`

☐ `HKLM\Software\Microsoft\Windows\CurrentVersion\Extensions`

☐ `HKLM\Software\Microsoft\Windows\CurrentVersion\ExtShellViews`

☐ `HKLM\Software\Microsoft\Windows\CurrentVersion\Internet Settings`

☐ `HKLM\Software\Microsoft\Windows\CurrentVersion\ModuleUsage`

☐ `HKLM\Software\Microsoft\Windows\CurrentVersion\RenameFiles`

☐ `HKLM\Software\Microsoft\Windows\CurrentVersion\Setup`

☐ `HKLM\Software\Microsoft\Windows\CurrentVersion\SharedDLLs`

☐ `HKLM\Software\Microsoft\Windows\CurrentVersion\Shell Extensions`

☐ `HKLM\Software\Microsoft\Windows\CurrentVersion\Uninstall`

☐   HKLM\Software\Microsoft\Windows NT\CurrentVersion\Compatibility

☐   HKLM\Software\Microsoft\Windows NT\CurrentVersion\Drivers

☐   HKLM\Software\Microsoft\Windows NT\CurrentVersion\drivers.desc

☐   HKLM\Software\Microsoft\Windows NT\CurrentVersion\Drivers32\0

☐   HKLM\Software\Microsoft\Windows NT\CurrentVersion\Embedding

☐   HKLM\Software\Microsoft\Windows NT\CurrentVersion\MCI

☐   HKLM\Software\Microsoft\Windows NT\CurrentVersion\MCI Extensions

☐   HKLM\Software\Microsoft\Windows NT\CurrentVersion\Ports

☐   HKLM\Software\Microsoft\Windows NT\CurrentVersion\ProfileList

☐   HKLM\Software\Microsoft\Windows NT\CurrentVersion\WOW

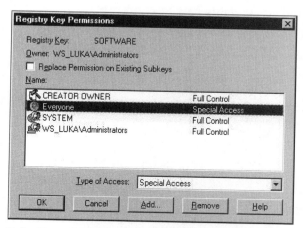

Fig. 5.4. Changing access rights to the system-registry keys

To minimize the possibility of "Trojan horses," just do not allow them to register themselves in the Windows registry. This can be done by means of editing the default access rights to the above-listed registry keys. In Windows NT/2000, this task is performed using the built-in Regedt32.exe utility, while, in Windows XP, the same task is performed using Regedit.exe (Fig. 5.4).

Selecting Data on Important Files and Folders

For each file or folder, it is necessary to have a sufficient amount of information in order to control all the changes that the file undergoes. This information must include information on the file location (note that this must be a fully qualified path name rather than a relative path). For example, a change introduced to the system variables will result in all of the programs that use relative addressing (despite the convenience involved) being replaced by other programs, possibly modified or tweaked (Fig. 5.5).

Other information (Fig. 5.6) that can be of interest includes:

❑ Alternative paths, such as links, alias names and shortcuts
❑ Folder contents
❑ File size (in bytes)
❑ Date and time of file creation and last modification
❑ File owner and access rights

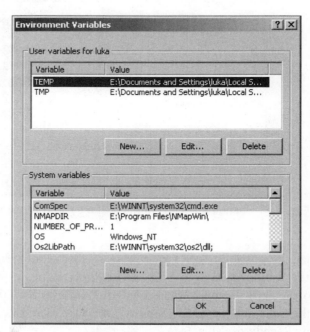

Fig. 5.5. The system variables

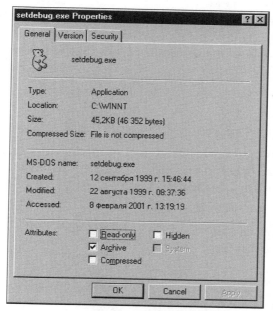

Fig. 5.6. Parameters of the controlled files

We have already mentioned the minimum information required to control file and folder integrity. For vitally important files, it may be necessary to know the values of the checksum that can be obtained using various tools intended for integrity control (such as Tripware, MD5, L5, System Scanner and so on). This information, along with backup copies of the log files, network map and other important data necessary for intrusion detection infrastructure, must be stored on the write-protected media (this topic will be covered in detail in *Chapter 7*). Before you begin selecting this information, it is necessary to determine which data for which files must be controlled. Otherwise, integrity-control system could end up consuming all available system resources and track the parameters of all files. For example, when dealing with log files, there is no need to check the creation date and time, size and checksum, since this data is constantly changing. However, for such files, it is necessary to control parameters such as file location, owner and access rights.

Integrity Control for Files and Folders

For integrity control, it is necessary to compare the current file parameters, described in the previous section, to the stored standard values of these parameters, so that you can identify any file-system characteristics that were changed since the last check.

Detection of the replacement or alteration of operating system or application software files can be done using the operating system's built-in utilities. For example, the `find` utility (in UNIX) allows the detection of files that were changed during a specified time period [CIAC1-94].

```
Luka# find /. -mtime -ndays -ls
```

or

```
Luka# find / -ctime -ndays -ls
```

The `cmp` utility built-in to UNIX is just another tool that enables you to detect changes to specified files or directories. This utility can be used to compare the current versions of files with their standard copies:

```
Luka# cmp /home/luka/vi /usr/bin/vi
```

If you are working with Windows NT or Windows 2000, you can use the similar built-in OS tool named `comp`:

```
comp c:\winnt\system32\drivers\etc\hosts d:\integrity-archive\OS\
30.12.2001\hosts
```

Integrity control can be performed using various methods — from the simplest to the most complicated. It is up to you to select the optimal method to provide a reasonable balance between a high level of security and the efficiency of the system that you are protecting.

Analysis of Log Files

Quite often, intruders leave traces of their activity in various log files. Viewing these logs on a regular basis is sometimes the only possible way to detect intrusions. Log files can contain evidence of various unauthorized or unexpected activities taking place in a system or a protected network. Log records can show that someone has compromised your system, or at least attempted to do so. By analyzing logs regularly, you can identify most attacks that have or are taking place and implement procedures to counteract them. It is necessary to distinguish between event log files and transaction log files. Transaction log files allow not only the registration of the event types, but also log actions performed by a specific user on a specific object. Because of this, in Windows NT/2000/XP, you can not always determine exactly what a specific user has done. For example, using only the Windows NT/2000/XP log file, you can state that your accountant has opened the file named Salary.xls (event code 650) for reading, writing or deleting. On the other hand, using only the Windows NT/2000/XP log file, you can not determine what modifications that particular user has made to the file.

Log-file management comprises three stages, in which you need to determine the following:

❏ The information you need to know about your system
❏ The log files that contain the required information
❏ The attack indicators you are going to use

Consider, for example, a case in which you want to determine who has attempted to exploit the expn vulnerability in the sendmail implementation. This is the first stage. You have determined what you need to detect. At the second stage, you need to open the /etc/syslog.conf, where the paths to the log files are specified [Spitzner1-00]. In the case of sendmail, this is /var/log/maillog (in Linux 7.2). The line shown in Listing 5.1, serves as an indication of unauthorized activity.

Listing 5.1. Exploiting the expn Vulnerability in Sendmail Implementation

```
Aug 18 04:03:44 luka sendmail[5453]: NOQUEUE: luka@infosec.ru[200.0.0.200]:
expn root [rejected]
```

Methods of log-file analysis depend on the type and volume of data to be processed. When the volume of data is small, it is possible to analyze these files manually (as was done before) using any text editor or a built-in event-log manager (such as the Event Viewer tool in Windows NT/2000/XP). It is also possible to use spreadsheets (such as Excel) of database management systems (Access, Oracle and so on), enabling you to perform various operations on the data being analyzed (filtering, selection, sorting, building dependencies and so on). However, this method of analysis is rather time-consuming and tedious since, in order to detect a single record providing evidence of unauthorized activity, you normally need to view hundreds or thousands of records. For example, when you double-click a text-file shortcut in the Windows NT/2000/XP GUI, this file will be opened using the WordPad or Notepad programs. In the course of this procedure, more than 20 events related to file access are registered in the log file (for WinWord there will be even more events). During business hours, there might be several thousand events like these that will cause significant growth in the log file.

Besides normal database management systems, it is possible to use specialized systems for the analysis of log files (so-called "log checkers"), which are specially designed for the analysis of log files in a manner very close to the real-time mode. Examples of these systems include SWATCH and Cisco IDS Host Sensor. The next generation of these systems is in the form of log checkers that support mechanisms for semantic compression, which allow one to join several related events within a single one and output that event to the console. For example, five events of a "logon failure" type can be united as a single instance of "password cracking." The RealSecure Server Sensor, for example, in implementing the SecureLogic and Local Fusion mechanisms, works according to this principle.

I would like to provide an example that I encountered personally in November 2000. One morning, when viewing logs on one of my computers (I have two systems; on one of them I installed RealSecure Server Sensor and, on the other one, I have RealSecure Desktop Protector), I noticed six `Brute_Force_Login_Attack` events, logged over the previous two days, meaning that the RealSecure Server Sensor system had detected brute force password attacks on my computer. Additional analysis showed that each of these events appeared as the result of a semantic compression of eight successive failed logon attempts over a short time interval. The RealSecure system had defined these events as `Failed_login-bad_username_or_password` (I hope that you remember the difference between an attack and a security event, which were described in *Chapter 2*). If I had not been using the intrusion detection system, I would have had to view several thousand events logged in the Windows NT security log (I now work in Windows 2000, but the event logging system has not improved significantly). The filtering of events (the result shown in Listing 5.2) is not always convenient. This is especially true when you need to control several hosts located in different network segments simultaneously.

Listing 5.2. Failed Attempts to Logon to Windows NT 4.0 (Fragments of the Security Log File)

Date	Time	Source	Category	Code	User	Computer
27.11.00	19:19:38	Security	Logon/Logoff	**529**	SYSTEM	NT-IIS
27.11.00	19:19:29	Security	Logon/Logoff	**529**	SYSTEM	NT-IIS
27.11.00	19:19:21	Security	Logon/Logoff	**529**	SYSTEM	NT-IIS
27.11.00	19:19:12	Security	Logon/Logoff	**529**	SYSTEM	NT-IIS
27.11.00	19:19:03	Security	Logon/Logoff	**529**	SYSTEM	NT-IIS
27.11.00	19:18:55	Security	Logon/Logoff	**529**	SYSTEM	NT-IIS
27.11.00	19:18:46	Security	Logon/Logoff	**529**	SYSTEM	NT-IIS
27.11.00	19:18:37	Security	Logon/Logoff	**529**	SYSTEM	NT-IIS
27.11.00	18:32:14	Security	Logon/Logoff	**529**	SYSTEM	NT-IIS
27.11.00	18:32:05	Security	Logon/Logoff	**529**	SYSTEM	NT-IIS
27.11.00	18:31:56	Security	Logon/Logoff	**529**	SYSTEM	NT-IIS
27.11.00	18:31:47	Security	Logon/Logoff	**529**	SYSTEM	NT-IIS

27.11.00	18:31:38	Security	Logon/Logoff	**529**	SYSTEM	NT-IIS
27.11.00	18:31:29	Security	Logon/Logoff	**529**	SYSTEM	NT-IIS
27.11.00	18:31:20	Security	Logon/Logoff	**529**	SYSTEM	NT-IIS
27.11.00	18:31:11	Security	Logon/Logoff	**529**	SYSTEM	NT-IIS
27.11.00	16:28:07	Security	Logon/Logoff	**529**	SYSTEM	NT-IIS
27.11.00	16:27:58	Security	Logon/Logoff	**529**	SYSTEM	NT-IIS
27.11.00	16:27:49	Security	Logon/Logoff	**529**	SYSTEM	NT-IIS
27.11.00	16:27:40	Security	Logon/Logoff	**529**	SYSTEM	NT-IIS
27.11.00	16:27:31	Security	Logon/Logoff	**529**	SYSTEM	NT-IIS
27.11.00	16:27:22	Security	Logon/Logoff	**529**	SYSTEM	NT-IIS
27.11.00	16:27:13	Security	Logon/Logoff	**529**	SYSTEM	NT-IIS
27.11.00	16:27:04	Security	Logon/Logoff	**529**	SYSTEM	NT-IIS
27.11.00	14:22:00	Security	Logon/Logoff	**529**	SYSTEM	NT-IIS
27.11.00	14:21:51	Security	Logon/Logoff	**529**	SYSTEM	NT-IIS
27.11.00	14:21:42	Security	Logon/Logoff	**529**	SYSTEM	NT-IIS
27.11.00	14:21:33	Security	Logon/Logoff	**529**	SYSTEM	NT-IIS
27.11.00	14:21:24	Security	Logon/Logoff	**529**	SYSTEM	NT-IIS
27.11.00	14:21:15	Security	Logon/Logoff	**529**	SYSTEM	NT-IIS
27.11.00	14:21:06	Security	Logon/Logoff	**529**	SYSTEM	NT-IIS
27.11.00	14:20:57	Security	Logon/Logoff	**529**	SYSTEM	NT-IIS
27.11.00	12:15:54	Security	Logon/Logoff	**529**	SYSTEM	NT-IIS
27.11.00	12:15:45	Security	Logon/Logoff	**529**	SYSTEM	NT-IIS
27.11.00	12:15:36	Security	Logon/Logoff	**529**	SYSTEM	NT-IIS
27.11.00	12:15:27	Security	Logon/Logoff	**529**	SYSTEM	NT-IIS
27.11.00	12:15:18	Security	Logon/Logoff	**529**	SYSTEM	NT-IIS
27.11.00	12:15:09	Security	Logon/Logoff	**529**	SYSTEM	NT-IIS
27.11.00	12:15:00	Security	Logon/Logoff	**529**	SYSTEM	NT-IIS
27.11.00	12:14:51	Security	Logon/Logoff	**529**	SYSTEM	NT-IIS

Code 529 corresponds to a "failed logon" event. A complete list of logged events can be downloaded from the Microsoft web server [Microsoft1-00, Microsoft2-00].

A potential danger also lies in the fact that, as the current log file grows, older records are overwritten by newer ones. Thus, if you do not view log files on a regular basis, you will miss a large number of events. I should mention that, recently, Microsoft has begun supplying a new product — Microsoft Operations Manager (http://www.microsoft.com/mom/), which is intended for managing log files located on remote hosts. However, this system is not oriented towards solving security problems either.

However, even semantic compression mechanisms do not always provide the level of analysis necessary for the efficient investigation of security incidents. When performing such an analysis, you can not just use the log checker or intrusion detection system alone. As shown in the previous example, the investigation of unauthorized activity is impossible without human attention, even though intrusion detection systems automate the analysis process. For instance, in the example we just considered, the intrusion detection system could not determine that password cracking was most likely attempted using some form of automated tool. Manual analysis, on the other hand, permitted the detection of this fact at first glance, since each logon attempt took place nine seconds after the previous one. Obviously, it is impossible to manually enter eight passwords in a nine-second interval, so there is clear evidence of the fact that an automated tool was used for this purpose.

Furthermore, to do a comprehensive analysis, it is necessary to use different log files from different systems, which most intrusion detection systems are currently unable to do. Correlating of data from dissimilar systems and different software still remains an unattainable dream, despite the fact that the first attempts at providing such a solution have already been made — RealSecure SiteProtector, netForensics, and so on. Consider, for example a situation in which the log file of a banking system contains a number of records indicating that one of the operators has made several payments on Wednesday, between noon and 1 p.m. The information would seem to be evidence of normal activity, typical for that employee. However, the operating-system log file (or that of the security system) contains other record(s), from which it is clear that the operator was not at a workstation during that time (there was a lunch break, for example). This discrepancy is hard to detect without additional manual analysis of the log files. Let us consider another example. Suppose that the system administrator performed some operations on server A at 14:00:12, and then performed other operations on computer B at 14:07:35. At first glance, this activity is quite normal. However, computers A and B are located in different buildings, and at least 10 minutes are required to get from the first location to the other. This is suspicious, and the results of an analysis reveal the fraud — several employees were working using the same user account, which is a security policy violation. Finally, let us return to the earlier example. Analysis of the Windows NT/2000/XP security-log file (SecEvent.evt) reveals attempts to access specific files, but it is impossible to state what changes, if any, were made to the file. However, if the file is analyzed in combination with the log files of the file integrity-control system, it is possible to determine the details of any writing to that file. Furthermore, by comparing the file's size before and after modification, you can determine whether the user was adding or deleting information.

Once again, I would like to mention that, unfortunately, log-file records themselves can not state that specific actions were unauthorized. Log files only register the information that is required to perform the analysis. Further results depend on the security policy of your organization.

Network Traffic Analysis

In this chapter, we are not going to concentrate on this topic. First, many aspects of network traffic analysis were already covered in *Chapter 4* when discussing attack indications. Secondly, there are two excellent books on this topic, which I would gladly recommend to anyone — [Northcutt1-00] and [Coopper1-01]. In these books, all aspects of network-traffic analysis and detecting attack indications are covered in great detail. So let's here discuss some topics that are rarely discussed in various publications or other sources of information.

Notification Analysis

It is necessary to investigate carefully any warnings or notifications from system or network monitoring systems. Despite the high probability of errors or false positive warnings, and the seeming uselessness of this work, this information can serve as an efficient method of preventive notification of specific types of security policy violations. For example, messages concerning disk space or RAM shortage can be evidence of the occurrence of DoS attacks. Warning messages on decreased network throughput can be of the same character.

Analysis of Processes, Services, and Ports

Process analysis is aimed at checking to determine whether the actions performed by the processes correspond to the intended ones that were implemented by the developers (here, I do not take into account self-modifying systems, such as those based on genetic algorithms, for example). A process with behavior that does not correspond to its design and intent might indicate potential security policy violations. The investigation of processes is a rather complicated and time-consuming problem, which requires high qualifications, skill and a large amount of resources. The level of process investigation depends on the amount of information on normal process behavior that you have at your disposal. Generally, you need to search for the following data:

❑ Absent processes
❑ Additional processes (for example, the presence of the patch.exe process in Windows-based operating system is evidence that the NetBus "Trojan" server component is running on that computer)
❑ Unusual behavior by the process or resource

And so on... Because of the large number of processes and rapid changes that are characteristic for the majority of them, constant control of the system does not make sense. Furthermore, the amount and contents of the information that you can gather during this process are too large to be stored. This means that it is necessary to use automated mechanisms to simplify the tasks of gathering data and controlling processes. In multi-user systems, for displaying the current state of processes and tracking information on these processes for short time intervals, you can either use the OS built-in capabilities (for example, Task Manager for Windows NT/200 or `ps` for Unix) or install third-party software, such as solutions supplied by SysInternals.

There are several sources of information that can help you when analyzing processes:

❐ Log files of specific programs, containing the following information:
  - Data on the programs (who started the specific program and when, how long did it run and which resources it accessed)
  - Attempts to logon or establishing network connections
  - Attempts to access protected data and resources
❐ Results of running programs, which provides the following information:
  - The current state of system processes
  - The Configuration of resources and devices on your computer
  - Which resources and devices are currently used by processes, and how they are used
  - Files that are currently opened by the processes
  - The program state and activities related to the currently opened network connections
❐ System and network monitoring programs, which indicate that they have detected one of the following:
  - Unexpected labels and resource types used in the system
  - Attempts to logon using a privileged user account
  - Attempts at accessing important system files or protected resources
  - Unexpected labels and types of network traffic
  - Network interfaces working in promiscuous modes
  - Other unexpected changes in hardware configuration

Detecting Unauthorized Devices

Intruders are constantly attempting to bypass security systems. After all, why break the firewall if you can bypass it by connecting to an unauthorized modem, or by intercepting the authorized user's password using a sniffer and then providing it at the firewall?!

Regular Revision of the Devices

To eliminate one of the possible ways of penetrating a protected corporate network by bypassing the installed security tools, it is necessary to perform a complete revision of all systems, network and peripheral devices (for example, remote access servers or modems) at least once per month (and sometimes even more frequently). This revision can be performed using network management systems, as will be shown in *Chapter 7*. Naturally, if you are planning a revision, it is necessary to have the network map prepared beforehand.

Sometimes, you might need not only to implement a remote inventory using automated systems, but a local revision as well, in order to make sure that a specific device is physically present. This will allow you to guarantee that the intruders will be unable to use remote inventory procedures. When you are getting prepared for such procedures, do not inform anyone except for the persons who actually need to know about your preparations. This will prevent intruders from hiding or temporarily removing unauthorized devices.

Special mention should be made of the difficulties that you might encounter when taking an inventory of wireless devices, which have become more and more common. Unfortunately, at the time of writing, the tools for scanning wireless networks are not many. Among these, I will like to note the WaveStumbler freeware utility (http://www.cqure.net/tools08.html), and one commercial product — Wireless Scanner, from ISS.

Warstorming — the New Word in Hacking Wireless Networks

Australian hackers from Perth feel rather comfortable on board a small plane at a height of 460 meters. What could be hacked there except the plane's systems? You might ask. The answer is easy. Currently, there are lots of companies using wireless networks, and their number is tending to grow. Wireless networks are very convenient, but most companies simply do not pay sufficient attention to their security. As a rule, their wireless networks are not protected at all. Everyone who wants to connect is free to do so. Thus, the hackers decided to fly over the city, and found about 95 hosts, using only iPaq a notebook with the appropriate software installed. Previously, hackers had tried to search for wireless networks using cars or bikes, or simply by walking with their notebooks and PDAs. This occupation became known as "warstorming" (a combination of "wardriving" and "barnstorming"). The origin of the term "wardriving" is interesting: in the past, hackers dialed using a list of phone numbers, in the hopes of dialing a phone number with a modem. This occupation became known as "wardialling." Walking in search of wireless networks is called "warwalking," and doing so with a car is "wardriving."

Controlling Modems

To detect the presence of modems in a network, you can to use special programs that use various methods to perform remote checks on dozens, or even hundreds of hosts. Usually, such programs use one of two main operating principles. The first one is the well-known class of efficient programs, such as "wardialers", "carrier scanners," or "pbx scanners." These programs dial the specified range of phone numbers in search of modems installed at the other end of the line. Examples of such programs are THC Scan; PhoneSweep, from Sandstorm Enterprises; or TeleSweep Secure Scanner, from SecureLogix Corporation. Other systems, such as, for example, Internet Scanner, implement a mode that searches for active modems installed on workstations and servers by analyzing the system registry. (Obviously, this method only applies to the Windows platform). A separate category of products includes tools for searching remote access systems, for example, Remote Access Perimeter Scanner (RAPS) from Symantec.

Like an inventory, it is recommended that you run these programs on a regular basis.

❗ *Uncontrolled Modem Usage*

When performed auditing procedures in large banks, I detected several computers to which modems were connected. In the course of the investigation, it became evident that the presence of only one of these modems was authorized (the device was installed to provide access to a remote database). All other modems were installed by the bank employees, who used them for accessing the Internet, bypassing the firewall system of the bank's LAN. One computer with a modem connected was found to have the pcAnywhere program installed, enabling the employee to access confidential data from his home computer.

It is necessary to identify traffic with sender or recipient addresses belonging to external networks in relation to the protected network, but not registered by the firewalls or perimeter routers. This will allow you determine whether unauthorized modems are present in your network. For example, employees might use unauthorized modems to access the office network from home or to access the Internet by bypassing the firewall. There are lots of tools suitable for the detection of such traffic: intrusion detection systems, internal network equipment log files and various decision-support systems. For example, the SAFEsuite Decisions system, belonging to the last category, can detect attacks that were not detected and stopped at the firewall, but were noticed within the internal network.

Controlling Access to Physical Resources

Most of us suffer from basic mental habits, due to which we often forget quite simple questions. Naturally, the information in computer systems has the form of zeros and ones "roaming" in the networks. However, do not forget that the same information can be contained on diskettes, CDs or other media, including carbon copies. These physical devices also might become potential targets for intruders. Thus, it is necessary to provide physical protection for all components of the informational system.

Analysis of External Sources of Information and System Behavior

In organizations that are careful about security, the users are instructed and educated (this topic will be covered in detail in *Chapter 7*). These users then inform administrators of all suspicious events. Administrators must pay attention to this information and analyze it along with the data obtained from other sources, such as security bulletins and reports published by various response teams, which were mentioned above. Proper attention to notifications received from system users significantly improves the security administrator's ability to control the information resources. Educated users, most probably, know best which resources are critical and which events must be considered as suspicious. Do not neglect user information, even if their notifications and alarms prove to be false later. By ignoring warnings a number of times you could find yourself in the situation where users stop reporting what seems to them to be suspicious because they fear their warnings will be ignored or ridiculed. When analyzing user notifications, do not rely entirely on a single report. It is best to confirm reports with information obtained from other sources as well — security tools, log-file information and notifications from other users. Correlate information from these sources and try to find matches. If the notification is not well grounded, you can disregard it, but do not forget to thank the user for his or her help. The next time, this user, noticing that you are carefully investigating his or her notifications, might inform you of something really important.

Do not forget that intruders might select your network as a starting bases for attacking other networks. They might infect your system with a "Trojan horse," through which they can later implement attacks on the information resources of other organizations. Or, for example, some hosts within your network might be compromised using "zombie" programs and become the base for attacks on other hosts. Investigate all materials and bulletins obtained from incident-response groups, and use various security analyzers. Your network could prove to be vulnerable to some problems identified by these sources.

Collect as much information as possible. Sometimes it may be necessary to contact the user (for example, one of your clients) or organization (ISP, for example), that has published information on a suspicious event. Analyze log files and, if you find clear evidence of an attack, initiate reaction procedures immediately.

Summary

In this chapter, we have discussed the approaches to detecting security policy violations without using specialized automated tools for detecting unauthorized activities. We have also considered the aspects that deserve special attention. However, in large corporate networks, "manual" detection becomes rather inefficient and, quite often, even impossible. From the purely physical point of view, it is impossible to control the integrity of thousands of files manually or, for example, analyze network traffic in real-time. This is the point where the automated intrusion detection systems become invaluable. Such systems will be covered in detail in the following chapters.

CHAPTER 6

Classification of Intrusion Detection Systems

"A scorpion will sting because it has poison; a soldier can be brave when he can rely on his equipment. Therefore when their weapons are sharp and their armor is strong, people will readily go to battle."

Zhuge Liang, "The Way of the General."

In the previous chapter, we considered manual methods of intrusion detection, along with the application of some specialized universal automatic tools. The inefficiency of these methods was clear — they can be applied only if the automated tools can not handle the situation, or when it is necessary to perform additional analysis, and so it is necessary to discuss specialized systems designed specifically for intrusion detection.

There are several ways of detecting and defending against security policy violations. The first and the most common method is the detection of attacks that are already occurring. If we return to the main stages of attack implementation discussed in *Chapter 2* (see Fig. 2.10), then, according to the suggested classifications, this method is associated with the second stage of attack implementation. This approach is used in "classic" intrusion detection systems (such as, for example, RealSecure Network Sensor or Cisco IDS 4200), firewalls (such as Check Point Firewall-1), information security and protection systems (such as SecretNet) and so on. However, the main drawback of the systems of this type lies in the fact that attacks can be repeated. Of course, they will also be detected and blocked. This process can continue indefinitely, which is inefficient and wasteful in terms of time, money and human resources. It is much more efficient and effective to prevent attacks before they are implemented. This is the basic idea of the second approach. This approach involves the detection of vulnerabilities (i.e. potential attacks) that may be used in implementing attacks. Finally, there is the third approach — detecting attacks that have already occurred and preventing them from being implemented in the future. Thus, systems for the detection of security policy violations can be classified on the bases of the stage of the attack (Fig. 6.1), as described below:

❏ *Systems functioning at the first stage of attack implementation and enabling the detection of information-system vulnerabilities that can be exploited by the intruder.* The tools belonging to this category are known as security-assessment systems or security scanners. Internet Scanner and SATAN are examples of this type of system. Some authors argue that it is not correct to classify security scanners as intrusion detection systems. However, if we follow the classification principles described above, then it makes sense to classify them in this way.

❏ *Systems functioning at the second stage of attack implementation and allowing the detection of attacks during the course of their implementation, i.e., in real-time mode (or very close to real-time).* These are intrusion detection systems according to classical definitions. Apart from of such systems are RealSecure Network Sensor or Okena StormWatch. Besides this, there is also a relatively new class of intrusion detection systems — deception systems, which will be covered in detail later. Examples of such systems are RealSecure Server Sensor and DTK.

❏ *Systems that appear at the third stage of attack implementation and detect attacks that have already been completed.* These systems can be divided further into the following two classes: integrity checkers, which check the integrity of the controlled resources; and log checkers, which are intended for log-file analysis. Tripwire and RealSecure Server Sensor are two examples of these systems.

As well as the system explained above, there is another manner by which systems for the detection of security policy violations can be classified — by principles of implementation: host-based, i. e, the detection of vulnerabilities or attacks directed at a specific network host, and network-based, which are directed at the entire network or a network segment. The classification of intrusion detection systems by implementation level is shown in Fig. 6.2.

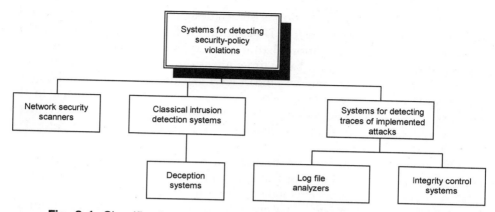

Fig. 6.1. Classification of intrusion detection systems by attack stage

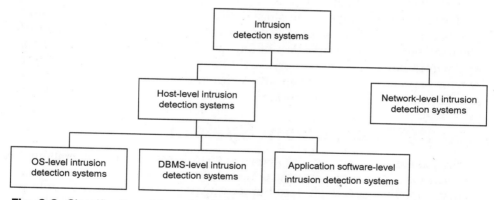

Fig. 6.2. Classification of intrusion detection systems by implementation principle

Normally, this level is the most detailed. However, based on the classification of information-system levels introduced in *Chapter 1*, it is possible to define three more sublevels:

❑ Intrusion detection systems at the application software level (application-based intrusion detection systems), which detect attacks on specific applications (such as Web-server). RealSecure OS Sensor and WebStalker Pro are two examples.

❑ Intrusion detection systems functioning at the operating-system level (OS-based), which detect intrusions there. Examples of these systems are DirectoryAlert and ServerAlert from NetVision intended for intrusion detection in NetWare networks.

❑ DBMS-based intrusion detection systems, detecting attacks at the DBMS level.

Classifying intrusion detection systems designed to detect attacks directed at the DBMS into a separate category is based on the fact that contemporary DBMS are characteristically something more than normal applications, and are closer to operating systems themselves. At the same time, intrusion detection systems (or, to be more precise, security scanners) at the DBMS level can function both locally, at the protected host, and via the network (for example, the Database Scanner). In turn, the network-level intrusion detection system can be localized to detect attacks directed at a specific host rather than at the whole network segment. RealSecure Desktop Protector represents an example of such system.

Of course, this classification can be disputed. Most specialists are of the opinion that security scanners should not be classified as intrusion detection systems. A similar situation exists for integrity control systems and log-file analyzers. Such systems help in intrusion detection, but, on the other hand, they are different from the IDS [Shiepley 1-00]. I do not want to argue this statement, but I would like to mention that, taking into account the steps of attack implementation, this classification is logical and reasonable.

Furthermore, even the terminology in this area has not been agreed upon yet. Each manufacturer, wishing to emphasize that its system is unique and that it outperforms all other solutions, creates a new class of intrusion detection systems. For example, this is how hybrid intrusion detection systems (such as Prelude), virtual intrusion detection systems (such as IntruShield from IntruVert), multitiered IDSs, stateful IDSs, and even specification-based IDSs have appeared.

Security Assessment Systems

Security assessment systems, also known as security scanners or vulnerability scanners, perform a comprehensive investigation of the resources under control in order to detect vulnerabilities that might result in security policy violations. The results produced by security scanners represent snapshots of the system state for a specified time period. Despite the fact that these systems can not detect an attack as it starts and evolves, they are capable of detecting the potential danger of attack attempts.

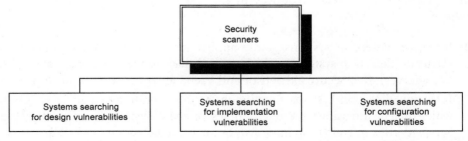

Fig. 6.3. Classification of security scanners by the type of vulnerability detected

Security scanners can be classified by the types of vulnerabilities they detect (Fig. 6.3). These vulnerabilities were described in *Chapter 2*.

Systems Searching for Design Vulnerabilities

As was mentioned in *Chapter 2*, these vulnerabilities are especially dangerous, since they are hard to detect and eliminate. In this case, the vulnerability is characteristic of an information-system project or a program algorithm and, consequently, even perfect implementation (which is virtually impossible) can not eliminate the inherent vulnerability. Depending on the subject to be analyzed, it is possible to use various tools for detecting design vulnerabilities. As a rule, when searching for design vulnerabilities in the information system, we have the following two aims:

❑ Analysis of the algorithm of the software and hardware complex
❑ Analysis of the corporate system project

The first aim is achieved relatively easily, since it is possible to use the existing techniques in the field of software verification during detection of the software-algorithm vulnerabilities. The second aim is much more difficult to implement but, even in this case, there are special tools that enable the analysis of design vulnerabilities.

Project Analysis

Table 6.1 outlines advantages and drawbacks of such systems.

Table 6.1. Advantages and Drawbacks of the Project Analysis Systems from the Standpoint of Information Security

Advantages	Drawbacks
Automation of problems that are difficult to formalize	The quality of the results depends on expert information built into the system
	Expense
	Limited area of application

The CRAMM system (CCTA Risk Analysis and Management Technology) is one of the best-known systems in this class. It was developed in 1985 by BIS Applied Systems Ltd., as a result of a research project initiated by the British government. The product, based on the CCTA methodology, was modified several times according to the security requirements of the systems it was being used to analyze. Currently, there are different versions of this product intended for government organizations, military organizations, private companies and financial institutions.

Besides the above-mentioned systems, there are other solutions intended for undertaking risk analysis, including design-vulnerability analysis. These systems include the following: RANK-IT, @RISK, ALRAM, ARES, LAVA etc. These systems are covered in detail in [Stang1-93] and [Nist1-91].

Algorithm Analysis

The PVS (Prototype Verification System) developed in the Computer Science Laboratory at the Stanford Research Institute (SRI), which is famous for creating intrusion detection systems like NIDES and EMERALD, is the most common among the systems of this class. The PVS system has the built-in language of formal software descriptions, along with a subsystem intended for proving theorems.

Systems Detecting Implementation Vulnerabilities

Quite a large number of attacks, such as buffer overflow, are based on hardware and software implementation errors. Because of this, the detection of such vulnerabilities is very important. Initially, security analysis (or, to be more precise, a search for software implementation errors) was conducted using standard methods, which implied software verification (i.e., finding proof of its accuracy). Using special methods and demonstrating that the initial and final conditions were satisfied, the investigators proved the software's health. However, despite their ability to detect specific errors, these methods can not be used for finding a number of vulnerabilities, particularly backdoors intentionally introduced into the software code. This is mainly due to the fact that, currently, there is no formal vulnerability description. The scientists suggested several different approaches to solving this problem, which can be classified into the following two main classes: analytical and experimental (Fig. 6.4). Systems of the first type are used to prove the existence of vulnerabilities by mathematical methods or analytical methods. This method is reliable and efficient, since it enables the investigator to determine specifically if any vulnerabilities are present in the system under consideration. However, the common drawback of these systems is the fact that they are hard to implement. Experimental methods enable the researcher to detect vulnerabilities present during the testing, which can be conducted in a virtual test environment (the sandbox in Java technology can be though of as an analog of this technology) using test generators, syntax and semantic analysis, etc.

Searching for vulnerabilities at the stage of software development allows the avoidance of many future security problems. Not only software developers can use the systems described in this section to provide information security, but also various organizations certifying hardware and software tools. Since my intent is to describe the most popular systems — those that can be employed by most users — I will briefly describe those used in certification laboratories.

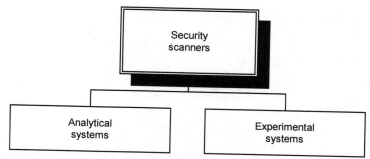

Fig. 6.4. Classification of the methods for searching for implementation vulnerabilities

Testing and controlling tools, in turn, can be classified depending on the availability of the source code of the program being analyzed (Fig. 6.5).

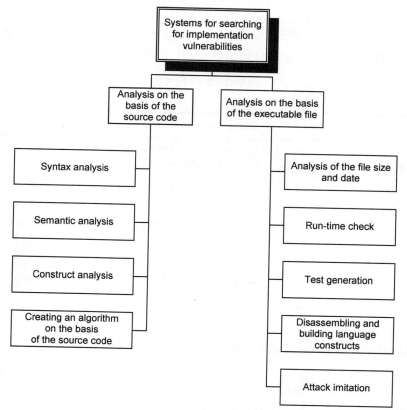

Fig. 6.5. Classification of the tools for searching for implementation vulnerabilities

Analysis of the Source Code

To create error-free software and hardware, it is necessary to organize the design and development process of the product correctly. This requirement, however, is not always met, due to the desire to release the product as soon as possible (or to accomplish obligations undertaken according to a contract). In this case, one generally uses various formal methods of describing the algorithm implemented by the product, the accordance of which is checked during the entire development process. Furthermore, one can check for vulnerabilities in the release version of the product. Examples of such systems are SLINT, RATS, and flawfinder. Quite often, if the source code of the software to be analyzed is not available, the product is disassembled. The resulting listing is then analyzed using standard source-code analysis methods.

The main drawback of source code analysis is the possibility of introducing various distortions into the software code when compiling and building programs. Even software that can be considered perfect from the point of view of the software code can have vulnerabilities introduced at the stage of compilation and building. Table 6.2 outlines the advantages and drawbacks of systems based on source-code analysis.

Table 6.2. Advantages and Drawbacks of Systems Based on Source-Code Analysis

Advantages	Drawbacks
Automation of the vulnerabilities search	The quality of the system functioning depends on the methods that it implements
	Each programming language requires its own analyzer
	Limited area of application
	Not practical for analyzing large amounts of the source code
	Such systems require qualified skilled personnel
	When compiling and building the software project, various deviations can be introduced, which are virtually unnoticeable at the stage of the source code analysis

Analysis of the Executable Code

In most cases, software is provided without the source code. Furthermore, source-code analysis requires qualified personnel. As well as this, the lack of efficient analyzers prevents investigators from performing their research at a high-quality level. Because of the above-mentioned factors, systems intended for detecting vulnerabilities in the source code are highly popular. As already mentioned, executable-code analyzers can be classified in the following categories:

- Analysis of file size, date and other attributes
- Run-time check
- Test generation
- Disassembling
- Attack imitation

File-Attribute Analysis

This method is very simple to implement. It simply compares the size and date of the file being analyzed with the data stored in the file database of existing vulnerable files. If these values match, the system decides that a vulnerability is present. For example, System Scanner performs a range of checks using this method.

Run-Time Check

Systems utilizing this approach (for example, BoundsChecker Pro, HeapAgent, and Purify NT) detect various errors (including vulnerabilities) that are hard to detect during source-code analysis. Although syntax and semantics analysis enables the detection of most errors with a high level of probability, some errors are still missed by these analyzers and can only be detected at runtime.

Test-Generation Systems

Test-generation systems apply a range of external actions to the software under analysis and investigate the system's response to these tests. Quite often, these tools analyze the system's reaction to various boundary values of the input data, including the following:

- Buffer overflow
- Array indexes exceeding array boundaries
- Lack of argument check
- Incorrect memory access
- Invalid arguments passed to critical procedures

The need for such tests is clear, since, according to statistics, most implementation vulnerabilities relate to the above-mentioned errors (for example, buffer overflow). Table 6.3 lists the main advantages and drawbacks of this method.

Table 6.3. Advantages and Drawbacks of Test-Generating Systems

Advantages	Drawbacks
Able to test software without needing the source code	Detects only specific classes of vulnerabilities and errors
Relative simplicity of implementation	The presence of some errors is not always an indication of vulnerability

Disassembling

The process of disassembling itself is not very helpful when detecting vulnerabilities, since, in this case, the amount of code to be analyzed will significantly exceed the amount of the source code written using higher-level programming language. However, the disassembled code can be used as a source of information for higher-level analyzers.

Exploit Checking

Attack simulators are intended for modeling various unauthorized activities directed at the components of the information system. These systems are the most popular all over the world, since they are relatively simple and not very expensive. Using such simulators, it is possible to detect most vulnerabilities before they can be exploited to implement an attack. Systems in this class include SATAN, Internet Scanner, etc.

Attack simulators are equally successful in detecting both implementation vulnerabilities and configuration vulnerabilities. Consequently, the information provided in the next section (which is entirely dedicated to searching for configuration vulnerabilities) is also applicable to attack simulators. These products are the most popular with users.

Systems for Searching for Configuration Vulnerabilities

As shown in Fig. 6.2, security analyzers in general, and configuration vulnerability scanners in particular, can function at all levels of the information infrastructure, i.e., at the network level, operating-system level, database level and application-software level.

The most popular systems in this class are security scanners for network services and protocols. This is chiefly due to the fact that the most popular protocols are universal and they support open standards. Thus, overall usage and open information on such protocol stacks as TCP/IP or SMB/NetBIOS enable the efficient checking of the security of the information system running within a specified network environment independently from the software running at higher levels.

Operating-system security scanners are the second most popular security scanners. This is a result of the fact that some operating systems are rather common and universal (this relates to both UNIX and Windows NT-based operating systems). However, since each manufacturer introduces some custom features into each release of the OS (the large variety of UNIX clones illustrates this point), OS-security analyzers usually investigate parameters characteristic to the whole family of the operating system. System-specific characteristics can not always be taken into account.

Security scanners for DBMS and application software are currently less numerous than is desirable. At the time of writing, these solutions existed only for the most popular application software, including Web browsers (Netscape Navigator, Microsoft Internet Explorer), DBMS systems (Microsoft SQL Server, Sybase Adaptive Server), and so on.

When analyzing security, vulnerability scanners use two strategies. The first — passive — is implemented at the level of operating system, DBMS and application software. It implies an analysis of configuration files and system registry for incorrect parameters, scanning password files for the presence of the passwords that can be easily guessed, and the investigation of other system objects to detect security policy violations. The second — active — strategy is mainly implemented at the network level and allows the reproduction of the most common attack scenarios and the analysis of the system's response.

Experience has shown that the most popular of these are configuration-vulnerability analyzers (implementation-vulnerability scanners are next in terms of popularity). This is due to the fact that the end user deals with this stage of the life cycle of various software and hardware products. Because of this, I will cover the systems in this class in more detail.

Network-Level Security Analyzers

Interaction between users in any network is based on network protocols and services that determine the procedure for information exchange between two or more hosts. In early 1970s, when most network protocols and services were emerging, developers practically ignored security requirements. Because of this, reports on new vulnerabilities detected in various implementations of these components appear constantly. Consequently, it is necessary to constantly check the security of all network protocols and services used in a corporate network.

Security analyzers perform a series of remote tests to detect vulnerabilities. These tests are similar to the methods used by intruders when implementing attacks on corporate networks. Scanning begins with obtaining preliminary information on the system being tested, including allowed protocols, open ports, and OS version. Quite often these tests include the simulation of an intrusion using the most common attack types (such as brute force, for example).

Network-level security scanners are not limited to testing the possibility of breaking into a corporate network from public networks such as Internet. These tools are just as effective when used to analyze specific segments or hosts within the organization's internal network. Network-level security scanners can identify an application for evaluating the security level of the organization and controlling the efficiency of network hardware and software configuration. These two fields of applications are the most common for security analyzers. However, other applications can be found. For example, external auditing or consulting companies can use security scanners to investigate their customer's networks. Besides this, there are other interesting possibilities, such as the testing and certification of specific software and hardware products. This approach is rather popular when various test labs evaluate the quality of network equipment, firewalls, etc.

Currently, there are more than 100 programs available that automate the procedure of detecting vulnerabilities in network protocols and services. Some tools are oriented towards detecting a wide range of different vulnerabilities, while others are intended to detect specific vulnerability categories. For example, Internet Scanner, which is one of the most popular products of this type, detects more than 1,300 different vulnerabilities belonging to a range of categories: Denial of Service, Brute force, FTP, LDAP, SNMP, RPC, NIS, NFS, DNS etc. Whisker, on the other hand, was designed specifically for scanning web servers and to detect vulnerable CGI scripts [Shipley1-00].

The first network-level security scanners appeared in early 1990s, at the beginning of the period when TCP/IP-based networks became widespread. The most popular among them is SATAN (Security Administrator Tool for Analyzing Networks), the free tool released on April 5, 1995, by two professionals in the field of information security, Wietse Venema and Dan Farmer [Freiss1-98]. Among other similar tools of note are the Internet Security Scanner (later renamed into Internet Scanner), Nmap and Queso.

Network-level security scanners analyze for vulnerabilities in network services and protocols existing in system and application software as well as in network hardware and software including web servers, FTP servers, mail servers, firewalls, browsers, routers and switches.

A typical scheme for network-level security-scanner implementation (here, the example is Internet Scanner) is shown in Fig. 6.6.

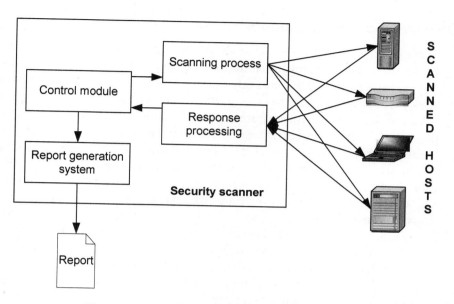

Fig. 6.6. Network-level security scanner

Advantages and drawbacks of systems belonging to this class are outlined in Table 6.4.

Table 6.4. Advantages and Drawbacks of Network-Level Security Scanners

Advantages	Drawbacks
Detects security gaps for a wide range of different platforms and systems supporting unified network protocols.	Analyzers and scanners of this type do not take into account vulnerabilities above the network level. Quite often, they are less precise than security scanners running at the OS, DBMS or application level.
Independence from the platforms and systems used within the organization network.	Can negatively impact network performance.
Easy to use from the organizational point of view, since agents are not present at the hosts being scanned.	If used incorrectly, these systems can disrupt the function of some network hosts.
	Incomplete coverage of the existing protocols. For example, only a limited number of programs support IPX.

OS-Level Security Scanners

Tools of this class are designed to check operating-system settings that have a bearing on security. Such settings include user-account settings, such as password requirements (minimum lengths, and other policy settings, such as minimum and maximum age), permission for users to access critical system files, vulnerable system and configuration files, system registry parameters, and patches installed. The methods for the application of OS-level security scanners are similar to strategies for using network-level security scanners utilized by security departments, auditing companies and the like.

In contrast to network-level security scanners that perform external scanning, these systems scan the internal components of the system being analyzed. This means that they simulate attacks by intruders who have already penetrated the first (network) line of defense. For this purpose, it is necessary to install a special agent in each host to be scanned. This agent will run all required system checks. Beside detecting vulnerabilities and providing recommendations for the elimination of detected security gaps, some OS-level security scanners (for example, System Scanner) allow the automatic elimination of at least part of the problem automatically or the correction of system parameters that do not satisfy security policy requirements.

As already mentioned, OS-level security scanners are less numerous than network-level security scanners. Among the best known systems of this class is the COPS (Computerized Oracle and Password System) system developed by Dan Farmer (one of the authors of the above-mentioned SATAN system) in cooperation with Eugene Spafford, the director of the Purdue CERIAS (Center for Education and Research in Information Assurance and Security) and the founder and director of the COAST Laboratory. Another well-known system in this class is System Scanner, from Internet Security Systems, Inc.

The main advantages and drawbacks of systems in this class are listed in Table 6.5.

Table 6.5. Advantages and Drawbacks of OS-Level Security Scanners

Advantages	Drawbacks
Produce an accurate, host-specific list of vulnerabilities.	Analysis methods are platform-dependent. Thus, they require very precise configuration for each host type used in organization.
Detects vulnerabilities omitted at the stage of network-level security analysis.	Operation and updates often require much more effort than network-level analysis.
	Not applicable for equipment that does not run an operating system.
	Not applicable for network hardware.

DBMS-Level Security Scanners

Initially, security scanners were developed only for network and operating system levels. Currently, these systems are quite numerous. This is largely because popular network protocols and operating systems are not numerous enough to allow the efficient development of tools for analyzing their vulnerabilities. The necessity of security scanners for DBMS has become strong recently, as companies have began to use databases to retrieve information via public networks.

The developers of these tools have taken into account all of the advantages and drawbacks of network and OS-level security scanners. As a result, DBMS security scanners implement most of the features characteristic of the previous two classes. In particular, they are able to analyze DBMS server security both locally and remotely. Database Scanner, SFProtect and SQL<> Secure Policy are a few examples of these tools.

Application-Level Security Scanners

Despite the fact that tools of this class are absolutely necessary, they have only begun to appear recently. Both network- and OS-level security scanners implement functional abilities for analyzing application security. However, these functional abilities are quite limited and cover only the most common application software. For example, System Scanner provides checks for Microsoft BackOffice, Microsoft Office and Symantec antiviral systems.

Working Mechanisms

There are two basic mechanisms that the scanner uses to check for vulnerabilities – passive and active testing. These are also known as scanning and probing, respectively.

Scanning — a passive analysis mechanism, which the scanner uses to attempt to detect vulnerability on the basis of implicit indications, without actually proving their presence. This method is the fastest and the simplest to implement. In relation to Cisco, the scanning process identifies open ports found on each network device and assembles banners detected when scanning each port. Each banner is then compared to the table of rules for detecting network devices, operating systems and potential vulnerabilities. Based on the results of this comparison, the system then identifies a vulnerability. Checking access rights to the password file, which can indicate cases of information-system vulnerability, is another example of passive scanning.

Probing — an active analysis mechanism, which enables you to determine whether a vulnerability is present on the host being analyzed. Probing operates by simulating an attack to exploit the vulnerability being checked. This method is slower than scanning, but it is also almost always more reliable. According to Cisco, this method uses information collected during scanning ("logical output") for a detailed analysis of each network device. It also employs common methods of attack implementation to confirm the supposed vulnerabilities and detect other points of weakness that can not be detected using passive methods, for example, vulnerability to DoS attacks. Another example of active testing is are password-system checks that simulate brute-force attacks.

Beside classifying security analyzers by method used (active or passive), these systems are able to perform both local and remote tests. Local tests run at the same host where the security scanner agent is installed (for example, System Scanner Agent), while remote methods are intended for remote hosts (such as Internet Scanner) [Polk1-92].

In practice, the above-listed mechanisms are based on the methods that will be described in the following few sections.

Banner Checking

This mechanism, which is usually utilized by network-level security scanners, involves a series of scans enabling you to determine whether vulnerabilities exist, based on the banner information in the response returned to a scanner request. A typical example of this type of examination is the analysis of Sendmail or FTP-server banners to determine their version number. Based on this information, it is possible to determine whether vulnerability exists. This method of checking for vulnerabilities is the fastest and the simplest to implement. However, this simplicity can also conceal a number of problems.

The efficiency of banner check is problematic. First of all, it is possible to modify the banner text by deleting the version number or other information used by the scanner. Although cases of banner replacement are relatively rare, this danger should not be ignored. This is especially true if you have security specialists who understand the danger of using default banners. Secondly, version information contained in the response banner often does not mean the software is vulnerable. This relates to software that is supplied with the source code (for example, the GNU project). You can eliminate vulnerabilities by modifying the source code, but forget about modifying the version-number information contained in the banner. Finally, elimination of vulnerability in one version does not automatically mean that this vulnerability will be eliminated in future releases. The mechanism under consideration is the first and the most important step in the course of performing a network scan. It does not result in the disruption of the operations of the network or its specific hosts. However, do not forget that the administrator can modify the text of banners returned in response to external requests.

Active Probing Checks

The active probing-check mechanism is also related to the scanning methods. However, the checks that it implements are based on a comparison of the digital fingerprint of the software to the digital fingerprint of the known vulnerability, rather than on a comparison of the software version information in the banners. This technique is similar to the one used by antiviral systems, which compare the fragments of the software being scanned to the signatures of the known viruses stored in a special signature database. Checks for file size and date implemented in the OS-level scanners are another variant of this method.

A specialized database (in Cisco terms, it is known as the network-security database) contains information on the known vulnerabilities and methods of exploiting these vulnerabilities to implement attacks. This information is complemented by data on the methods of eliminating these vulnerabilities, which enables you to decrease the risk of a successful attack in the event that such vulnerabilities are detected. Quite often, this database is used both by the security scanner and by the intrusion detection system. Both Cisco and ISS use this approach. This method is also relatively fast, but is still more difficult and time-consuming to implement than the banner-checking method.

Exploit Checking

These methods are classified as probing methods and are based on exploiting various bugs in the software. Some vulnerabilities, which are difficult to detect in the source code, manifest themselves clearly in the executable code. Similarly, there are vulnerabilities that never manifest themselves until someone tries to exploit them. To perform this kind of check, real attacks are attempted against the suspected service or host. Banner checks only perform network "reconnaissance," while the exploit-check method enables you to simulate real attacks, instead of using banner information, thus detecting vulnerabilities more reliably (but at the same time, it runs slower). Attack simulation is a more reliable method of security analysis than banner checking, and is usually more reliable than active probing checks.

Sometimes, however, situations arise when exploit checks can not be implemented. These situations can be classified in two categories: situations when the test results in a DoS attack on the host or network being analyzed, and situations when vulnerability can not be detected by means of an attack simulation.

As a matter of fact, many security problems can not be detected without locking or even crashing the service or computer during the scan process. Therefore, in some cases, an exploit check is undesirable (for example, to analyze critical hosts for a business), because this might result in significant expenses and extended downtime for the corporate network components crashed by the test attack. If this is the case, it is appropriate to use other checking methods, such as active probing or banner checking.

Some vulnerabilities (for example, vulnerability to packet storm attacks) can not be detected without the danger of causing a failure of the service or computer being tested. In this case, the developers lock such checks by default and provide the user with the choice of enabling such tests optionally. For example, this approach is implemented in the CyberCop Scanner and Internet Scanner systems. In Internet Scanner, such checks are bundled within a separate category named Denial of Service. When the user enables any of the checks belonging to this category, Internet Scanner displays the warning message: "WARNING: These checks may crash or reboot scanned hosts."

Configuration Checks

This kind of check can be performed both by local and remote security scanners. However, they are most often performed locally. Security scanners use these checks to test various configuration files (for example, inetd.conf), startup files (such as autoexec.bat or config.sys), system registry and so on.

Security-Scanner Architecture

All security scanners can be classified in several categories. Security scanners belonging to the first category run remote checks from a single host (Fig. 6.7). SATAN is a typical example of such systems.

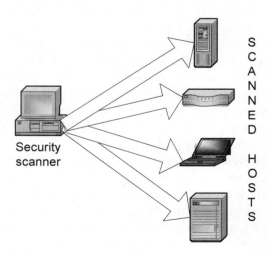

Fig. 6.7. Security-scanner architecture (type 1)

Systems of the second type are based on another principle. All hosts are scanned from the so-called security-scanner server, where all templates and results of previous scanning sessions are stored. Checks are run from the console, which is installed on a separate computer (Fig. 6.8). Nessus and Internet Scanner are examples of products based on this type of architecture.

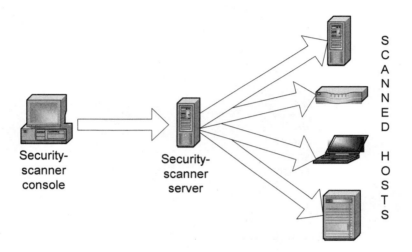

Fig. 6.8. Security-scanner architecture (type 2)

The CyberCop Scanner system utilizes an interesting architecture. As well as the main component of the security scanner, which implements the checks, there is a so-called "sentry" component, responsible for checking the results of the scanning (Fig. 6.9). Using this component, the system investigates the security level of firewalls and intrusion detection systems located between the main and auxiliary components of the security scanner.

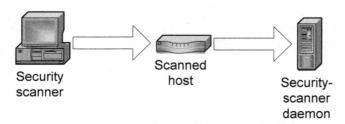

Fig. 6.9. Security-scanner architecture (type 3)

Host-level security scanners are built using a somewhat different scheme. System agents responsible for performing the checks specified from the console are installed in the most critical points of the corporate network. All management tasks are performed from the centralized console, to which all alerts are sent in cases where vulnerabilities are detected (Fig. 6.10). System Scanner is a typical example of a product that uses this scheme.

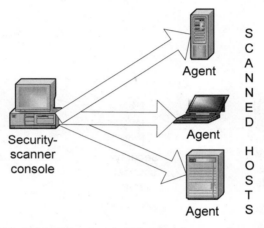

Fig. 6.10. Security-scanner architecture (type 4)

Introducing just another checking level (Fig. 6.11) can extend the scheme explained above. The Enterprise Security Manager from Symantec Corporation is an example of a product that utilizes this architecture.

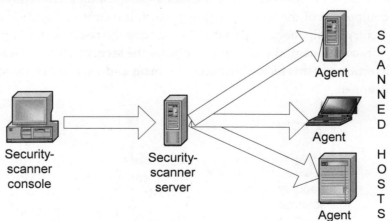

Fig. 6.11. Security-scanner architecture (type 5)

Classical Intrusion Detection Systems and Log-File Checkers

In this section, I would like to concentrate on the class of systems considered by users as "classical" intrusion detection systems.

Historical Overview

James P. Anderson was the first researcher to suggest the use of log files to ensure information security. This was in 1980, when the U.S. Navy adopted his concept, known as "Reference Monitor."

From 1984 to 1986, Dorothy Denning and Peter Neumann developed an abstract model of the real-time intrusion detection system known as IDES (Intrusion Detection Expert System). In 1987, Dorothy Denning published a document describing the use of intrusion detection systems to ensure information security. Like many other scientific research projects, this work was conducted in the laboratories of the U.S. Department of Defense (in this particular case, in the U.S. Navy's Space and Naval Warfare Systems Command). The IDES system was based on profiles and implemented various statistical methods enabling the description of normal and anomalous behavior by system objects (these were, for the most part, users). The IDES system ran on TOPS-20 computers. During the period from 1992 to 1994, the SRI International laboratory developed an enhanced version of this system, known as NIDES (Next-generation IDES).

In 1986, IBM specialists designed the Discovery expert system, intended for detecting problems in the TRW financial database. The Discovery system was based on the IBM 3090 and the COBOL programming language. The design goal of this system was to control daily financial transactions and detect unauthorized payments. To be more precise, this system related more to fraud detection systems than to intrusion detection.

In 1988, the US Air Force Cryptologic Support center sponsored the development and implementation of the Haystack anomaly detection system. The research project and system implementation were initiated by Tracor Applied Sciences, Inc. (1987–1989). Haystack Labs (1989–1991) continued the research work before being transferred to the Trusted Information Systems and Network Associates companies. The Haystack system supported the IBM AT platform and was implemented using the ANSI C programming language and Oracle DBMS. This was one of the first systems to be oriented toward PCs.

The MIDAS (Multics Intrusion Detection and Alerting System) was developed in 1988 by employees of the National Computer Security Center (NCSC) to detect anomalies in the Dockmaster network run by the center. This network was based on the Multics operating system on a Honeywell DPS 8/70 platform. Like all previous systems, MIDAS used statistical methods to provide the ability to detect anomalous behavior of system objects based on the records stored in log files. MIDAS was the first intrusion detection system that controlled hosts connected to the Internet. Because of this, it was able to detect external attacks.

In 1990, the National Los Alamos Laboratory developed the NADIR system (Network Audit Detector and Intrusion Reporter) intended for controlling the activities of a user connected to the ICN (Integrated Computing Network). This system ran on Sun Unix hosts and used the Sybase DBMS to support its functions. NADIR is one of the few tools developed in the late 1980s and early 1990s that still remains in use.

A new concept in intrusion detection systems was presented in 1990, along with the release of the NSM (Network Security Monitor) system, currently known as Network Intrusion Detector (NID). In contrast to its predecessors that used log files, this concept suggested using network traffic to detect unauthorized activities. The NSM system was developed in UC Davis and run on Sun UNIX workstations.

In 1991, the DIDS (Distributed Intrusion Detection System) was released. It was able to obtain data from several intrusion detection systems, in order to detect coordinated attacks directed at several network hosts. The main advantage of the DIDS system lies in the fact that it allows the simultaneous collection of data both from agents that control system log files and from agents that register network traffic. The research work required to implement this system was sponsored by the U.S. Navy, the National Security Agency (NSA) and the U.S. Department of Energy. Among project participants were the U.S. Air force Cryptologic Support center, the Lawrence Livermore Laboratory, UC Davis and the Haystack laboratory.

In 1994, Mark Crosbie and Gene Spafford introduced the idea of autonomous agents, which enabled them to enhance the following characteristics of intrusion detection systems:

❑ Scalability
❑ Efficiency
❑ Fault-tolerance

Another approach that simplified the scaling of the intrusion detection systems was introduced in 1996, in the form of the GrIDS (Graph-based Intrusion Detection System). This system simplifies the actions required to detect large-scaled, coordinated attacks. Like many other above-mentioned intrusion detection systems, the GrIDS system was developed at UC Davis.

In the late 1990s, there appeared a large number of new approaches to intrusion detection that differed from the classic ones existing at the time. These approaches include genetic algorithms and neural networks for detecting security policy violations. Currently, these approaches have exceeded the range of research works. For example, the work of James Cannady in the field of neural networks has created the possibility of significantly increasing the probability of detecting unknown attacks using the Real-Secure Network Sensor system.

The examples provided above are of principal importance for intrusion detection. These tools, developed as part of scientific research projects, were later used as prototypes for popular commercial intrusion detection products, such as RealSecure and Cisco IDS 4200.

Introduction to Classification

There are several different classifications of intrusion detection systems. Furthermore, each manufacturer determines its own classifications based on its own achievements in this area. The following few sections will cover the most common classifications of intrusion detection systems.

Classification by the Level of the Information System

As with security scanners, intrusion detection systems can also be classified by the level of information infrastructure at which security policy violations are detected.

Application and DBMS Level

Intrusion detection systems working at this level collect and analyze information from specific applications, such as DBMS systems, web servers or firewalls (for example, WebStalker Pro).

Advantages and drawbacks of systems of this class are listed in Table 6.6.

Table 6.6. Advantages and Drawbacks of Application-Level Intrusion Detection Systems

Advantages	Drawbacks
Enables you to concentrate on a specific activity that is difficult to detect using other methods (for example, improper activity by a specific user, such as fraudulent payments in the payroll system).	Application-level vulnerabilities can compromise intrusion detection at this level.

continues

Table 6.6 Continued

Advantages	Drawbacks
Detects attacks that are missed by tools running at lower levels.	Attacks implemented at lower levels (such as OS or network) are not covered.
Such tools allow the reduction of resource consumption by controlling a specific application rather than the whole set of programs running on the system.	

OS Level

OS level intrusion detection systems collect and analyze information that reflects various activities taking place in the operating system on a specific host (for example, RealSecure Server Sensor or Intruder Alert). As a rule, this information is represented in the form of the OS log files. Recently, systems running at the OS-kernel level have become increasingly popular, since such systems, thanks to "diving" mechanisms, provide a more efficient method of detecting security policy violations. The LIDS intrusion detection is one example of this type of product.

Advantages and drawbacks of systems belonging to this class are outlined in Table 6.7.

Table 6.7. Advantages and Drawbacks of OS-Level Intrusion Detection Systems

Advantages	Drawbacks
Systems of this class can control access to the information resources in a form specifying which user has access to which resources.	OS vulnerabilities can compromise intrusion detection technologies at this level.
These systems create the capability to display anomalous activity by a specific user for any application.	Attacks implemented at lower or higher levels (network or application) are not covered by tools of this class.
Tracking changes of the operation modes related to possible misuse.	Starting auditing mechanisms to register all types of events in log files might require additional resources.
The ability to work in environments that use encryption.	When log files are used as data sources, they can require quite significant storage space.
Such systems are capable of working efficiently in dial-up networks.	These methods are platform-dependent.
These methods enable you to control a specific host without wasting efforts on other, less important hosts.	Expenses related to supporting the operation and management of such systems are, as a rule, significantly higher than expenses required by other systems.

continues

Table 6.7 Continued

Advantages	Drawbacks
100% confirmation of the success or failure of the attack.	Tools of this class are practically inapplicable for detecting attacks to routers and other network equipment.
Detects attacks missed by tools running at other levels.	If data is lacking, these systems might miss specific attacks.
The ability to performing autonomous analysis.	

Network Level

Network-level intrusion detection systems collect information from network traffic. These systems can run on standard PCs (for example, RealSecure Network Sensor or Net-Prowler), on specialized computers (RealSecure for Nokia, Cisco IDS 4200 or AirDefense Server Appliance) or can be integrated into switches or routers (for example, Cisco IOS Firewall Feature Set or Cisco IDS blade, also known as Cisco Catalyst 6500 IDS Module). In the first two cases, the system analyzes information gathered by capturing and analyzing packets. Notice that access to network interfaces takes place in promiscuous mode.

The advantages and drawbacks of systems belonging to this class are described in Table 6.8.

Table 6.8. Advantages and Drawbacks of Network-Level Intrusion Detection Systems

Advantages	Drawbacks
Data is supplied without any special requirements for auditing mechanisms.	Attacks implemented at higher levels (OS and applications), are not covered by this category of tools.
The usage of these tools does not influence on existing data sources.	Systems of this class are not applicable in networks using link-to-link or even end-to-end data encryption.
Systems of this class can control and detect network DoS attacks (for example, SYN flood or packet storm attacks) designed to bring down network hosts.	Systems of this class are inefficient in dial-up networks.
The systems of this class can simultaneously control a large number of network hosts (as in cases with shared network media).	Systems of this class depend significantly on specific network protocols.

continues

Table 6.8 Continued

Advantages	Drawbacks
Relatively low operating expenses.	Contemporary approaches to network-level monitoring can not function at high speeds (for example, Gigabit Ethernet).
For the intruder, it is rather difficult to conceal traces of unauthorized activity.	
Detection of the attack and reactions take place in real-time mode.	
Detection of suspicious events (such as external IP addresses).	
Detects attacks missed by the tools running at other levels.	
Independence from the operating systems and application software used in the organization, since they interact using universal protocols.	

Integrated Approaches

As I mentioned above, until the present time, all existing intrusion detection systems could be classified as network-based or host-based. However, the ideal solution would be a combination of these two technologies. Using this combination, the intrusion detection system agent installed at each controlled host would trace attacks directed at this host both at the application level (OS, DBMS and applications) and at the network level. This approach (hybrid IDS) has several advantages when compared to existing solutions.

First, high-speed network media would no longer represent a problem, since the agent is able to view the traffic of a specific host rather than the traffic of the entire network. Second, the packets are decrypted before they reach the application level. Finally, since the agents reside at the host that is to be controlled, dial-up networks no longer create any limitations on the usage of the intrusion detection systems.

Some intrusion detection systems combine the capabilities of tools running at the network, OS, DBMS and application-software level. This group of products includes RealSecure Server Sensor from ISS [ISS2-99], and the Centrax system from CyberSafe. These systems combine the characteristics of network sensors working in real-time mode with the advantages of the system-level sensors.

Other Criteria

There are other criteria for intrusion detection system classification, which will be covered in greater detail in *Chapter 9*.

Architecture of the Intrusion Detection System

All intrusion detection systems can be classified as being members of one of two categories — stand-alone or client-server systems. Products associated with the first category collect information, analyze it and react to events at a single host. Systems from the second category are built according to another principle. The intrusion detection modules (sensors) are installed at the most critical points of the corporate network. These modules detect attacks and react. All management tasks are carried out from the centralized console, to which all alerts are sent. The architecture of this intrusion detection system is rather simple. It is shown in Fig. 6.12. It includes seven modules, each of which is responsible for a specific task. The data-source processing module is responsible for interaction with the log file, network adapter or OS kernel to obtain data, on the basis of which the system determines presence of an attack. The second module manages all components of the intrusion detection system and organizes their interaction.

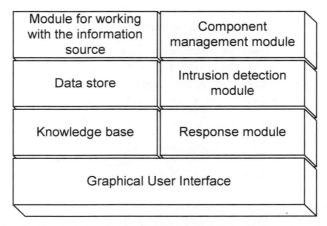

Fig. 6.12. Architecture of the intrusion detection system

The data is stored in a normal log file, storing all information on registered attacks and suspicious events. This log file can have a normal text-file format (like, for example, the Snort system) or be stored in the database. The database can be local (as, for example, the MS Access database in the eTrust IDS system) or client-server (like Oracle databases in Cisco IDS 4200, or MS SQL in RealSecure Network Sensor). The knowledge base contains information based on which the system decides if it should report an attack on the basis of the information from a specific data source. Depending on the analysis methods implemented, this database can store attack signatures, user profiles, etc. Comparison of the rules stored in the knowledge base to records from a specific data source is performed by the intrusion detection module, which, based on the results of the comparison, can issue commands to the reaction module. A graphic user interface makes administrative tasks intuitive and convenient to perform. Using the GUI, you can collect information from all intrusion detection system components as well as perform management tasks. In some intrusion detection systems (especially those implemented for Unix), the graphic user interface is lacking (for example, in the Snort system). If the intrusion detection system is built as a stand-alone agent, then all above-mentioned modules reside on the same computer. If the system was designed taking into account the client-server architecture, it has two basic levels — the sensor, which is also known as the agent or tracking module (engine), and the console. The sensor is responsible for detecting attacks and reacting to them, and then transferring the data on the detected unauthorized activity to the management console (Fig. 6.13).

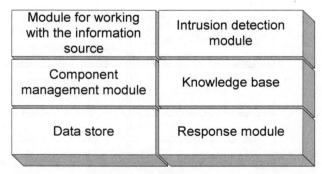

Fig. 6.13. Architecture of the intrusion detection system sensor

Usually, the sensor starts as a service or daemon and runs 24 hours per day. Since it transmits alerts of detected attacks to the console, it has no GUI module for displaying this data on the sensor.

The console is designed to control the sensor and collect information from all sensors to which it is connected (Fig. 6.14).

Usually, a single console can coordinate an unlimited number of sensors. Similarly, any sensor can send information to several consoles simultaneously, thus making the console fail-proof. Many intrusion detection systems, such as RealSecure Network Sensor or Cisco IDS 4200, are structured according to this principle (Fig. 6.15).

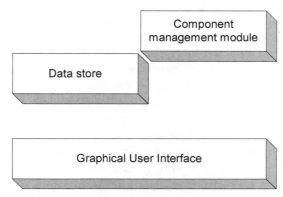

Fig. 6.14. Architecture of the intrusion detection system console

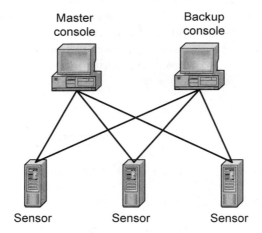

Fig. 6.15. Console fault-tolerant implementation

To prevent two consoles from changing the settings of the remote sensor simultaneously, one of them must have special status. Only the console that is assigned this status is permitted to change the configuration of a remote sensor and perform other management operations. This mechanism is similar to the principles implemented in the Check Point Firewall-1 system. According to these principles, only one administrator at a time can connect the firewall with Read/Write capabilities. Other administrators work only with Read capabilities.

The data storage contains information collected from all sensors. It is clear that the console lacks modules responsible for gathering data from the data sources, analyzing this data and reacting to the attacks. All the above-mentioned functions are delegated to sensors. This is done in order to prevent the disruption of the functions of the data channels between the console and sensor in the event of data channel or console failure. Thus, in case of such a failure, the sensors continue to function autonomously. Even if this happens, the sensors continue to detect attacks and react to them. When the connection to the console is restored, the sensors then send it all the accumulated information. Unfortunately, this fact has not yet been understood by all intrusion detection system developers. For example, I once had to investigate a system built according to a different principle. Sensors for this IDS only collected data from log files or from network traffic, while all processing is performed on the console (Fig. 6.16). There is no need here to explain the results that this structure can produce. In the event of a failure in the console or the communication channel between the console and remote sensor(s), the latter turn into useless programs that reside in the RAM and collect information, but can not accomplish anything, since all of the processing is centralized on the console. Furthermore, when the connection to the console is restored, a vast amount of information from all of the sensors floods to it. Besides network overload, this might cause the console to fail once again, since it will prove unable to process such a large amount of information. The situation can continue indefinitely, and the failures will persist.

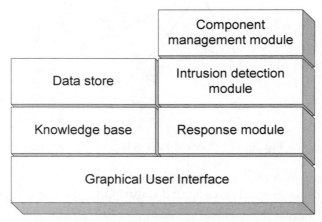

Fig. 6.16. Incorrect architecture in the intrusion detection system

A classic two-level "console/sensor" scheme is oriented toward a relatively small number (up to a few dozen) of sensors connected to a single console. This scheme is ideal for remote offices or affiliates that perform security management for themselves, or for small companies with centralized management of all sensors. As a further advance in this model, Cisco has suggested a new approach, which significantly improves the integration between centralized and decentralized sensors in the intrusion detection system. This scheme is especially advantageous for companies with hierarchical structures in their information-security departments. Usually, such organizations have, by default, a centralized department that develops a unified information-security policy and controls all security departments located in the remote affiliates.

The configuration of the hierarchical intrusion detection system developed by Cisco is shown in Fig. 6.17.

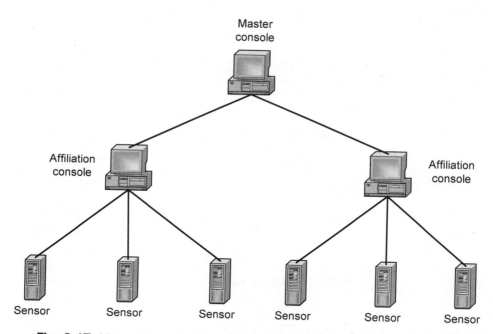

Fig. 6.17. Hierarchical management of intrusion detection system sensors

When the sensor detects an attack, it immediately sends information about this attack to the affiliate-management console. In this aspect, the scheme suggested by Cisco does not differ significantly from the classical two-level scheme. However, if the sensor detects an attack it considers to be particularly dangerous (or any other attack specified by administrator), it sends an alert to the affiliate console, as well as to the centralized console located in the headquarters of the information-security department.

Besides the above-mentioned architectures, there is yet another scheme, also known as the "sensor/control server/administrator console" architecture (Fig. 6.18). In this case, sensors send information about the detected attacks on the controller server rather than on the administrator console. The advantage of this scheme lies in the fact that all data on the security policies loaded to the sensors, as well as events registered by the sensors and other information, are stored on the controller server rather than on the administrative console. The role of the administrative console can be delegated to any computer, while the server is normally a powerful and fault-resistant system, on which the probability of failure is significantly lower than that in any other server or workstation. The NetProwler intrusion detection system is built according to this scheme.

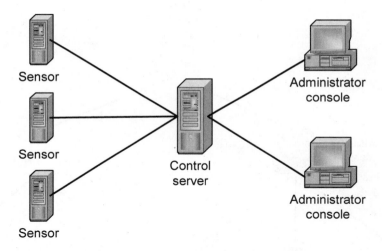

Fig. 6.18. Three-level sensor-management scheme

Host-Level Intrusion Detection Systems

These intrusion detection systems run on the protected host and control various security events. Most often, these systems operate with the operating system log files (for example, the Intrusion Alert system), application log files (RealSecure Server Sensor) or DBMS log files. Thus, all these systems depend on the contents of the log files. Consequently, if the log-file data is incomplete (or, even worse, modified by the intruder), these systems will be unable to detect an attack. Some less common systems (such as EMERALD) are modeled on detecting anomalous behavior, comparing the current user session (issued commands and other parameters) statistically to the standard profile of normal behavior. For detecting deviations from normal behavior, such systems utilize sophisticated algorithms. Besides this model, there are other intrusion detection systems that operate over network traffic sent or received from a specific host (for example, RealSecure Server Sensor).

Recently, systems built into the OS kernel have become common. Since such systems can control all system calls, they provide you with the ability to detect and lock all unauthorized activities quickly. The list of such systems includes Cisco Host IDS Sensor and StormWatch, developed by Okena.

There are several categories of host-level intrusion detection systems, which function at different levels of the information system.

Operating System Level

These tools are based on the monitoring of the operating system's log files, filled in the course of a user session or as the result of other activities carried out on the controlled host (for example, Swatch). Generally, these intrusion detection systems use the following criteria for detecting unauthorized activities:

❑ User's working hours (logon time)
❑ Number, types and names of the created files
❑ Number, types and names of accessed files
❑ Types of logon and logoff events
❑ Running applications
❑ Security policy changes (events such as the creation of a new user or user group, password changes and so on)

Events registered in the log file are compared to the signature database using special algorithms, which may vary depending on the intrusion detection system. The system classifies suspicious events and sends administrative alerts when these events occur. As a rule, the intrusion detection systems under consideration run on the server. Note that it does not usually make sense to run these systems at workstations because of the high demand they place on resources.

Sometimes, intrusion detection systems of this class control user activities in real-time mode (for example, HostSentry system from Psionic). However, this mechanism is rarely implemented. These systems usually analyze only OS log files. Quite recently, solutions have appeared that are not based on log-file analysis alone.

Some operating systems (for example, FreeBSD or Linux) are supplied with their source code. Thus, developers of intrusion detection systems can modify the OS kernel in order to add to the capabilities for detecting unauthorized activities. Examples of such additions are OpenWall and LIDS. These systems are built into the Linux kernel and enhance the default security mechanisms of this OS. The LIDS system, for example, can detect an instance of a protocol-analyzer installation or a change in the rules of the built-in firewall system, and react appropriately by blocking these activities.

Application and DBMS Level

There are two ways to implement systems of this class. In the first case, they analyze the records in the log file of a specific application or DBMS and are very similar to the OS-level intrusion detection systems. The main advantages of this approach are simplicity of implementation and that support is provided by any application program or DBMS that can register events in the log file. An example of this type of system is the RealSecure Server Sensor. However, this simplicity also conceals the main drawback associated with such an approach. In order to make the system work efficiently, you will have to spend a lot of time and effort customizing it for a specific application. Also, almost any application has a unique log-file format. The second method of implementing these systems is integrating them into a specific application or DBMS. In this case, the IDS becomes less universal, but more functional as a result of the close integration with the controlled software. An example of such a system is WebStalker Pro, developed by Trusted Information Systems (TIS) and then bought by Network Associates. Unfortunately, this system is no longer available. However, some of its elements are built into the CyberCop Monitor system.

Network Level

Besides performing an analysis of log files or system activities, intrusion detection systems of this class can operate with network traffic. In this case, the intrusion detection system does not analyze all network packets but, instead, considers only those that are directed to or from the controlled host. Because of this, the network interfaces of the controlled hosts can function in mixed mode as well as in normal mode. Since these systems control all incoming and outgoing network connections, they can act as personal firewalls. Examples of such systems include RealSecure Desktop Protector from ISS and PortSentry from Psionic.

Working Mechanism

The working mechanism of intrusion detection systems that implement the principle of information logging is quite simple — when a new record is written to the log file, an alert is sent to the intrusion detection system, which analyzes this information in relation to the attack-signature database (Fig. 6.19). Methods of network-traffic analysis will be covered in detail later in this chapter in the discussion of network-level intrusion detection systems.

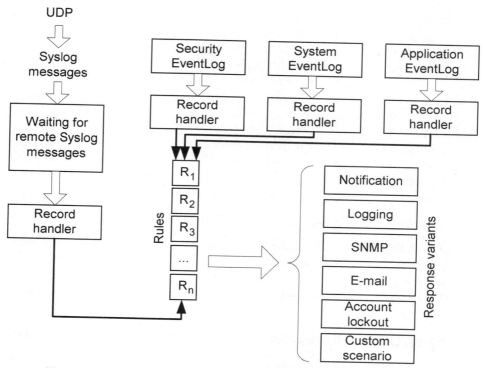

Fig. 6.19. Components of the host-level intrusion detection system

Advantages of the Host-Level Intrusion Detection Systems

Naturally, each intrusion detection system has specific advantages and drawbacks.

Confirming an Attack

Since intrusion detection systems based on log-file analysis operate only with events that have actually taken place, systems of this class can determine with a high level of precision whether an the attack really took place. In this respect, host-level intrusion detection systems ideally complement network-level intrusion detection systems, the strong points of which will be covered later. Such a combination provides preventive alerts based on the network component and the detection of an attack's success based on the system component.

Control over Specific Host Activity

These systems control user activity, file access, changes to file-access privileges, attempts to install new programs and attempts to access privileged services. For example, they can trace all user logons and logoffs. Using network-level systems, it is very difficult (or simply impossible) to implement this level of event details. System-level intrusion detection tools can also control the administrator's activities, which normally are not controlled by anyone. Operating systems register any event, when user accounts are created, deleted or modified. Intrusion detection tools of this class can immediately detect specific events when they take place.

Furthermore, host-level intrusion detection systems can control changes introduced to the key system or executable files. Any attempts to overwrite these files or install Trojan horse programs can be detected and blocked in a timely manner. Note that network-level intrusion detection systems sometimes miss this type of activity.

Detecting Attacks Missed by Other Tools

Systems of this class are capable of detecting attacks that can not be detected by network-level tools (for example, attacks originating from the attacked host). Additionally, some systems (for example, RealSecure Server Sensor) can detect network attacks directed at a controlled host that were missed for some reason by a network-level intrusion detection system.

Working on Dial-up Networks and Networks with Channel Encryption

Since these intrusion detection tools are installed on different hosts in the organization network, they can solve some of the problems that arise when operating network-level intrusion detection systems in dial-up networks or networks with channel encryption.

Dial-up connections permit the management of a globally distributed network in relatively small network segments. As a result, it might sometimes be difficult to determine the best place to install the system for detecting attacks in network traffic. Sometimes special ports (mirror ports, managed ports, and span ports) located at the switches can be helpful. However, this is not always the case. The detection of attacks at the system level allows more efficient work in the dial-up networks, since it enables you to place the intrusion detection systems only on those hosts where they are really necessary.

Encryption also creates a problem for network-level intrusion detection systems, since they may remain "blind" and miss some encrypted attacks. Host-level intrusion detection systems are not subject to this limitation, since the traffic at the OS level is already decrypted.

Detecting and Reacting in a Mode Close to Real-Time

Although intrusion detection at the system level does not allow for true real-time reactions, it can function in a mode very close to real time, provided that the system has been properly configured. In contrast to legacy systems that check the status and contents of the log files once in a specified time interval, most contemporary applications get an interrupt from the OS immediately after the new record is added to the log file. This new record can be processed immediately. Thus, the time delay between the identification of an attack and the system's reaction can be decreased significantly. The only remaining delay is the interval between the moment when the OS logs the new event that when the intrusion detection system identifies the attack. However, in most cases intruders, can be detected and stopped before they can cause any significant damage.

Low Prices

Despite the fact that network-level intrusion detection systems analyze the traffic of the whole network, quite often they are too expensive, in some cases exceeding $10,000 in price. On the other hand, host-level intrusion detection systems usually cost only a few hundred dollars per agent and can be purchased as needed.

Network-Level Intrusion Detection Systems

As follows from the historical overview of intrusion detection technology, initial investigations were carried out by means of the analysis of the log files created by the operating system and various applications. This analysis was aimed at finding specific records that characterize potential attacks or anomalous activities. In practice, however, intrusion detection systems based on log-file analysis have proved unable to detect many attacks. Because of this, developers have concentrated their attention at the network level.

The main limitation of the first intrusion detection systems was that log files were only accessed at the level of the OS, DBMS and specific applications. The further growth of networks requiring control at all levels of the information-system infrastructure led to the development of so-called kernel-based and network-based intrusion detection systems, i.e., intrusion detection systems running at the OS-kernel level and at the network level.

Thanks to the algorithms implemented in network-level intrusion detection systems, they have access to all data transmitted via the network. Since such systems run at a different computer than the controlled host, there is no negative impact on the controlled host's performance.

Working Mechanism

As the analysis of currently available network-level intrusion detection systems shows, all of these systems use the network traffic as their data source and analyze it for attack indications. It is also possible to analyze log files created by network hardware and software (such as routers, firewalls or protocol analyzers) that register all of the traffic that it processes. Ideally, these tools are able to function in any network but, in practice, these intrusion detection systems identify security policy violations in shared media networks, where a single connection line is used by several computers, one computer at a time. These systems function on the basis of Ethernet (and, consequently, Fast Ethernet and Gigabit Ethernet) technologies, Token Ring and FDDI. This is because of the fact that, in such networks, one computer can access all packets transmitted within a network segment. This property significantly reduces the cost of intrusion detection systems, since the traffic between these hosts can be controlled by a single intrusion detection system independently from the number of networked hosts within the network segment.

When hosts are connected by individual lines (such as ATM), it is necessary to install the intrusion detection system between each pair of interacting hosts. But the expense involved in such a system makes it a less attractive option. Because of this, current examples of network-level intrusion detection systems support network technologies with shared media. On the other hand, there are also ATM solutions, such as Dragon Sensor.

Two network-level intrusion detection systems that have appeared quite recently deserve special mention. These are AirIDS (http://www.internetcomealive.com/clients/airids/general.php) and AirDefense (http://www.airdefense.net/products/index.shtm). Both systems are intended for intrusion detection in wireless networks based on the 802.11b standard.

Besides this, intrusion detection systems are characterized by another limitation — they are only able to analyze the most common protocol stacks. Among currently available intrusion detection systems, approximately 95% support the TCP/IP stack, while the remainder support SMB/NetBIOS. Commercial systems supporting IPX/SPX, not to mention other, even less common stacks, are quite rare.

The working mechanism of a network-level intrusion detection system is shown in Fig. 6.20. It comprises four main components, responsible for the following functions:

❑ Packet capturing
❑ Filtering and assembling fragments

❏   Intrusion detection
❏   Reacting to attacks

If the network's equipment (for example, Cisco Catalyst 6500 IDS Module (in switch) or Cisco IOS Firewall Feature Set (in router) implements the intrusion detection system, then one of the network components takes the place of the network adapter. If the intrusion detection system is based on the principle of analyzing the log files created by the network equipment, this role is delegated to the appropriate log file (for example, the TCPdump log file). Depending on the source of the data for analysis (from the network adapter, switch components or the log file), the system component responsible for packet capturing might be based on different implementations. However, other components (filtering, recognition and reaction) remain unchanged.

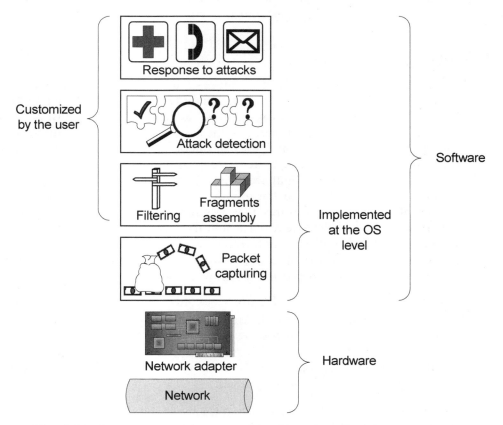

Fig. 6.20. Components of the network-level intrusion detection system

The IDS software has two components.

❏ The kernel that interacts with the network adapter, part of the network equipment or the log file storing the network traffic. The kernel is responsible for data capturing. In sophisticated intrusion detection systems that capture data from the network interface, this interaction is carried out by the intrusion detection system driver, which replaces the operating system driver. As well as improved efficiency, this enables the implementation of add-on functions such as stealth mode, which prevents the intruder from detecting and attacking the intrusion detection system itself. Simpler intrusion detection systems use and analyze data obtained from the operating system driver. In relation to the range of problems it solves, this kernel is similar to the protocol-analyzer kernel.

❏ Software that decodes and analyzes the protocols used by the network adapter. The same software also implements the system logic used when the system detects an attack and reacts to it.

Packet Capturing

The first stage of the procedure is the capture of the network packets. As already mentioned, this algorithm can be implemented in different ways, depending on the source from which network packets are captured. At the time of writing, most network-level intrusion detection systems were built on the basis of normal or specialized computers running specialized software on a normal operating system and capturing network traffic from network adapters. Systems such as RealSecure Network Sensor, NetPowler, Snort, and so on are built according to this principle. In some other cases, the operating system is reduced to the minimum required set of functions in order to eliminate all unnecessary features that might intervene with the IDS's operation. This approach was used by the developers of RealSecure for Nokia and the VelociProwler Intrusion Detection Appliance (unfortunately, after Symantec purchased Axent, this solution was abandoned). In all cases, network traffic is captured from a normal network adapter, which can operate in the following two modes:

❏ Normal mode, in which the NIC processes only the packets that are addressed to it

❏ Promiscuous mode, in which the network adapter processes all packets transmitted within the network segment

If the intrusion detection system is set up in network equipment, network traffic can be obtained from the following sources:

❏ Network-equipment backplane (Cisco Catalyst 6500 IDS Module is set up according to this principle)

❑ Software servicing network equipment (Cisco IOS Firewall Feature Set is based on this principle)

Filtering

Despite the fact that intrusion detection systems have access to all captured network packets, not all such packets are subject to processing. For example, the system can not process packets for unsupported protocols. Another example is that of fragmented packets, which can also not be processed by some intrusion detection systems. The filtering module is responsible for ruling out packets that should be ignored by the intrusion detection system (for example, IPX traffic).

There are two types of filters:

❑ **System filters.** These allow you to eliminate (or, conversely, to control) network traffic based on the data of the signatures to be recognized. For example, if the ColdFusion attack recognition system is operational, then the filtering module will trace HTTP traffic at TCP port 80.

❑ **User filters.** User filters eliminate or, conversely, control traffic satisfying the predefined rules set by the intrusion detection system administrator. For example, if the controlled network contains only Windows hosts, then there is no need to search for the Tribe Flood Network attack within this network, as this attack is characteristic of the Linux or Solaris operating systems.

Attack Detection

The attack detection and recognition module is an important component of any intrusion detection system. The efficiency of the whole intrusion detection system depends on the effectiveness of this module. The recognition module uses various methods and criteria, which were covered in detail in *Chapter 4.*

Analysis of network traffic can be implemented using two methods — syntax parsing of specific network packets using regular expressions, or analysis of the entire session. Systems using the first method capture raw packets and pass them through a syntax analyzer, which searches these packets for matches with a specific pattern or signature [Graham1-00]. An example of such a pattern is the text fragment "etc/passwd," characteristic of an attempt at a brute force password attack or a request for transmission of the password file via the network.

These systems function on the basis of the following algorithm [NetworkICE1-00]:

1. The system selects one network frame from the captured traffic in order to scan it for signatures.

2. Beginning with the first byte of the network frame, the system selects a group of bytes of the same length as the signature under consideration. It then compares the two sets of bytes — the signature and selected packet fragment (Fig. 6.21).

GET /cgi-bin/./phf
AF7*Hy289s820800B9v5yt$0611tbhk76500801293ugdB2%00397e39
↑

Fig. 6.21. Comparison to the pattern (the second step)

3. If the two groups of bytes are identical, then an attack has been detected.
4. If the groups do not match, the system shifts one byte forward in the network frame sequence, and the process is repeats until the sequence ends (Fig. 6.22).

GET /cgi-bin/./phf
AF7*Hy289s820800B9v5yt$0611tbhk76500801293ugdB2%00397e39
↑

GET /cgi-bin/./phf
AF7*Hy289s820800B9v5yt$0611tbhk76500801293ugdB2%00397e39
↑

Fig. 6.22. Comparison to the pattern (fourth and subsequent steps)

5. When the intrusion detection system reaches the end of the network frame, it begins a comparison to the next signature, and proceeds until the end of the database is reached.
6. If no matches for known signatures have been found in the first network frame, the system starts analyzing the second frame, and the whole process repeats from the beginning.

The advantages and drawbacks of this method (which has become widely known as pattern matching) are outlined in Table 6.9.

Table 6.9. Advantages and Drawbacks of Pattern Matching

Advantages	Drawbacks
Ease of implementation	High percentage of false positives

continues

Table 6.9 Continued

Advantages	Drawbacks
High performance	Does not work when attack undergoes minor modifications
High precision of detection	Inapplicable to flow traffic (such as HTTP)
Independent from the protocol used	

However, network traffic is more than simply a sequence of network packets. Therefore, systems based on analysis of the entire protocol are oriented toward the context of a network session, thus resulting in a reduction of false positives. They can distinguish between harmless and dangerous events. For example, they can distinguish between a security bulletin received via e-mail and containing text fragments such as "GET /CGI-bin/phf" from an HTTP request such as "GET /CGI-bin/phf." Session analysis can be done using one of two methods. The first method has become known as stateful pattern matching. Systems using this technology check each packet and trace their order. For example, suppose that the search pattern (GET /CGI-bin/phf) is divided into two packets — "GET /CGI-b" and "in/phf." The classical pattern-matching method will not detect this attack, since it is divided into two packets, neither of which matches the signature. Using stateful pattern matching, on the other hand, will enable you to detect this attack even if it is fragmented into 10 packets. The advantages and drawbacks of this method are described in Table 6.10.

Table 6.10. Advantages and Drawbacks of Stateful Pattern Matching

Advantages	Drawbacks
Ease of implementation	A relatively high percentage of false positives
High performance	Will not work if the attack is slightly modified
High precision of detection	
Independent of the protocol used	
A system using this method is harder to deceive	

The next method, known as protocol decode-based analysis, is relatively easy to describe. It is based on searching for deviations from the RFC that describes specific protocols. Thus, everything that is not described in the RFC is considered a violation, and the system reports it using this principle. Certainly, contemporary intrusion detection systems can use any of these methods, depending on the situation. With respect to the attack indicators described in *Chapter 4* — the exceeding of threshold values or network anomalies — special methods were developed for detecting attacks of these types. For example, the method using mathematical statistics became known as heuristic-based analysis [Cisco1-02].

The working mechanism of these systems differs from the previous one. An example of an algorithm illustrating this difference is outlined below:

1. The system selects one network frame from the captured traffic to scan it for signatures.

2. Knowing the format of the network frames characteristic for the Ethernet and higher-level protocols, we can decrease the number of possible operations, since it does not make sense to search for attack matches in the first bytes of the Ethernet frame, which contain source and destination addresses. Thus, the system goes to 13th and 14th bytes of a specific frame to determine the type of network-level protocol. In our case, this is the IP protocol with the value of 0x0800 (Fig. 6.23). It is important to note that, in this example, we are considering the Ethernet DIX (Ethernet II) frame format, which is used by default on workstations for transmitting IP traffic over the Ethernet. The size of the field identifying the higher-level protocol is 2 bytes. How can we detect which data format is in use — Ethernet DIX or, for example, 802.3/LLC, where this location contains the frame length field? Solving this problem is relatively easy. The Ethernet frame length can not exceed 1,500 bytes, and therefore, if a value exceeding 1,500 bytes (for an IP — 0x0800) appears in this field, then we are dealing with the Ethernet DIX (II) format.

AF7*Hy289s820800B9v5yt$0611tbhk76500801293ugdB2%00397e39

↑

Fig. 6.23. Analysis of the protocol as a whole (the second step)

3. The 10th byte of the IP header (24th byte from the beginning of the frame) identifies the transport-level protocol. The size of this field is one byte, and the value contained in this field is 6, which means that the higher-level protocol is TCP. Notice that, here, we have also filtered out some fields of the IP header, which are not necessary for the analysis (Fig. 6.24).

4. In the next step, we analyze the first two pairs of bytes in the TCP packet header. These are the source and destination ports (bytes 35 through 38 of the initial

network frame). In our case, the destination port is port 80, which identifies the HTTP protocol (Fig. 6.25). If a non-standard port is used, the time required to detect the protocol will increase, which will result in a worse performance.

AF7*Hy289s820800B9v5yt$0611tbhk76500801293ugdB2%00397e39

Fig. 6.24. Analysis of the protocol as a whole (the third step)

AF7*Hy289s820800B9v5yt$0611tbhk76500801293ugdB2%00397e39

Fig. 6.25. Analysis of the protocol as a whole (the fourth step)

5. Skipping the next 20 bytes of the TCP packet header, we go directly to the data field (55th byte), which (for the HTTP protocol) starts with URL. It is necessary to note that, to decrease the size of the network frame being considered, some bytes were deleted. Here, we are looking the match for the "GET /cgi-bin/./phf" signature (Fig. 6.26). Naturally, when operating in alert mode, it is necessary to analyze TCP header flags and other parameters. Right now, however, I will only demonstrate a more efficient method of analyzing network traffic in comparison to the byte-to-byte analysis of each frame.

AF7*Hy289s820800B9v5yt$0611tbhk76500801293ugdB2%00397e39

Fig. 6.26. Analysis of the protocol as a whole (the fifth step)

6. When the intrusion detection system reaches the end of the network frame, it begins a comparison with the next signature, and repeats the process until the database end is reached. This aspect is rather important, and I would like to draw special attention to it. The steps described here are repeated for each signature found in the IDS database and applicable to the HTTP protocol. Consequently, the more signatures are there in the database, the slower the system will operate.

7. If no matches for any of the known signatures have been found in the first network frame, the system starts analyzing the second network frame, and so on.

It is clear that, in contrast to the first algorithm, which requires 55 operations to accomplish the task, this algorithm allows the achievement of our purpose in only five steps.

However, systems in the first category have some advantages over protocol analysis systems. Since they analyze all traffic, they are able to detect attacks missed by other systems. For example, if the corporate web server is configured to use a non-standard port (for example, 8080 rather than 80), then an intrusion detection system based on protocol analysis will likely miss an attack to this server, as it will not compare the traffic of the non-standard port to the HTTP traffic (provided that it is not using the modified algorithm described above). Systems that analyze each packet are not bound to port numbers and can detect attacks in traffic directed to any of the available 65,535 ports.

Responding to Attacks

Simply detecting an attack is not enough; it is also necessary to react. When the intrusion detection system registers an attack, it provides a wide range of response options — from sending an alert to the security administrator and the network-management console, to reconfiguring routers and firewalls. These options vary from system to system. However, the most common types of reaction include sending an administrative alert to the console or via e-mail, closing the connection to the attacking host and/or logging the current session for subsequent analysis and collecting evidence and reconfiguring the network equipment.

Advantages of the Network-Level Intrusion Detection Systems

Network-level intrusion detection systems have some advantages over host-level intrusion detection systems. Most customers opt to purchase network-level intrusion detection systems because of the low operating expenses and quick reaction to suspicious events. Listed below are the main factors that make a network-level intrusion detection system one of the most important components of security policy implementation [ISS3-99].

Low Operating Expenses

Network-level intrusion detection systems do not need to be installed on each host. Since the number of hosts at which it is necessary to install IDS to cover the entire network is relatively small, the total operating cost of these systems in a corporate network is lower than that for the host-level intrusion detection systems. Moreover, in order to control a network segment, it is sufficient to have just one sensor, regardless of the number of hosts within the segment.

Network Attack Detection

Host-level intrusion detection systems generally do not process network packets and, thus, can not detect these types of attacks. Products such as RealSecure Server Sensor or Centrax are exceptions, since they include network components able to detect network attacks directed at a specific host. These intrusion detection systems can investigate the contents of packet data fields by searching and finding commands used in specific attacks. For example, if the intruder tries to find the BackOrifice server components in computers that are not currently infected, this becomes clear in an investigation of the data body of the packet. As was mentioned above, system-level tools do not usually work at the network level and, therefore, are unable to detect these attacks.

Difficulties in Concealing Traces of Unauthorized Activities

Once a network packet leaves the attacking host, it can not be returned. Thus, systems working at the network level analyze "live" traffic and detect attacks in real-time mode. As a result, intruders can not remove traces of unauthorized activity. The analyzed data includes information about the method of attack, as well as information that can be used to identify the intruder and serve as evidence in court. Since most intruders have a sound knowledge of system-authentication mechanisms, they are rather skillful when it comes to tweaking system logs in order to conceal traces of unauthorized activities. Consequently, this can have a negative impact on the efficiency of the system-level tools that rely on this information in order to detect attacks.

Real-Time Attack Detection and Response

These systems detect suspicious events and attack as they occur. Therefore, they send alerts and react much faster than systems that analyze log files. For example, an intruder carrying out a Denial of Service attack on the basis of the TCP protocol can be stopped by a network-level intrusion detection system, which sends a TCP packet with the Reset flag set in the header. Thus, the connection to the attacking host will be closed before the attack causes any damage to the target. Systems based on log file analysis do not detect attacks before the appropriate record appears in the log file and, thus, take response actions only after the event has been registered. Note that, by this time, important systems or resources might already have been compromised, or the computer running the host-level intrusion detection system might have already failed. Real-time notification allows quick response actions according to predefined parameters. The range of response actions varies from immediately stopping the attack to allowing the penetration in order to collect information on the attack and attacker.

Detection of Failed Attacks or Suspicious Activities

Network-level intrusion detection systems installed outside the firewall can identify attacks directed at the resources protected by the firewall, even if the firewall itself is able to thwart the attack attempt. Information collected by such a system might be very important for developing, evaluating and improving a security policy. Further, it is be helpful when evaluating the skill of the intruder.

Platform-Independence

Network-level intrusion detection systems do not depend on the operating systems installed in the corporate network, since they operate with the network traffic between all of the hosts within that network. For such intrusion detection systems, it does not matter which OS generated a specific packet, provided that the packet corresponds to the standards supported by the intrusion detection system.

Tools for Detecting DoS Attacks

Because the interest in tools for detecting and thwarting DoS attacks is constantly growing, I have decided to classify these tools as a separate category. This approach is additionally justified by the fact that these tools are actually different from other intrusion detection tools. Furthermore, some specialists even think that they are using a new approach, different from signature- or anomaly-based approaches to intrusion detection [Gong1-02]. Their main distinguishing feature lies in the fact that such systems, besides detecting an attack, are capable of thwarting or at least weakening it. Most companies that supply such solutions owe their success to the DDoS attack epidemics that took place in 2000. The list of these companies includes Mazu Networks, Asta Networks, Arbor Networks, etc. (http://www.network computing.com/1225/ 1225f3.html). Other companies are also competing for this prospective market. For example, such solutions are supplied by TopLayer Networks, Radware, and ISS as well. Other market leaders also pay significant attention to this segment of the IDS market. For example, in late 2001, McAfee made an agreement with Mazu Networks, Asta Networks, and Arbor Networks to cooperate in the field of developing new methods of detecting.

Since such tools are oriented towards weakening or completely locking the attack, they are usually implemented in the form of a separate appliance, installed between the protected network and public networks. Thanks to this, such appliances are able to control all the network traffic. Such devices are also known as inline IDS.

The easiest method of locking attacks is to block the traffic between the two networks totally. However, this will result in locking all access to the protected devices.

In other words, a device intended for protection against DoS attacks will itself present an obstacle to the normal operation of web servers, application servers, and so on. Because of this, this approach is only suitable for protection against a limited number of attacks (mainly those based on the ICMP protocol).

The second method of blocking DoS attacks implies traffic filtering based on the IP addresses of the intruders. This method is the most efficient. However, it works only if you are absolutely sure that the IP address in the header of a packet containing an attack really belongs to the intruder. Since tracing each unique address is quite a difficult, complicated, and resource-consuming task, some manufacturers use a simpler approach: They filter packets based on address ranges. However, when using this approach, you might not only lock access to intruders, but also to authorized users. But, for the moment, it is justified and viable.

The third method allows you to restrain network traffic and from time to time pass small fragments into a protected network. Although the part of traffic that is passed into the protected network might contain malicious traffic, the fact that there is so little will not allow protected hosts to fail. This method is rather efficient against a SYN Flood attack.

The last method of thwarting a DoS attack is similar to the methods used by classic intrusion detection tools. In this case, the system filters network traffic based on predefined attack indicators (the source port, TTL, the packet identifier, and so on).

It should be mentioned that tools of this type are not always implemented as standalone devices, such as FireProof from Radware (http://www.radware.com/) or TrafficMaster Enforcer from Mazu Networks (http://www.mazunetworks.com/). Sometimes these mechanisms are built into network equipment — into workload balancers, for example. This approach was adopted by Foundry Networks (http://www.foundrynetworks.com/) in ServerIron 400, and TopLayer Networks in AppSwitch 3500. Quite an interesting solution is supplied by Reactive Networks (http://www.reactivenetworks.com/). This company has created its own IDS, Flood-Guard, which is based on Dell hardware and the Linux operating system. However, this device does not itself block an attack. Rather, it uses access control lists on Cisco routers. Also note that any security mechanisms and additional equipment increase network workload, which results in a loss of performance.

Network Intrusion Detection Systems and Firewalls

Quite often, security administrators try to replace network intrusion detection systems with firewalls, hoping that the firewalls provide the necessary level of protection. Do not forget, however, that firewalls are simply systems based on predefined rules that allow or prohibit specific traffic to pass through them. Even firewalls based on "stateful inspection" can not determine for sure if an attack is indicated by the controlled traffic. All the firewall can determine is whether the traffic corresponds to the rule. In other words, firewalls, like any other security tools, have their own advantages, drawbacks and optimal areas of employment.

Consider a firewall that is configured in such a way as to block all connections except for TCP connections at port 80 (i.e., HTTP traffic). Thus, any traffic at port 80 is legal by the firewall's definition. On the other hand, an intrusion detection system also controls this traffic but, in contrast to firewall, also searches for attack indications in this traffic. The intrusion detection system ignores the question of the intended port This means that, despite the fact that an intrusion detection system works with the same data source (network traffic) as the firewall, they perform complementary functions. For example, an HTTP request such as `GET /../../../etc/passwd HTTP/1.0`, most likely indicates unauthorized access to a password file, while `http://www.domain.com/asp`. indicates an attempt to exploit the MS IIS vulnerability. Practically every firewall will permit this request and the usage of the specified URL. The intrusion detection system, on the other hand, will recognize this attack and block it.

The most common question about intrusion detection systems concerns the manner in which they can complement. One answer to this question is that they provide the classification of the security violations by attack source, independent of the question of whether the attack originates from an external or internal network. Firewalls act as a barrier between corporate (internal) networks and the outside world (public networks such as the Internet). They filter network traffic according to a predefined security policy. As was already demonstrated in *Chapter 1*, firewalls can not detect internal attacks or external attacks bypassing the firewall or exploiting firewall-configuration vulnerabilities. For intrusion detection systems, the origin of the attack is irrelevant. They function efficiently against attacks from within the internal network or from an external network.

Consider the following analogy. Think of a firewall as a metal detector set up at the entrance to the company's main building (analogous to your internal network). However, beside the main entrance, there are back doors and windows. Through technical methods or by deceiving the security services, an intruder can get by the metal detector carrying prohibited items. Thieves can also penetrate the building using the back doors or windows. Because of this, most buildings also have motion detectors and internal security personnel. In the same vein, it is necessary to have intrusion detection systems, which complement the protection provided by firewalls, which are a necessary, but not sufficient, component of network security.

Listed below are several advantages of using firewall/intrusion detection system combinations:

❏ Double-checking of the firewall configuration and detecting configuration vulner-abilities (if network sensors are installed both before and after the firewall)
❏ Detecting attacks that pass the firewall on a legal basis (for example, attacks against web servers, malignant applets etc.)
❏ Detecting internal intruders

Taking these facts into account, some IDS manufacturers have started to integrate mechanisms for detecting network attacks into their firewalls (for example, the Cisco IOS Firewall Feature Set). However, as I mentioned above, most attempts at combining two technologies result in the inefficient operation of both. For example, it is not difficult to create attack signatures using the INSPECT language built into CheckPoint Firewall-1. However, CheckPoint has adopted another approach. It has concluded an agreement with ISS, licensed the RealSecure Network Sensor, and started to supply the CheckPoint RealSecure system to its customers. In April 2002, CheckPoint declared that it is going to develop its own IDS — SmartDefense — with an interface very similar to that of RealSecure. By the way, the similarity of the interfaces is a sore subject for many manufacturers. For example, some specialists think that the Cisco Secure Policy Manager interface is very much like that of CheckPoint Firewall-1.

Deception Systems

Usually, when it comes to deception in the field of information security, we immediately think about attempts by intruders to exploit vulnerabilities, or "back doors," to bypass the existing security mechanisms. This can include password theft, working on the account of legitimate users or unauthorized use of modems. However, intruders are not the only people for whom deception might prove to be useful. On the contrary, deception can be used with equal success to protect information resources. We do not usually think of as a security mechanism. Generally, when speaking about security and protection, we immediately think about contemporary firewalls, which block hackers' attempts to penetrate protected networks. Some even provide examples taken from science fiction, where Artificial Intelligence systems adapt to the behavior of the intruder and take adequate counter-measures. For example, William Gibson describes such a system in his novel "Neuromancer." But, if security is vital, you can not rely on firewalls to provide the required level of protection. If you need a truly powerful security system, you must also consider additional, non-standard protective mechanisms.

This will help to deceive intruders accustomed to commonly known and actively promoted security tools.

There are many ways to use the deception for this purpose. Basing on the Dunnigan and Nofi classification [Cohen1-98], deception mechanisms are as follows:

❏ Concealment
❏ Camouflage
❏ Misinforming

In one way or another, these mechanisms are useful in the standard activities of information-security departments. However, these mechanisms are also applied to ensure security in other areas (physical, economic, etc.) than information security.

In the field of information security, the first method — concealment — has found widespread applications. Concealing network topology using a firewall is an illustrative example of the use of this method for ensuring information security. Examples of "camouflage" include, for example, the usage of a UNIX-like GUI in a system running Windows. Intruders encountering such an interface will attempt to implement attacks that are effective against UNIX. This will increase the time required to implement a successful attack.

As a matter of fact, in most blockbuster movies about hackers, they could determine the OS type immediately — a brief look at the system prompt to enter the user name and password was usually sufficient. In contrast to other movie tricks, this is not an exaggeration. Generally, each OS has its own, system-specific method for identifying users. The login interface differs by font type, size, color login prompt text, position on the screen, etc. Camouflage allows you to protect yourself from attacks of this type.

Finally, as an example of misinformation, the usage of banners that inform the intruder of non-existent vulnerabilities is one example of note. For example, if your network uses Sendmail version 8.9.3, and the header that it returns states differently, intruders can waste a lot of time and resources attempting to exploit vulnerabilities characteristic of earlier sendmail versions (before 8.9.3).

Here, we will consider only the second and third classes of deception methods, because they are the least common and most interesting. Systems utilizing these methods actually emulate typical vulnerabilities that are non-existent in the protected objects. The use of tools based on camouflage or misinformation usually has the following effects:

❏ They increase of the number of operations performed by the intruder. Since the intruder can not determine if the vulnerability found is real, additional time and effort is lost. Even additional efforts do not always help. For example, an attempt to initiate a brute-force attack on a non-existing or falsified file using a special password-checking utility (such as Crack for UNIX or L0phtCrack for Windows) will result in lost time without producing any effective result. The attacker will think that he or she was unable to crack the password, while the cracking software has actually been deceived.

❏ They permit tracing of the attackers. While the intruders are trying to check the vulnerabilities detected, including falsified ones, security administrators can trace the whole sequence of their actions and take appropriate counter-measures.

Usually, an information system uses from five to 10 reserved ports (numbered from 1 to 1024). These ports include those responsible for services such as HTTP, FTP, SMTP, NNTP, NetBIOS, Echo, Telnet, etc. If the deception system emulates the usage of 100 or more ports, the time required for port scanning will increase proportionally. Now the intruder will find 100 or more open ports rather than five to 10. Besides this, detecting open ports is not sufficient. It is also necessary to take into account any vulnerabilities related to that port. Even if the intruder automates this task using the appropriate software (Nmap, SATAN etc.), the number of operations he or she must perform increases significantly, which makes the work less productive. At the same time, the intruder is constantly at risk, because he or she can be detected at any moment.

Deception systems have another specific feature. By default, attempts to access unused ports are ignored. Thus, active security tools might miss attempts at port scanning. On the other hand, if you are using a deception system, such actions will be detected on the first attempt.

Using deception systems, you can defeat intruders with their own weapons, and the situation does not aid the intruders, who earlier were one step ahead of security specialists. Including deception tools in security infrastructure is an interesting approach, and it can be very efficient, provided, of course, that it is used correctly. To improve the efficiency of a security system, it is recommended to combine a deception system with the intrusion detection system. This not only allows the detection of the intruder with the first attempt at an attack, but also provides time for a security administrator to trace the intruder and take efficient counteraction measures.

There are two classes of deception systems. Systems of the first class emulate services or vulnerabilities locally (i.e., on the same computer on which they run). Examples of such systems are the RealSecure OS Sensor, running in the so-called decoy mode, WinDog-DTK or the Deception Toolkit (DTK) system. Deception systems of the second class emulate whole computers, or even network segments, containing virtual hosts running various operating systems. An example of such a system is CyberCop Sting, or Honeyd. For misinforming, one can use the UkR.Nate system, which replaces the standard headers of common services (ftp, finger, pop3, smtp, telnet, ssh, lpd) and mimics the operating system on a protected host such as Linux, SunOS, FreeBSD, Windows NT, Digital Unix, SCO UnixWare, OpenBSD. This system also uses open ports characteristic to specific operating systems (for example, port 1433 for MS SQL in order to imitate Windows NT). Furthermore, this system uses an interesting mechanism of resisting remote OS fingerprinting — UST.AntiNmap.

But remember that deception systems are not universal tools that can prevent any attack. They simply help in cases of simple, unsophisticated attacks performed by beginners. However, if a qualified and skillful hacker attacks you, deception systems usually lose their efficiency. Preliminary traffic analysis allows intruders to detect fictitious ports. Modeling attacks and comparing the results with those produced by the real attacked system also allows the detection of the usage of deception tools. Furthermore, the incorrect configuration of a deception system will help the intruders to detect the fact they are being watched, and the intruders will stop the unauthorized activity. However, highly qualified hackers are not numerous, so the usage of deception systems can be helpful in most cases.

Currently, experts tend to use full-featured deception systems (honeynet) rather than standalone deception tools. This approach will provide a better and more detailed level of analysis. There is a special project named The Honeynet Project (http://www.honeynet.org), intended for studying hacker tools, methods, and motives.

The Deception Toolkit

The Deception Toolkit (DTK) is the first solution aimed at deceiving intruders attempting to penetrate the organization's network. This tool, developed by Fred Cohen, is intended to deceive automated security scanners by means of creating falsified vulnerabilities. Reports generated by security scanners can not help the intruder to determine which detected vulnerabilities are real and which are fictitious. Thus, the intruder will have to spend time and resources checking all detected vulnerabilities, which will help the administrator to detect the attempt in time and, perhaps, even to trace the intruder.

The DTK can be customized easily according to the requirements of specific users. Usually, this programming is simply the creating a set of responses to the actions of attackers. For example, it is possible to create the sendmail banner returned in reply to an attempt to establish a connection to a specific port. This banner might include standard information on the program version, which is used by most security scanners when seeking the presence of vulnerabilities.

The DTK represents a set of programs written in C and Perl, and implementing the above-described mechanisms for deceiving intruders. These programs can be customized according to user preferences. The DTK can run on all operating systems supporting the TCP/IP protocol stack and having the Perl compiler implementation. For example, the DTK can run on most UNIX clones. DTK customization is performed by editing configuration files using any text editor. The DTK is a shareware program, which can be downloaded from http://all.net/contents/dtk.html. The DTK-Pro, the advanced version of this package, has all of the capabilities of the DTK, along with the following enhancements:

❑ Centralized management of several DTK copies installed on different network hosts
❑ Graphic user interface for DTK-Pro administrator (Fig. 6.27)
❑ The ability to check the consistency of deception rules and several other functions

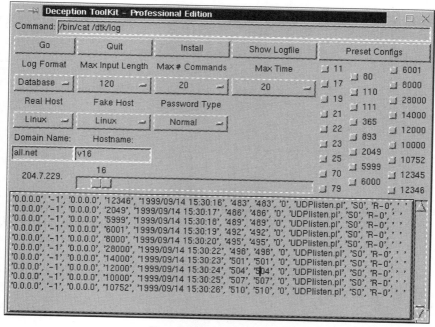

Fig. 6.27. DTK-Pro GUI

CyberCop Sting

The CyberCop Sting system was developed by Network Associates, and is intended to emulate an Ethernet segment containing Cisco routers with IOS 11.2 and servers running Windows NT 4.0 and Solaris 2.6. All packets sent to modeled virtual hosts are traced, which enables the administrator to detect and trace the intruders while they attempt to attack non-existent hosts.

CyberCop Sting "creates" a virtual network on a dedicated Windows NT host. For Unix, one can use the Honeyd deception system, which supports FreeBSD, Linux, NetBSD, OpenBSD, POSIX, Solaris, and SunOS. Each of the virtual hosts has one or more IP addresses, to which one can send network traffic and obtain a "real" response. In more complicated cases, the virtual host can play the role of a packet repeater, sending packets to the invisible, but real, computer, which replies to all of the intruder's requests. The main advantage of CyberCop Sting lies in the fact that, to model a "lure" for intruders, you do not need a large amount of hosts and routers. The whole system resides on a single computer (Fig. 6.28).

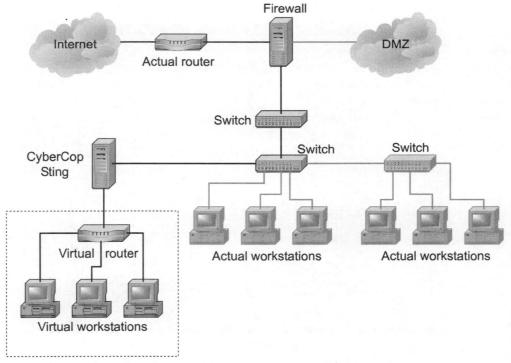

Fig. 6.28. The CyberCop Sting deception system

However, CyberCop Sting lacks the DTK's flexibility. For example, you can not specify emulated vulnerabilities and, even for standard network services that can be modeled by Sting, you will not be able to set specific responses for intruder requests.

Furthermore, both the DTK and Sting lack powerful log-analysis mechanisms. Consequently, you will have to view hundreds, or even thousands, of text records to find the information you actually need. Despite the fact that there are third-party products that can serve this purpose (for example, WebTrends Log Analyzer), it would be very convenient to have built-in tools for log-file analysis.

Consistency Checker Systems

If, despite the presence of classical intrusion detection systems and other protective measures, the intruder still manages to penetrate the protected system, he or she usually attempt to install Trojan horse programs, edit system files, or cause the security system to fail. In most cases, these actions are reduced to editing certain files (executable files, dynamic link libraries, drivers, configuration files etc.).

Target-based analysis, also known as file-consistency checking, relies on passive methods of checking the consistency of the system and data files with the system objects (data flows, databases, registry keys) and their attributes. These consistency-checking methods have no significant influence on the functions of the controlled system. Consistency checkers use cryptographic checks for control checksums (CRC) to identify proof of the tweaking or falsification of the most important system objects or files. Algorithms implemented in these checks are characterized by the fact that even minor changes in function input data produce significant differences in the result. This means that minor deviations in the flow of input data will result in a significant difference in the CRC generated by the algorithm. These algorithms are resistant, which means that, provided that the input value is predefined, it is practically impossible to obtain the identical result for any other input value. This prevents the most common attacks against relatively simple algorithms of CRC generation, when hackers conceal the changes in file contents in such a way that the same CRC is generated both for the original and the modified file.

Consistency checkers work in an endless loop by processing files, system objects and their attributes for generating CRCs, then compare these results to the results generated in the course of the previous iteration and search for inconsistencies. If any difference is noticed, the product sends an administrative alert and registers the most probable time of the change.

Consistency control enables the implementation of an efficient monitoring strategy, focusing on the systems where data and process consistency is a matter of primary importance (for example, database management systems). This approach allows for the control of specific files, system objects and their attributes for changes, paying special attention to the result of an attack rather than to the details of its evolution. Detailed information on the advantages and drawbacks of consistency checkers is provided in Table. 6.9.

Table 6.9. Advantages and Drawbacks of Consistency Checkers

Advantages	Drawbacks
Any successful attack, as a result of which some files were modified — even if rootkits or packet-capturing tools were used- will be detected independently of whether signature analysis or statistical analysis was used for attack detection.	Contemporary implementations of this approach tend to work in batch mode. Therefore, they can not provide real-mode reaction to an attack.
Since consistency control is independent from old records of working modes, it will detect attacks that can not be detected by other methods.	Depending on the number of files, system objects and their attributes, for which control checksums are calculated, systems of this type can still have a negative impact on the performance of the controlled system.
This method allows for the reliable detection of both the location and the presence of attacks that modify the system (for example, Trojan horses).	These tools are not suitable for real-time intrusion detection, since they control attack results, rather than the processes of attack evolution.
Because this mechanism does not have a significant influence on the performance of the controlled system, consistency control can be useful for monitoring systems with medium bandwidth.	
Consistency checkers are efficient for determining files that need to be replaced in order to restore the system, instead of complete reinstallation or restoring the system from the backup copy.	

There are many consistency checkers, available both commercially and as shareware. As an example, I will consider a number of such systems here.

Tripwire

Initially, Tripwire (http://www.tripwiresecurity.com) was a shareware product. Later, however, the system was further developed by Tripwire Security, and is currently a commercial product. This system has several differences from similar shareware products, the first and the most important of which is the support of client/server architecture. In contrast to other systems, which run in stand-alone mode, Tripwire comprises two components — HQ Connector and HQ Console. The first component must be installed on remote hosts running various operating systems. It performs consistency control over the specified actions. The second component manages remote agents, collects information from those agents, and performs a centralized analysis of this information, generates reports, and performs other functions. Another distinguishing feature of Tripwire, which most other consistency checkers lack, is Windows support (systems of this class usually provide support for a large number of UNIX clones, but "dislike" Microsoft products). Tripwire supports the following operating systems: Windows NT, Solaris, Linux, AIX, HP-UX, IRIX and Tru64. The third important feature is the availability of a special language for describing consistency checking policy (Enhanced Policy Language).

To meet user requirements, Tripwire Security has also a released freeware version of this product, as part of the GNU project. It is known as Tripwire 1.3 ASR, and has the following differences from the commercial release:

- ❏ No Windows support
- ❏ No capability for sending CRC-change alert via e-mail
- ❏ Limited number of controlled attributes (only nine, in contrast to the commercial version, which controls 14 attributes)
- ❏ Limited capabilities of the report generator (no sorting, no details)
- ❏ Lack of a centralized management console
- ❏ No capability of changing check priorities, does not protect its own files from unauthorized access

AIDE and L5

According to some specialists, the AIDE (Advanced Intrusion Detection Environment) system — available for download from http://www.cs.tut.fi/~rammer/aide.htmp — and L5 (ftp://avian.org/src/hacks) are the best alternatives to the freeware version of Tripwire.

Gog&Magog

In contrast to the tools considered above, the Gog&Magog system (http://www.multimania.com/cparisel/gog/) not only generates and checks the control sum (according to the MD5 protocol) for selected files (in automatic mode), but also controls other file parameters (access rights, owner and so on).

Summary

Different categories of intrusion detection systems have their own advantages and points of weakness. Combining various types of these tools helps to strengthen the advantages of some and eliminate the drawbacks of others, thus allowing the creation of an efficient intrusion detection infrastructure. Combining all these technologies will significantly improve the level of protection for corporate networks against attacks and misuse, make the security policy more stringent, and make network-resource operation more flexible.

CHAPTER 7

Anticipating Attacks, or Creating an Intrusion Detection Infrastructure

"Now the general who wins a battle makes many calculations in his temple ere the battle is fought. The general who loses a battle makes but few calculations beforehand. Thus do many calculations lead to victory, and few calculations to defeat: how much more no calculation at all! It is by attention to this point that I can foresee who is likely to win or lose."

Sun Tzu, "The Art of War."

So far, we have briefly considered all of the basic aspects of intrusion detection technologies and know what to look for and where, as well as how and using which tools. You might ask: "What else do we need?" This information alone, however, is not sufficient in order to create a truly efficient intrusion detection infrastructure. You need to know not only which intrusion detection systems are available and how they work, but also how to make the correct choice when evaluating the broad range of intrusion detection systems currently available on the market. By the most conservative estimate, the number of these systems currently available exceeds a hundred, and continues to grow. As well as this, it is necessary to have an idea of where to install these systems, how to customize them according to your information processing technology, and so on. And these, however, are simply organizational issues, as you will also need to put the system into operation, and maintain and support it. Finally, just detecting an attack is not enough, since you will also need to know how to react to this information by initiating investigative procedures within the proper time frame. The remaining chapters of this book are dedicated to the consideration of these issues. In addition, I would like to emphasize that you should not believe vendors' advertising slogans that state that all you need to do is install the product, and then forget about it completely. Maybe the system itself works like that, but do not forget that you still need to deploy and customize it, and then maintain its knowledge base, keeping it in the most current state. To achieve this, you will need human resources, time and, naturally, money. In other words, you will need to build the intrusion detection infrastructure.

To detect security policy violations efficiently, special preparation is required. These preparations must not only be related to the network environment itself (servers, workstations, routers, security tools and so on), but also to the personnel who are responsible for providing information security. In this case, it is necessary to remember that information security depends not only on the employees working in the information-security department (or in a department responsible for performing similar functions), but also on other specialists, including employees in the IT, communications and other functional departments, including the financial department. All employees must understand the organization's security policy, its role, and the basic procedures for ensuring information security (particularly within the range of their own duties).

In general, organizations that do not pay sufficient attention to preliminary tasks, and do not have an appropriate intrusion detection infrastructure, encounter the following problems:

❑ They are unable to notice traces of attacks because of the lack or incorrect configuration of appropriate intrusion detection tools and information on the standard functioning of the controlled system. Due to this, it is impossible to determine if an event is anomalous, as there is nothing with which to compare it.

❑ They are unable to identify attacks due to the insufficient theoretical knowledge, skills and practical experience of their security personnel

❑ They are unable to evaluate the duration of attacks or the damage caused by them. This significantly increases the time required to recover from attacks.

❑ In most cases, they are unable to restore the system after a failure using only their own resources.

❑ These organizations are likely to suffer serious damage, which might not be limited only to direct financial losses. For example, if your customers know that their confidential information or money is exposed to risk, they might go to your competitors, which will result in a loss of expected profit, and so on. You might even land yourself in court for inadequate protection of your resources and the interests of your clients. Quite often, intruders are able to use the vulnerable systems in these organizations as a basis for attacking other networks or hosts.

❑ Finally, the business reputation of such company might suffer serious damage.

In any case, adequate preparation can either entirely prevent an attack on your organization, or at least minimize the losses and damage due to the attack, and protect your system from similar intrusions in the future. This preparation involves the analysis of several basic components:

❑ The existing security policy and methods of ensuring that security procedures and security guidelines are being followed. If your organization currently has no such policy, it is high time to design one.

❑ Information processed within the information system.

❑ The components of the information system (workstations, servers, communications equipment, software, etc.).

❑ The corporate network and the segments that comprise it.

❑ The users of your information system. When considering users, you must take into account both internal users (company employees) and external users that have access to corporate resources (partners, clients, suppliers, etc.).

❑ Specialized tools used to ensure information security, including intrusion detection.

This chapter describes all of the preliminary actions that must be performed in the course of implementing an intrusion detection infrastructure. Simply following the recommendations provided here will help you prepare for creating an efficient information-security system, even if you are not planning to install the intrusion detection system right away. In practice, all of the preliminary actions described here are common procedures ahead of deploying practically any information-security infrastructure.

The list of actions to implement before creating the intrusion detection infrastructure includes the following:

❑ Educating and training your personnel. Note that it is necessary to provide education and training not only for employees working in an information-security department, but also for employees from departments in any way related to information security.

❐ Determining security policies and procedures that will prepare your organization for the detection of intrusions.

❐ The selection of mechanisms for system and network logon, which are the basis of intrusion detection technologies.

❐ Generating information that is required for the control of the integrity of information resources and for building an efficient intrusion detection infrastructure.

It is vital to note that, during the creation of a complex security system that includes intrusion detection, it is also necessary to perform a number of other actions, including activating access control systems and authentication servers, antiviral systems and firewalls, eliminating unnecessary services, using "strong" passwords, and limiting modem usage.

Training Personnel

The mechanisms employed in intrusion detection infrastructures, regardless of how powerful and efficient they are, are useless if your personnel are not able to use them correctly. The employees must know how to choose the appropriate security tool, evaluate, install and put it into operation. The majority of attacks implemented by intruders with computer skill of the same level as should be easy to detect. However, if you are dealing with an expert hacker, the situation is a lot more difficult. Fig. 7.1 shows the chances you have of tracing the intruder depending on his or her skills, and on the skill level of the security personnel. If the security specialists are more skilled and knowledgeable than the intruder is, then you have a good chance of detecting the intruder. Otherwise, this task becomes rather complicated, if at all possible. If the security administrator and the intruder have equal qualifications, everything depends on chance — the one who makes a mistake first usually loses.

An efficient intrusion detection system will most likely be able to detect an attack implemented by expert hackers. However, only trained and qualified security specialists will be able to understand system messages and take efficient measures to counteract the intruder. Therefore, it is rather important to ensure that employees responsible for intrusion detection are well trained and adequately prepared to detect intrusions, gather proof, investigate incidents, and react to them appropriately. According to the latest data, there are currently about 50,000 vacancies for security specialists in the U.S., and this number is constantly growing. One of the reasons for this is the rapid growth of the number of hacker attacks. John Gunn, the director of the Regional

Computer Forensic Laboratory, gives an even more pessimistic forecast: "The need for specialists in the field of computer crime is growing exponentially" [Chen1-00]. This problem is especially important for the various governmental structures responsible for the safety of citizens and upholding the law. Most such organizations have special departments responsible for investigating computer security incidents but, even so, the lack of qualified specialists is catastrophic. Most universities and training centers have already reacted to this growing need. By the way, highly qualified IS professionals receive quite generous salaries (at least according to the data provided by the SANS Institute (**http://www.sans.org**) [SANS2-00]).

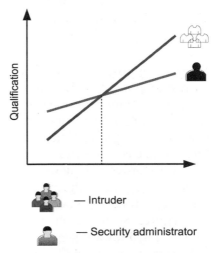

— Intruder

— Security administrator

Fig. 7.1. Chances of tracing an intruder based on the qualifications
of the security personnel

As was mentioned earlier, the process of completely automating intrusion detection systems is currently still in the realm of dreams rather than reality. In nearly all cases where an intruder is traced, security administrators use manual methods of intrusion detection, or customized programs that extend the capabilities of the security system. Because of this, manual methods of intrusion detection are still very important and were covered in detail in *Chapters 4* and *5*. According to the mass media, the U.S. Navy has assigned several experts to control network activities and detect intrusions not only based on data collected by security tools, but also on their own practical experience and intuition.

It is vital to educate and train your system's users (everyone who accesses your data, systems and networks). This training can be organized on the basis of your own organization, by third-party consultants, or through services provided by specialized training centers. The training (including training the users who access your data, systems, and networks) can take any form, including lectures, seminars (including online seminars on the Internet), role-playing and others. In the course of the training, normal users (those not specializing in information) have to master (as well as aspects related to correct password selection, general concepts of the security policy adopted by your organization, etc.) the following topics:

❒ What to expect when an external or internal intruder implements an attack
❒ How to identify suspicious activity, and whom to inform of it
❒ What to do to decrease the potential damage to the information, systems and networks caused by an attack

Before you start the training process, which can involve significant expense, you should perform your own evaluation of the level of skills and qualifications of the personnel that will operate your intrusion detection infrastructure. If your employees lack the required qualifications, it is important to interview the candidates for training and ask them what they need expect to get from the training. Although this advice might seem absurd at first glance, it makes sense and provides an opportunity to achieve the best results with minimum expenses, as it allows you to evaluate the level of knowledge of your employees correctly. Analyze the information that you have collected and develop a training program on aspects of information security, including intrusion detection strategies and procedures. Such a program should be divided into at least two parts, the first of which is oriented toward general users, while the second is intended for security specialists. After the program has been developed, apply it in practice and train your employees. Among other things, the training should be mandatory for all newly hired employees and encompass all aspects of the employee's functions and duties.

The CSC Will Train the Pentagon's Personnel

By the end of 2001, the Pentagon had signed a $86.7-million contract with the Computer Science Corporation (CSC) to train its personnel in the field of working with cyber-security tools. The CSC training course will cover a wide range of topics, including intrusion detection and investigating of cyber crime. 35 CSC trainers will teach the course over a period of eight years.

It is also important to check the level of efficiency and preparedness of your personnel in performing actions required to ensure the security of your information.

For this reason, it is necessary to organize regular training courses to improve the qualifications of your employees by modeling situations that are likely to arise in reality. This will help you to ensure that your employees know their duties and will be able to take adequate measures in critical situations.

Training Centers

To provide training for your employees, you can look to the manufacturer or vendor of the system you have chosen to operate, as well as to specialized companies that provide training services in the field of information security. Training programs can be expensive, so you should make sure beforehand that you are getting exactly the type of training service for which you are paying. Make sure that you select a training center that has specific experience and specializes in information-security training.

In general, there are two approaches to educating and training security professionals: developing universal specialists and developing professionals that specialize in one particular area of information security (intrusion detection, in particular). The first approach generally involves the study of specific products and their rules of operation. A specialist trained in this manner is usually familiar with specific software and the solutions provided by a specific vendor. As a result, these specialists are not always effective in other situations. CheckPoint certification programs are an example of this type of training. The second approach is more practical. As well as a general exam (the number of questions usually varies from 60 to 100), students in these courses must pass a test showing that they are able to handle real-world problems arising in the course of day-to-day activity. Specialists trained by this method will be able to solve intrusion detection problems using any tools. One example of such a course is the GIAC (Global Incident Analysis Center) program. There are also combined methodologies, combining the advantages of both approaches. Some examples are the programs provided by Internet Security Systems or Cisco Systems.

On-Line Training

On-line training is a relatively new field in education technologies that enables students to gain knowledge about to the latest achievements in the area(s) under consideration without leaving their home (or workplace).

Although, currently, the companies providing on-line courses are not numerous, they still exist. For example, the SANS Institute provides training with its "Intrusion Detection In Depth" course (http://www.sans.org/onlinetraining/track3.php), which allows you to become certified at the GIAC training center (http://www.giac.org) and obtain GIAC Certified Intrusion Analyst status.

On-Line Seminars

On-line seminars, also known as "Webinars" or "Webcasts" also represent a relatively new type of system that is oriented toward specialists that are unable to leave their workplaces even for a few hours. As opposed to distance learning, a Webinar lasts for only a few hours, and covers only one topic, whereas a distance learning course might take several days (or even months) and cover a wide range of topics. Such seminars solve problems such as finding a place to hold classes and limitations to class size (hundreds or even thousands of users can connect to web server on which the seminar takes place). Finally, users can attend an on-line seminar any time after it has finished, since its contents are saved into an archive.

Practically every company and organization working on the intrusion detection systems market conducts these seminars. This form of education is standard for ISS, Axent, Tripwire, SANS, etc. Cisco Systems has also recently started to conduct on-line seminars.

Seminars and Conferences

Seminars and conferences are a more traditional education format, enabling specialists to become acquainted with new achievements in the field of security. Note that this form of education is relatively inexpensive, and sometimes even free. Recently, there have been more and more such conferences, and so I will list only the most effective and best-known ones:

- ❏ SANS Network Security yearly international conference. Like other SANS projects, this one has a practical orientation. The conference has several sections dedicated to different aspects of the information-security question. Typical topics include information-security basics, firewalls, Virtual Private Networks (VPN), intrusion detection, response to incidents, network and system audits, Windows security and UNIX security. Beside the sections listed above, SANS Network Security conducts various training courses, including those dedicated to various hacking utilities.

- ❏ Recent Advances in Intrusion Detection (RAID) yearly **international conference**. This conference (http://www.raid-symposium.org/) is the first to be devoted solely to intrusion detection technologies. The conference is supported by representatives from universities and government and commercial organizations from a large number of countries from around the world.

- ❏ ISS Connect yearly international conference. This conference is rather similar to the previous ones, since it is also divided into different areas: organization security for top management, intrusion detection and incident response, risk analysis and development of security policy, etc.

❒ Computer Security Conference yearly international conference. This conference, conducted by the Computer Security Institute (CSI) also has several sections, each being dedicated to a specific area of information security.

Business Games

Business games are used to model various situations arising in day-to-day activity and to analyze all aspects that influence the decision-making process. Currently, the usage of business games in the information-security area is limited by the lack of the necessary skilled experts needed to predict various situations as well as assess the performance of business-game participants. In most fields, this role is delegated to computers. However, in the field of information security, there are no adequate programs able to serve this purpose. The efficiency of the business-game approach has been proved in practice. For example, the level of mastering of materials and practices as a result of participation in a business-game format is 79.3%, while traditional methods, including workshops, generate a figure of only 54%. Two weeks after participation, the amount of information retained for the two methods is 64.9% and 11.8%, respectively. After four weeks, the levels are 49% and 8.5%, while, after six weeks or more, the numbers are 32% and 5%.

ISS has developed a course known as "Enterprise Network Security", organized on the basis of business games. Students attending this course are divided into two groups. The first group plays the role of the intruders, imitating various attacks on the protected network. The second group plays the role of security administrator. These players try to detect and stop the attacks, and then investigate the security incidents. The groups then swap roles.

Certification of IS Professionals

Certification is necessary to confirm the completion of a certain educational program and the quality of the training. However, according to the KPMG report [KPMG1-02], 73% of IS specialists have no special certificate. Currently, there are two different certification schemes for security specialists that are similar to the training schemes. The first scheme is not associated with any specific product and covers various specific aspects of security technology. Certifications of this type include Certified Information System Security Professional (CISSP) and GIAC Security Engineer.

Certifications associated with the second scheme relate to specific products or solutions offered by different companies. This approach is common for many companies, including ISS, Cisco, CheckPoint, and others.

There are also mixed or combined certification schemes.

Defining Security Policy and Procedures

A security policy is a set of rules and procedures that must be observed when working with protected information, covering all specific features of information processing within the organization. A security policy can not be standardized, as it must always take into account the information processing technologies utilized by the organization, as well as the organization's aims, security requirements and so on. However, a detailed description of all of the aspects of security policy development goes beyond the scope of this book and deserves a separate discussion (http://www.sans.org/newlook/resources/policies/policies.htm). Here, I will describe only those topics that require your attention when preparing an intrusion detection system.

The procedures involved in preparing an intrusion detection regime include actions necessary for supervising components of the corporate network while searching for traces and indications of an attack. This takes the following forms: monitoring, inspecting, auditing and consistency checking. Besides the above-listed actions, there are also a number of other techniques (Table 7.1) [Kochmar1-98].

Table 7.1. Actions Aimed at Intrusion Detection

Action	Description
Filtering	The investigation of data flow between controlled systems, filtering unauthorized or suspicious actions from this flow and blocking them
Probing	Initiating attempts to establish connections to controlled systems and generating various requests
Scanning	Periodical probing of controlled systems
Monitoring	Monitoring specific events within the controlled area (including network traffic, log files etc.)
Inspecting	Investigating information resources or processes within the controlled systems
Auditing	Systematically investigating log data within the controlled system to detect already-known or expected behavior
Integrity checking	Controlling the system for integrity and preventing critical files from being changed
Notifying	Notifying the security administrator in cases where specific security events are detected within the controlled system using one of the above-listed actions

For efficient intrusion detection, it is necessary to create the documents that will be listed later in this chapter. Based on my own practical experience, I know that not all organizations will be able or willing to create these documents. Quite often, information-security specialists working in organizations have neither the time nor the ability to conduct the time-consuming and tedious work of collecting the required information and filling blanks in the information structure of the organization. However, this work is worth doing. The documents necessary for efficient intrusion detection (sorted in the order of importance to the information structure of the organization) are listed below. If you have no time, or lack the required skills to do this yourself, then you can delegate the writing of these documents to qualified third-party professionals or organizations.

First, it is necessary to prepare a document containing descriptions of attacks and vulnerabilities that could be implemented or found in your corporate network. I will like especially to mention the fact that this list should include only those attacks and vulnerabilities that are applicable to your resources, equipment, and software. These attacks and vulnerabilities must be described in a separate document as well as in the so-called protection plan. Beside the description of security events, the protection plan can also include other important data on the protected corporate network. These events are defined in the course of the risk analysis process. Through the risk analysis, you will define the most probable threats and evaluate the chances of their occurrence. There are two approaches to risk evaluation. The first approach focuses on the level of ensuring information security (the most probable scenarios of the corporate-network operation). If the basic level is not sufficient (for example, in real-time scheduling systems, banking systems, etc.), the second approach is used. This approach implies detailed investigation of the data-processing technologies, hardware and software used for this purpose. The first approach generally considers a typical set of probable threats (virus attack, hardware failures, etc.). In the second case, a more detailed list of potential threats is compiled, based on the results of a detailed analysis of corporate-network activity. It is likely that some threats will be deleted from this final list of potential threats later. The core of such a document could be information from the various statistical reports mentioned in *Chapter 2*. Most likely, your network is not so unique that it does not have shared resources (for a Windows platform) or that it does not use RPC and sendmail (for Unix systems). Because of this, you can use the following reports as a basis for creating your documents: SANS [SANS1-02], X-Force [ISS2-02] or Riptech [Riptech1-02].

Another necessary document, known as a network map, must include an inventory of all hardware and software used within the corporate network. The information contained in this inventory must be compared to the actual state of the corporate network on a regular basis. In the event of authorized changes in software or hardware configuration, these changes must be incorporated into the network map, so that it is always up to date. In the event that unauthorized changes are detected, it is necessary immediately to start incident investigation procedures. The method for creating the network map will be covered in more detail later in this chapter.

The third document that you must develop when creating an intrusion detection infrastructure assigns roles, duties, privileges and responsibilities to system administrators, network administrators and security administrators. It also describes user rights and responsibilities, in order to organize the efficient management of all data systems and networks when detecting attack traces.

The next document describes the actions that must be performed in order to detect intrusions into your corporate network (see Table 7.1). This document must cover all aspects related to hardware, software and the activities of responsible employees, including the following:

❑ The actions necessary to notify the proper individuals (network administrators, security administrators) in the event of the detection of security policy violations.

❑ The tools used for intrusion detection and their operations. These tools were covered in *Chapters 5* and *6*. The order of their usage will be covered later.

❑ The frequency of the operations intended to detect potential intrusions. For example, some tools must operate constantly (for example, network-level intrusion detection systems or host-level intrusion detection systems). Other tools need only to be used from time to time, although on a regular basis (for example, consistency checkers).

❑ The roles, responsibilities and duties of the employees responsible for the implementation of the intrusion detection plan. You must specify, by whom, when and how each of the above-listed actions should be performed.

Beside this, you must also create a document regulating the routine procedures for checking and analyzing logged data in order to detect attack traces. Additionally, this document must describe procedures for diagnosing and revising hardware and software in manual mode rather than automatically (consequently, they will be harder to falsify for the intruder).

For each of the intrusion detection tools, you must create a document that specifies and describes the procedures and rules for its usage. These documents must define the following (for each tool):

❑ Which resources (hosts, files, registry keys, network traffic, etc.) must be controlled

❏ How information on the state of controlled resources must be created, stored, analyzed and protected

❏ The frequency of running intrusion detection procedures (for example, in real-time mode or periodically on a regular basis)

❏ The roles, duties and responsibilities of the personnel operating specific tools. Here you must define who uses the intrusion detection tools, when, and how

The next document should define conditions for testing attacked and compromised systems and data, using intrusion detection tools. It is strongly recommended that this testing be performed in an environment isolated from the production network. This isolation can be created using physical or logical separation — for example, using a firewall or special rules specified for network equipment (for example, by using VLAN).

Finally, your intrusion detection plan must also contain a document describing the procedures and tools to be used for correlating information on attacks (i.e., definitions of facts when an attack or security event that is registered by a part of your system relates to an attack or security event that is registered in another part of your system). This aspect has become of primary importance with the arrival of distributed and coordinated attacks.

Notice that, despite the fact that this book considers only some aspects of security policy, these must not contradict other security rules. In the course of developing the above-described documentation, you must constantly analyze this question and discuss it with other interested parties (but not too many). By doing so, you will be able to ensure that the created documents are:

❏ Implementable within a reasonable time, while employing a reasonable amount of material resources

❏ Compatible to existing security policy within your organization (this requirement is not only limited to information policy)

❏ In line with the latest and most efficient intrusion detection technologies

❏ In accordance to all local and international standards and laws

❏ Able to provide a required level of legal protection for you and your organization in the event of difficulties

Revise your security policy (not limiting yourself to intrusion detection aspects) and its components periodically, including preliminary steps in intrusion detection, intrusion detection procedures and personnel training. In the course of such revisions, take into account all open sources of information, including information obtained from the vendor or manufacturer of the intrusion detection tools. These sources regularly inform the user community of new forms of attacks and vulnerabilities, trends in hacking technologies, methods of intrusion detection, and so on. The X-Force Security Alert mailing list is an example of this type of source. It is published by ISS and provides the latest information on recently detected vulnerabilities and attacks.

If your organization becomes the target of an attack that inflicts serious damage, revise the components of the intrusion detection plan to detect similar attacks and attempts at repeating these attacks quickly.

Selecting and Using System and Network Logging Mechanisms

Collecting and analyzing the data generated by the network, DBMS application or the operating system is a powerful and efficient method of intrusion detection. Further, this is sometimes the only possible approach. Log files contain information about all system, network or other events that have occurred during a specified time period. Neglecting the information from these logging mechanisms will significantly weaken your security system, to the point that it can render it virtually useless [CERT1-00]. Log files are necessary for:

- ❏ Notifying administrators that there has been an attack
- ❏ Helping to restore the system after an attack
- ❏ Performing investigations
- ❏ Obtaining proof that unauthorized actions are being performed

Initially, administrators and security professionals performed this analysis manually. Security personnel had to analyze large printouts in order to locate events indicating unauthorized activities. Naturally, by the time these events were located, it was already too late to stop the attack. Gradually, with the advances in information technologies, methods of automated analysis of log-file information appeared, and these methods were included in most commercially available systems.

Logged Information

Selecting the information that needs to be analyzed is the first step in using logging mechanisms. Next, it is necessary to define the logging mechanisms and the points where the logged information should be collected. Finally, the locations for storing the collected information must be defined.

Table 7.2 contains a general list of the most common types of log files and events registered there. Note that not all systems are capable of registering the information outlined in this table. This is especially true for custom application systems, which are generally designed without taking into account security considerations. On the other hand, it is pointless to register any useless information in a log file. If you are developing a custom application system with security in mind, you have to find a reasonable balance between the amount of data logged and the performance of the controlled system. This is necessary to avoid situations in which all of the controlled system's resources are being consumed by the task of logging an excessive number of events. This is where the network map becomes indispensable, since it contains a list of all information resources in the corporate network and specifies their level of importance. As a rule, the more important is a specific resource, the more information about this resource it is necessary to register. Further, the network map provides an understanding of the function performed by the controlled host, which simplifies the choice of information that needs to be logged. For example, if the host is a web server, then the actions of logging on to the server and accessing various HTML pages and CGI scripts are of primary importance.

Table 7.2. Types of Log Files and Information Contained There

Log-file type	Categories of logged information
User activities	System logon and logoff events (failed attempts, time and location of the logon or logoff), attempts to logon as privileged user
	Any attempts to change user information (password, privileges).
Process activities	Time and arguments of process startup
	User who started the process
	Time of process termination, termination status, duration of the process and the resources it accessed
	Files opened by the process and devices it accessed
System events	Actions requiring special privileges
	Errors and warnings issued by the hardware, software and file system
	Activities related to modem connections
	Any changes in the system status, including events such as shutdown and rebooting
	Information on system workload (average and peak values of CPU workload, consumed and free memory and disk space)

continues

Table 7.2 Continued

Log-file type	Categories of logged information
Network events	Information on attempts to establish connections with the system (who, when, from where, using which protocol and during which time) and on any open connections
	Additional data (network packet headers, packet size, contents of the data field, network interface, rule)
	Information on the network load (including the number of network errors)
	Network traffic information (workload by percentage, bytes, connections etc), sorting by various criteria (protocol, source and destination addresses)
File access	Any changes in file attributes (access rights, CRC, size, contents, path, permissions)
	Access (type, access time, duration, user or process name)
Application activity	Application-specific information (for example, mail traffic, firewall events, financial transactions etc.)

The Sufficiency of Built-in Logging Mechanisms

Determine which logging mechanisms are available in your system, what the names of the log files are and where are they stored. Note that the names of these files might differ from version to version of the same operating system.

Focus on creating a situation in which your logging mechanisms (both built-in and auxiliary) cover the entire range of events described in Table 7.2 by determining more precisely which categories of information are processed by specific logging mechanisms. It is most effective desirable when these logs even overlap. Although this will result in some redundancy of information stored and increase the space required to hold it, at the same time, it will increase the probability of detecting unauthorized activities. If the available logging mechanisms are insufficient (this is most likely to be the case if you use only the OS built-in logging capabilities), consider the possibility of installing auxiliary tools to extend and enhance the built-in logging function. This is particularly important when dealing with Microsoft operating systems, which do not generally log all of the necessary information.

Event Logging

At first glance, enabling the event-logging mechanism appears to be an easy task. However, this process is not as simple as it might seem. For example, you must determine when the logging mechanism will begin functioning at once (at system startup, as the case for Windows NT-based operating systems, or at specified times, as is the case, for example, for the Tripwire consistency checker or for System Scanner security scanner?) On top of this, you must also bear in mind that different logging tools provide different levels of detail when logging information. For example, CheckPoint Firewall-1 provides two options: Short Log and Long Log. The RealSecure Network Sensor system also permits two logging modes. Beside the classical logging mode (log without raw option), when only the name, date and time of the detection of an attack are stored in the log file, there is an enhanced mode (log with raw option), in which, in addition to the standard information, the logging mechanism also registers the contents of the entire traffic or all commands issued within the range of the registered security event. This mode enables an administrator to analyze the methods used by the intruder and to take efficient countermeasures. Be careful not to overuse the enhanced logging mode, however, since it will result in the log file quickly becoming full of useless data, which will consume a considerable amount of the storage space.

Pay special attention to the locations of the log files and their access rights and privileges. You must have a sufficient amount of free disk space for storing these files, or some records will not be logged. As a result, some of the collected data will be lost, and you will be unable to determine with any certainty whether the security policy has been violated.

Protecting Log Files

Since log files contain very important information that must not be accessible to anyone except for security administrators, it is necessary to protect them from unauthorized access. It would be best if even the administrator could not access these files directly, but only via special tools intended for log-file processing. This will prevent the administrator from deleting or modifying specific records without authorization. In this section, I will describe the proper methods for protecting the collected information:

❑ Store logged information on the dedicated host and make sure that appropriate measures of physical security are taken. Beside this, limit access to this host via the network.

❑ Write log files to write-once storage media (for example, CD-ROM) to eliminate the possibility of modifying this data. As well as this, you can also print out this information or register the output of "in-process" activity logs with devices that do not allow data modification. The last option will complicate the analysis significantly. Simply using a printer to provide a backup mechanism in the event of difficulties is sufficient.

❑ Prevent the possibility of changing any records already existing in the log files.

❑ Use encryption mechanisms to protect log files from unauthorized reading and, even more importantly, from unauthorized modification.

Storing log files on the hard drive is the simplest method. On the other hand, this method is also the least reliable. Despite this, it is the most commonly used method. The use of add-on encryption tools to protect log files stored on the hard drives improves reliability. However, this method has its drawbacks. In particular, since log files are constantly appended, integrity control becomes exceedingly difficult. During peak workload hours, dozens of records might be appended to the log file simultaneously, which might make the usage of encryption methods impossible. The usage of write-once storage media for recording log files is more complicated from the technical point of view, but, at the same time, is more reliable. If it is impossible to work with these media in real-time mode, consider recording the collected information periodically, when log files grow to a predefined size or when specific criteria are satisfied (for example, after a specified time period has elapsed).

If the host generating log-file records is different from the host for which these records are generated, you will need to provide protection for the entire connection through which the registered data is transferred from host to host. If the distance between two hosts is not great, it is a good idea to establish a direct cable connection between these two hosts (without any intermediate hosts). However, if the distance makes this option unrealistic (which is most often the case), you will need to use other methods. First, it is best to minimize the number of intermediate hosts along the route of log-file information, which means that you will need to customize the routing table. You will probably even dedicate a special VLAN for this purpose. Second, use encryption mechanisms to protect log-file information transferred via the network.

Another important consideration is the appropriate customization of the logging-mechanism settings. This is necessary to prevent any attempts at disrupting the operation of the logging mechanisms by organizing, for example, DoS attacks. For example, in UNIX, or in Windows NT/2000, depending on the logging mechanism settings, logging either stops or the older records of the log files are overwritten. To organize an attack on the logging mechanism, the intruder can attempt to generate a large number of events to fill the log files, and then perform unauthorized actions, which will not be registered anywhere. Filling up the log file can also bring the host down. To provide protection against this type of attack, you can employ different mechanisms. One option is to create several log files storing different kinds of information (like in Solaris). You can also download the data from the log file to a protected location or to the central management console. The Microsoft Operations Manager system functions according to this principle. The RealSecure Network Sensor system also operates in a similar way. As log files at each sensor are filling, RealSecure dynamically synchronizes them to the database stored on the central console (Fig. 7.2).

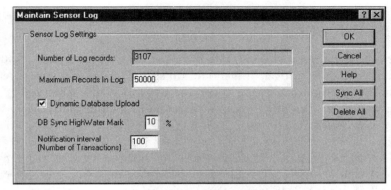

Fig. 7.2. RealSecure synchronization mechanism

Log-File Management Plan

All aspects related to the logging of all required information must be documented [CERT2-00]. The names of the resulting several sections correspond to the sections of the log-file management plan.

Managing the Volume of the Logged Information

It is usually recommended to log as much information as possible. However, as already mentioned, you should not follow this recommendation to the extreme.

First, this is the case because the amount of logged data will grow rapidly. Note also that it is difficult to predict which information will be the most important in case of attack. Initially, when enabling the logging mechanism, you will not be as aware of which events are the most important, and you will be forced to register them all. Some time later, when analyzing log files, you will understand which categories of events are critical and which are less important. Gradually, you will be able to stop logging events that have no relation to the security of the protected host.

Second, logging a large number of events has negative impact on the performance of the protected system. Therefore, it is highly recommended to find a balance between the amount of logged information and system performance. It is impossible to produce a universal set of practical recommendations in this case, and you can only achieve the necessary balance by assessing the operation of the system in actual conditions. To reduce the amount of information stored in log files, you can use physical or semantic compression methods. This way you will reduce the amount of free disk space reserved for storing log files and simplify the procedure of log-file analysis.

Assigning Priorities

If, while creating a network map, you have not determined which resources in your network are the most critical, you should do so now. Focusing your attention on the most important resources in the corporate network will enable you to use logging mechanisms more efficiently. Providing answers to the questions below will help you to solve this problem:

❑ Which functional tasks are delegated to the host or network segment? If this is a firewall, you should concentrate your attention on logging events related to the firewall. If this is DBMS server, then you must pay the most attention to events related to data input, output and data modification.

❑ How many users have access to this host? This will help you to evaluate the amount of logged information related to user logins and logouts.

❑ Will log files be used to restore the compromised system? This will help you decide whether you need to enable the transaction rollback mechanisms when logging events.

❑ Which programs and services can run at this host?

❑ What is the minimum acceptable host performance? Knowing this, you will be able to determine the resource requirements necessary for timely logging and processing of the collected log information.

Log-File Rotation

Log-file rotation includes periodic creation of the backup copies for all log files and saving them at a physically protected location, as well as periodic cleanup of the log files.

These actions will allow you to reduce the amount of data that needs to be analyzed in real-time mode in order to detect unauthorized activity while, at the same time, reducing the potential danger in the event of compromising the currently active log file.

Backing up the log files will allow you to access them whenever you need to. However, do not forget that you need to perform this operation before they are cleaned to economize space, since some part of the information will be lost.

You should encrypt log files in order to protect them from unauthorized access. Encryption should be applied both to the current log files (if this is possible) and to backup copies. Note that, as opposed to the current copies, for which encryption is not mandatory (especially if the system writes vast amounts of information into log files), backup copies must be encrypted.

When performing such routine operations (such as clearing log files), you must ensure that the information stored in these files is reliably wiped away. If you store log files on the hard disk, it is recommended that you use specialized programs for this purpose (such as Wipe). Write-once media that stores backup copies of log files can be physically destroyed.

Joining Log Files

In some cases, you may want to unite several log files into one. This will enable you to analyze data from several hosts or from several applications more efficiently. Such an approach may prove to be useful when detecting distributed attacks. However, such a merger might cause two problems:

☐ It may be necessary to convert several log files to a unified format. If you are joining several log files of a similar type (for example, logs from different hosts running the same OS), there are no difficulties created by this merging. However, if you are integrating log files from entirely different applications or systems, one or more of the log files may contain forms of data types that do not exist in the other log files.

☐ Time synchronization. If you are joining log files from systems located in different time zones, this will most likely also create problems with the uniting of this data and the subsequent analysis and correlation of the integrated log.

The netForensics system (http://www.netforensics.con/) from netForensics.com is an example of a system that integrates log files from different devices. This system will be covered later in more detail. Another system of this type, which joins log files from different hardware and supports time synchronization, is RealSecure SiteProtector from ISS.

To summarize all event logging, I would like to mention once again that the following aspects must be included into the security policy: "what", "when", "why", "where", and "how" should you react, as well as "who" is responsible for taking these steps.

Generating Information for Consistency Checkers

Precise and reliable information on the components of your system and data, starting from the moment of their creation up to the time of their deletion, is the key to the successful detection of security violations. This enables the security administrator to compare standard conditions to the current state and detect all unauthorized changes in time. All resources are monitored, including the data (both system data and user data), systems (both hardware and software), networks (both hardware and software), workstations (hardware and software), applications and operating systems.

Approaches to intrusion detection are usually based on detecting the differences between the current condition of a controlled object and that recorded previously, under normal conditions. Security personnel must always know where a resource is located, as well as its status and contents. Without detailed information of this sort, it is impossible to detect when something has been added, modified, or violated.

Unfortunately, most organizations neglect this stage of planning, due to the fact that the process of registering a large amount of required information on various components of the information can be somewhat time-consuming and tedious. Quite often, specialists in information-security departments do not have the appropriate skills for obtaining this information, or have no access to all of the equipment that is connected to the network. Therefore, they must cooperate with specialists from IT departments, telecommunications departments, etc. Only through such cooperation can specialists obtain all of the required information. As practice has shown, the network map (if ever created at all) is developed in most cases at the stage of designing the information system. But companies often do not keep their system maps up to date, rendering them practically useless as the basis for controlling unauthorized changes. Another common mistake is that, quite often, the network map and all related information is created and stored only in IT departments, so they are not available to security departments, which impacts their work negatively.

Network Map

If you have not done so already, it is absolutely necessary to perform a detailed inventory of all hardware and software of the corporate network. All information must be stored in a database, where it will be easy to compare the initial inventory results to the results produced by all subsequent inventories. In the case of authorized changes, such as adding new equipment, or the replacement or deletion of existing equipment, it is necessary to introduce a system of timely modification of the inventory list.

Network-architecture inventory must include the following information:

☐ Network topology for all devices, including active network equipment, servers and workstations, including their addresses (for example, IP addresses and MAC addresses)

☐ Routing table (information flows between devices)

☐ Description of the VLAN used and the principles according to which they are built (by ports, addresses, protocols, labels and so on)

☐ Information on the configuration of networks and devices (this must include access-control lists and other security settings)

☐ For communication equipment ports, indications that they belong to various network segments

☐ Availability of SPAN ports and their configuration

☐ Used protocols, traffic characteristics (for example, peak, minimum and average values for the network workload) and throughput value

☐ Description of the physical location of all network devices, workstations and servers, including the designation of floor and room numbers

☐ Information on the public networks by which your information is transferred and/or to which your corporate network has been connected

The description of the network's architecture is the basis for the network map. Additionally, the network map might contain the following information:

☐ List of all software installed on servers and workstations

☐ List of users and their privileges

☐ For network segments, an indication where they belong to specific departments, and a description of their functional tasks

The network map is not simply a document storing all of the required information. Instead, it is more like an atlas that includes different maps describing the same territory from different points of view (geographical, political, economic, etc.). In the same sense, the network map describes various aspects of the corporate network's operation.

To create the network component of this map, it is best to use various network-management systems (such as HP OpenView, SPECTRUM, Visio, etc). Such tools include the AutoDiscovery function, which allows administrators to update network maps automatically and trace all unauthorized changes in the network configuration. Information on the protocols used and the traffic characteristics can be obtained using various protocol analyzers. Security scanners can also be very useful, since they allow the detection of the following:

❑ Network services
❑ Banners of the responding services
❑ OS types and version numbers
❑ NetBIOS shares
❑ Common security policy parameters

All devices detected within the corporate network must be grouped according to the following parameters:

❑ Organizational departments and hosts that logically belong to them (for example, all hosts for the financial department or personnel-management department)
❑ Network segments and host that belong to them
❑ Vulnerabilities to attacks of high, medium and low risk levels (for example, an external router carries a high level of risk, while the risk level for a department server is medium, and that for a workstation is low)
❑ Level of the device's importance (high, medium or low), in relation to the functional tasks assigned to that device (for example, a banking payroll server or router can be classified as having high importance, a file server solving an organization's subsidiary tasks as a medium-importance device, and a workstation as a low-importance device)

You can also use automated tools for composing an inventory of the hardware and software. For workstations and servers running Windows 9x or Windows NT/2000, these mechanisms are already built into the operating system. For UNIX, there are similar programs, such as Strobe (ftp://ftp.cerias.purdue.edu/pub/tools/unix/scanners/strobe/) and fremont (ftp://ftp.cerias.purdue.edu/pub/tools/unix/netutils/fremont/), which allow you to determine which devices are connected to your phone line, system and network. Furthermore, there are third-party tools with a broader set of functional capabilities, for example, LAN Auditor (http://www.lanauditor.com/).

Backing up Important Files and Directories

For each important or critical file or directory, you must have backup copies that allow you to trace all the changes introduced for those files and directories. You must be able to identify the following changes:

- ❑ File type
- ❑ File path
- ❑ Alternate paths, such as links, aliases, and shortcuts
- ❑ Contents of files and directories
- ❑ Precise file size
- ❑ Data and time when the file was created and last modified
- ❑ File owner and access rights

These changes can be traced using integrity-control tools that were covered in the previous chapter. The description of the backup tools themselves (such as ARCserver, Ghost, etc.) goes beyond the range of topics discussed in this book.

Critically important elements of the information system that must be backed up and controlled include the following:

- ❑ Operating system files
- ❑ Access control lists (ACLs) for the routers, firewalls and other protection tools
- ❑ Application files
- ❑ Security tools and data used for integrity control, and detecting traces of attacks
- ❑ Organizational data and records which can disrupt business activity or inflict severe damage on the company if lost or compromised (for example, financial reports, information on employees, marketing plans, and so on)
- ❑ User data
- ❑ Public information (for example, Web pages)

Protection and Integrity Control of the Inventory, Network Map, and Authoritative Links

These requirements are quite similar to the requirements that must be met for the protection of log files. Therefore, we will not repeat them here.

Summary

Intrusion detection is impossible without preparation, which includes the following measures:

- ❑ The education and training of all personnel within your organization in various fields of information security
- ❑ Defining an appropriate security policy that takes into account all aspects of your organization's business activity
- ❑ Selecting mechanisms for logging system and network activity
- ❑ Creating an inventory of software and hardware used in the corporate network and documenting the network map
- ❑ Purchasing the most advanced tools enabling the detection of security policy violations, at both the network and system levels

CHAPTER 8

The Life Cycle, Deployment, and Implementation of an IDS

The previous chapter described all the preliminary steps that need to be taken in order to deploy an intrusion detection infrastructure. Now it is time to consider various aspects that are directly related to purchasing an IDS and bringing it into operation.

Implementing an IDS is not as easy a task as it might seem at first glance. It requires an approach similar to the one used in deploying and implementing Enterprise Resource Planning (ERP) or Customer Pelationship Management (CRM) systems. This means that this task must be considered separately, as a special project that has its own life cycle (Fig. 8.1).

Obviously, the time it takes to bring an intrusion detection system into operation will differ for different customers. In the next chapter, I will concentrate on IDS evaluation criteria and describe the main categories of customers. For the moment, however, I'd like to just provide a table outlining the approximate time it should take to implement specific steps of this project (Table 8.1).

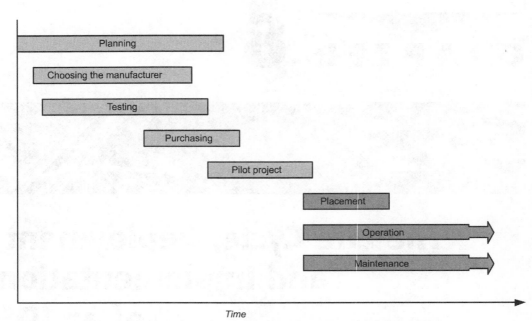

Time

Fig. 8.1. The life cycle of the IDS deployment project

Table 8.1. Approximate Implementation Times for Specific Steps of a Project Consisting of Deploying and Implementing an Intrusion Detection System (Man-Months/Months)

	Small business	Average and large companies	International companies	Service providers	Outsourcers
Planning	1/3	2/3	12/6	6/6	-
Choosing the manufacturer	1/1	1/1,5	1/2	1/1	-
Testing	1/1	1/2	1/3	1/3	-
Pilot project	-	1/2	2/3	2/3	-
Purchasing	0.5/1	1/3	6/6	6/3	-
Placement	0.5/1	2/3	12/12	3/6	6/9
Operation	3/-	6/-	48/-	24/-	24/-
Maintenance and support	1/-	3/-	6/-	6/-	3/-

Life Cycle of the IDS Infrastructure Project

Planning

Planning consists of providing a description of the criteria that must be satisfied by the intrusion detection system. Currently, there are no intrusion detection systems that can satisfy absolutely all criteria and absolutely all customer requirements. Because of this, planning is a very important step. Its results will serve as the basis for successful creation of the intrusion detection infrastructure. More detailed coverage of IDS evaluation criteria will be provided in *Chapter 9*.

This step is not complete after you form a list of criteria, but rather continues in parallel with such steps as choosing the IDS manufacturer and testing the system. According to the results produced at these stages, the list of criteria can be amended or even changed. At this stage, after obtaining information from the manufacturers and carefully testing the intrusion detection system, it is necessary to determine the financial parameters related to each of the tested systems, including the Total Cost of Ownership (TCO), the Return on Investment (ROI), etc. In the long run, this information will enable you to make your final choice and start implementing the pilot project.

Choosing the Manufacturer

After composing the list of requirements to the intrusion detection system, it is necessary to start searching for a manufacturer whose solutions can satisfy the requirements on your list. Taking into account the fact that this market is constantly growing and that new leaders are constantly appearing, I won't provide a list of manufacturers and their solutions. Instead, I recommend that you visit the following site: http://www.networkintrusion.co.uk/, where you can find a regularly updated list of intrusion detection systems, security scanners, deception systems, and integrity control tools. Another list of popular intrusion detection tools can be found at: http://www-rnks.informatik.tu-cottbus.de/~sobirey/ids.html.

After composing your list of potential manufacturers, it is necessary to send them Requests for Information (RFIs), in which it is necessary to provide an informal description of your requirements to the intrusion detection system. This document will be your first attempt to interact with the manufacturer, and from it the manufacturer (or vendor) will get information about your needs. If you have not completely formulated your requirements for the intrusion detection infrastructure, the manufacturer's response describing its solution will help you to add to your list of requirements or elaborate on some of them.

Despite the fact that according to Table 8.1, this step requires approximately one month, it does not mean that during this month you or your employees need to dedicate all business time to that task. This interval simply takes into account the moment that you send the RFIs and the time it takes to receive replies from the manufacturers interested in selling their solutions to you.

Testing

At the testing stage, which will be covered in detail in *Chapter 9*, you have to check the correspondence of the parameters and functions that the manufacturer claims to the ones that actually exist. Sometimes, after careful testing, you might change your opinion and begin examining another IDS.

In the course of testing, you might want to contact other companies that have already purchased the solution that you are currently testing. This will help you to detect problems that other customers encounter before they happen to you. Information on other customers can be obtained from the manufacturer. Note that if the manufacturer truly provides a valuable solution, there is no need to conceal information about other customers (if, of course, there are no agreements concerning privacy and confidentiality between them). In any case, practically all manufacturers publish so-called Case Study information on their websites, from which you can get information about successful projects.

The testing is finished when you send a Request for Proposal (RFP) to the chosen manufacturer. This document must contain more detailed requirements of the intrusion detection system. When answering this request, the manufacturer can elaborate on its answers to specific questions and provide more detailed data concerning the requirements satisfied by its system. The main difference between RFI and RFP lies in focusing on specific requirements.

Pilot Project

The placement of the IDS components can not start before the actual purchase of the intrusion detection system. However, it is possible to start the pilot project at this early stage. Why might you need to do this? Testing will show you whether the system implements (or does not implement) some of the declared properties and features. However, only a pilot project can show you how the system performs in your working environment. Since it is impossible to bring the system into operation simultaneously on all segments of your corporate network, it would make sense to choose a relatively small segment (usually a typical one) and place, set up, and start working with the chosen system within that segment.

Placement

This stage starts immediately after you have finished the pilot project (or when this project is very close to completion), and signals the fact that the chosen system suits your needs, and that you can start deploying it on all segments of the corporate network. This process will be covered in detail in *Chapter 10*.

Operation and Maintenance

After placing all the sensors and scanners within the corporate network, the continuous process of IDS infrastructure operation and maintenance starts, which will be covered in detail in *Chapter 11*. Various aspects of responding to detected attacks will be covered in *Chapter 14*.

Justifying Your Purchase

Let us suppose that you have chosen an IDS that satisfies all your requirements. After making your choice, you need to purchase the chosen system. At this step, you might encounter some misunderstandings with top management (the board of directors), who often underestimate the need for investing into intrusion detection system. In 1999, two companies — ICSA and SAIC — polled 745 respondents with a single question: "What is the greatest obstacle that prevents you from ensuring information security?" The most common answers and their frequency are outlined in Table 8.2.

Table 8.2. Most Common Reasons Preventing Companies from Deploying Intrusion Detection Systems (According to the Results of a Poll Conducted by ICSA/SAIC)

Obstacle	Number of organizations (%)
Budget limitations	29
Lack of managerial support	14
Lack of qualified security specialists, low qualification of end users	10
Low qualification of security personnel	9
Lack of correspondence to the internal security policy	8
Lack of authority	8
Technical complexity	6
Incomprehensible liabilities	4
Lack of reliable security tools	3
Other	9

The results of a similar poll conducted in 1999 by Information Week among 2700 respondents in 49 countries produced the results shown in Table 8.3.

Table 8.3. Typical Reasons Preventing Organizations from Deploying Intrusion Detection Systems (According to the Results of a Poll Conducted by Information Week)

Obstacle	Number of organizations (%)
Lack of time	17
Technological difficulties	16
Rate of technological evolution	11
Lack of support by top management	11
Poorly designed security policy	10
Financial expenses	8
Lack of cooperation between departments	8
Lack of knowledgeable end users	8
Low qualification of security personnel	6
Time expense and lack of human resources	5

From the results of these two polls, it is evident that lack of support by top management is one of the reasons that prevent organizations from deploying intrusion detection systems. Consequently, the better you can justify the necessity of investments into the intrusion detection infrastructure, the higher is the probability of the project's success. Thus, if you can compose a well-grounded budget for IDS deployment and implementation, and find proper arguments in support of your project when facing top management, you'll have a good chance of building a really efficient and reliable security system. Remember that upper-level managers of the company, such as the General Manager, the Chief Financial Officer, the Chairman of the Board of Directors, etc., are not usually technical experts, and can not quite understand all the technical details of intrusion detection technologies. The fact that some of them might seem to support your ideas of ensuring information security does not necessarily mean that they will continue supporting the idea of IDS deployment when it comes to their attention how much it will cost. Besides this, some of those in top management may have heard about the existence of freeware intrusion detection products. If this is the case, be prepared to answer the question, which is a quite logical and reasonable one from any financier's point of view: "Why should we invest money if we can use free solutions?" Thus, it is very important to carefully plan the budget for organizing the security infrastructure and provide a well-grounded basis for each item in the budget. If you speak IT language only, your managers will not understand you, and will not be able to understand your ideas without prejudice (of course, this only applies if they are not technical persons that come from the same technical environment as you). Try to explain the situation using financial language rather than technical, and they will understand you much better. Furthermore, if you succeed in preparing a good budget and carefully finding good reasons for the need to invest into the intrusion detection infrastructure, you will notice that the directors will value you, and provide your project with the required financial resources without discussing the technical details. Certainly, this is only possible if you manage to clearly explain all advantages that the company will get from IDS deployment and implementation, methods of controlling the investments, and evaluating its efficiency.

What is the goal of any company? Clearly, it is not purchasing and installing the most advanced and most expensive intrusion detection system. For most commercial companies and other organizations, the main goal is obtaining revenue, and naturally, all efforts are concentrated on achieving this aim. Information technologies (IDS infrastructure being one of its components) also aim at increasing the company's profit (which, roughly speaking, is the difference between the company's income and expenses). Thus, the company achieves its goal either by increasing its income or by decreasing expenses. An ideal situation is one where you can combine both approaches. However, this is not always possible. As a rule, expenses grow with the increase of income. Thus, the company will suffer financial losses from bringing a technology into operation only if the income from that technology does not exceed the expenses for deployment, operation, and maintenance of that specific system. You will thus have to calculate and evaluate the potential advantages and incomes expected from the deployment of the intrusion detection infrastructure, and compare them to the expenses required for these operations. The first task can be solved using the ROI (Return on Investment) mechanism, while the second one can be done using the TCO (Total Cost of Ownership) mechanism. However, you should note that even if calculating the TCO is not such a difficult task, it is rather problematic (if even possible) to calculate the efficiency of bringing IT technologies into operation, since intrusion detection systems do not directly participate in generating income. Furthermore, the task of comparing system states before and after deployment of the intrusion detection infrastructure is also rather difficult.

Total Cost of Ownership

The Total Cost of Ownership determines the planned and unforeseen costs related to ownership and usage of a specific system for its whole life cycle. Obviously, besides the direct expenses for an intrusion detection system, there are indirect expenses that appear during its operation. For example, according to the data of the Gartner Group, direct expenses make up only 15 to 21% of the total expenses of purchasing and operating an information system.

Total Cost of Ownership can be divided into direct and indirect expenses. Direct expenses include the following:

❑ Capital outlays for IDS hardware and software.

❑ Cost of additional software (DBMS, Internet browser, hardware setup and configuration tools, backup solutions, etc.) and required equipment (network cables, T-connectors, cable, etc.). This topic will be covered in more detail in *Chapter 11*.

❑ Cost of maintenance and training of personnel (if these expenses are not included into the cost of software and equipment). In addition, maintenance and training costs also include travelling expenses for visiting remote offices and setting up remote components of the intrusion detection system. According to Gartner Group data, this item can make up from 17 to 27% of the total cost.

❑ Expenses for IDS management, which include the salaries of the security administrator and other technical personnel that support and maintain the intrusion detection system. Besides which, this item of expenses can include the costs of outsourcing services and responses to attacks. As a rule, this item of expenses takes up about 9 to 13% of the TCO.

❑ Expenses required to bring the system into operation (including preliminary investigation and composing the network map). This item usually takes up about 20% of the TCO.

Indirect expenses might include the following:

❑ Losses incurred by inefficient work, when users start working with the system without proper knowledge and understanding of its working principles. This might result in possible malfunctions, loss of time, etc.

❑ Losses caused by the downtime of the intrusion detection system.

Thus, a choice in favor of a freeware intrusion detection system, which at first glance might seem logical and advantageous, is not necessarily the best solution. If you choose this approach, expenses for bringing such a system into operation, along with the maintenance and support expenses, can significantly exceed similar expenses for a commercial product (which at first might seem rather expensive).

The most important aspects that must be taken into consideration when calculating the Total Cost of Ownership of the intrusion detection system are listed below:

❑ The cost of the computer selected for installing the management console and control server (in three-tier architecture).

❏ The cost of the computer selected for installing the IDS sensor (if the sensor is not supplied as a separate security appliance or is not integrated with network equipment).

❏ Network equipment required for controlling network traffic (splitter, hub, and workload balancer). More detailed information on this topic will be provided in *Chapter 10*.

❏ Costs of add-on software and hardware, which will be covered in detail in *Chapter 11*.

❏ Purchasing additional hard disks for storing large amounts of data from system sensors.

❏ The decrease in the performance of controlled hosts and networks, and consequently, reduced incomes obtained as a result of the operation of the controlled hosts.

❏ The salary of the IDS operators, including expenses for supporting a 7×24 mode of operation.

❏ The salary of the personnel responsible for administering the intrusion detection system, incident response, and investigation.

❏ Expenses for development and implementation of the incident response plan.

❏ Expenses for recovery of the intrusion detection system in case it becomes an attack target.

❏ The cost of downtime caused by malfunctions of the IDS's components.

When composing a yearly budget, do not forget about depreciation, which, in the IT area, includes the obsolescence of computers and network equipment, as well as that of the software used. Now, practically everyone understands that since information technologies seem to evolve exponentially, both hardware and software become obsolete very soon. Remember that it was not so long ago when 20 MB hard disks were an unattainable dream of many users (and compare this situation to the current one, when it is hard to find a hard disk of a size less than 20 GB). The situation is similar with intrusion detection systems. Hardware appliances become obsolete and can not handle an increased amount of data within half a year after its implementation! Let's consider this situation using a practical example. Suppose that your network sensor started to experience performance problems, and in order to improve the situation, you need to increase the RAM installed on the sensor. Once again, you will need to justify the necessity of these additional expenses to someone who does not understand technical problems. In this case, it is the most likely that you will get a standard answer: "According to the norms and standards, the life cycle of the RAM module is 3 years. Your sensor was purchased only 6 months ago. Come back in two-and-a-half years." You will probably have quite a tough time advocating your point of view. And even if you do actually accomplish the impossible and prove to a person far removed from information technology that the addition is necessary, he or she still might not be able to help you, since the money for updating the sensor was not foreseen in the budget. On the other hand, if you correctly formulated the budget and included a special item of expenses for hardware or software upgrades, the situation might seem a little brighter.

Furthermore, the analysis and calculation of the TCO often helps you understand whether or not you will be able to operate an IDS efficiently relying just on your internal resources. If it seems that you will be able to, you should consider purchasing an outsourcing service. In other words, calculating the TCO allows you to justify the necessity of purchasing technical support or outsourcing services.

Return on Investment

Currently, it is common practice to measure the success of a specific project in terms of Return on Investment (ROI). ROI is the ratio of money earned to the sum invested into a specific area of activity, expressed as a percentage. This concept is easily understandable. However, behind this simplicity, there is quite a complicated procedure for calculating the ROI, which can not always be formalized. The calculation formula includes a large number of parameters, including ones directly related to the intrusion detection infrastructure, as well as the general financial parameters of your company. Thus, it is very important to know the total value of the corporate resources and revenues yielded by specific sectors of the company's business activity. When you lack this information, calculating the ROI gets much more complicated, or even becomes impossible. It is not always possible to calculate the ROI even if you do know all these parameters. An example of a situation in which you will have difficulty evaluating the ROI is when one specific technology or system yields indirect advantages that are hard to evaluate numerically. For example, if you migrate from the Snort intrusion detection system (which does not provide a graphical user interface and is hard to manage and maintain in a large distributed network) to another product, such as RealSecure or Cisco IDS, the advantages are obvious, but difficult to express in numbers. How can you calculate the cost of ease of use and administrator convenience? However, even in such a case, you must understand the advantages that the company will see after migrating to the new technology, starting from ease of use, convenience, and reduction of the response time, all the way up to a decrease in system maintenance and personnel training costs.

We can provide the following simplified model for evaluating the damage related to not using an IDS. The formula provided below calculates the total sum of the financial loss for a single host (for example, a web server). However, this formula can easily be rewritten for calculating the financial losses incurred by an attack on the whole corporate network. When calculating the total losses incurred by an attack on the whole network, all parameters will become global and will relate to all corporate resources.

The initial data will be provided below.

❏ Downtime caused by the attack, t_D (in hours)
❏ Time required to repair a system damaged by the attack, t_R (in hours)
❏ Time required to re-enter lost information, t_{RI} (in hours)
❏ The salary of the technical maintenance personnel (administrators, technicians, etc.), S_M
❏ The salary of employees maintaining the attacked host or segment, S_E
❏ Number of maintenance personnel administrators, technicians, etc., N_M
❏ Number of employees maintaining the attacked host or segment, N_E
❏ Sales made by the attacked host or segment, $SALES$ ($ per year)
❏ Cost of replacing equipment or spare parts, C_{SP}
❏ Number of attacked hosts or segments, I
❏ Number of attacks per year, n

The total sum of losses caused by the lost productivity of the employees of the attacked host is equal to:

$$C_L = \frac{\sum\limits_{N_E} S_E}{192} t_D$$

The cost of restoring the attacked host or network segment comprises several components:

$$C_R = C_{RI} + C_{RH} + C_{SP},$$

where C_{RI} is the cost of re-entering the lost information, and C_{RH} is the cost of restoring the host (OS installation and configuration, etc.).

These are calculated using the following formulas:

$$C_{RI} = \frac{\sum\limits_{N_E} S_E}{192} t_{RI}$$

$$C_{RH} = \frac{\sum\limits_{N_E} S_M}{192} t_R$$

The profit loss caused by downtime of the attacked host or segment is:

$$U = C_L + C_R + V$$

where

$$V = \frac{SALES}{52 \cdot 5 \cdot 8}(t_D + t_R + t_{RI})$$

Thus, the total damage caused by an attack on the host or segment of the corporate network is equal to:

$$L = \sum_{year} \sum_{1} U$$

Let's give an example that illustrates the procedure of assessing the damage caused by an attack on a protected object based on the following initial data.

- ❑ Downtime caused by the attack t_D (in hours) = 2 hours
- ❑ Time required to repair the damaged system after an attack, t_R (in hours) = 8 hours
- ❑ Time required to re-enter the lost data, t_{RI} (hours) = 8 hours
- ❑ The salary of the technical maintenance personnel (administrators, technicians, etc.), S_M ($ per month) = $5,000 [SANS2-00]
- ❑ The salary of the employees of the attacked host or segment, S_E ($ per month) = = $6,000
- ❑ Number of maintenance personnel (administrators, technicians, etc.), $N_M = 1$
- ❑ Number of employees of the attacked host or segment, $N_E = 4$
- ❑ Sales made by the attacked host or segment, $SALES$ ($ per year) = $1,000,000
- ❑ Cost of replacing the equipment or spare parts $C_{SP} = 0
- ❑ Number of attacked hosts or segments, $i = 1$
- ❑ Number of attacks per year, $n = 5$

The salary of an employee per hour will be 6,000 / 192 = 31.25, while the salary of the support personnel per hour will be 5,000/192 = 26.042. The cost of the lost productivity of the employees of the attacked host or segment will be $C_L = 4 \times 31.25 \times 2 = 250, while the cost of re-entering the lost information and restoring the damaged host will be $C_{RH} = 0$ and $C_{RI} = 1 \times 26.042 \times 8 = 208.34, respectively. Since the equipment was not replaced ($C_{SP} = 0$), the cost of restoring a host damaged by the attack will be $C_R = \$208.34$. $V = 1{,}000{,}000/2080 \times (2 + 8 + 0) = \$4{,}807.70$ and the total lost profit will be equal to $U = 250 + 208.336 + 4807/7 = \$5{,}266$. As a result, the total damage caused by 5 attacks on a segment per year totals $L = 5{,}226 \times 5 = \$26{,}330$, which justifies the purchase of an intrusion detection system for this amount.

As you can see, this formula does not take into account some probability parameters that increase or decrease the risk of losses, including the following:

❒ Labor turnover, which results in a lack of qualified personnel and an increase in expenses for training new employees.

❒ Internet access, which results in an increased number of possible attacks. Notice that the use of other security tools in combination with an intrusion detection system decreases this number.

❒ The availability of dedicated employees responsible for intrusion detection and response.

Sales made by the attacked host is not a single parameter that can be used in this formula. We can also take into account, for example, the amount of lost profit resulting from downtime and malfunctions, or what the company will have to pay because of the failure to carry out its responsibilities resulting from the failure of the attacked resource.

Such parameters as expenses for criminal prosecution due to a leakage of confidential information, lost productivity, loss of customer confidence (or what is worse, customer migration to the company's competitors), damage to the company's reputation, etc., are very hard to calculate. However, they also must be taken into account in this formula. Taking these parameters into account increases the total of the potential financial losses caused by lack of an intrusion detection infrastructure.

Finally, there are several other aspects that result from the deployment of an intrusion detection system, and their assessment will also help you to assure the management as to the necessity of investments.

First, IDS deployment and implementation (or migration to a newer IDS version) releases security administrators from having to perform a large amount of manual operations (beginning with the manual analysis of log files and network traffic, and ending with the updating of the signature database and remote host scanning according to schedule). As a result, administrators will work more efficiently, which can be expressed in the following financial formula:

$$P = \sum_{n} (t_M - t_A) \times S,$$

where P is the productivity of n administrators, t_M and t_A is the time required to perform intrusion detection operations in manual and automatic modes, respectively, and S is the salary of the security administrators.

Second, the automation of intrusion detection operations results in a decrease in the number of specialists who must participate in this process. Furthermore, tasks that earlier could only be delegated to qualified experts can now be performed by operators.

$$E_A = \sum_n \left(N_{before} - N_{after} \right) - S_A,$$

where E_A is the efficiency of n administrators, N_{before} and N_{after} are the number of administrators before and after deployment of the IDS, and S_A is the salary of security administrators.

By adding up the parameters listed above and subtracting the TCO from the result, you will get the effect of deploying the IDS, which must be more than 1. If the result is less than 1, using an intrusion detection system will not solve your problems, will not produce any effect, and will only complicate the current situation with corporate network security.

Bringing the IDS into Operation

So, you have finally managed to prove the necessity of deploying an intrusion detection system, succeeded in convincing management to purchase one, and started to deploy the intrusion detection infrastructure in your company. However, it is most likely that as soon as you begin implementing your plans, you will encounter quite a few difficulties and problems whose existence you did not even suspect. The more sophisticated your project, the more problems you will have to solve. It is commonly thought that intrusion detection systems are much easier to deploy and bring into operation than ERP or CRM systems. This is not the case, however. Creating a viable intrusion detection infrastructure according to the principles discussed in previous chapters is a rather difficult task, and you must consider and approach it seriously.

The well-known Lerman's Law of Technology states that "Any techical problem can be overcome given enough time and money." Lerman's Corollary goes on to say: "You are never given enough time or money." It is practically impossible to do anything quickly, cheaply, and well. Achieving the ideal simultaneously in all three areas is impossible. In most cases, even the goal of attaining the ideal of two of parameters can only rarely be achieved. Thus, the best approach is to choose a single criterion to take priority in your work (Fig. 8.2).

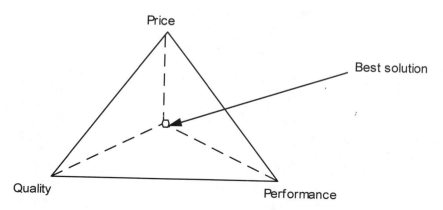

Fig. 8.2. The criteria to be used during deployment and implementation

Thus, when deploying an IDS infrastructure and bringing it into operation, it is necessary to adopt some well-known approaches and principles used to deploy other complex systems. In particular, you must do the following:

❑ Create a workgroup responsible for deployment. This group must include employees from the IT department, security specialists from the IS department, and representatives from management. The best approach is one that includes someone from top management into this team, since his or her authority will be very helpful when solving many of the organizational problems that will inevitably arise in the course of deployment.

❑ Carefully consider the possibility of inviting consultants or requesting services from third-party companies. Do not be too self-confident, and try to be objective when deciding whether you are able to implement the whole project on your own. If you fail to deploy and bring into operation an expensive system, this will be much worse and will cost your company much more than it would have cost to invite external consultants to help. It is impossible to be an expert in all areas, and because of this, using third-party services will likely play a positive role.

❑ Do not forget to test the deployed system. This will help you avoid a situation in which the system seems to operate properly, but in practice does not solve even one tenth of the problems it is supposed to.

CHAPTER 9

Selecting an Intrusion Detection System

*One should recruit one's army, reflecting that
"such is the army of my enemy; and this
is my army to oppose it."*

Kautilya, "Arthashastra."

In previous chapters, we discussed various aspects related to intrusion detection technology. This was pure theory. Now it is time to apply this knowledge choosing the proper technology to allow you to efficiently detect and stop various attacks. In this chapter, I'll describe the criteria for evaluating intrusion detection systems, and consider what questions you need to ask an IDS vendor when purchasing such a system. Then, we will discuss techniques of testing the purchased system [Edwards1-97].

Promotional materials for systems usually specify the attacks that they can register. However, these materials rarely provide information on the resources (time, financial, and human) required to make the system run smoothly and efficiently perform the declared functions. It is important to formulate these questions before you purchase the system. Otherwise, you could end up with a system that is able to perform its function and that does offer all of the capabilities it claims — just not in your network environment.

Real-World Example

Here is a case from my own experience. One of the top managers of a large organization had heard about a well-known intrusion detection system. He ordered that this system be purchased, only to discover after this was done that his IS specialists found the system useless for their particular organization! The sales representative for the product had stated at a seminar that the system detects TCP/IP attacks, including those ones directed at Novell NetWare networks. However, in the organization's network, the IPX/SPX stack, and not TCP/IP, was used as the primary protocol stack, rendering many of the system's features useless.

Only testing and qualified assistance from specialized companies will allow you to determine if a particular system actually meets your requirements for an intrusion detection system. Such questions include the time required to put the system into operation, Total Cost of Ownership (TCO), system performance, etc.

The first problem that you need to solve before installing an intrusion detection system is determining where it must be installed and what tasks it will perform. Without clear answers to these questions, even the most advanced and efficient tool is practically useless. Having determined this, you will have a clear understanding of which technology is preferable in your particular case — intrusion detection at the network, OS, DBMS, or application level. You will probably find an area of use for each of these technologies in different segments of your corporate network. However, before purchasing an intrusion detection system, you must get a solid understanding of *What* you are going to protect, *From Whom,* and *How.*

Regardless of the chosen intrusion detection system, you will need to consider the following aspects, most of which should already be described in the network map:

- Protected resources
- The most likely attacks
- Objects (protocols, addresses, ports, files, etc.) accessible from outside
- Subjects (users, applications, etc.) using the protected resource
- Availability and performance parameters for the protected resource
- Who will manage the intrusion detection system and how
- Scales of potential growth for the protected resource and, consequently, the scalability potential of the chosen intrusion detection system

This will enable you to quickly and correctly install and configure the intrusion detection system you purchase.

Preliminary Analysis
What Needs Protection?

Before purchasing expensive intrusion detection tools, you should determine which resources need protection. After performing such an analysis, you will probably realize that it does not make any sense to spend money on a system that you like but that offers functions you can handle easily enough using organizational measures and built-in security mechanisms. Each organization has its own specific resources that need protecting. However, you can generally divide these resources into the following categories:

- ❏ File servers
- ❏ Database servers
- ❏ Telecommunication servers
- ❏ Routers
- ❏ Firewalls and other perimeter protection tools
- ❏ Web, FTP, and mail servers
- ❏ Workstations that process critically important information (for example, in banking systems)

Even a simple listing of critically important resources is very helpful when you need to choose the right technology for intrusion detection for their optimal protection. For example, when it comes to securing file servers, integrity control tools are of primary importance, since they allow you to trace unauthorized file changes. For routers, network-level intrusion detection systems are of the highest priority. Table 9.1 lists the most common categories of important resources, along with the corresponding optimal intrusion detection technologies to be used to protect them.

Table 9.1. The Most Common Intrusion Detection Technologies and Their Areas of Application

Resources	Intrusion detection technologies
File servers	Integrity control systems
	OS-level intrusion detection systems
Database servers	DBMS-level intrusion detection systems
	OS-level intrusion detection systems
	DBMS-level security scanners

continues

Table 9.1 Continued

Resources	Intrusion detection technologies
Telecommunication servers	Network-level intrusion detection systems
	OS-level intrusion detection systems
	Network-level security scanners
Routers	Network-level intrusion detection systems
Firewalls and other perimeter protection tools	Network-level intrusion detection systems
	OS-level intrusion detection systems
	Network-level security scanners
	OS-level security scanners
Web, FTP, and mail servers	Application-level intrusion detection systems
	Network-level intrusion detection systems
	OS-level intrusion detection systems
	Integrity control systems
	Network-level security scanners
	OS-level security scanners
Workstations	OS-level intrusion detection systems

Protection against What?

Simply put, from attacks and misuse. However, as we showed in *Chapter 2*, there are too many types of unauthorized actions. Purchasing a system that offers protection against all types of attack is not very reasonable — even if such systems existed. Because of this, you need first and foremost analyze the attacks most likely to be directed at your resources. For example, suppose that you need to secure an application server running Windows NT/2000. In this case, you delegate the detection of network intrusions to a network-level intrusion detection system installed in the same network segment. This immediately narrows the range of possible attacks on your server. Thus, you need to select an OS-level intrusion detection system that analyzes log files or user activities. You must make sure, in this case, that the system you choose supports Windows NT-based systems. By performing this type of brief assessment, you will be able to reduce the number of possible systems to two or three products, thus simplifying the selection process and reducing expenses that you would otherwise incur by purchasing a system that performs functions or supports operating systems that are not applicable in your environment.

Protection against Whom?

Ask a layman this question, and the most common answer will be "hackers." Without delving into terminological details, the vast majority are of the opinion that the main threat to system security comes in the form of external intruders, who penetrate the computer networks of banks or military organizations, intercept control of satellites, etc. This somewhat paranoiac attitude is generated by the mass media, which has recently published a large number of reports about hackers and the threats associated with them. There is no question that this danger is real, so it should not be underestimated. However, it must not be overestimated either. Let us consider the statistical data that were provided in *Chapter 2*. These figures show that 70–80% of all registered cases of computer crime are internal security policy violations, meaning that they involve current or former company employees.

If someone on the outside has managed to find a security breach in the information system of some company or organization, they can penetrate the corporate network via this security hole and access financial data or information on the company's development plans. Generally, such intruders do not know what to do next, due to the fact that they are not professionals in the company's field of activities or research area. Thus, it is simply impossible to make any use of these megabytes and gigabytes of information. An intruder exploiting access vulnerabilities often just gets confused, not knowing what information is of real value and what is useless garbage.

The situation is different for a company's employees, who understand the situation and are able to assess the value of specific information realistically. Often, these are employees who have been granted privileges that are not necessary for them to do their jobs.

"Why would my employees want to steal from me?" is a question that arises for many managers in this situation, and the answers to the question can vary. The most common causes arise from disappointment with their position or salary, hidden dissatisfaction, envy, etc. Employees who feel that they are under-appreciated or underpaid have committed computer crimes resulting in tremendous losses for their companies. One example is an internal intruder involved in the well-known case of an attack on the Citibank network. Such cases, however, are often ignored in published reports of the incident, or are considered to be unimportant. Another common scenario involves an employee who is fired from a company and develops a plan to get revenge. If the employee had significant access rights and privileges, he or she is able to inflict significant damage on the company after leaving. If the employee's user account is not deleted, he or she will be able to access company resources for his or her own purposes. In the least harmful cases, the employee will use the company's resources without carrying out any destructive actions. For example, dismissed employees using company accounts to access the Internet are a common occurrence. This is generally the result of the administrator neglecting to change the password for the account used by the employee to perform his or her duties. Often, no one even notices that the former employee is continuing to use the company's Internet account, which is simply a minor financial loss for the firm. In one case, however, the company went bankrupt and could not pay the bills from its ISP. The ISP began to investigate the traffic and thus detected the security policy violation.

The most dangerous departed employees are those who were granted administrative privileges while still working for the company and had access to a wide range of information. Generally, these are technical personnel that worked in the IT or network communications departments. These people usually know all of the passwords to the systems used within the organization. If these people decide to use their knowledge and technical skills for negative purposes, the company can experience some very serious problems. These intruders are very knowledgeable and skilled, and therefore hard to detect. Because of the factors listed above, when designing your security infrastructure, it is necessary to consider protection against both internal and external intruders. You should always keep in mind that traditional security mechanisms (such as firewalls or authentication servers) are oriented toward the detection of external, not internal, intruders.

The answer to this question will enable you to determine appropriate priorities in detecting external and internal attacks. By the way, the answer to the question formulated at the beginning of this chapter as to the tasks to be solved will also enable you to determine the most important direction in which to apply your efforts. For example, if the your company's main activity is e-commerce (such as Internet shopping), you should concentrate on external attacks.

How to Protect?

Although this question appears to be simple, it is much harder to answer than it seems. You can, if you like, simply rely on the claims made by developers of security systems and just purchase a system, install it, and then go on working without giving the subject any more thought. If you feel your company can afford it, then why not? However, the proper usage of the tools at hand is just as important as your choice of tools in the first place. Worldwide organizations now deploy complex protection systems, which are organized in several stages. The first stage — information system investigation — is the most important. At this stage, it is necessary to figure out the most likely threats from which you need to protect the company. Here you should build a so-called "intruder model," which describes the characteristics of the most probable intruder, including skill level, tools utilized for implementing specific attacks, the typical time his or her activities will take, etc. From this profile, you can determine the answers to the questions posed earlier in this chapter: "Why do you need protection, and from whom?"

At this stage, you can also identify and analyze possible ways of implementing attacks, and evaluate the probability of these attacks and the potential damage that might be caused by them. Based on the results of this analysis, you will be able to develop recommendations for the elimination of detected threats, providing the opportunity to select and use the most effective protection tools. Before proceeding to the next stage, it makes more sense to use tools already at your disposal than to purchase expensive security systems. For example, if you have a powerful router as part of your network, it might make more sense to use its built-in security functions than to purchase a firewall.

Alongside analyzing existing technologies, you must also develop organizational documentation, which will provide a legal basis for security services and information security departments when performing a whole range of security and protection measures, including interacting and cooperating with external organizations in order to bring intruders to court. The result of the measures taken at this stage should be the development of your organization's security policy. Upper management must then approve this security policy, including aspects related to intrusion detection.

The next step in building a complex information security system is the purchase, installation, and customization of the security tools and mechanisms chosen during the previous stage. These include tools for protecting information against unauthorized access, cryptographic systems, firewalls, security scanners, and so on.

To ensure the correct and efficient use of the security tools that you install, your staff must be properly trained. To ensure this, you must train all employees working in your security service and information security departments, and make sure that they possess all of the practical skills required to detect and prevent security threats using the security tools you have purchased. Determining who will operate the intrusion detection system also narrows the range of available alternatives. If you can not assign an operator for tracking alerts in real-time mode, you should choose a system that allows you to perform an autonomous analysis.

However, even when this has been done, the process of ensuring your security is not yet over. Both hardware and software become outdated as new versions of security products appear, the list of known vulnerabilities and attacks is growing constantly, technologies used for information processing continue to evolve, and both software and hardware are becoming more and more advanced. At the same time, normal staff turnover means that some employees leave, and are replaced by new ones.

Because of this, it is necessary to revise your organizational documents on a regular basis. From time to time, it is necessary to investigate the information system and/or its subsystems to train new employees and to update security tools. By following the sequence of actions for building a complex information security system described above, you will be more able to ensure the necessary level of protection for your automated system.

What Tools Should Be Used for Protection?

The answers to the first four questions (what, from what, from whom, and how to protect) will enable us to narrow the range of available products that will meet our purposes. The appropriate options will generally consist of two or three systems, which will significantly simplify the process of making a decision, as well as speed up the testing process. Table 9.1 lists technologies that can be used to secure vital resources in the corporate network. Although you are free to choose any of these technologies, be aware that what appears to be the most obvious choice is not always the best. For example, suppose that you need to protect a file server. Here, an integrity control system would seem to be the most appropriate for your needs. However, imagine that stored files are changing every second. Any time such an event takes place, the integrity control system will check to determine whether the change is authorized. This will result in a significant degradation of the file server's performance. In the most extreme case, the integrity control system will end up consuming 100 percent of the server's resources, preventing users from accessing the server. In this event, it makes more sense to use an OS-level intrusion detection system, or to reduce the number of files whose integrity is to be checked by the integrity control system. Similar examples can be provided for other technologies.

Intrusion Detection System Customers

Let us consider typical groups of customers that require intrusion detection systems. This will help you in forming a list of criteria to use to make the right choice for yourself. Since each group has its own specific requirements for intrusion detection systems, which can differ significantly, this is an effective exercise. For example, if you are representing a small company with just a single Internet connection that is to be protected by the intrusion detection system, mechanisms based on the centralized management of remote sensors are of little or no value to you. For a large company, on the other hand, this system may be one of the most important.

We can classify IDS customers into the following categories.

❑ Small companies that have no remote affiliates or departments
❑ Mid-size and large companies whose affiliates and departments are geographically distributed all over the country

❏ Large international companies that are geographically distributed all over the world
❏ Internet providers
❏ Information security service providers (outsourcing companies)

It is also necessary to mention that in some countries, special requirements exist, which demand that security systems used in governmental, military, or other organizations be certified according to predefined rules. Quite often, this requirement is the key one, which has priority when choosing an intrusion detection system. Even the most efficient intrusion detection system can be rejected just because it fails to meet this requirement.

Small Companies

This category is the most typical among intrusion detection system customers. It includes small banks, IT firms, local governmental organizations, universities, etc. The distinguishing features of groups in this category are: a single point of connection to the Internet, a small number of hosts within a LAN, and the centralized management of all resources.

Large Companies with Remote Affiliates

Customers in this category usually have at least one remote affiliate located either in the same city as the headquarters or in another (Fig. 9.1). In this situation, the affiliate or department can manage its resources in-house, or resource management can be run centrally from headquarters. In some cases, remote affiliates located in isolated parts of the country might not have personnel qualified to carry out this task.

International Corporations

The conditions for international corporations are quite similar to those for large companies (Fig. 9.2), with the following two exceptions. First, the corporation might include several subsidiary bodies joined into a united whole. These subsidiary bodies may have quite different or even contradictory security requirements. Second, international corporations differ from large companies in that their offices are distributed all over the world. This, of course, significantly influences the intrusion detection infrastructure. For example, as was already mentioned, most intrusion detection systems provide cryptographic protection for interaction between sensors and the console. However, the use of encryption in different countries faces different restrictions, and must be in accordance with the various laws and regulations.

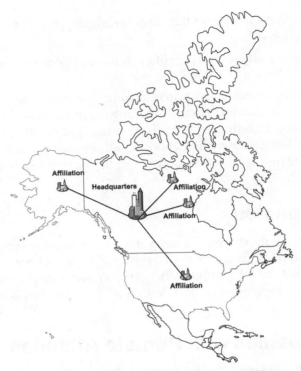

Fig. 9.1. A large company with remote affiliates

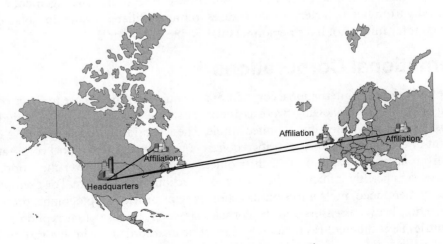

Fig. 9.2. An international corporation

Internet Service Providers

Internet Service Providers (ISPs), in contrast to the categories of companies above, operate mainly with the resources (including, of course, traffic) of their clients, rather than their own. This has a definite impact on the methods they must use when working with intrusion detection systems. Internet Service Providers, in contrast to end-users, handle a very large number of network connections and a very large number of users. Therefore, most current intrusion detection systems are not effective for them, since, as we already saw, network systems are oriented towards attacks targeting a single network segment or "listening" on several ports at switches and routers. ISPs normally have hundreds or even thousands of these switches. Beside this, the high speed of connection does not allow the provider to control all traffic. It does not make sense for ISPs to use a system that protects only some of its users and provides no protection for the remainder. Thus, an ISP will be forced either to purchase an intrusion detection system for each segment (switch), which is prohibitively expensive, or attempt to solve the problem of detecting intrusions and reacting to them using other methods. One such method is an IDS integrated into the network hardware (for example, RealSecure for Nokia or Cisco Catalyst 6500 IDS Module).

Service Providers

This option is a combination of an end user and an Internet Service Provider. Service Providers control the traffic of specific users, but at the same time, an outsourcer company centrally manages the IDS. End users rely on the outsourcing, since they require outside help when it comes to security mechanisms and technologies. Certainly, the help necessary depends on the degree of importance of the user's data and on the end user's sense of security. These services are becoming quite common. Most end users do not want to deal with the hassles caused by an intrusion detection system. It would be much easier for them to have such a system as part of a complex solution for ensuring network information security provided by an external organization and supported 24 hours a day, 7 days a week. A reliable intrusion detection system must be easy to use, and it must be designed in such a way that a technician can operate it. Currently, however, data analysis and developing responses still require a certain level of expertise. The lack of these protection skills prevents most organizations from ensuring security at a high technical level. Consequently, it is likely that more and more organizations will rely on outsourcing in the network security area. Various aspects of using services provided by outsourcing companies will be covered in greater detail later in this chapter.

Evaluation Criteria

In the following few sections, we will discuss various criteria that enable you to choose and evaluate the intrusion detection system that best meets your requirements [Jackson1-99]. I would like to note immediately that all requirements to the intrusion detection system can be classified into 3 groups — mandatory, desirable, and optional. Since there is no system that can satisfy all the requirements provided below, we recommend that you choose the one that meets mandatory requirements, regardless of the large number of optional requirements met. It is impossible to determine the necessity of satisfying specific criterion beforehand — your choice must depend on a wide range of conditions. As was shown earlier in this chapter, it also depends on the type of your company. The complete list of all evaluation criteria, along with their priorities for various users, will be provided in the end of this section. Certainly, this list is not indisputable truth, and can be changed according to your specific requirements.

All evaluation criteria can be classified into the following groups:

- ❏ Intrusion detection
- ❏ Responses to attacks
- ❏ Management
- ❏ Performance
- ❏ Self-protection
- ❏ Installation and configuration
- ❏ Additional capabilities
- ❏ Manufacturer/vendor

These groups form the basis for testing and evaluating intrusion detection systems.

The Point of Installation

The first criterion is the possible network location at which to install an intrusion detection system. As was mentioned in *Chapter 6*, there are two main locations for installing intrusion detection systems — on a network segment and on a specific host. Depending on the resource that needs protection (see Table 9.1), you should select either a network-level intrusion detection system or a host-level intrusion detection system operating at the OS, DBMS, or application level. For example, if you need to ensure file server security, integrity control systems must have priority. For application servers, systems for controlling log files are of primary importance. Note that in this case, the chosen system must control both system logs (EventLog or Syslog) and other log files. To secure web servers, you might choose two intrusion detection systems, based on the server location. For example, if your web server resides in a demilitarized zone along with other hosts (SMTP, FTP, and DNS servers), then the whole DMZ is controlled by a network-level intrusion detection system. At the same time, a specific web server can be controlled by the event log management system. If only one web server is installed in the DMZ, it makes sense to use an integrated solution, joining event log control and intrusion detection (such as RealSecure Server Sensor).

If it is necessary to protect both network and system resources, it would be best to choose an intrusion detection system that has both network and system components. The RealSecure Protection System family of products — which enables you to detect attacks at the network level (RealSecure Network Sensor), at the server level (RealSecure Server Sensor), and on workstations (RealSecure Desktop Protector) — is an example of such solution. Another representative of these types of products is a solution from Symantec, which supplies NetProwler network-level IDS and Intruder Alert (for controlling log files). Cisco Systems also provides solutions, including Cisco IDS and the Cisco IDS Host Sensor. However, at the moment of this writing, systems from the last two manufacturers could not be controlled from a single management console.

Information Sources and Methods of Analysis

Information sources (network traffic, log files, user activities, and so on), along with methods of analysis (misuse and anomaly detection), allow you to draw conclusions as to the existence of an active attack. They were covered in detail in *Chapter 4*.

Processing Time

The next important criterion influencing IDS selection is the time it takes for the system to actually processes data obtained from the specified sources of information.

Batch Processing

Security scanners, classical intrusion detection systems operating at levels higher than the network level, and integrity control systems operate according to this principle. When using batch-oriented (or interval-oriented) approaches, the auditing mechanisms of the OS, DBMS, and applications (or integrity control mechanisms) log information on each event in the appropriate log files, and the intrusion detection system periodically analyzes these logs to detect cases of misuse, anomalous activity, or checksum discrepancy. The advantages and drawbacks of tools working in batch mode are outlined in Table 9.2.

Table 9.2. Advantages and Drawbacks of Intrusion Detection Systems Operating in Batch Mode

Advantages	Drawbacks
Batch processing systems are suitable for networks where there is a relatively low risk of suffering from various attacks. Most frequently, users of such networks are interested in explaining problems rather than in an immediate response to suspicious events. Consequently, a batch-oriented analysis can be combined with another investigation process (such as identifying the attack source) in order to locate the individual responsible for the incident and start the appropriate inquiry process.	Users will rarely receive warnings and alerts on active attacks, since events are registered in the log files only after they actually occur. Thus there is practically no possibility of active incident registration in real-time mode for minimizing the damage caused by an attack.
Schemes of batch-oriented analysis result in a lower workload on the systems in comparison to a real-time analysis. This is especially true when the intervals are short and, consequently, the amounts of collected data are relatively small.	Information gathering in batch-oriented analysis requires quite a large amount of free disk space in the system performing analysis. This space is required to store the records of all events that take place during the interval between two starts of the batch processing system.
The batch-oriented approach to information gathering and analysis is preferable for organizations where human and system resources allocated for ensuring information security are limited. It is quite probable that organizations where there is no specially assigned employee(s) responsible for information security (or there is no way to have 24-hour monitoring) will find that real-time security alerts generated by intrusion detection systems are not really so necessary.	This method is inefficient when the auditing subsystem does not register all events (or some events are omitted in the course of logging).
Most contemporary methods related to gathering information on computer crime were developed based on the manual analysis of information gathered in batch mode.	

Working in Real-Time Mode

In this context, "real-time mode" means that the intrusion detection process is done relatively quickly, and the security administrator can manage to nip the attack in the bud. Systems operating in real-time mode provide a wider range of security warnings than systems operating in batch mode. Besides this, they give you the ability to foresee variants of automatic responses to detected attacks. Typical responses vary widely — from an ordinary security notification, to the termination of the connection to the attack source, or reconfiguring network equipment aimed at preventing any attempts at repeated attacks from a specific address. All systems of this type have their strong and weak points (Table 9.3).

Table 9.3. Advantages and Drawbacks of Intrusion Detection Systems Operating in Real-Time Mode

Advantages	Drawbacks
Depending on the analysis rate, attacks can be detected rather quickly, which enables the security personnel to stop them just in time. Quite often, attacks are detected before they achieve their goals.	Such systems require specially assigned security personnel to constantly monitor the messages generated by the IDS.
Intrusion detection systems of this type provide quite a wide range of possible variants of responses to detected attacks.	

Architecture

As I mentioned in *Chapter 6*, all existing intrusion detection systems — both network- and host-level — are based on the "agent-manager" scheme. Configurations in which both console and sensor run on the same computer are quite rare. This is characteristic of outdated and obsolete intrusion detection systems, such as SessionWall-3, or freeware systems such as Snort. A distributed architecture in the intrusion detection system provides for good scalability in the corporate network, including the installation of sensors in remote affiliates and offices. However, it would be a mistake to think that you should always choose distributed systems. In small businesses, for example, you can do just fine with an autonomous agent, and a distributed architecture is not required.

Supported Platforms

This evaluation criterion does not need detailed consideration, since the requirement of supporting the hardware and software platforms, network protocols, etc. that have been adopted in your organization is obvious.

Intrusion Detection

This group includes the following criteria:

- ❏ Number of detected attacks
- ❏ Updates to attack signatures
- ❏ Capabilities of creating custom attack signatures
- ❏ Monitoring additional events
- ❏ Notifications on false negatives
- ❏ Processing fragmented traffic
- ❏ Reference material on each attack
- ❏ Extended capabilities of customizing attack signatures

The Number of Attacks That Can Be Detected

It is strongly recommended that you never use the number of attacks that can be detected as the main factor when choosing an intrusion detection system. This parameter is much too subjective. To illustrate this statement, let us consider the following situation. Suppose that we have a computer that is vulnerable to infection by viruses and we must choose between two antiviral tools — Kaspersky Antivirus and AntiDIR. The first system detects about forty thousands viruses (as of the time of writing). However, it is not freeware. The second program is free, but is only able to detect one virus — DIR. The choice might seem obvious — Kaspersky Antivirus. However, things are not that simple in practice. For example, if you can determine for sure that the protected computer can only be infected with a DIR virus, then there is no reason to opt for Kaspersky Antivirus. In this case, AntiDIR is obviously preferable. First of all, it is freeware. Second, it works faster when detecting and eliminating the DIR virus, since it is optimized specifically for this purpose. Despite the fact that Kaspersky Antivirus finds and eliminates thousands of other viruses along with DIR, here its capabilities are pointless. A similar analysis can also be done for intrusion detection systems. If your network is based on the Windows platform and you have no hosts running other operating systems, you do not need an IDS that is capable of detecting attacks on UNIX hosts. These functional capabilities are redundant, and will probably never be used. Because of this, you should not rely on the number of attacks that can be detected as the only criterion when choosing an intrusion detection system. You should also note that IDS manufacturers use different approaches to evaluating the number of attacks that can be detected. Without naming specific vendors, I would like to provide one illustrative example. Three years ago, 25 NIS checks in one of the security scanners available on the market at that time were equivalent to a single check implemented in another scanner. Currently, with the appearance of the CVE database, the situation has improved, but you should still bear this fact in mind.

Signature Updating

Since attacks, just as vulnerabilities, are being constantly updated, it is important to update the intrusion detection database in order to detect attacks efficiently. This is just as important as updating antiviral software or installing patches, hotfixes, and Service Packs for operating systems. The same applies to the intrusion detection system. Only when regular and timely updates are performed will the system be able to provide the desired level of network security. Ideally, there should be no delay between the publishing of information on a particular attack by the various hacking information sources available and the inclusion of this signature into the attack database. Better yet, if the developers update their system before information on new vulnerabilities becomes common knowledge, they can stay one step ahead of the intruders. In practice, however, this does not always work so smoothly and seamlessly. It is the task of the manufacturer (or vendor) and user of the intrusion detection system to make this interval as small as possible. By the way, I would like to say that you should not rely completely on the vendor's ads and statements like "the system is able of detecting new and unknown attacks." Remember that system developers (who probably would be glad to provide you with honest and unbiased information on their product) are not the ones who are actually selling the IDS. On the contrary, this job is delegated to sales representatives, whose task is to sell as much as they can.

Despite the fact that the number of vulnerabilities or attacks detected by the intrusion detection system ca not serve as a criterion, all aspects related to the updating of the vulnerability database are extremely important, and directly influence the IDS's efficiency. It would seem that once a mechanism for adding custom attack signatures has been put in place, updating and correcting the IDS database are less important. However, as statistics show (for example, those published on the WhiteHats server, http://whitehats.com), this is not the case. As it turns out, over 52.31% of IDS users do not know how to create custom signatures. Another 34.23% of the user community does not even know that there are ready-to-use attack and vulnerability signature databases available for download from the Internet as freeware. Thus, over 86.54% of users do not create customized rules, even when their intrusion detection system provides such a mechanism.

Frequency of Updates

The first parameter that should be taken into account when evaluating the signature updating subsystem is the frequency of updates. The more frequent is the updating process (no less than once per month), the more secure are your resources, and the higher is the probability of your system being able to thwart new attacks invented by intruders.

Update Method

The method used to update your signature database is a second important factor for consideration. It is particularly important in distributed networks, where there are a large number of remote affiliates and a lack of qualified personnel. In this case, the question of updating in a timely manner not only the signature database, but also the sensor kernel, is of primary importance.

There are several types of updates available for intrusion detection systems (Fig. 9.3), which are briefly described below.

- ❏ *Via diskette or CD-ROM.* This method is the simplest to implement, but at the same time is the most inconvenient. Here, either the entire sensor or some of its components (such as the signature database) must be rebuilt. The Cisco Secure IDS operates according to this principle.
- ❏ *Via e-mail.* Updates are performed via the SMTP protocol (usually, only the signatures database is updated).
- ❏ *Using an FTP or HTTP server.* In this case, the component update must be downloaded from an FTP or, more frequently, HTTP server. In the latter case, either the HTTP or HTTPS protocol is used, HTTPS allowing for the establishment of a secure connection between the server and the component to be updated. This approach is used in the RealSecure intrusion detection system.

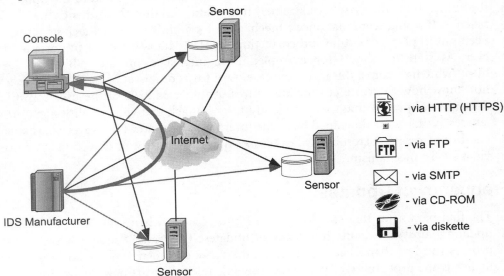

Fig. 9.3. Mechanisms for updating intrusion detection systems

Updates can be provided by both the IDS developer and the vendor. Large companies might support their own update servers, on which they publish all new releases of system components. From this server, the data are further distributed to sensors installed in the client's corporate networks (Fig. 9.4). This is especially convenient for companies where Internet access from some hosts is not allowed.

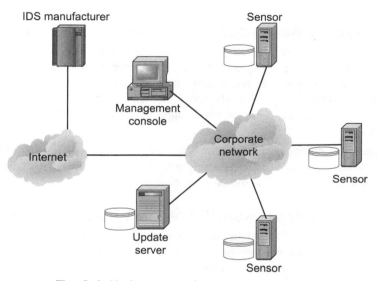

Fig. 9.4. Update center in a corporate network

The ways of obtaining the latest signatures desribed above can be set up using either manual or automatic mode. In the first case, the security administrator (or intrusion detection system operator) visits an HTTPS or FTP server from which he or she downloads the required modules (or orders them on a CD). Then the administrator updates the selected components of the intrusion detection system manually. The chief drawback of this method is the possibility that the administrator will forget to perform the update, which might result in a discrepancy between the current attack database version and the situation in the hacking community. Furthermore, if an administrator waits for the CD containing the updates to be delivered, this itself creates a delay. Also, difficulties related to delivery might arise if customs interrupts the CD shipment. Using the second approach, updates are carried out automatically via the Internet. A specialized module, which starts up according to a predefined schedule or in response to a command issued from the update center, downloads the updated version of the required component and installs it.

Secure Updates

There is little need to stress the fact that all updates — even those obtained from the manufacturer — must be duly protected. This can be done by transmitting the data via a secure channel, by using data integrity control with specialized algorithms (such as MD5), etc.

❗ *Companies Spread the Nimda Internet Worm*

In June 2002, Microsoft reported that it had detected the Nimda Internet worm in the distribution set of Visual Studio .NET. According to the information provided by Microsoft, the problem concerns exclusively Korean distribution sets of various Visual Studio .NET versions, as well as the Visual Basic .NET, Visual C++ .NET, and Visual C# .NET development environments. The worm is contained in one of the compressed help files of the Application Center Test component.

A similar situation has arisen with GameSpy.com — the popular gaming site that gave quite an unpleasant surprise to its users. Gaming fans that downloaded the GameSpy Arcade 1.09 program from that site got the Nimda worm along with it.

❗ *U.S State Department Spreads Viruses*

On May 21, 2002, the U.S. State Department admitted the fact of the presence of a computer virus that was spreading within the State Department and had infected computers of a large number of mass media and government organizations. The virus in question was one of the Klez versions, spreading via the Internet in the form of e-mail attachments. The virus does not destroy files stored on the computer, but can disrupt the operation of the mailing system in corporate LANs. Hundreds of infected e-mail messages were sent with return address of the State Department PR service. Supposedly, the virus first infected the computer to which e-mail from the State Department is delivered, and thus gained access to the mailing list used in the State Department. After that, the virus sent copies of itself using a fake return address. Virus makers often use such a trick, since people tend not to trust messages received from unknown persons. The State Department sent official apologies to all companies, organizations, and individuals that suffered from this virus attack.

Update Notification

The manufacturer or vendor must inform system users of new releases of or updates to the intrusion detection system. This notification can be sent by various methods (via e-mail, a mailing list, from the web server, at a conference, or by normal mail), depending on the circumstances and on the capabilities of the notifying and notified parties.

Declining Updates

When evaluating intrusion detection systems, users rarely pay attention to the capability of declining updates (or rolling the system back to its previous state).

Although this mechanism seems unimportant at first glance, this is not the case. I will provide a personal example. Until recently, I was using antiviral software that satisfied my requirements on all parameters. However, at some point, the software's virus signature database was complemented by signatures of the programs such as Remote Administrator, BackOrifice, NetBus, etc. This turned into a nightmare. The antiviral software began to warn me constantly of the presence of those programs on my hard disk. Even worse, besides the persistent warnings, the antiviral monitor would not allow me to start these programs, despite the fact that I needed them for teaching purposes. When I attempted to disable the detection of these programs, I discovered that there was not an option allowing me to do so. The ability to roll back to the setup before the database was updated with the signatures of these programs was not there. I ultimately stopped using that specific antiviral software, despite all of the advantages it offered. I would have gladly continued using it if it had simply allowed me to decline the updates.

Creating Custom Events

No matter how frequently the signature database for attacks or vulnerabilities is updated, there is always some delay between the time when a new attack or vulnerability is reported and the arrival of the signature for it. Reducing this delay is one of the most important problems that the department operating the IDS must deal with. One possible method of solving this task is to create custom signatures. There are two ways of doing this — using special attack (vulnerability) description language, or by directly specifying the attack parameters with the use of a specialized subsystem.

Mechanisms for describing custom checks, attacks, vulnerabilities, or other controlled events are very useful for system administrators who are trying to track vulnerabilities described in Bugtraq or other mailing lists. Thanks to this capability, it becomes possible to quickly formulate a new rule and apply it within the network. It should be pointed out, however, that although this capability is very useful, it is rather difficult to use in practice. There are very few organizations (other than government organizations, intelligence services, or organizations specializing in the field of information security) that can afford to hire the group of professionals necessary to perform research work in the field of new checks and detecting new attacks or vulnerabilities (or even a single professional of this qualification level). As for commercial companies, the employees responsible for information security usually have no serious background in programming. Besides this, their duties include quite a wide range of routine tasks (such as control over user activities, specifying access rights and privileges, etc.), and they simply have no time for such creative and difficult work as developing new signatures and rules.

However, if the intrusion detection system provides a vulnerability description language, this can be considered an additional advantage. The following few sections will provide brief descriptions of the most common languages that allow you to describe an attack or vulnerability. More detailed coverage of this topic is provided in [Eckmann1-00]. Unfortunately, these languages are rather exclusive, since signatures written in these languages can not be ported to other systems. The only exception to this is the language used in the Snort IDS, since this language can be understood by several other intrusion detection systems, such as RealSecure Network Sensor.

P-BEST

P-BEST (Production-Based Expert System Toolset) is an expert system providing a specialized language that can be used for describing various security policy violations. This system was developed by Alan Whitehurst, and was used as part of the MIDAS system for detecting attacks on the NCSC Dockmaster network. Later, through a contract with DARPA, this system was further enhanced in the SRI laboratory and incorporated into the IDES and NIDES intrusion detection systems [Lindquist1-99].

The attack and misuse description language implemented in the P-BEST shell is rather simple and easy to use. This language allows qualified administrators to quickly summarize nearly any type of unauthorized activity. For example, a failed logon attempt can be described in just 9 lines (Listing 9.1).

Listing 9.1. An Example of a Rule in P-BEST for Detecting Failed Logon Attempts

```
rule[Bad_Login(#10;*):
    [+e:event| event_type == login,
            return_code == BAD_PASSWORD]
==>
    [+bad_login| username = e.username,
                hostname = e.hostname]
    [-|e]
    [!|printf("Bad login for user %s from host %s\n", e.username,
    e.hostname)]
]
```

The first line of this code specifies the rule name (`Bad_Login`), its priority (`10`), and permission for multiple use (`*`). The remaining lines describe the failed logon event and the notification mechanism. Furthermore, the rules developed can be easily integrated with the C programming language, which gives P-BEST practically unlimited capabilities. In the over 10 years of its existence, the P-BEST shell has been integrated into a large number of the most popular intrusion detection systems, including the EMERALD system, which detects misuse and attacks on various operating systems, such as Multics and UNIX clones (SunOS, Solaris, FreeBSD, and Linux).

N-Code

The N-Code interpreted language was developed for the NFR system. It allows you to define reactions to different types of events that attract the attention of the system or network administrator. Besides attacks, this language can describe the following aspects:

- ❑ Intensity of mail traffic
- ❑ Network statistics (the number of packets transmitted via ICMP, ARP, and other protocols)
- ❑ Attempts to access specific services

Thus, the N-Code language can be used not only for intrusion detection, but also for controlling various aspects of network communications that might be of interest to IT professionals and security specialists [NFR1-99, NFR2-99].

Besides the standard variables, procedures, and lists, the N-Code language includes special built-in data structures that fully describe network packet formats for different protocols. For example, you can access the source of an IP packet directly by specifying a single parameter — `ip.src`. All processing, including Ethernet frame parsing and selection of the **Source Address** field from the IP packet header, is performed by the interpreter module implemented as part of the NFR system. This allows you to specify a compact set of rules for detecting specific events. Listings 9.2—9.4 provide typical examples.

Listing 9.2. An Example of a Rule for Detecting a WinNuke Attack Written in N-Code

---

```
filter oob tcp (client, dport: 139)
{
$urgpointer=long(ip.blob,16); #Offset == OOB
if ($urgpointer == 3)
  record system.time, ip.src, ip.dst to the_recorder;
}
```

Listing 9.3. An Example of a Rule for Detecting a Land Attack Written in N-Code

```
filter pptp ip () {
      if (ip.src == ip.dest )
      {
       record system.time,
           eth.src, ip.src, eth.dst, ip.dest to land_recrdr;
      }
}
```

Listing 9.4. An Example of a Rule for Detecting Attempts of Xmas Scanning Written in N-Code

```
filter xmas ip () {
      if (tcp.hdr){
      $dabyte = byte(ip.blob, 13);
      # If all SFAURP bits are set, this can only be a malicious packet
      if (!($dabyte ^ 63 )){
      record system.time, ip.src, tcp.sport, ip.dest, tcp.dport, "UAPRSF" to
      xmas_recorder;
         return;
         }
   }
}
```

Attack Signature Definition

The Attack Signature Definition (ASD) mechanism utilized by the NetProwler intrusion detection system is used to create attack signatures that are not in the existing database. This process comprises the following 4 steps:

1. *Generation and gathering of data.* All attacks that can be detected by the NetProwler system can be classified into the following two categories: connection-oriented (implemented via the TCP protocol) and connectionless (for UDP and ICMP). At this stage, traffic is generated, which is then analyzed and stored in a text file for further attack detection.

2. *Data analysis.* At this stage, the system identifies all information that will later enable you to describe the attack signature. Analysis is performed on the basis of the text file saved in the previous stage. Note that the analysis is performed

manually, and the specialist who performs it must have the knowledge and skills required to detect signs of an attack in the incoming traffic.

3. *Creating an attack signature.* When describing an attack signature, you should use the following parameters.

- *Attack type.* The following three types of attacks exist: Simple, Counter-based, and Sequential-based. The first type are simple attacks that can be described by a single network packet. The second type is used to describe attacks that operate using several packets during a specified time interval. For example, three failed attempts at remote logon during a 60-second period can be interpreted as an attack of this type. The last type includes the most complicated attacks, which span several network packets, and are directed at several applications (or from several applications) and in a predefined sequence. For example, sequential attempts at authentication using such services as Telnet, Rlogin, and Rsh performed within 180 seconds can be considered to be an attack of this kind.
- *Properties.* An extended description of specific attacks. For example, one of the properties can specify that 4 failed attempts at authentication from 4 different hosts do not represent an attack, while 4 failed attempts from the same host does.
- *Operating systems and applications.* Those that are vulnerable to this attack.
- *Priority.* This parameter enables you to assign a priority to a newly created attack signature — low, medium, or high.
- *Category.* Specifies the category of the newly created signature. You should note that categories in this classification are absolutely identical to the categories available in the RealSecure intrusion detection system. They include: "Denial of Service," "preparation for attack," "attempts at unauthorized access," "suspicious activity," "network protocol," and "miscellaneous."
- *Search criteria.* Such criteria include various additional signs that characterize an attack, such as keywords or regular expressions.

4. *Testing and debugging the signature.*

In the course of describing signatures, it is possible to use different predefined variables that can significantly simplify the tasks of a security administrator (for example, `IP_SRC_ADDRESS` or `ICMP_TYPE`). When working with these variables, you can apply arithmetic, logical, or other variables such as "AND," "OR," "NOT," ">=," "!=," "+," "/," etc. Listing 9.5 illustrates the use of predefined variables for describing the Land attack signature.

Listing 9.5. Fragment of the Rule DESCRIBING the Land Attack Using Predefined Variables

---

```
((IP_SRC_ADDRESS == IP_DEST_ADDRESS) AND (IP_SRC_PORT == IP_DEST_PORT))
```

RUSSEL

The RUSSEL language (Rule-Based Sequence Evaluation Language) is intended for describing rules that give you the ability to track unauthorized actions in log files. It is used in the ASAX system (Advanced Security Audit-trail Analysis on UniX), which supports the following two operating systems — SINIX and BS2000 from SIEMENS [Habra1-92]. This language has much in common with the P-BEST language. After a short training course, you should be able to create rules for detecting security policy violations in local or corporate networks quickly and easily (Listing 9.6).

Listing 9.6. An Example of a Rule Created Using the RUSSEL Language for Detection of Failed Login Attempts During the Specified Time Period

---

```
rule Failed_login (maxtimes , duration : integer)
# This rule detects the first failed attempt and calls the add-on rule
begin
if evt='login' and res='failure' and is_unsecure (terminal)
-> Trigger off for next Count_rule1 (maxtimes-1, timestp+duration )
fi ;
Trigger off for next Failed_login (maxtimes , duration)
end


rule Count_rule1 (countdown , expiration : integer)
# This rule counts the number of failed attempts
# It remains in force until the predefined interval expires
# or when the countdown variable reaches zero
if evt='login' and res='failure'
and is_unsecure(terminal) and timestp < expiration
-> if countdown >1
-> Trigger off for next Count_rule1(countdown-1, expiration) ;
countdown =1
-> SendMessage ("too many failed logins")
fi ;
timestp =?expiration
-> Skip;
true
-> Trigger off for next Count_rule1 (countdown, expiration)
fi
```

SNP-L Scripting Systems

The SNP-L Scripting System is a language that very closely resembles C. This language is used in the SecureNet PRO intrusion detection system, and is intended for attack descriptions. One of the distinguishing features of the SNP-L language is the presence of a so-called "sandbox," which has much in common with similar technology implemented in the Java programming language. All attack scenarios are executed in the "sandbox," which protects the computer on which the intrusion detection system is installed from script failures or from other undesirable effects [Intrusion1-00].

SecureLogic

The SecureLogic language, created on the basis of the Tcl language, is used in the RealSecure Server Sensor system for more precise customization of the signatures of detected attacks. Furthermore, SecureLogic provides the capability of a more detailed analysis of a situation resulting from the detection of a specific event. For example, using a SecureLogic script, it is possible to analyze an administrative logon in the protected system (see Listing 9.7). If the user name is contained in the list of allowed names, the system does not implement any response action and does not consider the event to be an attack.

Otherwise, the system implements a predefined response action — for example, blocking the user account — and sends a notification of the detected attack to the central console.

Listing 9.7. An Example of a SecureLogic Script

```
# List of allowed user names
Store __iss_trust_usr_list [list "Luka"]
# In this case, Luka is the only user with administrative privileges
# in the protected system. When Luka logs on
# no response is implemented, since
# this activity is normal.
# If anyone else logs on with administrative privileges,
# the sensor reacts to such an event.
if { [catch { Retrieve "__iss_trust_user_list" } trust_user_list] } {
set trust_usr_list ""
}
set user [GetData "User"]
if { $tcl_platform(platform) == "unix" }
foreach i2User $trust_usr_list {
if { [string equal $user $i2User] } {
# If the user is listed as trusted, the script
```

```
# returns 0
return 0
}
}
# Otherwise it returns ti 1 and the sensor
# reacts by the predefined action.
return 1
```

CASL

CASL (Custom Audit Scripting Language, formerly known as the Custom Attack Simulation Language) is both the name for a language and a subsystem implemented as part of the CyberCop Scanner. Both were developed by Network Associates (to be more precise, by Secure Networks) to enhance the capabilities of their Ballista security scanner, which was later renamed CyberCop Scanner. Recently, the CASL subsystem was made a stand-alone product that runs on Windows NT (Fig. 9.5) and Linux. This product is available for downloading from the Network Associates web server.

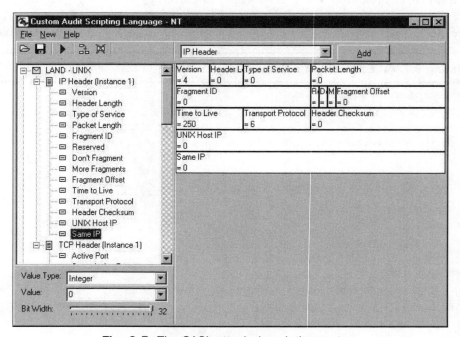

Fig. 9.5. The CASL attack description system

The CASL language is rather simple and easy to use. At the same time, it allows for the description of any fields of the packet headers for any protocol based on ICMP, IP, TCP, or UDP [CyberCop1-00]. CASL operates with variables, operators, and packets, and has much in common with N-Code. For example, the ip.src parameter in the N-Code language is similar to the ip_source parameter in the CASL language. An example description of hidden TCP scanning written in CASL language is presented in Listing 9.8.

Listing 9.8. An Example of a Description of Hidden TCP Scanning Written in CASL

```
#include "tcpip.casl"
#include "packets.casl"
for(i =1; i <1023; i =i +1){
    OurSYN = copy SYN;
    OurSYN.tcp_source = 10;
    OurSYN.tcp_destination = i;
    OurIP = copy TCPIP;
    OurIP.ip_source = 127.0.0.1;
    OurIP.ip_destination = 127.0.0.2;
    OurPacket = [ OurIP, OurSYN ];
    ip_output(OurPacket);
    OurFilter = [ "src host ", 127.0.0.2, " and tcp src port ", i ];
    ReadPacket = ip_input(2000, OurFilter);
    if(!ReadPacket)
        continue;
    if(size(ReadPacket) < size(IP) + size(TCP))
        continue;
    ReadIP=extract ip from ReadPacket;
    ReadTCP=extract tcp from ReadPacket;
    if(ReadTCP.tcp_ack != 1
            || ReadTCP.tcp_syn != 1
            || ReadTCP.tcp_rst == 1)
        continue;
    print("Port ", i, " is open");
}
```

NASL

NASL (Nessus Attack Scripting Language) is the attack description language developed for the Nessus security scanner. It has a lot in common with C. However, as its developers admit, in many respects (for example, in the speed of script execution) it is weaker than other languages, such as Tcl, Python, and Perl. Nonetheless, this language is very efficient when it comes to performing the tasks for which it was specifically created and optimized (see Listings 9.9 and 9.10). Like many other attack-description languages, besides variables, operators, functions, and other elements, NASL can operate with network packets, which significantly simplifies the work of the security administrator [NASL1-00].

Listing 9.9. A Fragment of an NASL Script Describing a Check for Detecting Web Server Vulnerability

```
if(is_cgi_installed("php.cgi")){
 display("CGI-script php.cgi is installed in /CGI-bin\n");
 }
```

Listing 9.10. A Fragment of the NASL Script Describing the Check to Detect FTP-Server Vulnerability

```
soc = open_sock_tcp(21);
if(ftp_log_in(socket:soc, user:"ftp", pass:"luka@"))
{
    port = ftp_get_pasv_port(socket:soc);
    if(port)
    {
        soc2 = open_sock_tcp(port);
        data = string("RETR /etc/passwd\r\n");
        send(socket:soc, data:data);
        password_file = recv(socket:soc2, length:10000);
        display(password_file);
        close(soc2);
    }
    close(soc);
}
```

VDL and VEL

Languages such as VDL (Vulnerability Descriptive Language) or VEL (Vulnerability Exploit Language) are very convenient for those end users that have no experience with languages such as C, Perl, or Tcl. Both VDL and VEL were developed by Cisco Systems, and are used in the Cisco Secure Scanner product. The checks described by these languages are based on simple logical expressions (Listing 9.11), and the user can add required rules in a few seconds. Unfortunately, Cisco no longer supplies this product.

Listing 9.11. An Example of a Rule Written in VDL That Detects the Presence of the Telnet Service

```
# Service description section: Telnet service found at the scanned host
port 23 using protocol tcp => Service:Remote-Access:my_telnet
```

This check describes a rule that determines the presence of the Telnet service at TCP Port 23 of the analyzed host. The next rule is more sophisticated. It identifies the obsolete SuperApp application by the header returned in reply to a request directed to Ports 1234 or 1235 (Listing 9.12).

Listing 9.12. An Example of a Rule Written in VDL That Detects the Presence of the SuperApp Application

```
# User-defined check: The SuperApp 1.0 application is started
# at the scanned host
(scanfor "SuperApp 1.0" on port 1234) || (scanfor "SuperApp 1.0 Ready" on
port 1235) => VUL:3:Old-Software:Super-App-Ancient:Vp:10003
```

This potential vulnerability (Vp), having its priority set to 3, is included in the category of "outdated (potentially vulnerable) software" (Old-Software), and is known as Supper-App-Ancient (this name is user-defined). The number 10003 is the unique number of the record in the vulnerability database of the Cisco Secure Scanner (Network Security Database, NSDB).

Using the VDL language, it is possible to give three categories of rules that allow for the identification of [Cisco1-99]:

❑ Network services
❑ OS type
❑ Vulnerabilities

Cisco Systems divides all vulnerabilities into the following two classes.

❑ *Potential* — those resulting from header checks and so called nudges of the service or host being analyzed. A potential vulnerability might exist in the system, but active probing checks do not confirm this fact. This type of check is identified by the Vp keyword.

❑ *Confirmed* — detected vulnerabilities whose existence on the scanned host is confirmed. The Vc keyword corresponds to this type of check.

Potential vulnerability checks are implemented via header checks and nudges. Nudges are used for services that do not return headers but react to simple commands, such as sending the HEAD command to obtain the version number of an HTTP server. As soon as this information is obtained, Cisco Secure Scanner enables a special mechanism known as the rules engine, which implements a specific range of rules that confirm or deny the existence of a potential vulnerability. Thus the administrator knows which vulnerabilities are actually present in the system and which require confirmation.

However, it is clear that the built-in language of the Cisco Secure Scanner intended for describing these rules is rather elementary, and can help only in the simplest situations. In more complex situations, when the check can not be written in a form that comprises a single rule, you will need to compose more sophisticated scripts, which can be done using other programming languages, such as Perl, Tcl, or C.

STATL

The STATL language (State Transition Analysis Technique Language) was developed at the University of California (http://www.cs.ucsb.edu/~rsg/STAT/). It provides you with the ability to describe an intrusion in the form of an attack scenario that is a sequence of transitions between the system security states. This method was first used in the USTAT and NetSTAT intrusion detection systems.

Perl, C, and Other Languages

Attempts at enhancing vulnerability description mechanisms, checks, and so on have been being made for a long time, and virtually every developer or vendor has attempted this. The first attempt was undertaken by Vietse Venema and Dan Farmer — the authors of the SATAN security scanner. In this system, the description of new vulnerabilities — or to be more precise, the checks for new vulnerabilities — was designed using the Perl language. This important task required extensive knowledge of the Perl language, the architecture of the TCP/IP protocol stack, and the operating system being scanned. The developers of the WebTrends Security Analyzer system proceeded in the same way (and once again Perl was used). The Perl language, like C, is also used in the Internet Scanner system. The advantages of the Perl and C languages lie in the fact that checks and rules written for one operating system can be transferred to another with practically no changes having to be made.

Monitoring Custom Events

Most intrusion detection systems enhance their functions by adding new capabilities. For example, systems such as RealSecure Network Sensor and Cisco IDS can be customized so as to control e-mail messages by various parameters, from the sender or recipient address or message topic to the keywords encountered in the message body. Finding keywords such as "job," "resume," and so on enables administrators to detect employees searching for new jobs during business hours. The same capability helps detect macro viruses and Internet worms in e-mail traffic.

The next add-on function that extends the range of usage of intrusion detection systems is the control of access to different Internet hosts. Using built-in mechanisms, it is possible to select traffic belonging to HTTP, FTP, and other protocols from among all of the network traffic (Fig. 9.6).

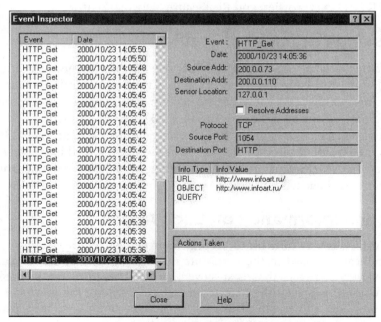

Fig. 9.6. Controlling access to HTTP pages
(using the example of the RealSecure Network Sensor system)

Besides the additional capabilities mentioned above, intrusion detection systems can also have functions allowing for the detection of viruses with active contents (Java, ActiveX) added to them. For example, the eTrust IDS provides built-in, fully functional antiviral software, which is just as effective as similar but better-known products. Systems such as RealSecure Network Sensor, Cisco Secure IDS, and others include mechanisms for detecting and locking malignant Java applets and ActiveX controls.

In my opinion, mechanisms such as antiviral protection and content control are basically stand-alone products that can, in turn, be integrated into an intrusion detection system.

False Negative Notifications

Notifying the IDS operator to the fact that the system can not handle an intense workload and is starting to miss events (for example, network frames) is rather important. Without this function, you will not be able to know in time that your system is experiencing problems and can not handle the workload. Unfortunately, this capability is not provided by all manufacturers. Some of the products that implement this feature are NFR NID, NetProwler, and RealSecure Network Sensor.

Processing Fragmented Traffic

In *Chapter 6*, when discussing the IDS network sensor architecture, I mentioned a module for processing fragmented traffic. I would like to draw your attention to the surprising fact that most intrusion detection tools, especially shareware and freeware (for example, Centrax 2.4 or NetProwler 3.5), lack this function, which results in the potential danger of causing such intrusion detection systems to fail by sending them fragmented traffic. Examples of such attacks were described in *Chapter 4*. A contemporary network-level intrusion detection system must provide a mechanism for processing fragmented packets.

Reference Information on Each Attack

Obviously, it is very difficult to become an expert on all the existing operating systems and applications used in the corporate networking environment. Learning about the entire variety of attacks that exist is even harder. Therefore, the availability of reference information on each of the detected attacks, describing the mechanisms of its implementation and vulnerable platforms, as well as variants of false positives and false negatives, are yet more important criteria that should be taken into account when choosing an intrusion detection system.

Extended Signature Customization

Even for the most efficient intrusion detection systems, supplied with the most complete signature databases, the need for additional customization of each signature still exists. This might be required, for example, to reduce the number of false positives. Because of this, a high-quality intrusion detection system must provide the required flexibility, allowing it to be customized according to specific user requirements.

Response

An intrusion detection system's reactions in response to detected and identified unauthorized activity can be classified into the following two categories.

❑ *Passive reactions*, which imply standard notifications sent to personnel when the IDS detects an attack, misuse, or other anomaly. This category includes: sending notification to the central console of the intrusion detection system, generating controlling SNMP sequences for network-management systems, registering events in the event database, etc.

❑ *Active types of response*, which include closing the network connection to the attacking host, blocking the user account used by the intruder to log in, reconfiguring network equipment and security tools, automatic elimination of the vulnerability, etc.

Notification

The first type of reaction that was implemented in intrusion detection systems was administrative alert — notifying the security administrator or intrusion detection system operator. Current intrusion detection tools provide quite a wide range of response types, from sending alerts to the central console of the intrusion detection system, to sending a voice message to the administrator's phone (Fig. 9.7).

Generally, intrusion detection systems provide two or three types of reactions: sending a notification to the IDS console, generating an e-mail message (via the SMTP protocol), and sending a message to the network management system (via the SNMP protocol) are the chief examples. Some developers provide other types of notification. For example, systems such as NetProwler and eTrust IDS provide alert mechanisms hooked up to the security administrator's pager. In eTrust IDS, each detected event can be further designated by a sound signal, or information on that event can be sent by fax. While the RealSecure system does not provide for sending notification by fax or by pager, it can be integrated with the AlarmPoint system by Singlepoint Systems (http://www.singlepointsys.com). This system is intended for facilitating various scenarios for notification of security administrators via various tools — fax, telephone, pager, cellular phone, e-mail, voice mail, etc.

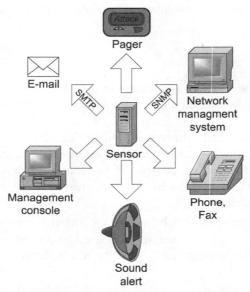

Fig. 9.7. Types of IDS responses to an attack

An interesting though rarely used capability is offered in the RealSecure OS Sensor and the RealSecure Server Sensor. Using it, a notification of unauthorized activity is sent to the intruder rather than to the administrator. According to the developers of the RealSecure system, this informs the intruder of the fact that he or she has been detected and stops the attack. RealSecure utilizes a different type of notification, where information about the detected attack is sent to the console of the firewall. The RealSecure Network Sensor intrusion detection system, which was developed by ISS, uses the Lucent Managed Firewall by Lucent. For RealSecure, released by the Check Point company through an agreement with Internet Security Systems, the Firewall-1 system is the firewall.

Taking into account the fact that mobile communications are becoming more and more popular, it is possible to predict that most advanced intrusion detection systems will soon implement an SMS notification mechanism.

Event Logging

There is no need to write extensively about the logging of detected events here, since this is a mandatory requirement of every intrusion detection system. Two aspects, however, warrant special mention — where the logged events should be written, and with what level of detail. You can select files in various formats to act as a log file, including a text file, a system log (as is the case with Cisco IOS Firewall Feature Set), a text file in a special format (as, for example, in the Snort system), a local MS Access database (as in the Internet Scanner system), or an SQL database (as with the Spitfire or RealSecure systems). For intrusion detection systems, it is desirable to have built-in database mechanisms oriented towards end users rather than towards database experts. Otherwise, a situation might arise in which, for example, the SQL database exceeds its storage limit and needs to be cleared or backed up, which can only be done by an SQL professional who is not currently available.

In all cases, it is necessary to consider the rate of data processing. Several thousands of messages must be saved in the databases per day. Therefore, if communication between the console and the database is inefficient, it will be rather inconvenient, or even impossible, to use the system.

▼ *Computer Failures in the NSA and NSWC Caused* ▪ *by Overload*

According to ComputerWorld data, in January 2000, the NSA experienced problems caused by computer failures due to an overload for about 3 days. The NSWC experienced similar problems in 1990.

Information stored in log files can be saved with the standard level of detail or the complete level of detail. In the first case, the type of logged event, date and time of detection, the sensor that detected that specific event, and the source and destination addresses related to the event are registered. Below are some examples of various log files at the brief detail level (Listings 9.13—9.16).

Listing 9.13. A Fragment of the TCPdump Log File

```
06:41:24.067330 stealth.mappem.com.113 > 172.21.32.83.1004: S
4052190291:4052190291(0) ack 674711610 win 8192
```

Listing 9.14. A Fragment of the Apache Web Server Log File Named access_log

---

```
193.56.123.47 — - [04/Apr/1997:16:39:06 -0500] "GET /etc/passwd HTTP/1.0"
404 139
```

Listing 9.15. A Fragment of the SecurityEvent Log File of a Windows NT-Based Operating System

---

```
Date    Time    Source Category   Code    User    Computer
27.11.0 19:19:38   Security  Logon/Logoff   529 SYSTEM NT-IIS
```

Listing 9.16. A Fragment of the Cisco IDS 4200 Log File

```
4,1025294,2001/01/16,16:58:36,2001/01/16,11:58:36,10008,11,100,OUT,OUT,1,
2001,0,TCP/IP,10.1.6.1,10.2.3.5,0,0,0.0.0.0,
```

The second type of log file saved involves registering the detailed content of all data fields related to the logged security event. For example, network-level intrusion detection systems register all network packets. Extended logging formats are available with a number of intrusion detection systems, including Snort (Listing 9.17), Cisco IDS 4200, and RealSecure Network Sensor.

Listing 9.17. A Fragment of the Snort Log File

```
[**] BACKDOOR Attempt- Subseven [**]
12/26-23:09:42.219109 0:90:27:F:22:A2 -> 0:40:5:F6:34:51 type:0x800
len:0x4E
216.192.29.30:3216 -> 206.18.108.130:1243 TCP TTL:64 TOS:0xD0 ID:11841
S***** Seq: 0x4908C6 Ack: 0x0 Win: 0x2000
TCP Options => MSS: 536 NOP WS: 0 NOP NOP TS: 0 0 Opt 9 (40): 0000 0000
0000 0000 0000 0000 0000 0000 0000 0000 0000 0000 0000 0000 0000
0000 0000
```

Do you need to trace packet dumps? Making this decision is important, since this feature consumes a lot of system resources. However, this function is rather useful, and can play an important role in the investigation of a specific incident. The contents of the packet will allow you to reconstruct the whole attack (as opposed to the event tracing mechanism, which does this job automatically). Furthermore, it will help you understand a situation in which there was a false positive (false positives now occur in every intrusion detection system).

Tracing Events

Sometimes, the security administrator needs to track all the actions of the intruder and all the commands that he or she has issued. This is hard to do using log files and reports created based on them. Because of this, some intrusion detection systems implement an event tracing mechanism that allows you to record all events in exactly the same sequence and at exactly the same speed at which the intruder was operating. After that, the administrator can at any time replay the required sequence of events (in real-time, accelerated, or slowed down modes) in order to analyze the intruder's activity. This will allow him or her to assess the intruder's skill, the tools at his or her disposal, and so on, in order to collect the required proof for an internal investigation or for court. An event tracing mechanism is implemented in such intrusion detection systems as RealSecure Network Sensor and SecureNet PRO, as well as several others.

Closing Connections

Closing the connection to the attacking host is one way to interrupt an attack. There are two possible ways of going about this. In a network-level intrusion detection system, the mechanism for terminating the connection is based on session hijacking, with a packet whose RST flag is set sent to both the attack target and the attacker (Fig. 9.8).

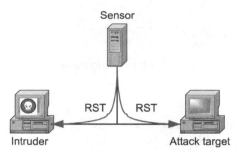

Fig. 9.8. Termination of the network connection

This type of response (utilized by intrusion detection systems such as RealSecure Network Sensor and Cisco IDS 4200) has two main limitations: it is available only for events that are made up of several packets, and only for fully established TCP connections. This approach is not effective against attacks that consist of a single packet only (such as WinNuke). It is also not effective in reacting to a SYN Flood attack, since no fully functional TCP connection is established in the course of such an attack.

In host-level intrusion detection systems, the above-mentioned response option is done by locking out the user account that was used to implement the attack. This locking out can be either temporary (for a specified time period only) or permanent. The permanent locking of a user account remains in force until the system administrator unlocks that account. Depending on the privileges used in setting up the intrusion detection system, account locking can be active either within the host representing the attack target only or within the entire domain or network segment.

Reconfiguring Network Equipment

The reconfiguration of the network equipment or firewalls is yet another type of active response to attacks (in Cisco Systems, this concept is known as shunning). If an attack is detected, the intrusion detection system sends a special command containing instructions to change the access control list to the router or the firewall (Fig. 9.9). Later on, all attempts to establish a connection originating from the attacking host will be rejected. As with locking out accounts, ACL changes can be temporary or permanent.

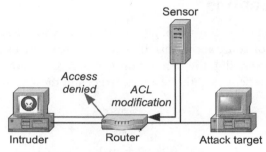

Fig. 9.9. Reconfiguring network equipment

Blocking Traffic

Some intrusion detection systems (RealSecure Server Sensor, for example), complement the set of existing active response methods with a feature allowing you to block network traffic in the same manner as firewalls do [ISS5-00]. This approach allows you to isolate both the traffic and the recipients that might need to access the resources of the protected host. Such an approach thus carries out the functions of a personal firewall as well.

Deception Technique

We already discussed the deception technique in *Chapter 6*, so there is no need to concentrate any more on it now. I just want to mention that this mechanism is utilized by some intrusion detection systems. For example, the RealSecure Server Sensor system provides the Decoy mechanism, enabling it to emulate various ports and network services.

Eliminating Vulnerabilities

The elimination of detected vulnerabilities is the result of using a security scanner. This can be done either manually or in an automated mode. The first mode is easier to implement, but requires extra time and effort from the security administrator, who must eliminate all detected vulnerabilities manually, on his or her own, in order of priority. Some intrusion detection systems attempt to automate this process by providing administrators with ways of automatically patching detected security holes. Such systems include SFProtect (the IntelliFix mechanism), System Scanner, and Desktop Scanner. In contrast to small networks, where this function is not vital, in large corporate networks where there is a lack of qualified personnel, this mechanism becomes a matter of primary importance.

Counter Attack

I would like to give special attention to this type of response and discuss it separately, because it is the response that causes quite a number of disputes among experts. At first glance, this solution can be easily implemented — just register the intruder's address and implement a counter attack against him or her.

▌ *A Counter Attack Attains Its Goal*

As was reported in the press release of the Conxion hosting company (**http://www.conxion.com/news/releases_16.asp**), during the period from November 30 to December 3, 1999, a political group identifying itself as "E-hippies" attacked the site of World Trade Organization (WTO), hosted by Conxion. The E-hippies attempted to cause the WTO's site to fail by implementing DDoS attacks directed from 3793 various IP addresses. However, the Conxion security engineers managed to redirect all of the traffic back to the E-hippies' site, which was brought down by this bombardment. At the same time, the E-hippies themselves appeared to have interpreted this redirected traffic as hits to their site in support of their activities.

Most specialists (for example, [Schneier1-01] and [Schneier2-01]) consider such actions justified self-protection. From the hacker's point of view, this reaction is also a justified measure that would teach a good lesson to beginner intruders who are just using freeware hacking tools without a proper understanding of what they are actually doing. By the way, there are plenty of tools on the Internet both for implementing DDoS attacks and redirecting them back. The PortSentry intrusion detection system, for example, provides this feature. Furthermore, most intrusion detection systems provide the capability of implementing customized responses, including counter attacks. Some governments have gone even further and are trying to legalize counter attacks.

▌ *Legalized DoS Attacks*

On June 25, 2002, the House of Representatives of the U.S. Congress started to discuss a bill on intellectual property, according to which music recording companies and other owners of intellectual property will have the legal right to force the disconnection of users that spread pirated content. In particular, this bill legalizes the redirection of pirate traffic, file locking, DoS attacks against pirate sites, and so on. The only action that is not allowed is the use of various tools for destroying computer systems or data.

DoS Attacks against Nazis

On April 10, 2001, the German Prime Minister declared that the German Intelligence Service can implement DoS attacks against neo-Nazi sites. A few days later, however, this statement was denounced, and it was declared that the government will find legitimate ways of neutralizing Nazi sites.

This point of view, however, is arguable. Some specialists think that a counterattack is similar to the lynch law, and therefore is not justified. Furthermore, according to the opinion of most specialists, the main problem here is correctly identifying the intruder's actual address (which will be covered in more detail in *Chapter 12*). In practice, intruders rarely attempt an attack from their real addresses — usually they use various proxies in order to conceal their location. Address spoofing (see Table 2.4) will result in a counterattack targeted against someone else (a company or individual who never did anything to you). If that company or individual suffers damage as a result of your counterattack, they can also file a lawsuit against you. However, there is one subtle feature here. If you redirect the intruder's requests back without changes, this could be seen as a refusal to receive the traffic, which is a normal function of network communications. On the other hand, if you modify these requests or implement your own counterattack, it might be considered breaking the law.

To conclude, I would like to mention that you should not neglect this type of response completely. Provided that some specific conditions are satisfied, it can be considered a viable solution.

Additional Types of Responses

Almost every intrusion detection system allows the user to create custom types of event handling, which provides for a practically unlimited range of various response types. For example, you can allow an event to be recorded not only in the IDS log file, but also in the system log, or start the antiviral software for a specific type of traffic. For example, quite an interesting type of response to distributed attacks such as Trin∅∅, TFN, Stacheldraht, Troj_Trin∅∅, and Shaft is implemented in the Zombie Zapper system from the Bindview Corporation. Knowing the default passwords for interaction between masters and daemons, Zombie Zapper sends commands to stop attacks against the selected target.

Creating Custom Responses

A well-designed intrusion detection system must allow the system administrator to add to the list of predefined reactions to detected attacks. This will allow him or her to significantly extend the system's effectiveness. For example, the addition of a function that performs administrative notification via a pager would be desirable for most companies that supply administrators with these inexpensive communication devices. Let us consider another example. Most manufacturers utilize so-called proactive variations of response, which allow the reconfiguration of network equipment. However, the list of this equipment is quite short (most often, it is limited to two or three items). The capability to reconfigure devices significantly improves the efficiency of the intrusion detection system. For example, earlier versions of the RealSecure Network Sensor intrusion detection system allowed for the reconfiguration of access control lists for series 7000 routers developed by Cisco Systems. In the current version, this function has been significantly enhanced and improved. Now, using the specialized Expect software tool, it is possible to reconfigure a wide range of network devices. This system (http://expect.nist.gov), which runs on Windows NT-based operating systems and on Unix clones, allows you to write various scripts using a language that is an extension of Tcl (Listing 9.18).

Listing 8.15. An Example of Script Written Using the Expect Language to Reconfigure Cisco Routers

```
## Usage:
## cisco <routerip> <routerpasswd> <configpasswd> <hostip>

spawn telnet [lindex $argv 0]  # Connecting via Telnet to routerip
expect "Password:"            # Waiting for Password prompt:
send "[lindex $argv 1]\r"       # Sending routerpasswd
expect "Router>"          # Waiting for reply
send "enable\r"
expect "Password:"
send "[lindex $argv 2]\r"       # Sending configpasswd
expect "Router#"          # Waiting for reply
send "config\r\r"
expect "Router(config)#"
# Adding a new rule to the Access Control List
send "access-list 101 deny ip host [lindex $argv 3] any\r"
expect "Router(config)#"
send "exit\r"
expect "Router#"
send "exit\r"
expect eof
```

Managing Sensors

Obviously, IDS sensors can be managed both remotely and locally. Local management might be necessary in one of two cases — when there is only one sensor (in a small company) or when remote management is impossible (for example, when communications with the console have been interrupted). In such cases, you can manage the sensor locally from the computer on which it is installed, either using a separate utility (such as Engine Manager in RealSecure Network Sensor) or an embedded management module (such as IDS Device Manager in Cisco IDS). However, local management becomes rather inconvenient if you have two or three sensors, to say nothing about controlling several dozens or hundreds of them. Because of this, remote control is used.

Remote Control

This criterion — remote control capability — is especially important for large geographically distributed networks with a number of sensors. As noted in [Jackson1-99], remote administration can be accomplished using the following two methods:

❑ *From any console.* Here, an unlimited number of consoles can be installed in the network. Each of these consoles can control remote sensors for the intrusion detection system. At first glance, this approach is very convenient. However, when operating such system in a real-world environment, you might encounter some problems. For example, intruders may be able to install a false console in the network and send commands to sensors in order to reconfigure them or perform other unauthorized actions.

❑ *From the central console.* In this case, only one console (a predefined central console) is capable of managing remote sensors, and any attempts to establish control from other locations are denied. The RealSecure Network Sensor system is based on this principle. During RealSecure's installation, the console and sensor exchange authentication keys. Later on, the RealSecure sensor will accept control commands only from the console for which it has the authentication key. Otherwise, all control commands are rejected.

You should note that console managing remote sensors can be supplied by IDS sensor manufacturers (as in systems such as RealSecure Network Sensor or NetProwler), as well as by other companies (for example, the Spitfire system allows you to manage sensors of other IDSs, such as RealSecure and Cisco IDS). Furthermore, there are also intermediate or mixed variations, which will be described below.

When evaluating this mechanism, you need to take yet another aspect into account, which comes onto the scene only during the actual operation and maintenance of the system. Sometimes, the capabilities provided by the developer are insufficient for supporting the remote sensor. For example, you might sometimes need to reboot the sensor or even the computer on which it is installed, view the system event log or CPU usage, etc. Of course, some of these actions can be performed from the management console. However, if you need to reboot the computer on which the sensor is running or view CPU usage statistics, you will need additional software. If you encounter such a situation, you will notice that Unix solutions are much more convenient than similar solutions for the Windows platform. Obviously, it is much easier to open an SSH or Telnet session than it is to start Remote Administrator or other Windows utilities for remote access. Of course, you can start a special service on a remote computer (especially in Windows 2000 or Windows XP) and manage all settings via it. However, if you do so, you are gaining convenience at the expense of the sensor's security.

Number of Management Consoles

In most organizations, IS management functions are distributed among several departments. For example, the IT department controls a limited set of specific network parameters, while the information security department monitors and controls other parameters. The sets of functions performed by these departments should not intersect, and maintaining this requires the presence of at least two management consoles, each of which must be customized for performing a specific set of tasks. In addition, a decentralized management scheme requires the presence of several consoles — both at the headquarters and at remote offices. More detailed coverage of this aspect will be provided in the next chapter.

Number of Managed Agents

If you are not planning to use more than 5–10 sensors, there is no significant difference between management consoles from various manufacturers. However, if this limit is going to be exceeded, you will encounter several problems, from the impossibility of tracing all alerts on the console and the event database filling up, to the failure of the console or the management server. Because of this, this criterion is important only in large networks that have dozens or hundreds of sensors. In small networks, a single console (or management server) can control all the sensors that exist in the network. Some intrusion detection systems can coordinate an unlimited number of sensors (for example, RealSecure SiteProtector), while in other systems the number of sensors is limited. For example, in the NetProwler system, the management server

(NetProwler Manager) to which remote sensors are connected (NetProwler Agent), can manage no more than 20 agents [NetProwler1-00].

Hierarchical Management

In large networks implementing a mixed management scheme, the headquarters (or central office) might control the activities of the remote affiliates, despite the fact that the main management is done from the regional information security departments. In other cases, it might be necessary to instruct the IDS sensor to transmit all messages during business hours to the local console installed in the regional office. At other times, during non-business hours, these messages would be transmitted to another console, monitored 24 hours a day by the IDS operator. In both cases, a hierarchical management scheme might be required, allowing the system to switch between two consoles automatically, without user intervention. Cisco IDS is one example of such a scheme.

Group Operations

This criterion becomes very important when it is necessary to manage a large number of sensors. In large, geographically distributed networks, it is very inconvenient to perform the following operations on a per-sensor basis:

❏ Updating the attack signature database
❏ Applying templates
❏ Starting and stopping the sensors

Because of this, your IDS must be able to perform these operations for groups of sensors.

Managing Events

Specifying Priorities

The same attack can have different consequences for different hosts within a corporate network. For example, a host running Solaris 2.5.1 is vulnerable to the Ping of Death attack, while a host running Windows NT is not [ISS4-00]. We can also give another example — the presence of a modem. If the modem is connected to the computer, according to all the information security requirements, the situation is considered normal, and does not require the security administrator's attention. On the other hand, if the modem is connected in such a way as to bypass the firewall, it must be removed immediately. Yet another example relates to the Telnet service. This service must be present on the router, but is absolutely unnecessary on most workstations. Because of these reasons, the IDS must provide the ability to specify priorities for detected attacks and vulnerabilities. Priorities can be specified both statically (as was shown above) and dynamically (this topic will be covered in more detail later). At the moment of writing this, all intrusion detection systems — with the exception of the RealSecure Protection System family — were only capable of assigning static priorities. With the release of RealSecure SiteProtector, security administrators obtained the ability to delegate the comparison of the log files created by the IDS and the security scanner to the Fusion Security Module included with RealSecure SiteProtector.

Another aspect of assigning priorities is found in the qualitative and quantitative characteristics of the detected vulnerabilities and attacks. There are two points of view on this problem — the generally accepted one and the non-standard one. Using qualitative characteristics (weights) in intrusion detection systems is nothing more than theory, since quantitative parameters (low, average, and high risk) are easier to interpret by the end user. Let us consider the following example: what sounds more possible — "high-risk vulnerability" or "vulnerability with a weight of 4"? In my opinion, the first concept better reflects the idea of intrusion detection systems. Because of this, quantitative characteristics are so widely used in contemporary intrusion detection systems. Experts that back the non-standard point of view are usually those working in various research organizations or in companies that do not work much with intrusion detection technologies on a practical level. As for qualitative characteristics, they also lack a unified classification, since each manufacturer uses its own approach. Still, most manufacturers tend to use three main categories of attacks — high risk/average risk/low risk. This approach, for example, is utilized in RealSecure Network Sensor, SecureNet PRO, Cisco IDS, eTrust IDS, etc. However, there are other classifications, such as information/warning/attack/error, used in NFR NID, information/suspicious/serious/critical implemented in RealSecure Desktop Protector, suspicious/probing/attack/error/breach/virus used in Dragon, etc.

Event Correlation

When considering the aspect of priorities, we mentioned that you have the ability to assign priorities dynamically. Why is this needed and why is not the static method sufficient? Suppose that there is a Guest user account on the computer. Under normal conditions, this vulnerability has a high priority. In practice, however, the priority of this vulnerability must change from high (if this user account is enabled) to low (if the Guest account is disabled). In this case, the priority can only be calculated during the process of security scanning, which means that it must be assigned dynamically.

Let us consider a more difficult example. Suppose that the intrusion detection system detects a Ping of Death attack (which normally has the highest priority), thus forcing the security administrator to react to this event immediately. Now suppose that the corporate network contains only Windows hosts. If this is the case, this attack will not cause any damage (although it still must be registered). What should you do in this situation? In order to figure out if the detected attack is dangerous, you must know if the attacked host is vulnerable to this attack. This can be accomplished manually, and this operation is usually done when creating the network map. However, as I mentioned earlier, administrators do not seem to care enough to perform this step in most organizations. This is where the automatic event correlation mechanism comes to the rescue. This mechanism provides you with the ability to analyze the log files of the intrusion detection system and security scanner without user intervention. Based on this information, the correlation mechanism draws a conclusion as to whether the attacked system is vulnerable. If the attacked host does not contain this vulnerability, the attack priority is dynamically lowered, thus changing the predefined responses for this attack, and vice versa. On the other hand, if an attack having low priority can still damage the attacked host, the correlation mechanism increases its priority, and additional responses are applied. The Fusion Security Module supplied with RealSecure SiteProtector operates based on this principle. As of yet, other intrusion detection systems have not implemented similar mechanisms. However, most leading manufacturers have declared that they are working on it. For example, after Symantec purchased the MountainWave company, it stated that it was going to implement the CyberWolf technology, which would enable you to correlate information from different security tools and to automatically react to the detected attacks.

Besides the correlation of data from scanners and intrusion detection systems, it is often necessary to use data collected by other security tools, such as firewalls. This goal can be achieved using specially designed correlation tools, which we will describe later.

There is yet another aspect related to correlation (one that is quite often neglected) — the time after which information on the attack or vulnerability becomes obsolete. For example, the WinNuke attack is currently rather rare. Why is this the case? Naturally, the main reason for this is the fact that the vulnerability exploited by this attack has long been known to almost everyone. This vulnerability has now been eliminated in most systems. Therefore, implementing such an attack is simply a waste of time and effort. Usually, intruders try to exploit the information on security holes immediately after they are reported, but before the appropriate patches are released. Therefore, the risk imposed by attacks and vulnerabilities decreases with time. It is desirable that the correlation module take this aspect into account and decrease the priority of a specific attack or vulnerability after a certain time interval expires.

As I mentioned in *Chapter 1*, one of the main drawbacks of traditional security tools, including firewalls, is the fact that they only block attacks, without providing the possibility of preventing them. If these tools could eliminate the vulnerabilities that result in the attacks, the level of security of the corporate network would be improved significantly. The possibility of reconfiguring firewalls helps to block specific attacks, but it can not prevent the intruder from resuming these attempts. It was this situation that led Internet Security Systems to create a new technology known as SmIDS (Smarter IDS) [ISS3-00]. This technology is the first example of the integration of intrusion detection systems and security scanners. Note that this integration is mutual. For example, when it detects an attack, the RealSecure network sensor issues a command to start the Internet Scanner security analyzer to investigate the attacked host. If it detects a vulnerability on this host, and this vulnerability allows for the implementation of the registered attack, the sensor notifies the security administrator or eliminates this vulnerability automatically (Fig. 9.10).

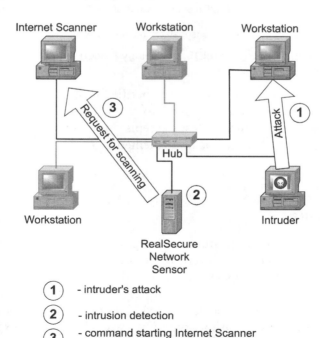

Fig. 9.10. The SmIDS technology (first implementation)

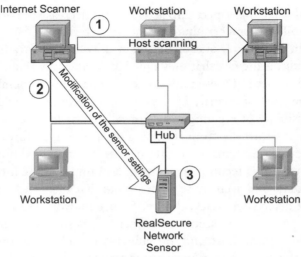

(**1**)   - host scanning and detection of a vulnerability

(**2**)   - modification of the settings of the RealSecure network sensor

(**3**)   - network sensor starts to detect new attacks

Fig. 9.11. The SmIDS technology (second implementation)

Alternatively, Internet Scanner scans specified hosts and, after detecting a vulnerability, immediately sends a command to the RealSecure network sensor in order to modify its settings. Network sensor accepts this command and initiates the procedure to detect attacks that may be implemented by exploiting the detected vulnerability (Fig. 9.11).

Trend Analysis

Trend analysis and the forecasting of changes of the security level of the corporate network are closely related to event correlation. Unfortunately, IDS manufacturers have only taken the first steps in this area, and can not really be proud of any serious achievements. However, some security scanners even now are capable of comparing the security status (the number of vulnerabilities of a specific risk level) on the same host or group of hosts at various time intervals. This enables experts to determine what influence specific security measures have on the overall security level of the corporate network.

Displaying Events

Event visualization is quite a sophisticated area, in which it is rather difficult to determine any evaluation criteria. Visualization is a method of representing data collected from the IDS sensors, and each user must determine which method of representing data is best for his or her purposes. It should be mentioned that a data visualization tool is a mandatory component of contemporary intrusion detection systems, especially in large distributed networks. This tool usually allows you to display data using various methods, from table views (like in the Internet Scanner system) and hierarchical tree-like structures (like the ones used in RealSecure Workgroup Manager), to graphical maps (like the ones used in CyberCop Scanner and Cisco IDS). Some systems do not provide such tools, and are limited to data logging and sending administrative alerts via e-mail to the central console. The popular Snort system is an example of such a system.

When choosing and testing the IDS, pay special attention to the method used to notify the administrator of possible attacks. This parameter is rather important, and it is hard to evaluate without testing the system under the conditions of your network. For a more precise evaluation, it is also good to implement stress tests, since they will demonstrate the convenience and ease of use of the system. For example, if there are not many events, you might not notice that in order to analyze a single event, you must click the mouse button 3 times. Consider, however, a situation where there are 5,000 such messages. Furthermore, some systems display events on the console as they are detected. For example, if the sensor has registered 100 attempts of remote scanning in an hour, the console will display 100 rows. But what if there are 10,000 events instead of 100? Even worse, what if these events were all registered during a small time interval, and came from 10 sensors? With an incorrectly designed console, you will get lost in such amounts of information. The only thing that you will be able to do is to watch the fleeting messages in dismay. If this is the case, the manufacturer of the system is to blame, since they were the ones who were supposed to perform the stress test and check the ergonomic parameters of the product under peak workload conditions. Various mechanisms for keeping the operator's attention at the proper level need to be implemented. As noted in [Shipley2-99], most IDS manufacturers do not test their products in large networks, since their interfaces and data visualization functions are very far from perfect. Intrusion detection systems designed with ergonomic requirements in mind (such as RealSecure SiteProtector or Dragon) do not display all events one after another. Rather, they simply specify the number of events of a specific type. As for the Cisco IDS console, it provides a special option known as freeze updates, allowing the administrator to temporarily stop the scrolling of a constantly updating event list. Besides this, the IDS must differentiate between various methods of issuing security alerts, including the following:

❏ Sound notification. It is best to have the capabilities of differentiating sound notifications for each detected attack. Otherwise, if there is only one customization parameter (enable/disable), the administrator will have to listen to a continuous beeping. Within several minutes these sounds will be perceived as background noise, and after an hour the operator will cease to pay any attention to it at all.

❏ Graphic notifications in the form of various icons.

Since events from all managed sensors are displayed in real-time mode, there can be a whole lot of them (probably several hundreds of thousands per day). This significantly complicates noticing and analyzing them. Moreover, most such events are due to false positives, and do not provide any significant information on the attacks. Thus, event filtering and sorting is a rather important characteristic of an intrusion detection system (and this is especially true for large networks). Filtering and sorting functions provide the capability of displaying only events of specific interest on the console (all events are still registered in the database). The operator must have the ability to customize this display according to his or her particular needs. Such a function, indispensable in large networks, is implemented in Cisco Secure Policy Manager. The developers of RealSecure SiteProtector have gone even further — they have integrated this function with a mechanism for grouping protected resources. This draws the operator's attention to really critical and serious attacks and vulnerabilities detected for a specific group of resources. In *Chapter 11*, we will consider the integrated operation of these two mechanisms (see Fig. 11.8). The function of displaying the events that occurred while the administrator was out (for example, at lunch or at night) will also always be rather useful.

Data visualization has one more aspect. The system console can be used to display data not only in real-time mode, but also when analyzing the data accumulated in the database. For example, Cisco Secure Policy Manager and RealSecure WorkGroup Manager are oriented towards working in real-time mode, while RealSecure SiteProtector is oriented towards analysis of accumulated information.

Grouping Protected Resources

In order to simplify the life of the security administrator, IDS must provide the ability to group all protected resources of the corporate network based on various factors:

❏ Geographic location (for example, resources of the headquarters and remote affiliates)

❏ Network topology (DMZ resources and internal network resources)

❏ Business tasks (resources of the commercial department, accounting resources, resources of the research department, etc.).

❏ Service (databases, UNIX servers, web servers, workstations, etc.).

Such a grouping allows us to focus our attention on the resources that are currently required, without distracting ourselves with irrelevant data. This significantly improves the efficiency of administrative work, especially when the console displays vast amounts of data.

When evaluating the system by this criterion, do not forget to determine how the information on all controlled hosts is registered. The best intrusion detection systems can provide a learning mode, in which the IDS collects information by investigating network packet headers. The same task can also be implemented by exporting data from network management systems, security scanners, firewalls, etc.

Central Management Console

The availability of a unified central management console is very important for large companies that need to create a complex and sophisticated information security system that combines several security tools. One of the best examples of such a system is the CheckPoint solution. Unfortunately, at the moment, there is no unified management console that can integrate all security tools. Because of this, this requirement relates only to intrusion detection systems and security scanners that must be managed from a single console. And if this goal can not be always achieved when using security tools from different manufacturers, this requirement is mandatory for tools provided by the same manufacturer. Unfortunately, however, not all manufacturers provide a unified management console.

Quite an interesting situation exists for the IDS solutions provided by Symantec. This company, after purchasing L-3, Axent Technologies, and Recourse, now supplies the following tools:

❏ The NetRecon network-level intrusion detection system

❏ The Enterprise Security Manager (ESM) host-level security scanner

❏ The NetProwler network-level intrusion detection system

❏ The Intruder Alert OS-level intrusion detection system

❏ The ManHunt intrusion detection system

❏ The ManTrap deception system

However, this long list lacks the products that were originally developed by Symantec. The first four systems were released by Axent, while NetProwler was originally developed by the Internet Tools company, and was initially was supplied under the name ID-Trak. The last two items on this list are solutions from Recourse. At the moment of writing this, these 6 systems did not have any central "control point" (although some steps in this direction have been taken), and you have to use 6 different management consoles. A similar situation exists with other manufacturers that promote solutions purchased along with smaller companies.

Report Generation

Like the data visualization subsystem, the report generation subsystem is a very important component of any IDS. The lack of this component complicates the process of determining the attacks that are registered most frequently and the hosts that most often become targets of intruder attacks. Based on the information created by the reporting subsystem, the administrator plans all further activity — changes in security policy, elimination of vulnerabilities, reconfiguration of network equipment, preparation of reports for management, etc. An advanced report generating subsystem must have the following properties:

❐ The availability of both text and graphic information in reports, which can satisfy practically all requirements for creating meaningful and illustrative reports.

❐ The capability of including into the reports information on the detected attack or vulnerability along with the operating systems vulnerable to it, cases of false positives, methods of elimination, links to manufacturer sites, and additional reference information. Recently, specifying the correspondence between the detected problem and its related information in the CVE database has become a rule.

❐ The possibility of selecting only the required data from the entire set of accumulated information according to specified criteria (time interval, attack or vulnerability name, risk level, operating system, type of attack or vulnerability, and so on).

❐ Functions of data sorting according to various parameters (by name, by date, by risk level, by the source or destination address, etc.).

❐ The possibility of creating reports for different categories of specialists. At the least, we need to choose three such categories: the upper-level management of the company, managers, and technical personnel. Reports of the first category should not include any technical information on the detected vulnerabilities or attacks. Such reports must contain only a description of the general status of the corporate network security. Reports that fall into the second category can contain more detailed technical information, for example, a description of the detected vulnerabilities or attacks, however, without specifying the steps required to eliminate them. The same category also includes a so-called trend analysis, showing the trends in the changes in the security level of specific hosts within the corporate network. The third class contains technical reports that include detailed information on each detected problem, recommendations for their elimination, and to references for additional information sources. This type of report is produced by the Internet Scanner and Cisco Secure Scanner.

❑ Export capabilities. Besides printing the reports on printers and saving them as files, some intrusion detection systems can export reports into formats of other applications, such as Lotus Notes or MS Exchange.

❑ Support of various report formats. Usually, intrusion detection systems are limited to two or three formats when creating reports: HTML, CSV, and the native format of the IDS. However, depending on the operating system under which the IDS runs, and on the installed applications and other parameters, the intrusion detection system might create reports in other formats, such as Microsoft Word, Microsoft Excel, ODBC, and DIF (Data Interchange Format), etc.

❑ The possibility of creating report templates. Quite often, the existing templates are insufficient, such as when your organization has adopted a custom report template (with the company logo, report author, date and time of creation, sensitivity level, and so on). In this case, the intrusion detection system you choose must have a mechanism for creating custom report templates. These mechanisms are provided by Internet Scanner, RealSecure, Cisco Secure Scanner, etc. The function for creating custom templates is implemented differently in different systems. For example, Internet Security Systems products use third-party software for this purpose — the Crystal Report system from Seagate. Cisco Systems uses built-in functions of the operating system, i.e., report templates are normal HTML files [Cisco1-99].

Time Synchronization

This criterion is rather important for international corporations and companies with a large number of affiliates around the world. If this requirement is met, the events are displayed on the console using the common unified time system. The confusion caused by viewing events from sensors installed in different time zones significantly complicates and slows down event analysis and attack response. The necessity of information correlation (especially when dealing with distributed attacks) requires that you perform time synchronization for all sensors, or display all events on the central console using a single reference point.

Automating Routine Tasks

When employees responsible for the intrusion detection system can not pay sufficient attention to it, it is best to automate the process of the IDS's operation. Automation is especially important for security scanners, whose efficiency depends on the frequency of their use. However, administrators quite often forget to or just are not able to start the scanner in due time, which results in discrepancies between the actual and supposed states of security of the corporate network. Thus, the most important aspect in such situations is the possibility of the IDS's automation, which can be implemented using built-in mechanisms (like in the Enterprise Security Manager system), or by starting IDS components from the command line.

Automatic updating of the signature database is a mandatory requirement for any intrusion detection system. If this capability is not provided, the attack and signature database will not be maintained in its most up-to-date status.

Ease of Use and Customization Capabilities

Such criteria as "ease of use" or "intuitive and user-friendly interface" are rather subjective characteristics very closely related to the visualization of registered data, which we covered earlier in this chapter. It might be said that almost each person has his or her own idea as to what "ease of use" means. For example, one security professional may have no problem working with the command line, manually entering all commands, and changing the configuration files, while other users just can not do without a graphic console and a mouse. The chosen system must be convenient for the end-user, rather than for its vendor or a third-party consultant. This requirement is the most important, and you must properly evaluate its convenience and ease of use during the testing procedures. According to the opinions of most experts [Shipley1-00], this parameter is one of the most important these days. It does not much matter how many signatures are stored in the IDS database or how fast the system identifies them. If the system provides an excessive amount of information to the operator, and it is impossible to make efficient use of this information, such a system is practically useless. On the other hand, if the console hides most of the important information from an operator who has to spend time and effort to retrieve the required information from the database, this also is not good. To form your own opinion as to the requirements for convenient and ergonomic user interfaces, consider the screenshots shown in Figs. 9.12—9.14.

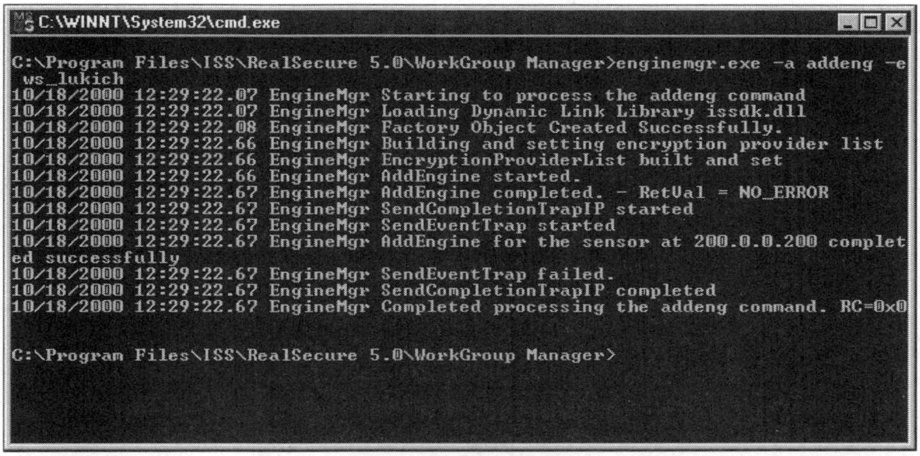

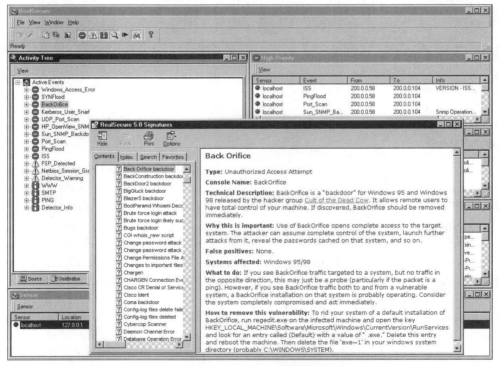

Fig. 9.12. Managing the RealSecure intrusion detection system from the command line

Fig. 9.13. Managing RealSecure using the RealSecure Workgroup Manager
graphic console

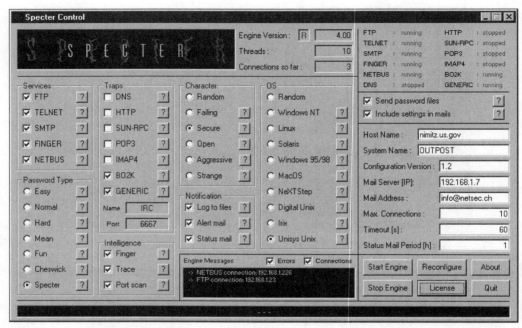

Fig. 9.14. Managing Specter using a graphic console

Templates

Let us suppose that you need to analyze the security status of the three segments of your corporate network. The first segment is located at a significant distance from headquarters, and the number of hosts within it is unknown. The second segment is the "demilitarized zone," containing Web, FTP, SMTP, and DNS servers. The third segment is localized within headquarters' network and contains database servers. This task can be solved by starting all the checks for each of the analyzed devices. First of all, however, it is necessary to determine the list of analyzed equipment, i.e., to perform a network inventory. Then, you must classify all the scanned devices by OS type and the software that they are running. This will allow you to reduce the required number of checks and speed up the security scan. Templates that describe the required procedures for each category of devices are intended for just this purpose. The best implementation of this scheme belongs to Internet Security Systems, who have introduced the concept of so-called security levels, which significantly simplifies management of the information security infrastructure. This concept is based on the principles listed below.

❑ It is impossible to ensure security without knowing the network topology, protected resources, and information flows.
❑ For most devices of the corporate network (workstations, for example), there is no need to implement expensive and labor-intensive measures to ensure security.
❑ The most critical devices need serious protection at all levels of the information infrastructure.
❑ Malicious insiders are the most dangerous.
❑ The security infrastructure must be implemented on all levels.

At the first step, you will have to analyze the existing network devices, workstations, servers, and so on. This will enable you to find an answer to the question of "What needs protecting?" This analysis is one of the components of the process of creating a network map. At the next level (ensuring minimal security) you need to prevent external attacks on the protected host. A medium security level includes protection against insiders that are able to implement various attacks and misuses. The highest security level is intended for the most critical hosts within the corporate network — in particular, against failures or against Denial of Services that occur because of them [ISS8-00].

Thus, at the lowest level, it is necessary to identify and classify absolutely all devices of the corporate network (including ones located in remote affiliates). For these devices, you will need to implement a minimal security level. Minimum security is usually ensured for workstations. At the next security level, the range of devices protected against external attack narrows. This list includes internal servers, network equipment, and other important devices on which the corporate network operation depends (application servers, DMZ devices, network equipment). Finally, the strongest security is intended for hosts that form the core of the whole corporate network (servers for accounting, billing, payroll systems, perimeter devices).

This concept is practically implemented in seven levels, used in all ISS products. The first five levels are applicable for the Internet Scanner system that performs remote security scanning. The levels from the second to the seventh are implemented in the Database Scanner system, which also performs remote analysis. However, since this system is used to analyze specific devices (DBMS), the inventory and classification stage (level 1) is not used in the Database Scanner. The System Scanner product is intended for detecting internal vulnerabilities that exist on the analyzed host, and therefore this system uses levels 3 to 7. This structuring allows you to identify and select the devices for which security requirements are different.

A similar task arises for other categories of intrusion detection systems. For example, depending on the location of the intrusion detection system (DMZ, Unix segment, and so on) and on the tasks delegated to it (detection of attacks, control over Internet access, etc.), it might be necessary to include specific signatures or implement specific response types. Templates provide you with the capability of replicating them.

Protection against Unauthorized Access

Despite the fact that an intrusion detection system is a protection tool itself, it also needs protection against unauthorized access, since, should it fail to operate, the whole network is exposed to the risk of intrusion.

Integrity Control

Since unauthorized modification of IDS components can result in it being compromised and, consequently, rendering it impossible to use the data gathered by the IDS as a reliable source of information on the actions of the intruders, it is necessary to provide the intrusion detection system with the ability to control the integrity of all of its components. If this is impossible, you should at least specify the control checksum values for all files included with the system in the documentation or in a separate file. This will enable you to check their integrity using third-party tools, such as Tripwire, or the OS's built-in tools (mainly Unix utilities).

Stealth Mode

Stealth mode makes the intrusion detection system invisible in the network. This is activated by installing two network adapters into the computer on which the network sensor is installed. One of these adapters will function in promiscuous mode, without TCP/IP stack support. Thus, this network adapter will not have an IP address, but will monitor all network traffic within the controlled segment. This adapter is connected to the switch, hub, splitter, etc. The second adapter must be bound to the TCP/IP stack and used to loopback to the management console, sending notifications via e-mail, SNMP control sequences, and the implementation of other types of responses (Fig. 9.15).

The invisibility of the intrusion detection system enables the improvement of protection levels in the network segment in which the intrusion detection system is installed, protects it from attacks by intruders, and prevents these intruders from compromising the IDS.

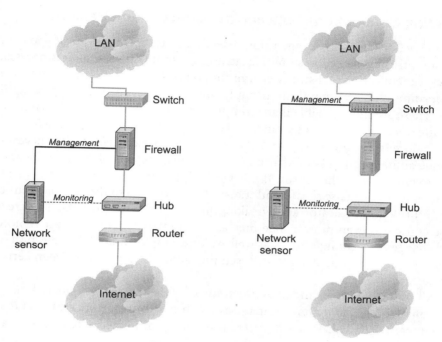

Fig. 9.15. Stealth mode

Controlling Access to IDS Components

Since the intrusion detection system is one of the most important components of the information security infrastructure, it is necessary to limit the list of individuals who have access to system components and to the data collected by the IDS. Unauthorized access to these components can result in configuration changes or in important information, such as the vulnerabilities of the corporate network, being revealed.

Access control can be implemented using different approaches. For example, in the NetProwler system, requests for the user ID and password are carried out several times — when starting the management console, when connecting to the management server, and when connecting NetProwler agents (sensors) to the management server. In the RealSecure SiteProtector system, this mechanism is implemented differently — it allows you to specify the roles of IDS users, such as operator, administrator, analyst, etc. Each of the user roles has its own field of activity. In Internet Scanner, this mechanism is somewhat simpler — it can only be installed and started by a user belonging to the Administrators group. Requests from all other users are blocked.

Protecting Connections between the Console and Sensors

If you need to control your intrusion detection system remotely, or if you have to control an intrusion detection system located in a remote office, then it is necessary to use strict authentication and strong encryption to prevent the IDS components from being compromised. For authentication, apply single-use passwords or cryptographic protocols. These are more reliable than a simple request for an identifier or password, which is quite often transmitted as plain text. For example, when running the RealSecure system, before initiating interaction between the console and sensor, it is necessary to exchange authentication keys. If you do not do this, the console will not be able to connect to and manage the sensor. If this kind of protection is lacking, the intruder might be able to install a false sensor and transmit falsified data to the console, thus deceiving the security administrator and wreaking havoc on the logged data. The creation of a false console is even more dangerous, as it can intercept control over remote sensors and change their configuration, as well as, for example, disable the detection of specific events or the function charged with sending administrative alerts when certain events are detected.

All of the data transmitted between the console and sensors (including updates to the vulnerabilities and attack signatures databases) must be encrypted and subject to data integrity control. This will help to prevent unauthorized access to this data and its modifications.

Control over the IDS Components Activity

The intrusion detection system is one of the most critical components of the information security infrastructure. Because of this, it must be protected from various external influences and interruption of the communication between the management console and the sensors. Although the sensors continue operating even if this connection is interrupted (see *Chapter 6*), you need to ensure mechanisms for detecting such violations and protecting the IDS against them.

In a geographically distributed network, where IDS sensors are installed far from the management console, it is necessary to provide the capability of controlling their activities. The failure of a particular sensor, the interruption of the connection to any sensor, and other errors of this type must be registered immediately and reported to the intrusion detection system operator. Such mechanisms are implemented in most intrusion detection systems, including RealSecure and Cisco IDS.

One such mechanism uses TCP (or another similar protocol), which allows you to establish a virtual connection between the sensor and the console (or management server). If this virtual connection is interrupted or terminated, it will immediately become obvious. Cisco has developed a rather interesting UDP-oriented Post Office protocol for its Cisco IDS product. Using this protocol, each component of the Cisco IDS is specified by a unique address, comprising three parts: "Organization," "Host," and "Application." This addressing scheme serves as the basis for the point-to-point protocol, which ensures up to 255 alternate routes between Cisco IDS components. As soon as the system detects that the connection between the sensor and management console (or between two consoles) has been interrupted, it automatically switches to an alternate route, etc. If the interrupted connection is restored (using the HeartBeat mechanism) the system switches back to the restored connection. All missed packets are sent anew. The Post Office protocol is used for implementing hierarchical management in the Cisco IDS 4200 [NetRanger1-99].

Fault Tolerance, Availability, and Reliability

In mission-critical applications, for which it is necessary to ensure high availability and fault tolerance, it is possible to utilize intrusion detection systems that implement backup, standby, and clustering mechanisms. There are three types of standby mechanisms. Hot standby provides the ability to automatically switch between the main and the backup intrusion detection system. Using hot standby minimizes the possible downtime of the intrusion detection system. Warm standby requires small configuration changes before switching between the main and backup intrusion detection systems. Cold standby requires significant configuration changes. Both intrusion detection system sensors (Fig. 9.16) and their consoles (Fig. 9.17) are subject to backup.

Backup consoles are used in Cisco Secure IDS and System Scanner, while the RealSecure for Nokia system is an example of sensor backup. As its name implies, this IDS was created by the cooperation of Internet Security Systems and Nokia. Here, two or more sensors can be joined into a cluster, thus improving the reliability of the intrusion detection system in networks with high requirements regarding availability.

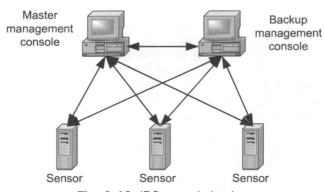

Fig. 9.16. IDS console backup

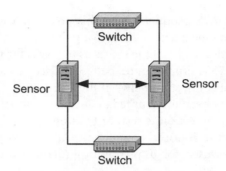

Fig. 9.17. IDS sensor backup

Another example of sensor backup is demonstrated in the Cisco Secure Integrated Software, which is built into the Cisco Systems network equipment. Since backup capabilities (such as using the Hot Standby Routing Protocol (HSRP) are included in most products from Cisco, this function is also automatically implemented in the intrusion detection system (although in a somewhat limited mode).

Besides employing backup devices, other methods that often are not related to a specific intrusion detection system can be used. Such mechanisms include a fault-tolerance level, which is present either at the software level (Compaq solutions) or at the hardware level (solutions from Intel, 3Com, etc.).

Compaq's Advanced Network Error Correction Support for Windows NT mechanism provides network-level fault tolerance for network adapters, cables, and hubs [Compaq1-98]. Compaq's Advanced Network Control Utility and NetFlex-3 Device Driver Controller are used to configure coupled network adapters on Compaq Proliant servers. These configuration changes are carried out at the following levels:

❒ Network adapter
❒ Cable
❒ Hub

This mechanism, designed for RealSecure Network Sensor and supplied with Compaq servers, functions according to the following principle: one of the network interfaces is designated as the primary interface, while the other is designated as secondary. When the driver detects the failure of one of the cards, it automatically switches to the other card. This can occur due to the following reasons:

❒ Cable failure
❒ User-initiated switching
❒ NIC performance degradation
❒ Other hardware problems

3Com provides fault tolerance in its network adapters using a custom approach. The company has developed the DynamicAccess technology, which is integrated into server NICs such as 3Com EtherLink Server NIC 3C980, 3C980B-TX, and 3C980C-TC. These adapters provide mechanisms that improve the reliability of the network sensor.

☐ *Self-Healing Drivers*. These ensure the reliable operation of the network sensor by monitoring network connection performance and other parameters. When necessary, these drivers perform corrective actions. Situations leading to failures include access collisions and carrier loss. Corrective actions include driver reloading, checking connection integrity, and switching to another adapter.

☐ *Resilient Server Link*. This provides the capability of restoring the connection in the event of network adapter failure and redistributing the traffic between the adapters that remain in operation. This procedure is absolutely seamless and transparent to the user. As long as this task is performed quickly enough, it ensures continuous network operation.

Intel has introduced the AFT (Adapter Fault Tolerance) technology, which incorporates functions similar to those in the DynamicAccess technology. This technology is used in the Intel PRO/100 and Intel PRO/100+ families of adapters.

Integration with Other Tools

Not every intrusion detection system is the primary tool for network protection, and even the primary security system might play a minor role in the general communications infrastructure. Quite often, security departments are subordinate to IT departments. In organizations where this is the case, a network management system is adopted as the corporate standard (HP OpenView is one example). These corporations usually try to integrate all other tools (including security tools) with this system. Therefore, when choosing an intrusion detection system, it is necessary to take into account its ability to be integrated with network management systems and other products used within your organization.

Network Management Systems

As I mentioned above, some intrusion detection systems can be integrated with network management systems. For example, in Cisco IDS, coordination with other components is performed via a console (Cisco IDS Director), which is the plug-in module of the HP OpenView system (for managing Cisco IDS, it is also possible to use Cisco

Secure Policy Manager and Cisco IDS Device Manager). Besides using plug-in modules, integration can be done using the SNMP protocol. This capability is provided by practically every commercial intrusion detection system — for example, in RealSecure Network Sensor, NetProwler, etc.

Other Management Systems

Besides using the above-mentioned systems, management can be carried out using other products. For example, Cisco Secure IDS Sensor can be managed by the Cisco Secure Policy Manager (instead of Cisco Secure IDS Director), which also has priority over Cisco Secure PIX Firewall, Access Control Lists (ACL) for Cisco routers, Cisco VPN tools, and Cisco Secure Integrated Software [Schaer1-00]. The only thing that complicates this situation is the availability of two CSPM versions with the prefixes *i* and *f*, which are responsible for managing intrusion detection systems and firewalls, and ACL and VPN, respectively.

Another example of a management system is the Spitfire system developed by the Mitre Corporation in response to an order from the 609th information warfare force of the U.S. Air Force Electronic Systems Center and Hanscom AFB [Spitfire1-99]. Other users of this system are NAVAL and Army Land Information Warfare Activity. Despite the fact that Spitfire is not a commercial product and is available only to U.S. government organizations, I would like to provide a brief description of this system. The system is designed to gather data on attacks and cases of misuse from two intrusion detection systems adopted by the U.S. Department of Defense — RealSecure and Cisco Secure IDS (NetRanger). Special MITRE Alarm Loader agents are installed on computers running RealSecure WorkGroup Manager or Cisco Secure IDS Director management consoles. These agents are responsible for converting and transmitting records from RealSecure and Cisco Secure IDS log files to an Oracle database (Fig. 9.18).

The Spitfire management console is created using PowerBuilder. It is responsible for rendering an analysis of data from RealSecure and Cisco Secure IDS network sensors (Fig. 9.19), as well as for managing and controlling these sensors. All management is performed using the IP*Works system developed by devSoft. The Spitfire system supports operating systems such as Windows NT and Windows 95/98.

Another example of a product that can manage intrusion detection systems is the well known Firewall-1 (VPN-1) firewall from Check Point, which was designed with the OPSEC initiative in mind. This initiative allows developers to integrate different security products. For example, intrusion detection systems such as RealSecure Network Sensor, NetProwler, eTrust IDS, and Anzen Flight Jacket can reconfigure CheckPoint Firewall-1 via the SAM protocol.

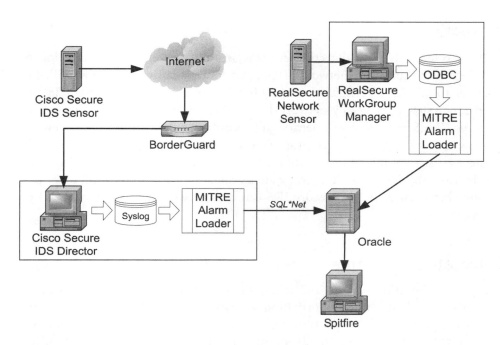

Fig. 9.18. Architecture of the Spitfire system

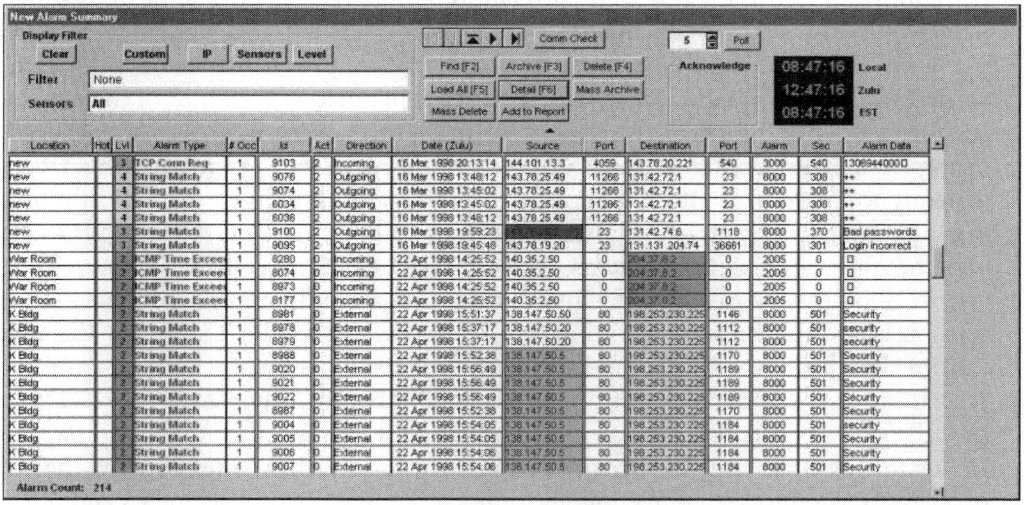

Fig. 9.19. Graphic user interface of the Spitfire system

Protection Tools

Quite often, intrusion detection systems are united with other protection tools installed in the corporate network. This provides the ability to create a unified complex center to provide information security for the organization. Most often, intrusion detection systems (especially network-level IDSs) work together with firewalls. For example, RealSecure Network Sensor can reconfigure the Check Point Firewall-1, Net-Prowler can integrate with Raptor, eTrust IDS can configure Check Point Firewall-1 and eTrust Firewall, and Snort can alter rules created on the IPCHAINS screen. Besides firewalls, intrusion detection systems can also be integrated with other protection tools. For example, Cisco Secure IDS can change access control lists (ACL) on Cisco routers.

Correlation Systems

Intrusion detection systems and security scanners create detailed reports on potential points of weakness in the information security system, and are able to react to attacks in real-time mode. Firewalls allow only specific types of traffic to pass. All information registered by these tools is vitally important, since it enables security administrators to develop an efficient security policy and evaluate the capabilities of a policy to be implemented.

Unfortunately, the gathering, correlation, comparison, and analysis of all of the data from numerous independent sources is time-consuming, and requires skilled personnel. This is due to the fact that different types of products are not compatible or related to each other and are unable to create a generalized "snapshot" of the network's security status or reconfigure network security tools in response to an attack or a change in network configuration. Even more important, they can not use the data they generate to implement efficient changes in the security system by dynamically changing the settings of the attacked hosts or performing a security analysis in order to make sure that there are no other systems vulnerable to the detected attack.

To unite the data from different security tools, including intrusion detection systems, it is possible to employ various correlation systems, which allow for the collection of data from security scanners, intrusion detection systems, firewalls, and other security tools located at different points of a distributed corporate network. This approach provides you with an overview of the security status of the network as a whole. Using this system, security personnel can concentrate their attention on the main problems related to the vulnerabilities found at the most critical segments and hosts of the corporate network.

The list of such systems includes:

❏ SAFEsuite Decisions from Internet Security Systems. This system is oriented towards ISS security products.

❏ netForensics from the company of the same name (http://www.netforensics.com). This system is oriented towards security tools provided by Cisco Systems.

❏ Private I from Open Systems (http://www.opensystems.com).

❏ Security Manager from Intellitactics (http://www.itactics.com).

❏ SPECTRUM Security Manager from Aprisma Management Technologies (http://www.aprisma.com).

All these systems support a wide range of security tools. However, they all have one significant drawback — they are all unable to change the settings of the supported systems according to the analysis results. The only exception is the RealSecure SiteProtector system, which not only analyzes the data received from different security tools, but can also manage their settings.

When choosing one of the above systems, bear in mind that they also need to updated, just like the security tools that they support. Furthermore, the correlation system must update its knowledge base with information on new attacks and vulnerabilities each time an IDS or security scanner update is released; otherwise it will be unable to analyze unknown events. Note that most advertising materials never mention this fact, only specifying that the product supports various intrusion detection systems, firewalls, proxy servers, and so on.

Performance

Most manufacturers will try to assure you that their systems are capable of handling 100 Mbit/sec traffic, or even "operate at the speed of the physical channel." The real situation, however, is not quite as remarkable (I will cover this aspect in more detail in *Chapters 10* and *12*). However, I would like to mention that this criterion is not that important for organizations that plan to use an intrusion detection system at the network perimeter, since the total inbound traffic does not even come anywhere near that speed. On the other hand, internal traffic not only reaches this value, but quite often exceeds it.

The Influence on the Performance of the Network or Host

The IDS's influence on the performance of a controlled host or network is a criterion that is rather difficult to describe. First, the chosen IDS must not significantly degrade the performance of the controlled system. The reason for this is obvious. When selecting and testing an intrusion detection system, you should first estimate the maximum workload on the system to be controlled in order to preview the behavior of the chosen tool under these conditions. It should be mentioned that this criterion is applicable mainly to host-level intrusion detection systems, since these systems are the ones for which performance degradation is a matter of primary importance. As a rule, an IDS decreases the performance of a protected host by 1–5%. However, with an incorrect configuration, this parameter can grow to up to 20% or even more. On the other hand, the IDS/9000 system developed for detecting attacks on hosts running the HP UX OS decreases the performance of protected host by less than 1%.

Installation and Configuration

Normally, this group of criteria is not tested carefully for the chosen IDS. However, this is a big mistake. In a large network, unskilled installation can drive even the most friendly and good-natured administrator crazy. In part, this topic is covered in *Chapter 11*. Here I will just point out some specific aspects that need special attention:

❑ *Remote installation.* Check to see if the chosen system implements a mechanism that allows you to perform remote installation without the presence of the security administrator. Certainly, the installation process does not always run smoothly, and sometimes it might need the administrator's intervention. Sometimes, however, this capability might be necessary (especially if you need to install the IDS on hundreds and hundreds of workstations).

❑ *Automatic installation.* This criterion is also very important to systems installed on a specific host. After installing an IDS once and saving all system prompts and your answers in a special file, you will be able to replicate this file along with the system distribution, and thus significantly simplify the process of installing the system on a computer with an identical configuration.

❑ *Access control.* As I already mentioned, the IDS itself must be protected from attacks. Because of this, it is desirable to create the appropriate IDS user accounts and specify the appropriate access rights during installation.

❑ *Predefined configuration.* In order to reduce the time required for deploying the system and bringing it into operation, you should have a mechanism for creating a predefined configuration. Depending on the system, this mechanism can be implemented in different ways. For example, when installing integrity control systems, it is advisable to create checksums for all protected files (naturally, before doing so, you have to make sure that the host is not infected by a virus or compromised by Trojans or Internet worms). Quite an interesting mechanism is implemented in the NetProwler system, which scans the hosts of the controlled segment and determines their operating systems. When this operation is complete, the system enables only those signatures that are applicable to the detected operating systems. The availability of standard templates on the basis of which the administrator can create custom templates for a protected host or network segment is also a benefit.

❑ *Distribution of authentication keys.* When dealing with an IDS based on a client/server architecture, you need to solve the problem of the distribution of authentication and encryption keys. This problem must be solved while installing the IDS components.

If the IDS requires additional software (such as Internet Explorer, virtual Java machine, databases, etc.), this additional software must be included into the distribution set. If this condition is not met, you might encounter problems during installation. A most frustrating situation is one in which it becomes evident during installation that this additional software costs quite a bit.

Availability of API and SDK

The availability of an application programming interface (API or SDK) is an additional criterion that becomes important if your company has qualified programmers who integrate purchased tools with custom software, or if the company needs to perform this integration for a customer. In the latter case, you can use API to implement the management of the IDS sensors from the custom management system. Usually, IDS manufacturers rarely implement such an API, since this requires additional expenses that thus might not bring the expected profit. Therefore, only a limited number of manufacturers provide a built-in API or SDK. However, you should not confuse the abovementioned SDK and API with a similar term introduced by the WebTrends Corporations in its WebTrends Security Analyzer product. This company provides the so-called POST initiative (Platform for Open Security Testing) SDK, which is intended for writing custom vulnerability checks [WebTrends1-00, WebTrends1-98].

Technical Support

Even if you choose the most efficient intrusion detection system, from time to time you might need technical support from the manufacturer or vendor. The technical support service might include consulting services by phone or e-mail, software updates, maintenance work at the customer's location, and informational support, training, technical seminars, and so on. High-quality technical support is very important, since quite often several days elapse before obtaining an answer to a request sent. Often, the fact that the client's request has been received is not even confirmed, and therefore the customer does not know what to think when there is no answer for two or three days. These questions might be vitally important to the operation of the whole network. Although it is rather difficult to cover all the criteria for evaluating the quality of the technical support, I will briefly describe the most common ones.

Support Levels

Manufacturers usually offer from two to five support levels, which differ in the range of services provided, response times, etc. The first level includes only software updates as new versions are released (this level is provided by the Check Point company). The services provided at the second level (which some companies include in their first-level support services) also include technical support services. These are also provided at the next level, but there the response times are much shorter. For example, you generally have to wait from 12 to 24 hours for a response at the second support level, while the wait at the third level is from 6 to 12 hours, at the fourth it normally does not exceed 6 hours, and responses at the fifth level generally come within 1 hour.

Support Method

Methods of supporting IDS users also can differ, starting with the usual methods of corresponding via e-mail or phone, and progressing to on-line chats and tracing incidents via the Web. Depending on the support level and the cost, the support service provider might delegate a support specialist to work with the customer on an individual basis. A rather good source of information is the so-called knowledge base, which stores descriptions and solutions to common problems encountered by other customers.

Business Hours

The business hours of the technical support service are the most important parameter of technical support. There are two possibilities — 5×8 (business hours only) or 7×24 (twenty-four hours). The first is the most common, since it is easier to implement. However, in such a case, time delays are inevitable, especially if the customer and service provider are located in different time zones. If there is 7×24 support, this problem does not arise.

Mailing Lists

Mailing lists are an additional element of technical support, which simplify the job of IDS users. The creation and posting of the mail can be performed either by the manufacturer or the IDS vendor. In the first case, this usually is done in the form of a mailing that contains general news, information on upcoming releases, etc. Manufacturers may also generate mailing lists, answers to most frequently asked questions, and answers from technical support services or from other users that have encountered similar problems and managed to solve them themselves. Such lists can also be published in the form of a Web conference on the company's web server. The vendor can also operate a localized mailing list that is oriented toward foreign customers.

Attack Database

Attack or vulnerability signature databases are compiled and published on the Internet by practically every vendor that offers intrusion detection systems. These databases enable users to become acquainted with the late breaking news and technological advances both in the field of hacking technologies and in the field of data protection. Examples of this type of database are those supported by ISS (the X-Force group — http://xforce.iss.net), Symantec (the SWAT group), and Cisco Systems.

Training

We have covered training in great detail, so we will not repeat it here. Just be aware that most system developers and vendors offer at least some training on the basics of operating and using their systems.

Cost

Cost is, perhaps, one of the most important criteria that needs to be taken into account when selecting an intrusion detection system. Quite often, organizations choose a cheaper solution rather than one of the more efficient ones available. Clearly, this is not the best practice, but price must be taken into account. Because of this, most manufacturers offer special programs aimed at potential customers. The most common methods of this marketing approach (without mentioning the vendors that apply these methods) are listed below.

❑ Arranging payment for the chosen system on an installment plan.
❑ Discounts for customers purchasing several tools from the same manufacturer.
❑ Special prices for educational institutions.
❑ Discounts for customers switching over from a competitor's product.

Flexibility

Even the most efficient intrusion detection system can not satisfy absolutely all user requirements. Because of this, a high-quality IDS product must provide flexibility, to allow users to customize it according to their specific requirements. There are several chief mechanisms that determine an IDS system's flexibility.

Other Criteria

Quite often, we think about intrusion detection systems in a very narrow sense. Most times, people think that intrusion detection systems are only for protecting corporate resources. In practice, however, this is not so. Intrusion detection systems are vitally important components of a corporate network. If this component fails, the whole network is at risk. Because of this, when creating (or choosing) an intrusion detection system, it is necessary to consider all aspects that are characteristic for all critical systems.

Assigning Priorities to Criteria

Most of the above-described criteria can be included into the following table, describing their importance (on a scale of 1 to 3) for various categories of users (Table 9.4).

Table 9.4. Priorities of IDS Selection Criteria for Different Categories of Users

Criterion	Small businesses	Large companies	International corporations	ISPs	Service providers	Government organizations
Attack database updates	3	3	3	3	3	3
Update method	1	3	3	2	3	3
Creating custom events	1	2	2	3	3	2
Monitoring of custom events	3	2	1	1	1	1
False negative notifications	2	2	2	3	3	2
Creating custom responses	1	2	2	2	3	1

continues

Table 9.4 Continued

Criterion	Small businesses	Large companies	International corporations	ISPs	Service providers	Government organizations
Remote control	1	3	3	2	3	3
Unlimited number of managed sensors	1	2	3	2	3	3
Hierarchical management	1	2	3	1	1	2
Group operations over the sensors	1	2	3	2	2	2
Event correlation	1	2	3	1	3	3
Dynamic priority changes	1	2	3	1	3	3
Trend analysis	1	2	3	1	3	3
Event representation	3	3	3	2	3	2
Grouping of protected resources	1	2	3	1	3	2
Centralized management console	1	2	3	3	3	3
Time synchronization	1	1	3	1	3	3
Automation	1	2	3	1	2	2
Template support	1	2	3	1	3	3
Protection against unauthorized access	1	2	3	3	3	3
Fault tolerance	1	3	3	3	3	2
Integration	1	2	3	3	3	2
Installation	1	2	3	1	1	3
Training availability	2	3	3	1	2	2

Testing

Each new release of security tools (including intrusion detection systems) is more sophisticated than the previous one, which increases the risk of failure due to more implementation bugs. However, clients do not normally test purchased software (or if they do, they do not do it thoroughly enough). Why does this happen? Quite often, the customers tend to rely on the manufacturer or vendor (especially if this is a well-known brand, such as Cisco or Sun). Some customers do not consider this task a very important one, while others simply are short on time and human resources. For example, I have many times encountered the situation in which the client demanded that a purchased system be brought into routine operation within a month. The quite a reasonable recommendation to test the system in order to analyze its behavior in the customer's network often caused indignation and misunderstanding: "What for? We paid good money; it should work fine." Furthermore, the lack of testing experience is also a rather important aspect.

At the time of writing this book, there were no standards for testing intrusion detection systems. However, certain steps in this direction have already been taken, and research in this area continues. This is due to the fact that the technology under consideration is relatively new, and as of yet, developers have not achieved a mutual understanding. The lack of a mathematical basis for intrusion detection technology also prevents researchers from complete and detailed testing of the tools. Ways of testing that utilize statistical methods are those that are being studied in the most detailed manner and that have been developed most extensively. Such systems include profile-based intrusion detection systems. It is important to note that most research work in the field of testing intrusion detection systems has been carried out in the last three to five years.

There are virtually no open sources that provide descriptions of testing methods, since each organization performing tests is using its own testing methods. These methods are the commercial, intellectual property of the individual company, and therefore are kept top secret. The only exception to this rule is the Lincoln Laboratory, which is developing a standard for testing network-level intrusion detection tools. However, access to these materials is limited, they are very hard to obtain, and quoting from them is prohibited. If you are interested in becoming acquainted with these tools, visit the following web server (with limited access): http://ideval.ll.mit.edu.

Quite recently, a new evaluation standard appeared — the Open Security Evaluation Criteria (OSEC), which is intended for testing and evaluating information security tools. The evaluation criteria for network intrusion detection systems (http://osec.neohapsis.com/) were the first to be released.

The lack of a unified testing methodology results in a large variety of testing methods, since each organization develops its own. Because of this, some quite interestuing situations, in which the same system shows different results in different tests, might occur. This happens because each test lab differs not only in the tests performed, but also in the environment in which the testing takes place, in the qualification level of the testers, the priorities of the evaluation criteria, and so on.

Sometimes there are even more serious situations. It is no secret that each manufacturer wants its product to be praised as the best, and IDS manufacturers are no exception. Certainly, if you are rated as the market leader, it is much more probable that the customer will choose your products. Not all companies can afford full-feature testing of the security system they are going to purchase. This is why manufacturers themselves often become customers of so-called "independent" consulting companies, test labs, and so on (although they certainly try not to advertise this fact). As a result, the analysis can not be considered objective, since it is naive to think that the company that sponsored the testing will not be proclaimed the market leader. Without mentioning specific names, I would like to mention that, recently, I have encountered reports from "respectable" consulting firms, released at the same time, but that give different companies the title of market leader. Also note that it is practically impossible to prove that a specific consulting firm is not correct, since their testing methods are their own "know-how," which must not be revealed, and therefore can not be checked for correctness. This is why it is so important to develop a unified method of IDS testing and evaluation.

Of course, for the moment, there are many good publications dedicated to IDS testing, such as [Shieply1-01], [Yocom1-00], [Jackson1-99], [Denmac1-99], [ICSA1-00], [Newman1-98], [Hurwicz1-98], [SC1-00], and [NSS1-02]. However, all of these and similar tests must be interpreted critically, just because all of them are not conducted in your network and can not take into account all the specific features of your organization. Moreover, a system that was considered by the testers to be the best one might be unsuitable for your organization. As was shown earlier, each customer must have their own priorities — parameters that are vitally important for one customer might be of little or no importance to another. For example, at the beginning of the test described in [Shieply1-00], the NFR system lost 2 million frames during the first 48 hours of operation, while the eTrust system showed that it requires a processor 4 thousand times as powerful as your 700 MHz Pentium III. Because of this, you should not rely completely on the manufacturer's advertisements, but rather test all the facts and parameters yourself.

How should you perform the testing? This question is the one most frequently asked by security administrators who do not want to rely completely on the vendor's word. All tests can be classified according to the above-described groups of criteria, for example:

❏ *Intrusion detection.* This class is one of the most important ones, and these tests are conducted by all test labs. As I have already mentioned, it is not the number of signatures that is of primary importance, but rather the efficiency of detecting attacks in normal traffic. The same category of tests includes the detection of intrusions typical for your network, the capability of customizing existing attack signatures and creating new ones, etc. If you can not afford to check all possible attacks, at least try to check the attacks from the SANS Top 20 list — The Twenty Most Critical Internet Security Vulnerabilities [SANS1-02]. One might suppose that manufacturers would pay the most attention to these attacks. However, as was shown in [NSS1-02], this is not always so, which is rather surprising.

❏ *Performance.* The efficiency of the IDS is not limited to the ability to detect attacks in normal traffic. A well-designed IDS will show quite good results under conditions of stress tests, during which the traffic intensity is significantly higher than under normal conditions. For example, the NSS laboratory [NSS1-02] conducted its tests with workloads of 25, 50, 75, and 100 Mbit/sec, while the Miercom company tested systems with workloads of 40, 60, and 90 Mbit/sec [Yocom1-00]. Only those intrusion detection systems that are capable of detecting attacks in heavily loaded networks can be considered efficient. Packet length is yet another parameter that must be considered during tests. When testing network-level intrusion detection systems, the packet transmission mode with a minimum packet length for each protocol is the most complex test, allowing you to test IDS functionality under the toughest conditions. For example, if we return to the NSS test, there are 3 tests that are used to evaluate this criterion — ideal conditions (the length of all IP packets is the maximum, and is equal to 1514 bytes for the Ethernet), the worst conditions (the IP packet length is equal to 64 bytes) and normal conditions, under which the average packet length is about 300 bytes. By the way, all things being equal, IDS will work more efficiently in FDDI networks than in Ethernet networks. This relates to the fact that MTU value for FDDI is equal to 4,352, while for Ethernet it is 1,500 bytes (see Table 10.3).

❏ *Self-protection.* Being a security tool, the intrusion detection system must not itself become a cause of lessened security of the corporate network that it is meant to protect. Therefore, the third class of tests should include the self-protection capabilities of the intrusion detection system — i.e., checking its operation in stealth mode, protection of the collected data and the data transmitted between the sensors and the management console, the capabilities of role-based access control, etc. There is also another intermediate class of tests intended for checking the system's ability to detect attacks, specially designed to bypass the IDS (Stick, Snot, ADMutate, etc.).

❏ *Manageability.* This class of tests is rather important, especially in large, geographically distributed networks that contain several dozens of sensors.

❏ *Functionality.* This class of tests includes all the other tests that were not included in the other categories, and this approach is justified. Manufacturers, in order to attract as many customers as possible, try to provide not only intrusion detection functions, but also a wide range of other functional capabilities intended to achieve customer satisfaction.

The simplest example of a test bench for evaluating network-level intrusion detection systems is shown in Fig. 9.20. Note that for the sake of simplicity, this variant does not provide testing for the IDS's integration with other security tools, various schemes of sensor management, and so on.

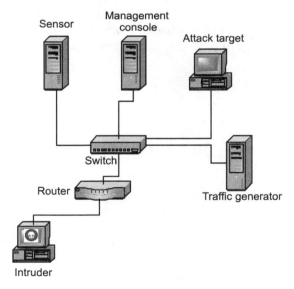

Fig. 9.20. An example of a test bench for evaluating
network intrusion detection systems

Various software tools can be used for testing intrusion detection systems. For example, quite an interesting solution is provided by the IDS Informer system from Blade Software. However, if you can not afford to purchase such specialized testing systems, you can use normal security scanners to imitate a hacker's activities. If this method is also not available, you can download exploits from any hacker site and use them to test your IDS. When using this approach, remember that if you undertake such an attack without proper care, you might cause your network some significant damage. Therefore, it is recommended that you run such tests in a specially prepared, isolated test environment.

Summary

In this chapter, we have covered IDS evaluation criteria that are vital to information-security professionals in the process of choosing the right tool for their specific environment. In no case should you rely solely on the information provided by the vendor. Like anyone else in sales, their first concern is selling the product, and their being more interested in seeing the client find a solution that adequately fits their aims and purposes than in piling up higher sales numbers is rare. Hopefully, the evaluation criteria described in this chapter and the recommendations provided here will enable specialists to make the right choice from among the tools covered here, as well as those that go beyond the range of tools discussed in this book.

CHAPTER 10

Placement of the Intrusion Detection System

"Knowing the land is the soldier's best ally; but the power of estimating the adversary, of organizing the victory, and of shrewdly calculating difficulties, dangers, and distances constitutes the test of a great general."

Sun Tzu, "The Art of War."

In using an intrusion detection system within a corporate network, one of the key things to consider is where to place it. Understanding the principles involved in correctly positioning intrusion detection system components (network and system sensors, security scanner agents, and deception systems) will allow you to fully control the most important resources of a protected network. Otherwise, you might encounter a situation in which you are unable to detect certain vulnerabilities or attacks. As a general rule, the IDS components should be placed on network segments or hosts containing critical information resources. I will start this chapter with a brief overview of the preferred location points of IDS network sensors, since this topic is the one that tends to lead to the most questions.

Placing IDS Sensors

Classical intrusion detection systems operate at the network and host levels. With regard to host-level intrusion detection systems, the answer to the question of where to put the IDS sensors is easy, since they must reside on the most important network hosts (database servers, web servers, and so on). The issue that interests us, therefore, is the problem of correctly placing IDS network sensors. This topic will be covered in detail in this section.

As a rule, network sensors of an intrusion detection system are installed on the following network locations:

❑ Between a router and firewall
❑ In the "demilitarized zone" (DMZ)
❑ Behind a firewall
❑ Near a remote access server or near a modem pool
❑ On the network backbone
❑ Within key segments of an internal network
❑ In remote offices

The Network Sensor between the Router and Firewall

Protecting corporate networks against external attacks is one of the most important functions of IDS network sensors. This task determines the first way to install the network sensor — between the router and firewall (Fig. 10.1). This type of installation will allow you to control all traffic in the corporate network (including the traffic passing through the demilitarized zone), as well as all outbound traffic, which is not locked by a firewall. This solution also allows you to protect the firewall, which quite often also becomes a target of external attacks. However, this position does not allow the network sensor to control the traffic that is isolated by the firewall and router, circulating within the LAN and the demilitarized zone, and outbound from the DMZ into the local area network. Furthermore, bear in mind that the traffic coming into the network through a point that is not controlled by the network sensor (for example, via a backup connection or modem) will not be analyzed, and consequently, attacks present in such traffic will not be detected.

In this case, the network sensor is absolutely unprotected, since it is located outside the area protected by the firewall. To secure the sensor, it is recommended that the user take the following measures:

- ❏ Enable Stealth mode
- ❏ Change the default port numbers of the ports used in communications between the sensor and management console
- ❏ Make sure that the network interface responsible for accepting the commands from the management console and transmitting information on registered events back to it is connected to the internal network or to a separate interface of the firewall
- ❏ Use non-routable addresses (RFC 1918) for the management interface

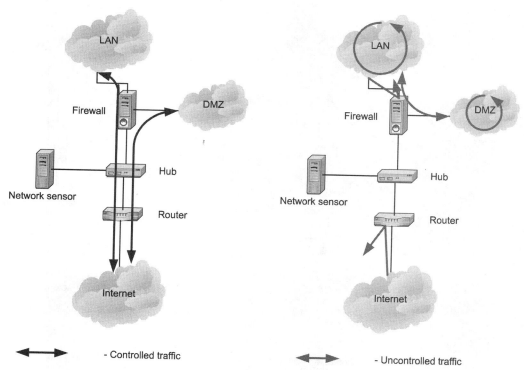

Fig. 10.1. Placing the network sensor between the router and firewall

The Network Sensor in the Demilitarized Zone

Another important function of network sensors (Fig. 10.2) is their role in protecting devices located in the demilitarized zone (DMZ). The list of such devices includes Web, FTP and SMTP servers, an external DNS server, and other hosts that must be accessible to external users. Obviously, the IDS network sensor does not analyze traffic that does not pass through a controlled zone. I should point out that this solution is not common, because financial resources assigned for purchasing IDSs are usually rather limited. As a rule, most clients prefer to invest in a network sensor installed behind the firewall or between the firewall and router. However, placing the IDS network sensor in the demilitarized zone is justified for companies that actively use external Internet resources (e-shops, Internet portals, etc.)

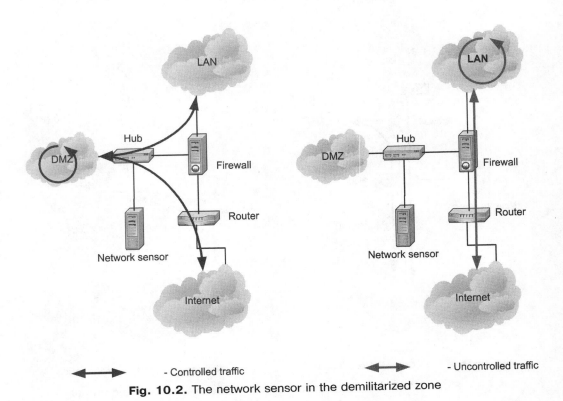

Fig. 10.2. The network sensor in the demilitarized zone

The Network Sensor behind the Firewall

The network sensor is usually placed behind the firewall (on the side of the LAN), as shown in Fig. 10.3, and the first approach that we have discussed is also employed. In this case, it is possible to track the changes in the firewall's operation and to view all traffic passing via the firewall. The network sensor in this configuration lets the administrator make sure that the firewall is correctly configured and that no one can penetrate it in attempts to enter the corporate network. This means that the network sensor controls the firewall configuration and efficiency of its operation. Simultaneous logging of the same events on both sensors (behind and beyond the firewall) enables you to compare the number of attacks detected on both sides of the firewall, thus allowing the detection of problems with the security rules that the administrator created.

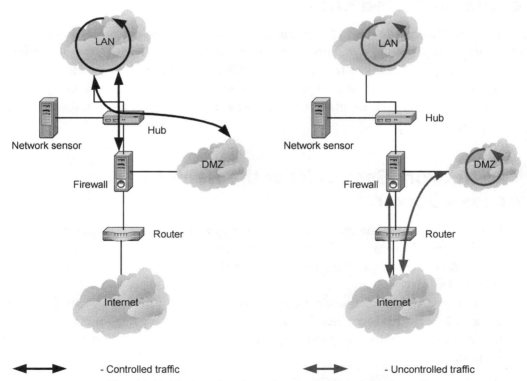

Fig. 10.3. Placing the network sensor behind the firewall

This configuration enables the administrator to control all inbound and outbound traffic in the demilitarized zone, as well as traffic circulating within the LAN segment adjacent to the Internet gateway. The network sensor does not analyze external traffic locked by the firewall or inbound traffic directed to devices located in the demilitarized zone. This approach is even rarer than the previous one, since in this case the firewall is not protected from external attacks. Furthermore, such a configuration does not allow you to trace attacks thwarted by the firewall (for example, port scanning), which could serve as evidence of an intruder's attempts to investigate the company's security system. Early detection of such attempts can help security personnel to take all the required preventive measures in a timely manner.

Network Sensors in Key Segments of the Protected LAN

The most common type of configuration can be seen when network sensors are located within the key segments of an internal network connecting valuable resources or critical applications (such as ERP and CRM). As I mentioned earlier, the most significant damages are usually caused by attacks originating from within. To prevent such losses, be sure to place network sensors within the most critical network segments.

The Network Sensor Near the Remote Access Server

In most companies, the remote access server provides access to corporate resources. When network sensors are located near remote access servers, they are able to control attacks initiated by users accessing the corporate network via those servers (Fig. 10.4).

This method is used quite rarely, since it allows administrators to detect only those unauthorized activities initiated by a limited range of users (those who log on to the network using modem connections). All other intruders are not even noticed.

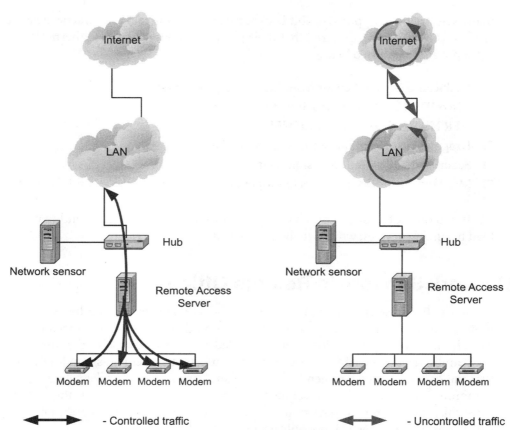

Fig. 10.4. The Network sensor placed near the remote access server

The Network Sensor on the Backbone

Network intrusion detection systems can not efficiently function on most backbones since they are based on different networking principles. ATM, Frame Relay, X.25, and others are modern technologies for building Wide Area Networks (WAN), including backbones that have no relation to multiple access data communication networks.

If Gigabit Ethernet is used as the backbone technology, the situation improves somewhat, but only in a rather insignificant way. Another problem immediately arises. On the backbones, network traffic is rather fast, and the transmission rate significantly exceeds the capabilities of most intrusion detection systems. There are not many sensors that support Gigabit backbones, despite the fact that practically all leaders in this market have declared that their products support Gigabit Ethernet. Some of these products are listed below:

- ❐ RealSecure Gigabit Sensor from Internet Security Systems
- ❐ Cisco IDS 4250 from Cisco Systems
- ❐ NFR NID-320S or 320D from NFR
- ❐ Dragon Sensor Appliance from Enterasys Networks
- ❐ SecureNet 7000 from Intrusion.com
- ❐ ManHunt from Recourse Technologies, purchased by Symantec on July 2002

If you can not afford to purchase gigabit sensors, I would recommend that you use load balancing devices, which will be covered later in this chapter.

Network Sensors in Remote Offices

Placing network sensors in remote offices and affiliates is yet another approach to building an IDS infrastructure. This configuration does not have any specific features, since in this case the network sensor is installed either before or after the firewall, or in the demilitarized zone (if there is one). One important aspect you should remember is that the data exchange between the console and sensors usually takes place via public communication channels. Consequently, you will need to protect all the traffic. Besides this, the amount of data transmitted between remote sensors and the management console can exceed all possible limits.

The recommendations provided here concern the standard placement of IDS network sensors. The particular configuration of the IDS infrastructure depends on the corporate network configuration and on the security policy adopted in the organization.

Using Load Balancing Devices

Load balancing devices let you distribute network traffic to several devices (firewalls, servers, traffic analyzers, etc.) and process it at the same time. Such devices can be both applied to intrusion detection in backbones and used for several other purposes that will be covered later.

TopLayer Networks supplies one of the most popular solutions of this type. It allows the administrator to organize parallel processing of Gigabit Ethernet traffic by several network sensors (Fig. 10.5).

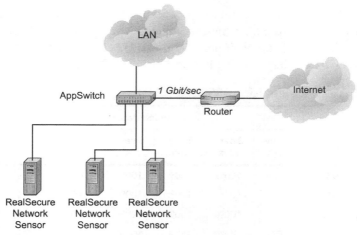

Fig. 10.5. The solution developed by TopLayer and Internet Security Systems

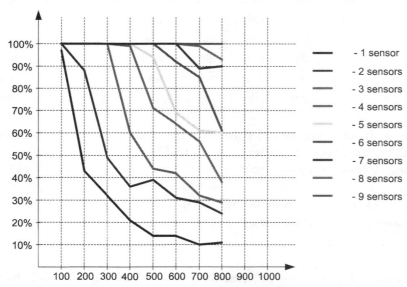

Fig. 10.6. The results of AS3502 AppSwitch testing

According to Internet Security Systems and Top Layer Networks' test results, the AS3502 AppSwitch device can support up to 9 network sensors. This provides the capability of tracing all network traffic, depending on the gigabit channel's workload [ISS10-00]. Later, this solution was transformed into IDS Balancer (http://www.toplayer.com/ Products/ids_balancer.html), providing significant advantages, including the ability to aggregate the traffic from several network segments or even the VLAN, and transmit it to a group of network sensors. At the time of this writing, two IDS Balancer models were available — AS3531 (12 100-Mbit ports) and AS3532 (12 100-Mbit and 2 Gbit ports). Test results for AS3502 are shown in Fig. 10.6 and in Table 10.1.

Table 10.1. Test Results for AS3502 AppSwitch

Workload		Intrusion detection (%)								
Mbit	**%**	**1 sensor**	**2 sensors**	**3 sensors**	**4 sensors**	**5 sensors**	**6 sensors**	**7 sensors**	**8 sensors**	**9 sensors**
100	10	96%	100%	100%	100%	100%	100%	100%	100%	100%
200	20	44%	88%	100%	100%	100%	100%	100%	100%	100%
300	30	32%	49%	100%	100%	100%	100%	100%	100%	100%
400	40	21%	36%	60%	99%	100%	100%	100%	100%	100%
500	50	14%	39%	44%	71%	94%	100%	100%	100%	100%
600	60	14%	21%	42%	64%	69%	92%	100%	100%	100%
700	70	10%	19%	32%	56%	61%	85%	89%	99%	100%
800	80	11%	14%	29%	38%	60%	61%	90%	93%	100%
900	90	n/a	n/a	n/a	n/a	n/a	n/a	n/a	n/a	n/a
1000	100	n/a	n/a	n/a	n/a	n/a	n/a	n/a	n/a	n/a

The main advantage of IDS Balancer is that additionally, it can send the same traffic to different groups of sensors and even to different groups of devices. For example, incoming data can be redirected to:

❏ Sensors responsible for detecting Denial of Service attacks
❏ Sensors responsible for detecting HTTP attacks
❏ Protocol analyzers

A similar approach — i.e., parallel processing of the fast traffic by distributing it between several analyzers (including IDS network sensors) — is also suggested by NetOptics (http://www.netoptics.com) and several other manufacturers of load-balancing devices. However, you should take into account that such devices might be based on two different load balancing principles — packet-by-packet balancing and flow balancing. Only devices based on the second principle are suitable for using with network intrusion detection systems. For example, IDS Balancer "understands" the traffic of the whole session received from different ports (for example, from different splitters), which allows it to be processed and sent to the sensor so as to let the sensor view the bidirectional interaction as a whole.

These same devices can be used to improve the reliability of the IDS network infrastructure. Connecting a group of sensors to such a load balancing device eliminates any risk of failure. If one of the sensors fails, the device will stop redirecting traffic to it and switch to one of the other sensors of the group. Therefore, you will have to ensure some redundancy when planning the number of sensors to be connected to the balancer. Thus, the failure of a single sensor will not cause other sensors to be overloaded with excessive traffic. To calculate the required number of sensors, use the following formula [Edwards1-02]:

```
Sensor number = ((connections number * network speed * duplex coefficient) /
    IDS performance) + redundancy factor
```

The duplex coefficient can take a value of 1 or 2, depending on the controlled connection type — half-duplex or full-duplex. If the controlled connection is full-duplex, the amount of traffic increases twofold, and the coefficient takes a value of 2. In most cases, the redundancy factor (an integer) is equal to 1.

For example, to control 4 half-duplex Fast Ethernet connections (from splitters, for example) with a network workload factor of 0.8 (80 Mbit/sec), you must use 5 network sensors providing a performance of up to 90 Mbit/sec:

```
((4 * 80 * 1) / 90) + 1 = 4.56
```

If we neglect the redundancy factor by assuming that it is equal to zero, then 4 sensors will be sufficient. In cases when the IDS is overloaded and fails to thwart all attacks (some solutions, such as RealSecure Network Sensor, notify the administrator if such a situation arises), it is possible to connect additional sensors to the load balancing device. Thus, scaling becomes rather easy.

Specific Cases

In recent years, most companies have begun to pay special attention to the matter of having network elements in reserve, since networks perform business-critical tasks. A network infrastructure failure results in financial damages and loss of morale and customer confidence, among other things. There have been several documented cases of bankruptcy that were caused by network failures.

A Case of Bankruptcy Caused by Network Failure

In January of 2002, intruders attacked CloudNine Communications, one of the most widely known British Internet Service Providers. It became a victim of Distributed Denial of Service

(DDoS) attacks, which had already gained some notoriety. DDoS attacks are different from DoS attacks in that the traffic intended to overload the ISP equipment originates from hundreds or even thousands of Internet hosts. CloudNine, a company with 6 years of experience in this segment of the market, was forced to close down and sell the clients' database to its competitor — Zetnet.

Besides backing up the network equipment, there are two other popular methods of improving network reliability. These methods significantly affect the selection of positions for IDS network sensors:

❑ Connecting to the Internet via two different ISPs
❑ Usage of asymmetric routes

Till recently, these cases were quite rare in real-world practice. Currently, however, more and more companies are using such methods of improving their networks' reliability. As a result, I'd like to cover such solutions in more detail.

Quite recently, Cisco announced a new set of functions for its IOS operating system — Globally Resilient Internet Protocol (GRIP). These functions provide for automatic network recovery in case of failures (http://www.cisco.com/warp/public/732/Tech/grip/). The most important functions of GRIP include Nonstop Forwarding, Stateful Switchover, and Gateway Load Balancing Protocol. Considering that Cisco network equipment is widely used all over the world, we can assume that this technology will quickly find supporters, and security specialists will have to consider it when selecting positions for IDS components. However, I would like to draw attention to the fact that the methods described in the following few sections are also applicable to networks using GRIP.

Connecting to Multiple Internet Service Providers

Creating a backup channel for Internet connection and automatically switching between channels can be implemented in different ways — both by using the settings of routing protocols (BGP, for example), and with the help of special equipment (such as LinkProof from Radware company). In this case, one can use the simplest approach — install the sensors at any Internet connection point. However, this solution is rather expensive, and not all organizations can afford it. Using load balancing devices, which allows the traffic from several channels to be merged and redirected to a sensor or group of sensors, is an efficient way around this issue (Fig. 10.7).

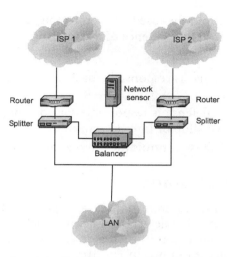

Fig. 10.7. Intrusion detection when using backup Internet connections

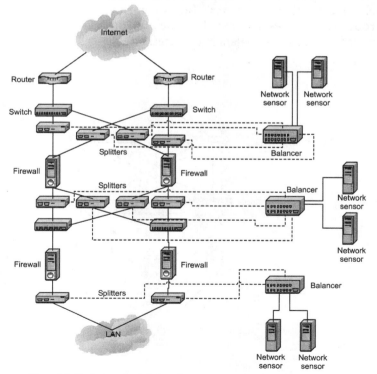

Fig. 10.8. Intrusion detection on e-commerce hosts

A similar scheme can be used for protecting e-commerce hosts (Fig. 10.8). The only difference lies in the presence of multiple lines of defense when applying load balancing devices:

☐ The first line of defense is responsible for external traffic coming into the firewalls from the Internet.
☐ The second line of defense is responsible for control over the demilitarized zone (a web server of an e-shop or Internet bank).
☐ The third line of defense controls the internal network.

Using Asymmetric Routes

In asymmetric networks, omnidirectional traffic goes by different routes. This causes several problems for intrusion detection systems, which can not get complete information on the network interaction in such a case. This might result in false positive or false negative problems. As shown in Fig. 10.9, packets leaving the LAN might follow any of four possible routes. Because of this, installing a network sensor on one of the channels or activating the router's built-in intrusion detection system (when using Cisco routers) produces no effect. Like the previously described case, the situation can be corrected by using load balancing devices.

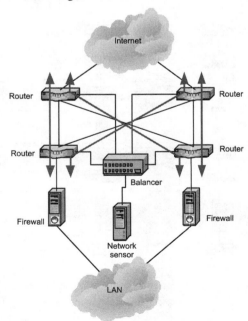

Fig. 10.9. Intrusion detection in asymmetric networks

Using IDS Sensors in Switched Networks

Previously, networks were based on a common bus using hubs, which repeated frames received by one port to all other ports (Fig. 10.10). Hubs have become inefficient in large networks that comprise hundreds and thousands of computers, since access delays grow exponentially with the growth of network hosts. Experiments have shown that the number of hosts within a segment with traditional traffic (text data) must not exceed 30 (for Ethernet networks). This number is even lower for multimedia data. As the number of hosts grows, traffic intensity increases, and network performance degrades, since most of the time the network is busy detecting and processing collisions.

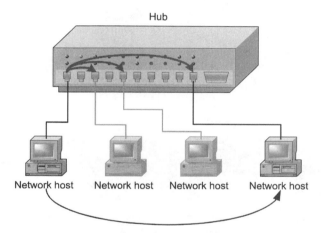

Fig. 10.10. Hub operation

Using network sensors in such environments does not present any problems. The sensors can be switched to any port of the hub and then "listen" to traffic on all other ports.

To eliminate limitations specific to multiple access media, several different devices have been developed, particularly, bridges and switches that translate frames from port to port and analyze the destination addresses specified in those frames (Fig. 10.11).

These devices simplify the lives of network administrators in large networks, but complicate them for security administrators, since connecting a network sensor to one of the switch ports only allows one to listen to the traffic directed to this port. Since normal traffic will not be directed to the network interface responsible for monitoring, IDS will see only broadcast packets and packets with a destination address unknown to the switch. In cases when VLAN is used, practically nothing will be directed to the "listening" port except for broadcast traffic of the local virtual network. The following methods of efficiently positioning sensors in networks with switching can be recommended:

❑ Using the SPAN port on the switch
❑ Connecting an additional hub
❑ Using a splitter
❑ Integrating the IDS with a switch
❑ Using load balancing devices
❑ Using system sensors controlling specific hosts

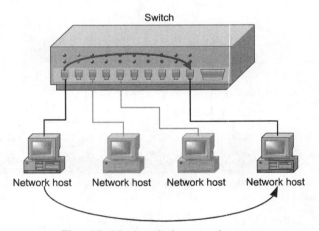

Fig. 10.11. A switch operation

Using the SPAN Port

This mechanism is intended for switching the traffic from several switch ports to a single dedicated port, known as the SPAN port (Switch Port ANalyzer), which is generally used for connecting traffic analyzers (Fig. 10.12).

Some manufacturers use other terms for this port, such as mirror port, manage port, monitor port, or analyzer port. Notice that traffic commutation from controlled ports to a span port can be done using the following two methods:

❑ By directly configuring the switch (using, for example, commands such as the port monitor or set span for Cisco Catalyst 2900XL/3500XL and Catalyst 4000/5000/6000 switches, respectively.

❏ By using third-party software, for example, NetScout Manager Plus. NetScout uses the term "roving" for this mechanism.

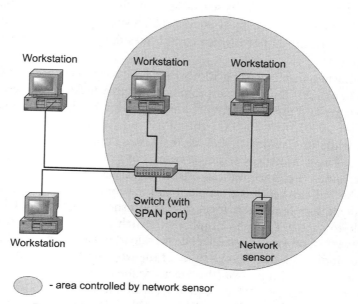

Fig. 10.12. The network sensor and span port

SPAN port usage partially eliminates the problem of monitoring networks with switching; however, there are several important aspects that seriously influence the efficiency of IDS operation.

First, not all switches support SPAN ports (for example, for fiber optic networks), although most contemporary manufacturers build such mechanisms into their solutions (especially in the newer models of switches).

Second, it is the fastest port of the switch that must be designated the SPAN port. For example, if the switch is equipped with mostly 10 Mbit ports, and just one 100 Mbit port, this port must be selected as the SPAN port. Otherwise, one may have to deal with the system simultaneously transmitting data from several 10 Mbit/sec ports to the SPAN port (also 10 Mbit/sec). Since at 10 Mbit/sec, the SPAN port will not be able to process information at speeds exceeding 10 Mbit/sec, data will wait in the internal buffers of transmitting ports until the SPAN port is ready. When the internal buffers of any switch overflow, all packets coming into the port will be discarded. This will degrade the performance of the networks connected to the switch and that of the switch itself, and/or lead to a loss of the data processed by the sensor (if these data are not retransmitted).

This problem is especially important when non-locking switches are used. That's why the fastest port must be selected as the SPAN port. In the case described above with parallel processing of network traffic by several sensors, the AppSwitch AS3502 was connected to the Gigabit SPAN port of the Catalyst 6000 switch. Bear in mind that errors are not translated to the SPAN port, which complicates the process of detecting network problems in time.

Third, when implementing VLAN, it is necessary to ensure that the SPAN port belongs to the VLAN that you want to protect from attacks. However, depending on the manufacturer and the switch model, this limitation might be eliminated. For example, in Catalyst 2900XL or 3500XL, the SPAN port can not control traffic in multiple VLANs, while in Catalyst 4000/5000/6000, this shortcoming does not exist. In addition, VLAN also influences response types. For example, sending an RST packet in order to terminate a connection can only be done via a controlled VLAN. Otherwise, the RST packet will not reach the recipient and the connection will not be terminated.

Finally, a simple mathematical calculation shows that even a Gigabit SPAN port is only able to switch a limited number of switch ports. How can we define this limit? To achieve this, one must consider the workload of each controlled port. For Ethernet, the factor indicating the average value of the workload is 30%, and in reality this value is even smaller — about 10% (the precise value of the port workload can be obtained using a network analyzer). Consequently, at first it seems that a Gigabit SPAN port can switch 100 ports (of 100 Mbits each), rather than 10 as in our example. However, there is an empirical rule which holds that an IDS network sensor on a Fast Ethernet network efficiently handles a workload of 60–80 Mbit/sec. Sensor performance on the Gigabit Ethernet network drops to 40–60%, i.e., 400–600 Mbit/sec. Therefore, 40–60 (rather than 100) would be a more realistic number of ports that could be switched to a single Gigabit SPAN port and efficiently handled by the sensor. Naturally, this is averaged data (a precise formula for calculating sensor performance will be provided at the end of this chapter), which depend on many factors. However, it demonstrates the general level of performance for network-level intrusion detection systems. One way to solve this problem (besides using another SPAN port) is to use the load balancing devices described earlier.

It is much simpler to use hubs. When the network workload coefficient increases, the delays of frames' access to multiple access media also grows exponentially. Critical values of the coefficient (excluding cases where a computer is connected directly to a hub) are as follows:

- ❑ 40–50% for Ethernet
- ❑ 60% for TokenRing
- ❑ 70% for FDDI

Since IDS sensors are able to handle such workloads, particular problems with sensor performance in multiple access networks do not arise, since the Ethernet technology itself protects the IDS from overloading.

Furthermore, there are several other drawbacks related to the usage of SPAN ports.

❏ As a rule, switches have only one SPAN port. However, most manufacturers allow you to use 2, 3, or even 4 SPAN ports.

❏ This port is vulnerable to attacks. A specially formed packet sent to a SPAN port can, under certain conditions, cause an intrusion detection system to fail.

❏ Controlling ports operating in full-duplex mode can cause difficulties, since communicating hosts can transmit their traffic simultaneously. This will have a significant effect on the SPAN port operation, since traffic intensity doubles.

❏ Since the SPAN port is implemented to operate in unidirectional mode, some response types can not be implemented (such as terminating the connection to the attacking host). In this case, it is necessary to employ an additional network interface responsible for control.

❏ Physical-level errors are not reproduced on the SPAN port.

❏ Using SPAN with an intrusion detection system prevents you from using network analyzers and other tools that are usually connected to this port, and vice versa. For example, if you are using a network analyzer connected to the SPAN port, this might prevent you from connecting the IDS sensor to the switch. A shortage of SPAN ports might result in a conflict of interest between the IT and information security departments. It is quite rare that this conflict is resolved to the benefit of the information security department.

Using SPAN ports can also have a negative impact on switch performance (despite what the manufacturer may claim). Depending on the specific features of its design and on network traffic, switch ports can slow down their operation. Usually, this is true for older models (for example, Catalyst 2900XL or 3500XL). Newer switch models (such as Catalyst 4000/5000/6000) are free of this drawback.

When making a decision whether or not to use the SPAN port to which you want to connect IDS sensor, I recommend that you go over the documentation provided by the manufacturer, since each manufacturer usually supplements its products with additional functionalities. For example, Cisco Systems has implemented the Remote SPAN (RSPAN) mechanism in Catalyst 6000, which allows you to control ports of remote switches. More detailed information on the implementation of SPAN technology in Cisco equipment can be found at the following address: http://www.cisco.com/warp/public/473/41.html.

Connecting an Additional Hub

This approach involves the combined usage of switches and hubs. When using this method, an additional hub is installed between the host or segment controlled by the IDS sensor and switch. The IDS network sensor is connected to the hub (Fig. 10.13). This approach is applicable in cases where there is no SPAN port on the switch. Considering the low cost of 4-port switches, this solution is rather functional. The limitations of this approach are obvious, since you can only control one port of the switch. If the switch is used for monitoring more than one connection, loops might occur. Furthermore, connecting an additional device degrades the whole configuration's reliability. Finally, an increased number of collisions caused by a full-duplex connection between the sensor and the switch also presents a problem that may occur when using this solution.

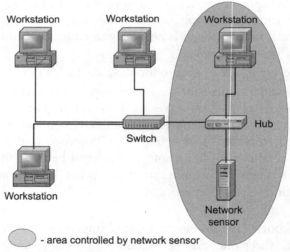

Fig. 10.13. Combined usage of a hub and switch

Using a Splitter

A splitter (also known as a tap) is a device that duplicates the traffic transmitted between two or more network hosts (Fig. 10.14). TAP is an acronym that stands for Traffic Analyzer Port.

The equipment connected to the splitter port can not transmit data via this port. However, it also can not be attacked via that port, since the splitter does not allow direct calls to the network sensor or any other device connected to it. Furthermore, the intruder will not even be aware of the presence of a splitter between the switch and controlled host, since it operates on the physical layer and has neither a network nor a data link layer address.

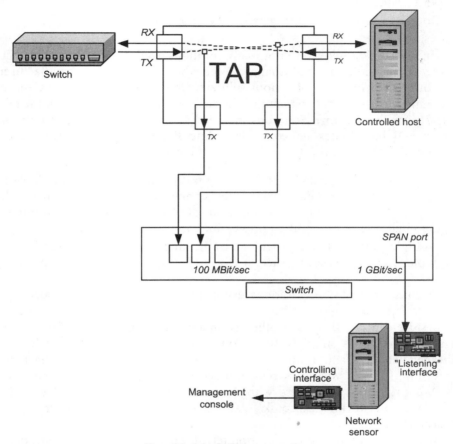

Fig. 10.14. Splitter operation

Splitters are ideal tools for intrusion detection. In fact, splitters are the devices that most IDS manufacturers recommend. They provide the following advantages:

❏ Operate both in networks with switching and in global networks (such as Gigabit Ethernet or ATM)
❏ Provide the capability of processing traffic from different VLANs
❏ Operate efficiently in full-duplex networks

❏ Have no negative effect on the controlled network
❏ Allow the information security department to have an independent copy of all network traffic
❏ Do not require reconfiguring network equipment (such as switches)

Until recently, there were not many solutions available on the market. Currently, however, the situation has changed, and there are several manufacturers, each promoting their own line of various splitters. One such solution is the Century family of products from Shomiti, which the Finisar Corporation purchased in the fall of 2001 (http://www.finisar.com). Solutions included in this family can operate both in full-duplex and half-duplex networks, including Ethernet, Fast Ethernet, and Gigabit Ethernet. This line of products includes the following solutions:

❏ Single-port Ethernet splitters providing traffic duplication from a single Ethernet, Fast Ethernet, or Gigabit Ethernet connection to a single network sensor (Fig. 10.14). These splitters support full-duplex Ethernet operation mode, including single-mode and multiple-mode fiber optic and twisted pair.
❏ Multiple-port splitters, providing traffic duplication from several (8–12) full-duplex Ethernet, Fast Ethernet, or Gigabit Ethernet connections (Fig. 10.15).

Various types of configurations using single-port and multiple-port splitters are shown in Figs. 10.16 and 10.17.

Besides Finisar, there are other companies that provide similar solutions. For example, NetOptics supplies 10 various splitters, including 4 models for Gigabit Ethernet networks and 1 model for ATM networks. Another manufacturer, Rioco Direct Ltd. (http://www.rioco.co.uk/), based in England, supplies Rioco Data Tap — 100-Mbit full-duplex splitters with 1, 4, and 12 ports. Finally, Network Critical (http://www.networkcritical.co.uk/) supplies one- and four-port splitters for Ethernet/Fast Ethernet networks.

Still, this solution is also not absolutely flawless; the most important problem being the fact that there are several types of attack responses that you can not implement (such as closing the connection to the attacking host). To overcome this, you should use a second network interface or additional equipment (Fig. 10.18). In this case, the sensor sends the RST packets to Splitter 2, which duplicates and retransmits them to Switches 3 and 1. Since Switch 3 is not able to transmit traffic further via Switch 1, there will not be any loops or duplicated routes.

The second shortcoming (see Fig. 10.14) is attributable to the fact that the sensor connected to the splitter can only see unidirectional traffic (TX). Obviously, this results in a false positive and false negative problem. Let us consider a typical situation. Suppose that some host attempts to establish a TCP connection to another host by sending an SYN packet to the port of the recipient. If the port is closed, the recipient replies by sending the RST packet, and the connection is terminated. However, if a splitter is used, RST packets will not reach the sensor, which will result in the detection of a SYN Flood attack and a false positive case. A similar result can be observed for several other events related to the ARP protocol.

Fig. 10.15. The Shomiti Century 12-Tap

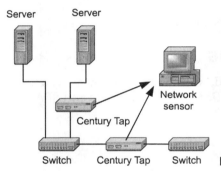

Fig. 10.16. Using splitters and a network sensor

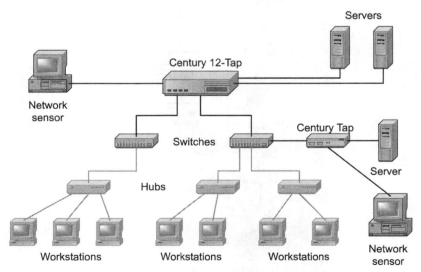

Fig. 10.17. Using a Century 12-Tap and network sensor

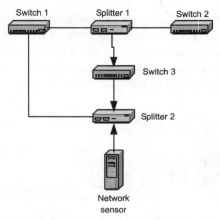

Fig. 10.18. Closing the connection using splitters

Using Load Balancing Devices

The load balancing devices we just described, such as IDS Balancer, can be used in networks with switching. In particular, traffic from both splitters and SPAN ports

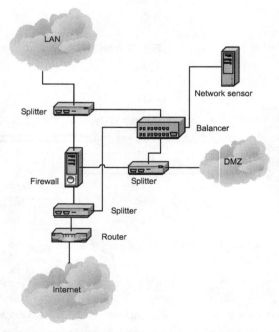

Fig. 10.19. Using a load balancer to protect a set of controlled segments

of several switches can be directed to the input of such a load balancing device. This allows users to be free from the case of "one switch = one sensor." In a similar way, switching traffic from several 100-Mbit SPAN ports to the Gigabit sensor will allow you fully utilize its capabilities.

Using splitters and load balancing devices together lets security administrators create rather complicated schemes of protection without having to purchase additional IDS sensors. For example, Fig. 10.19 shows a scheme for protecting an Internet gateway.

The same solution allows you to resolve possible conflicts between IT and IS departments competing for precious Gigabit SPAN ports. To solve this problem, it is sufficient to connect the load balancing device to the Gigabit SPAN port and redirect all traffic to both IDS sensors and network analyzers (Fig. 10.20).

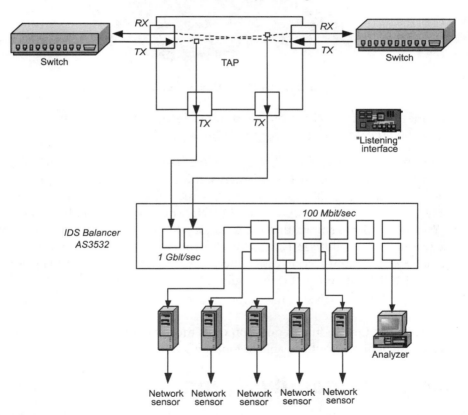

Fig. 10.20. Connecting a splitter to a load balancing device

Integrating Network Sensors into Switches

Direct integration of IDS network sensors into switches is another interesting method of employing IDS sensors. For example, Cisco Systems has adopted this approach, and at the end of 2000 they released the Catalyst 6500 IDS Module (formerly known as Cisco Secure IDS Blade), which is meant to cooperate with the Catalyst 6500 switch (Fig. 10.21) from the same manufacturer (Cisco models 6006, 6009, 6506, and 6509).

Fig. 10.21. The Cisco Catalyst 6000 IDS Module

Besides the features characteristic of other intrusion detection systems, the Cisco Catalyst 6500 IDS Module provides the following two advantages:

❑ High performance and no threat of switch bandwidth degradation. According to information provided by Cisco Systems, this module is capable of processing traffic at a rate of 47,000 packets per second (the average packet size is about 484 bytes). Testing conducted by Network World Global Test Alliance [Yocom 1-00] has shown that the Catalyst 6000 IDS Module can process traffic at a speed of 200 Mbit/sec (in full-duplex mode), which is twice that assessed by Cisco Systems. However, in cases where it is necessary to control a Gigabit port (or a set of 100-Mbit ports), this throughput becomes insufficient.

❑ The capability of analyzing the traffic of several VLANs.

However, as the module in question costs more than $15,000, not every company, especially small ones, would be able to foot the bill.

Placing the Security Scanner

As compared to classical intrusion detection systems, the placement of security scanners creates fewer problems. There are a limited number of variants of positioning in such systems. Still, there are lots of factors to take into consideration, especially with respect to network-level security scanners (Internet Scanner, Nessus, etc.), since host-level security scanners create no problems.

First, scanning the same host from different locations of the corporate network might produce different results. Let us consider a typical example: scanning the corporate web server. The first position for placing a security scanner that you will probably think of is the local area network in which the scanned host is located. Most often, security administrators proceed in this manner. The second way to position scanners is to place them in the same network with the scanned host (in the case under consideration, this is the demilitarized zone). The third way is to place the scanner at a remote affiliate. This approach is generally used for scanning remote offices that lack qualified security specialists (Fig. 10.22).

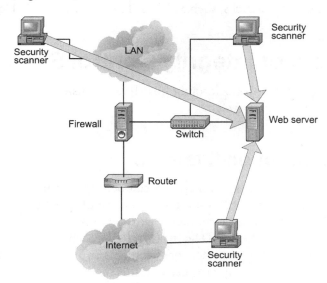

Fig. 10.22. Placement of a security scanner

However, placing the scanner there is potentially dangerous and involves several risks. For example, if there are security tools between the scanning and scanned hosts (such as a firewall or filtering router, or even network-level intrusion detection systems) or network devices, they might prevent the scanner from performing certain checks. This is especially true when the scanning and scanned hosts are located in zones with different security requirements (and note that this is rather common).

The second problem relates to scanning via public networks, since most ISPs lock such attempts. Furthermore, they can even lock all subsequent attempts to connect to the Internet (even to send e-mail). Therefore, when performing remote scanning in such a way, it would be a good idea for you to notify all providers between the scanner and scanned host(s) beforehand.

The second problem is due to VLANs, which, besides offering some advantages (including security advantages), also present some complications for security administrators. This fact was already mentioned in the section dedicated to selecting the right place for IDS network scanners.

Yet another problem might arise if the scanning and scanned hosts are installed in different network segments based on dissimilar architectures (for example, Ethernet and Token Ring). Not all checks available for Ethernet can be implemented in Token Ring. For example, Internet Scanner can not check Token Ring networks for vulnerabilities to some DoS attacks, such as Land, Teardrop, and SYN Flood.

Placement of Integrity Control Systems

The same approaches to positioning host-level intrusion detection systems are applicable to integrity control systems.

Placing Deception Systems

As we saw earlier, the deception system can be implemented using one of two methods. The first approach is based on the emulation of specific services or vulnerabilities located only on the computer where the deception system is running (for example, RealSecure Server Sensor or DTK use this approach). The second method implies emulating other hosts or even network segments containing virtual hosts (systems like CyberCop Sting or ManTrap are based on this method). In the first case, when the deception system is placed on the protected host, selecting its location does not present any problems, while systems of the second type may not be as straightforward.

Recourse Technologies (http://www.recourse.com), recently purchased by Symantec, has come up with quite an interesting solution. Its original deception system, known as ManTrap, is located in a separate segment of the corporate network. The traffic that passes via the firewall is split into two directions. Normal queries (for example, SMTP or HTTP) are transmitted as usual — into the demilitarized zone. All other queries, which should not reach the production servers (Telnet, for example), are directed to the deception system, which serves as a signal of unauthorized activity (Fig. 10.23). To implement this redirection, one can use the built-in router mechanisms (for example, the built-in mechanisms of the Cisco IOS 12.x operating system).

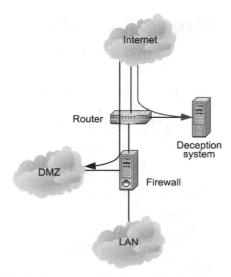

Fig. 10.23. The first approach to deception system placement

However, this configuration does not replace the classical model of intrusion detection systems in any way, since attacks against existing applications or services will not be redirected to the deception system.

Another way to place the deception system is to position it in a controlled network segment (Fig. 10.24). The host with the deception system is connected to the same switch or hub as the production hosts, and has a slightly different address from those of the production hosts. For example, the IP address of the database server, file server, and domain controller are 192.168.0.100, 192.168.0.254, and 192.168.0.1, respectively, while the address of the deception system is 192.168.0.200. When the intruder falls into a trap while determining an attack target by means of network mapping, this serves as a signal to the security administrator. Besides an IP address very similar to those used in the production environment, the deception system might have a DNS name that is phonetically similar. Several different names or IP addresses can map to the same system using aliases.

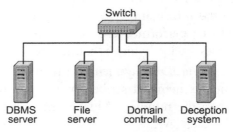

Fig. 10.24. The second approach to positioning the deception system

Placing Management Consoles

Although the main problem with deployment of IDS components concerns choosing the correct positions for network sensors, you still must not forget about management consoles. This problem becomes especially important in large, geographically diverse networks.

One of the first questions that needs an answer is: how many management consoles do you actually need? The answer to this question depends on the following parameters:

- ☐ *The number of managed agents.* Even if technically the console is able to support an unlimited number of agents, inherent human limitations in information procession may not be conducive to adequately tracing events from a large number of agents. In large networks, it is not advisable for more than 50 agents to be connected to the same console.

- ☐ *Types of agents.* Network and system components are intended for controlling different events, which results in different amounts of data transferred to the console. Network components transmit much more frequently — approximately 10 times more event data than a host-level IDS running on a specific host.

- ☐ *Types of responses.* Depending on the response types used and the IDS operators' capabilities, you might need to use more than one management console. For example, when focusing attention on a real-time response, the user should not connect more than 10–15 network sensors to a single console. If the user must concentrate on further analysis of events, then it is possible to connect 20–25 network sensors to a single console. For system sensors, these numbers must be increased by 5–7 times.

- ☐ *Interaction between departments.* This parameter is more organizational than technical. In most organizations, information security functions are distributed between several departments. The IT department monitors specific network parameters, while the information security department traces other parameters. Most operations to be performed are independent, which requires at least two management consoles, each of which is configured to perform specific tasks.

- ☐ *The necessity of hierarchical management.* If the organization implements the hierarchical management scheme, described in *Chapter 6*, the number of consoles must be no less than the number of management hierarchies, and there can be multiple consoles at each level.

However, I can not give any universal recommendations in this area. Depending on several factors, the recommendations provided here might not prove to be useful. For example, grouping sensors and protected resources implemented in the RealSecure SiteProtector system allows one to overcome the limitation of 10–15 network sensors per console. However, even in this case connecting too many sensors to a single console is still not the best idea.

One more aspect must be considered in relation to the management console. If all sensors use a separate network interface to interact with the console, it makes sense to localize all management within a single VLAN, which would improve system security and quickly detect any problems that may arise.

Factors to Consider when Setting up an Intrusion Detection System

An intrusion detection system is a critical component of a complex information security system. Correctly selecting the positions for its components seriously influences how efficiently it operates. Suppose that you have chosen where you want to detect attacks (for example, let us say it is the demilitarized zone). What do you need to know in order to be able to place sensors efficiently? It is not enough to simply understand which traffic will be controlled and which will pass through. Besides this, it is necessary to answer several questions, which I'd like to cover now. Generally, since an intrusion detection system (especially its network component) relates to network equipment, it is necessary to consider various aspects of the network when choosing the places for its sensors. Considering the fact that planning locations for security tools must be kept in mind at the stage of planning the network layout, this should not cause any serious dilemmas.

Network Workload and Traffic Intensity

These parameters are rather important. Without knowing them, you would be unable to tell for sure whether or not a sensor installed in a controlled segment is able to process the controlled traffic. If a threshold value is exceeded, the sensor will not be able to perform its tasks. It will either start overlooking attacks (false negative) or simply fail to operate (these aspects will be covered in more detail in *Chapter 12*). You are lucky if the sensor notifies you during a false positive event (for example, RealSecure Network Sensor provides such a mechanism) and you will be able to understand that some steps must be taken. But what if you are not so lucky?

In order to forecast and predict situations that might cause the IDS to fail, one should know the network workload's average and peak values. For example, the sensor might handle an average workload of 40 Mbit/sec, but at peak workload of 90 Mbit/sec it might start to pass suspicious packets. The frequency of peak workloads depends on various parameters, including the traffic type.

Types of Traffic in the Controlled Segment

The traffic in a controlled segment can be classified by the following two types: flow traffic and pulsating traffic. Applications that generate flow traffic are characterized by highly predictable workload peaks. Traffic such as IP telephony or multimedia (audio and video) data transmission, is ideal for a network intrusion detection system, since data are transmitted at a predictable speed, thus reducing the relation of peak-to-average workload to practically zero. Pulsating traffic (e.g. FTP protocol, e-mail transmission, Web browsing, etc.) is characterized by unpredictable peaks of the network workload — from zero to peak values. Unfortunately, most attacks are implemented in segments with pulsating traffic. This is the main reason why users should test intrusion detection systems at average and peak network workloads.

Average and Peak Processor Workloads

In contrast to network sensors, one should consider the processor workload's average and peak values for host-level sensors. It might even be impossible to install system sensors on servers running applications that heavily load the CPU. I would also advise you to thoroughly assess the processor workload when purchasing and testing the IDS. This will prove to be useful not only when planning sensor positions within the corporate network, but also in thwarting internal attacks. The collected statistics will help you to prove to the specialists from the IT department that performance problems that they are experiencing are not related to the intrusion detection system.

Average Packet Size in a Protected Segment

Let us suppose that you believe the manufacturer's claims that their intrusion detection system can process 100 Mbit traffic without problems. You install this system in your network and use it to protect the IP telephony segment or DNS server managing the whole corporate network (more than 1000 addresses). And what happens? The system can not even handle half of the planned workload. Why did this happen and who is responsible? The answer lies in the fact that the size of the DNS query and

DNS response packets is usually not larger than 50 and 90 bytes, respectively (neglecting the sizes of UDP and IP headers). Thus, you have not solved the problem, but the manufacturer did not deceive you. The problem is that the manufacturer measured IDS performance under laboratory conditions, and in your environment, the average packet length proved to be significantly smaller. However, some manufacturers prefer to pull an even simpler trick — they measure performance at the maximum possible values of packet length rather than at the average values (Table 10.2). Knowing the average packet size allows you to detect various anomalies, including attacks, as was shown in *Chapter 4* in the description of a Loki attack. It should be noted that there is no universal average packet size. In each segment, these values can significantly differ. For example, in the NSS tests [NSS1-02], the average packet size was equal to 300 bytes, while in other tests conducted by Shieply [Shipley1-99], 40% of all packets had lengths of less than 75 bytes, and only 30% were more than 1,426 bytes.

Table 10.2. Average Packet Lengths for Different Protocols

Protocol	Average packet size (in bytes)
ARP	28
ICMP Address Mask Request and Reply	12
ICMP Timestamp Request and Reply	20
ICMP Destination Unreachable Error	36
ICMP Echo Request	64
ICMP Time Exceeded, Parameter Problem, Source Quench, Redirect	36
DNS Query	40–50
DNS Response	70–90
TFTP	516
BOOTP	300
HTTP	400–1500
Telnet	64–1500
NFS	64–1500
Multimedia	400–700

When determining the type of traffic controlled by the sensor, you must not only take into account the network's average packet sizes and higher-level protocols, but also the MTU values (Table 10.3) for the type of network architecture used in the controlled segment [RFC1-90]. Notice that typical packet sizes for different protocols can vary in different networks. For example, in the Ethernet network, the size of an IP packet is limited to 1,500 bytes, while in the FDDI network this value increases to up to 4,772 bytes.

Table 10.3. MTU Values for Different Networks

Network type	MTU value (in bytes)
Token Ring (16 Mbit/sec)	17,914
Token Ring (4 Mbit/sec)	4,464
FDDI	4,352
Ethernet	1,500
Ethernet IEEE 802.3/802.2	1,492
X.25	576
NetBIOS	512
Point-to-Point	1,500 or 296
SLIP	1,006

Thus, you must ask the manufacturers at which packet length they measured the performance of their intrusion detection system. Practically all manufacturers process packets with a length of 1,500 bytes (maximum size of the Ethernet frame without a header), but not every product can handle 46-byte packets (minimum Ethernet frame without a header). Furthermore, some intrusion detection systems even fail when processing such small packets. Although small packets (runts) are quite rare (IP-telephony has not yet been developed enough), one should not exclude this possibility. Some manufacturers (such as Cisco Systems) specify this information in their promotion materials. Besides needing to know the average packet size, one should also have an idea of the number of such packets processed by the intrusion detection system per second. Based on these two parameters, one can approximately evaluate the throughput of the network-level intrusion detection system. This value, measured in Mbit/sec, can be calculated using the following simplified formula:

```
Throughput = number of processed packets * packet size (in bits) / 1000000
```

For example, if the packet size is 1,500 bytes, and the intrusion detection system processes 30,000 packets per second, the throughput of this IDS will be 360 Mbit/sec. At first glance, this is not too bad. However, in reality, the traffic comprises packets of different sizes, including service packets that are significantly smaller in size. Taking this fact into account, if the system processes the same number of packets per second, but the packet size drops to 64 bytes, the IDS throughput will be only 15.36 Mbit/sec. Actually, there is another aspect that ought to be considered when evaluating the IDS throughput, but we will leave this to be covered in detail in *Chapter 12*.

Acceptable Response Time

You should remember that, despite its importance, ensuring security is secondary to ensuring business continuity. Because of this, the installed intrusion detection system must not introduce any delays or otherwise influence the circulation of traffic. This especially relates to those active intrusion detection systems installed between protected and public networks. The list of applications susceptible to delays includes:

- ❏ Financial and other transaction processing applications
- ❏ Scheduling systems
- ❏ Systems for exchanging audio and video data
- ❏ IP telephony
- ❏ Multiplayer games
- ❏ Any other interactive applications

The Presence of Networks with Switching

This problem was already covered in detail earlier in this chapter. However, you should remember that there is no universal intrusion detection solution in networks with switching. It is possible that you will need to implement other methods of intrusion detection. In particular, you can use network analyzers (including RMON-based ones). The solution from NetScout (NetScout Probe) is an example of such an analyzer, in that it analyzes the data from which the *n*Genius Performance Management System can make the decision as to whether network anomalies exist [NetScout1-02]. Thus, it is possible to detect the malicious activity of worms such as Red Code or Nimda.

The Presence of Asymmetric Routes

This problem, already considered earlier in this chapter, is similar to the one that arises when using splitters, and will be covered in detail in *Chapter 12*. Consequently, it is necessary to know whether asymmetric routing is used within a controlled segment.

Scalability and Extensibility

Each network changes with time: information flows change their routes, new hosts and network segments are added, etc. This all influences the design of the intrusion detection system's infrastructure. As nothing in the world remains constant and unchanged, it is wise to consider future changes when choosing locations for IDS components. Obviously, it is impossible to predict and forecast everything. However, it is desirable to avoid situations in which adding another sensor will require you to move the management console to another location. Furthermore, any upgrade requires resources (time, human, and financial), which might exceed all possible limits if you do not plan the IDS infrastructure with scaling in mind.

Compatibility with Existing Software and Hardware

You can spare both effort and expense if you efficiently integrate the intrusion detection system with the existing network equipment and software. For example, instead of terminating the connection to the attacking host, the intrusion detection system can send an appropriate command to the firewall or filtering router. Let us consider another example. If your network is mainly oriented towards Microsoft DBMS products (MS SQL Server), then selecting an intrusion detection system using an Oracle database as its data store is not the best solution (although this decision might be made on account of other reasons).

The Availability of Channel and Subscriber Encryption

As will be shown in *Chapter 12*, like any other conversion of controlled traffic, encryption leads to the inability to detect any attack indications within it. One can proceed quite easily by simply disabling the transmission of encrypted traffic within the corporate network. However, what should you do in respect to access to protected web servers? Or what about for VPN connections between headquarters and remote offices? You will have to either stop using the IDS network component and solve the problem by installing a host-level component, or try to find where traffic is transmitted in plain-text mode. In any case, you must know beforehand whether or not encryption is used in the controlled segment.

Distribution between the Management Console and the Sensor

If you plan to install IDS agents in remote offices (away from headquarters, where the management console is installed) with access via the Internet, then it is necessary to bear in mind the following two aspects: the amount of data transmitted between the console and the sensor, and this data's protection. In contrast to the first issue, which has begun to lose its significance (most large companies now have communication channels of a significant bandwidth), the second problem must never be underestimated. The information circulating between the sensor and the console is both very important and confidential, since knowledge of system vulnerabilities would certainly help intruders implement a successful attack on your corporate network.

Security Tools between the Console and the Sensor

Even if the information exchange between agents and the management console is performed via the corporate network and stays there, one important problem still remains: the presence of the security tools between them. As was already mentioned, the presence of a firewall or IDS between the security scanner and scanned hosts can lock some attacks (including DoS attacks). It also might be a problem if the firewall locks all unknown traffic. Such traffic might include all interactions between the management console and the sensor. Because of this, you should know in advance which ports are used by the IDS components, and what the directions of interaction are. This data is required to create appropriate rules for the firewall or filtering router.

Dynamic Address Assignment in the Controlled Segment According to the DHCP Protocol

The arrival of the DHCP protocol has significantly simplified the process of automatic assignment of IP addresses. However, this protocol introduces specific features into the deployment of the IDS infrastructure. With the dynamic assignment of addresses, each host is assigned an IP address for a limited time — a so-called lease duration. When this period expires, this address can be assigned to another host. There are some possible issues that may have to be dealt with, including:

- ❑ Those related to the detection of the real address of an internal intruder.
- ❑ Problems with respect to the analysis of the attacking host addresses (which change dynamically).

❏ Problems regarding the reconfiguration of network equipment and security tools. To tell the truth, it is not a good idea to employ these tools in networks with dynamic address assignment.

❏ Issues related to security analysis by IP address.

Since log files of the intrusion detection system store the information on the IP address of the attacked or attacking host taken from the packet IP header, this IP address might already be assigned to another host while this information is being analyzed. As a result, it will be impossible to get an adequate response to the incidents. Therefore, it is extremely important to register not only the IP address, but also the MAC addresses along with DNS and NetBIOS names.

Keep in mind that if you use static (both manual and automatic) address assignment, these problems never arise.

Interaction with the IT Department

All the problems described above are related mainly to technical aspects, and successfully solving them depends on the existence of a previously composed network map, described in detail in *Chapter 7*. However, do not forget that besides the technical component, the network's infrastructure also has an organizational component, which is no less and sometimes even more important. One of the most serious organizational problems that might arise is interaction with the IT department (if introduction of the sensors is delegated to the IT department). One possible conflict was already described earlier in this chapter — IT department employees might form the opinion that the intrusion detection system degrades network performance. By the way, it may very well do so if you place the network sensors and connect them to the SPAN port of the switch incorrectly. Another conflict might arise between the IT and information security departments, as both may demand to use the precious Gigabit SPAN port. You need it for the intrusion detection system, but the IT department also needs it to connect to the network analyzer. Solutions to most of these and other problems strongly depend on your skills at finding mutually acceptable solutions and in a word — compromising. Note that it is only by working in this way that you will be able to build a truly efficient intrusion detection infrastructure.

CHAPTER 11

Using Intrusion Detection Systems

The most frequently reported security violations are due to the incorrect configuration of security tools in corporate networks, including their incorrect placement. According to statistics for 1999 collected by International Computer Security Association (ICSA), 70 percent of all firewalls are vulnerable, due to their being incorrectly configured or improperly placed. By analogy, this figure can be extended to intrusion detection systems (although concrete statistics on this were not available at the time of writing). An analysis of different publications that discuss intrusion detection systems will reveal that they actually omit such topics as the practical use of such systems. In a way, this is similar to a driving course in which an instructor teaches the pupil the rules of the road, the car's components, what to do to make the car start and stop, etc. However, the pupil is not taught how to drive in such a way as to enjoy the process without exposing other people to danger. This last skill you will have to gain from experience, or after attending a specialized course for advanced drivers (for example, an extreme-driving course).

This is analogous to the field of information security. Books and documentation describe the IDS components and the available settings, but do not discuss the practical applications of these systems in a particular user environment, taking into account that user's information processing technologies. At the same time, these aspects are matters of primary importance to IS professionals. The previous chapter discussed aspects of choosing the correct places for the components of the intrusion detection system within the corporate network. This chapter will cover the most important aspects related to the practical use of intrusion detection systems. Although each organization differs in the specifics of its IDS, there are several important topics that are characteristic for almost all users.

It should be noted here that most aspects covered in this chapter relate to intrusion detection systems, including security scanners working at the network level. However, the tips provided here will, in addition, certainly be useful for implementing other approaches to intrusion detection.

Selecting the Correct Host for an IDS

Assuming that an intrusion detection system has been chosen according to the recommendations in *Chapter 9*, and that the network location for installing the system has also been chosen, you now need to purchase the selected IDS, select the correct hardware and software platforms for it (only for a network-level intrusion detection system), and install and configure the hardware, software, etc. Therefore, you must perform all the steps described in *Chapter 8*.

Choosing the Platform

Network-level intrusion detection systems — with the exception of systems such as Cisco's Catalyst 6500 IDS Module, which is integrated into the network equipment — can run on two types of hardware platforms:

❏ A standard, general-purpose computer
❏ A specialized computer, known as a security appliance

Currently, the first solution is the most common and the most attractive, due to the commonly held opinion that, in this case, all you need do is purchase the IDS software and install it on any suitable computer within the organization. In practice, however, it is quite difficult to find a free computer that satisfies these demanding system requirements. For this reason, the computer on which the IDS software is to be installed must be purchased along with the IDS itself. Installing and configuring the operating system must follow this — which also costs time and money. Only after these steps can IDS installation proceed. In other words, using a standard PC for installing an IDS is not as simple as it may seem at first.

For this reason, specialized solutions, known as security appliances, have recently become more popular. These solutions are a combination of software and hardware, stripped of unnecessary functionality and optimized to perform a specific set of tasks. They are run either by a general-purpose or specialized operating system. (As a rule, such specialized operating systems are based on FreeBSD or Linux.) Specialized solutions provide several advantages, including:

❑ **Simplicity and ease of implementation.** Since practically all devices of this type are supplied with a pre-installed operating system and preconfigured security mechanisms, it is usually sufficient to connect them to the network (a process that usually takes no longer than a few minutes). Although most devices will still require fine-tuning, the time taken will be significantly shorter than installing and configuring the system from scratch would.

❑ **Performance.** Because all unnecessary services and subsystems are eliminated, the device operates more efficiently and more reliably in terms of overall performance.

❑ **Fault tolerance and high availability.** IDSs on specialized machines allow the implementation of fault tolerance and high availability on the level of both software and hardware. Moreover, such devices can be joined into clusters fairly easily.

❑ **Security focus.** Solving network-security problems does not necessarily involve the extensive use of resources needed to perform other functions, such as routing. Trying to create a universal device to solve several tasks with the same, fairly high level of efficiency does not usually produce a good result.

Currently, many vendors supply devices that are more or less universal. For example:

❑ Cisco Systems — IDS 4210 Sensor, IDS 4235 Sensor, IDS 4250 Sensor (Fig. 11.1)

Fig. 11.1. Cisco IDS 4200

❒   Internet Security Systems — RealSecure for Nokia (Fig. 11.2)

Fig. 11.2. RealSecure for Nokia
(based on IP740, IP710, IP530, IP330, IP120, IP71, and IP30)

❒   Intrusion.com — SecureNet 7000 (Fig. 11.3), SecureNet 5000, SecureNet 2000

Fig. 11.3. SecureNet 7000

❒   NFR — NID-320, NID-315, NID-310 (Fig. 11.4)

Fig. 11.4. The NID 300 family

❒   Enterasys Networks — Dragon Appliance (based on Intel NetStructure Appliance)

Some manufacturers, such as ISS and NFR, also supply combinations of hardware and software solutions, while others, such as Cisco, concentrate exclusively on hardware solutions.

According to a report published by the Gartner Group in June 1997, by the end of 2002, about 80 percent of companies with a yearly revenue of between $20,000 and $200 million will chose custom solutions over universal ones. The main advantage of these solutions lies in the fact that custom solutions provide the same level of security as universal solutions, but are less expensive. The simplicity and ease of use of custom solutions are other advantages that simplify their integration into a pre-existing corporate network. Finally, such devices can easily be mounted in a 19-inch rack, which makes it easy to mount them in communication racks alongside other network equipment. Therefore, the Total Cost of Ownership is significantly lower than for non-custom solutions. At present, most manufacturers are promoting custom solutions.

However, it must be pointed out that, for most small business, custom, hardware-based solutions are still rather expensive, even taking into account the above-listed advantages. (Table 11.1 provides a comparison of the advantages and drawbacks of such systems.) This is largely because most companies still do not purchase a separate computer in order to install an IDS, but instead use existing equipment. Furthermore, the software installed on such a computer is often not licensed. It is hoped that this situation will improve over time.

Table 11.1. Comparison of Universal and Specialized Intrusion Detection Platforms

	General-purpose computer	Specialized computer
Advantages	Unlimited extensibility	High performance
		Simplicity of deployment and implementation
		Ease of use
		Fault tolerance
Drawbacks	Average performance	Minimal extensibility
	Operating system vulnerability	
	Low level of fault tolerance	

It is very important to note here that a specialized computer is not the same thing as a router that performs some IDS functions (such as Cisco's IOS Firewall Feature Set). For router manufacturers, improving traffic speed and traffic optimization always have priority — only after these are accomplished is it possible to try to implement security functions. Because of this, when choosing between routing and security, a developer always chooses in favor of routing. Practical experience has shown that implementing built-in security mechanisms on routers actually significantly decreases performance. Security functions will be limited if a manufacturer can not afford to include them. (Cisco's IOS Firewall Feature Set is based upon this principle. In contrast, its "elder brother," IDS 4200, it identifies only the 59 most common types of attacks. A similar situation is found when implementing security functions in switches.)

Using a Dedicated Host

The best practice is to install the IDS' network sensor and network-level security scanner on dedicated hosts. This improves sensor performance and protects both the system and its data from unauthorized access. The network sensor and the management console must be run on different computers, since both are intensive users of processing and RAM resources. A host specially designated for the IDS also allows it to be used in stealth mode, which significantly strengthens its security.

It is also good to assign dedicated hosts as system consoles, since otherwise the chances of a successful attack on them increase significantly. However, it is possible to combine the management consoles of several security systems — including IDSs, security scanners, firewalls, etc. — on one computer. For example, I took part in a project in which one host was used for the management consoles of the following security systems: Internet Scanner security scanner, RealSecure IDS (this was before the arrival of the RealSecure SiteProtector centralized management system), the Check Point Firewall-1 firewall, and the Cisco Secure Policy Manager system, which controlled the Cisco IDS 4200 IDS and Cisco PIX Firewall.

Purchasing an IDS

Purchasing an IDS comprises several steps that must be undertaken in order:

❏ Purchasing appropriate software and hardware
❏ Purchasing an IDS
❏ Purchasing documentation
❏ Purchasing technical support services

Purchasing Appropriate Software and Hardware

Before deploying an IDS in a corporate network, you will need to buy all the necessary software and hardware. Here, the term "software" is used in a broad sense — i.e., not just the IDS itself. In addition to the IDS, the software also includes the operating system in which the IDS will run, along with add-on application software, such as Internet Explorer or Oracle. Purchasing a specialized hardware-software combination (a security appliance) solves this problem, as it comes with all the required software pre-installed, and the only remaining job is to buy add-on software for the management console.

In terms of hardware, it is recommended that you choose reliable equipment that has a good reputation. This is not an item on which to economize, especially given the fact that IDS failure due to unreliable equipment or manufacturing defects can result in serious damage. In my practice, I have had the experience of having to handle a case in which a vendor supplied defective computers to one of my clients. One of the computers failed after two weeks of running the IDS. One week later, we had to replace the second computer. The client suffered no serious damage and managed to thwart attacks, but only thanks to multiple-layer security made up of access-control lists on Cisco routers, a combination of the advanced firewalls — Check Point Firewall-1 and Cisco PIX Firewall — joined into clusters, and the Cisco IDS 4200 and RealSecure Network Sensor IDSs.

Since an IDS is an intensive user of available resources — especially RAM, hard-disk space and network adapter resources — and given that the protected network segment will inevitably increase in size over time, it is advisable to purchase scalable hardware and software. If you have chosen reliable, fault-tolerant hardware, it is also desirable to provide a fault-tolerance level that will allow a failed component to be replaced within a reasonable period of time. Although such a solution may seem somewhat redundant, it provides a sufficient level of support to the security system. If spare parts of backup equipment are difficult to come by, consult the vendor for information on replacing the failed components. All major brands — Cisco, Compaq, IBM, Hewlett Packard, etc. — usually have enough stock available to allow them to supply spare parts with minimum delay. (Cisco, for example, guarantees such supplies within one day.)

It is impossible to deploy and bring into operation an IDS without purchasing all the required software and hardware components. For example, although it may be possible to bring an IDS into operation with insufficient amount of RAM, in a high-throughput network or when analyzing the security of a large number of hosts, some attacks may remain undetected, or even worse, the IDS may fail. Moreover, when the missing components are purchased, the whole IDS will have to be reconfigured.

IDS hardware may include the following components:

❑ *CPU.* Experience has shown that the more processors are installed on the host running the IDS, the more efficient is the analysis of network traffic or remote hosts. In contrast to relatively small networks — which can survive with a single-processor system and compensate for the lack of extra processors by the amount of RAM — in large networks or backbones, two-processor or four-processor systems are recommended. This approach has been adopted by Compaq, which supplies hardware with RealSecure Network Sensor pre-installed. Based on this, it should be noted that, although the IDS may theoretically use 100 percent of processor resources, under normal conditions this value should not exceed between 2 percent and 10 percent.

❑ *RAM.* Like processors, more RAM makes an IDS more efficient. This is especially true for networ sensors. The amount of RAM required for a host-level IDS does not exceed the amount required by the operating system itself. In practice, such systems consume from 1 MB to 5 MB of available RAM. For other types of IDS, this element is not as important, since security scanners, integrity control systems, and other similar applications are not characterized by consistently high levels of activity. Rather, they consume resources intensively only when specific events occur, after a predefined time period, or at the request of the security administrator. From personal experience, I can say that when setting up a network sensor, you will need to optimize its settings for the efficient support of a large amount of RAM.

❑ *Peripherals.* (CD-ROM drive, floppy disk drive, keyboard, monitor, etc.) These components are required for installing and operating the IDS. For IDS network sensors, a keyboard and monitor are usually optional, since network sensors are managed remotely from the central console. This also applies to an IDS' management server and security scanners based on three-tier architecture.

❑ *Hard-disk space.* The amount of hard-disk space needed depends on the type of operating system installed, the IDS chosen, any add-on software, the log-file size, frequency of event logging, and frequency of log-file rotation. As a rule, the hard disk must be at least between 4 MB to 6 MB. It is best to combine hard drives into RAID arrays, or another distributed storage systems, which ensures fault tolerance and a high level of performance.

❑ *Network adapters.* Similar to the rule that "the security of the network is equal to the security of its weakest link," it is possible to say that "network performance is equal to the performance of the slowest device." The network interface is one such device. Consequently, IDS performance depends directly on the performance of the network interface. It is recommended that you use PCI-compliant network adapters in promiscuous mode. PCI has become the architecture of choice, as the speed of data exchange between the bus and RAM is the critical factor that influences the performance of the network-level IDS, and PCI devices are characterized by a better performance than other architectures, such as Sbus. The overall performance of the IDS depends on the performance of the network adapter, and therefore,

it would be best ito choose a server configuration for the network sensor that increases the level of network traffic processing significantly — i.e., by 30 to 40 percent. This performance can be achieved with a built-in processor that significantly
reduces the PC processor workload by eliminating the need for transmitting
frames from the RAM to the network. Examples of such adapters include Intel's
PRO/100 (1000, 100+) Server Adapter, or 3Com's Fast EtherLink Server, which are
based on Intel Adaptive Technology and Parallel Tasking II, respectively. Another
important criterion in choosing a network adapter is the amount of on-board
RAM: 1 MB will be enough to monitor a high-speed network. Management functions — such as SNMP, RMON, DMI, ACPI, WfM, Remote Wake-Up, and so
on — are not mandatory for an IDS, and purchasing them is solely dependent on
an organization's standards and on the amount of money available. One network
adapter is sufficient for an IDS' or security scanner's system console, as well as for
a control server, in a three-tier scheme. For network sensors, however, two network adapters are best, in order to allow the implementation of stealth mode, although it is possible to manage with a single adapter if two prove too expensive.
Although it may seem obvious, the network adapters must operate at the speeds
adopted by the network. Otherwise, a 10-Mbit network interface could be connected to a 100-Mbit port in the network switch — in this case, the network sensor
will work inefficiently, and most attacks will go undetected.

❏ *Backup hardware.* (CD-ROM drive, streamer, etc.) These devices store log files,
which contain information on the IDS' logged events and distribution sets, including all the configuration files and rules for traffic processing and analysis.

❏ *Power supplies.* Power supplies, UPSs, backup power supplies, etc. ensure the IDS's
independence from the organization's power supply. This is especially important
for the system's most critical components, which must be available at all times.

The hardware requirements for the computer on which the IDS' network sensor is
to be installed are determined by the following factors (partially discussed in the previous chapter):

❏ The amount of traffic transmitted in the protected segment
❏ The average packet size within the protected segment
❏ The types of traffic (e-mail, files, multimedia, etc.)
❏ The number and type of signatures in the relevant template (dependent on the
protocols, services, and operating systems used in the protected segment)
❏ The methods used for log file or network traffic analysis

❑ The predefined response types

❑ The network topologies — Ethernet, Fast Ethernet, FDDI, Gigabit Ethernet, etc. — used in the protected segment

❑ The number of hosts in the protected segment

❑ The average and peak values of the network workload

Manufacturers develop their recommendations based on the average statistical values of these parameters. For example, Compaq recommends the following configuration for installing an IDS' network sensor (particularly for installing the RealSecure Network Sensor):

❑ Standard configuration (for low bandwidth networks):

- Proliant 1600 server

- 1xPentium II 450 processor

- 128 MB RAM

- 1x9.1-GB hard disk

❑ Enhanced configuration (for high-speed networks):

- Proliant 1600 server

- 2xPentium II 450 processors

- 256 MB RAM

- SmartArray2 controller

- 3x9.1-GB hard disks (for implementing RAID-5)

Although the situation has changed in the four years since these recommendations were published, the approach suggested by Compaq illustrates the trends described above quite well.

The software platform for an IDS may include the following components (besides the components of the IDS itself):

❑ *Operating system.* In contrast to host-level IDSs, for which the solution is obvious, this choice for a network-level IDS (with the exception of a security appliance) is more important. Experience has shown that, despite the wide range of alternatives (Table 10.2), the following are the most common choices: Windows NT (although recently Windows 2000 has become more prevalent), Solaris, or a shareware Unix clone such as Linux or FreeBSD. The last option is generally preferred under limited budget conditions, whereas the first two are usually preferred by large customers with stable finances. I can not make a definitive recommendation for any one specific system, as it depends on a large number of parameters (operating systems already in use, the vendor, financial resources, the IT personnel's knowledge and skills, etc.). In the past, I have recommended Solaris for heavily loaded networks: For example, this is the best choice for an internal Web or database server with thousands of users. However, since the release of Windows 2000, the situation has changed, and for the moment, the following advice is the least that I can give: for a 100-Mbit network, it is preferable to use a Unix clone (Solaris in particular), while a host running Windows 2000 should undertake the monitoring of a Gigabit network. Table 11.2 lists all the operating systems that can be used for installing the various components of an IDS.

Table 11.2. Operating Systems Used by IDSs

IDS	Operating system
	Security scanner
Internet Scanner	Windows NT, Windows 2000
System Scanner	Management console — Windows NT, Windows 2000
	Agents — Windows NT, Windows 2000, NetWare, Linux, HP UX, AIX, Solaris, SCO OpenServer, SCO UnixWare, Sequent DINIX/PTX, NCR Unix, Digital Unix
NetRecon	Windows NT
Enterprise Security Manager	Console — Windows NT, Windows 2000, Windows 95/98
	Management server — Windows NT, Windows 2000, OSF/1, IRIX, HP UX, AIX, Solaris, NetWare, OpenVMS
	Agents — NetWare, OpenVMS, Windows NT, Windows 2000, HP UX, AIX, Solaris, NCR Unix, OSF/1, IRIX, Sequent DINIX/PTX, Digital Unix, Compaq Tru64
Nessus	Console — FreeBSD, Linux, Solaris, Windows NT
	Management server — FreeBSD, Linux, Solaris
CyberCop Scanner	Windows NT, Windows 2000, Linux
Kane Security Analyst	Windows NT, NetWare
Expert	Windows 95/98, Windows NT
STAT	Windows NT
BindView HackerShield	Windows NT, Windows 2000, NetWare, OS/400

continues

Table 11.2 Continued

IDS	Operating system
	IDS
RealSecure	Console — Windows NT, Windows 2000
	Network sensor — Windows NT, Windows 2000, Solaris
	RealSecure for Nokia — Customized version of FreeBSD
	OS Sensor — Windows NT, Windows 2000, Solaris, HP UX, AIX
	Server Sensor — Windows NT, Windows 2000, Solaris
Cisco IDS	Console — HP UX (HP OpenView NNM), Solaris (HP OpenView NNM), Windows NT (Cisco Secure Policy Manager)
	Sensor — custom OS
NetProwler	Console — Windows NT, Windows 2000
	Management server — Windows NT
	Sensor — Windows NT
Dragon	Console — Web interface
	Network sensor (Sensor) — Linux, FreeBSD, OpenBSD, Solaris, HP UX
	System sensor (Squire) — Linux, FreeBSD, OpenBSD, Solaris, HP UX, Windows NT
NFR	Console (Administrative Station) — Windows NT, Windows 2000, Windows 95/98
	Central Station — Solaris
	Sensor — OS on the basis of BSD
Intruder Alert	Console — Windows NT, Windows 2000, Windows 95/98
	Management server — Windows NT, NetWare, HP UX, AIX, Solaris, NCR Unix, OSF/1, IRIX
	Agent — Windows NT, NetWare, HP UX, AIX, Solaris, NCR Unix, OSF/1, IRIX, Sequent DINIX/PTX
eTrust IDS	Console — Windows 95/98, Windows NT
	Sensor — Windows 95/98, Windows NT
CyberCop Monitor	Console — Windows NT
	Sensor — Windows NT, Solaris, HP UX, AIX

continues

Table 11.2 Continued

IDS	Operating system
SecureNet PRO	Sensor — Red Hat Linux
Kane Security Monitor	Sensor — Windows NT
Centrax	Console — Windows NT
	Sensor — Windows NT, Solaris
Snort	Linux, *BSD, Solaris, SunOS, HP UX, AIX, IRIX, Compaq Tru64, Windows NT
LIDS	Linux
Integrity-control system	
Tripwire	Windows NT, Solaris, AIX, HP UX, IRIX, Compaq Tru64, Linux
Deception system	
CyberCop Sting	Windows NT
DTK	Various Unix clones
ManTrap	Console — Windows NT, Windows 2000, Windows 95/98, Solaris
	Sensor — Solaris
RealSecure OS Sensor	Windows NT, Windows 2000, Solaris, HP UX, AIX
RealSecure Server Sensor	Windows NT, Windows 2000, Solaris

❑ *Operating system and software updates.* These software components (patches, hot-fixes, and service packs) eliminate known vulnerabilities and errors in the operating system and application software, thereby strengthening system security and improving reliability.

❑ *IDS updates.* As noted previously, the efficiency of an IDS depends on frequent updates of its database of attack and vulnerability signatures. IDS purchasers should make sure that the system is supplied with the developer's latest updates.

❑ *Drivers for all required devices.* (Network adapters, streamer, CD-ROM, etc.) To avoid hardware compatibility problems, which can lead to the IDS malfunctioning, drivers released by the software or hardware manufacturer are preferable.

❑ *Software/hardware customization software.* Practically all combinations of software and hardware require customization. This can be performed using both built-in software and add-on tools. Usually, add-on tools are supplied with the system, but sometimes come at an additional cost (especially for sophisticated combinations of hardware and software).

❑ *Protocol analyzers and attack-modeling tools.* These tools, which test that the IDS is operating correctly, include Dragon Sensor Workbench from Enterasys Networks and nidsbench from Anzen. The latter program — a set of utilities running under BSD, Linux, and Solaris — is especially interesting. It includes three utilities:

- TCPreplay — used for analyzing the IDS' performance by sending real network traffic containing attacks. It allows the user to set traffic transmission speed, and can increase or decrease this speed. In addition, TCPreplay is compatible with the previously mentioned TCPdump.

- FragRouter — analyzes the efficiency of a network-level IDS by sending fragmented packets containing attacks, as well as other attacks described elsewhere [Ptacek1-98], [Paxson1-98]. The program can be downloaded from the developer's Web site (http://www.monkey.org/~dugsong/fragroute/). (This server was the victim of an unpleasant hacking incident: The hacker who compromised the server modified the source codes of the FragRouter and dsniff utilities with a Trojan that allowed a user with the IP address 216.80.99.202 to run commands remotely on the host on which the modified programs are installed. The source codes were modified on May 17, 2002, and all copies of FragRouter downloaded since then have contained the Trojan code.)

- IDStest — used for evaluating network-level IDS efficiency by testing the means of sending real attacks to the IDS. In effect, it is no different from the various attack modeling scanners.

One other system is worth mentioning. At the time of writing, Blade Software's IDS Informer was one of the best testing kits available.

Purchasing Documentation and Support Services

Depending on the complexity of the IDS, the technical staff's skill levels, the system, and other factors, an organization may need technical support from the manufacturer or vendor, training services, and so on.

Users who are unfamiliar with the technologies and principles upon which the chosen IDS is based will always be prone to err, which can cost an organization quite a lot. Such errors can result in delays in installation and deployment, and furthermore, can complicate the operation and maintenance of the IDS. Therefore, it is advisable to purchase documentation and technical support services at the same time as the IDS. (This is especially true for large companies.)

It is not a good idea merely to purchase the bare minimum (usually just the CD and instructions). Most system administrators are usually short on time, and therefore, do not even study the documentation supplied with the system. This lack of knowledge can result in the IDS actually simplifying penetration into the network instead of protecting it. Manufacturer support is especially important should difficult situations not described in the documentation arise. Technical support often doubles as training, which can provide a large amount of valuable information in a short time.

Most companies, such as ISS and Cisco, provide high-quality technical service. For example, each request to the technical support service is answered by a message confirming receipt of the request and promising to answer it within a set period of time (depending on the services paid for). This guarantees that the client's request is being processed by a group of highly qualified specialists.

As was mentioned, the technical support provided by a manufacturer usually includes several layers that differ in their response time to client requests. The following types of support are commonly used:

❏ Consulting via phone and e-mail
❏ Support via the web server
❏ Software and hardware updates
❏ On-site support and maintenance

Based on real-world practice, most manufacturers have adopted the following technical support parameters as standard:

❏ Support during standard business hours (9 a.m. to 6 p.m., Monday through Friday).
❏ A technical support warranty valid for the first year after purchase. When this runs out, the agreement is usually extended for another year, and so on.
❏ Average technical support prices usually are anywhere from 20 to 25 percent of the total cost of the IDS, although this figure can be as high as 50 percent. This mainly relates to the so-called Platinum Support Level, which guarantees a response within one hour, with technical support available 24 hours a day.

When discussing the IDS' technical support agreement, it is worth considering similar support for other software and hardware, in order to avoid an unpleasant situation in which the IDS runs smoothly, but problems with the working environment constantly disrupt its operation. Moreover, it is worth making sure that the technical support agreement includes a paragraph relating to periodic updates of the IDS and other software. Subscribing to the IDS manufacturer's mailing list is also useful, as it keeps the user informed of all news related to the IDS and companion software.

Installation and Deployment

IDS installation includes several steps. If the chosen IDS is an exclusively software solution (for example, RealSecure Network Sensor or Nessus), the process is made up of two steps:

❑   Installation and customization of the operating system
❑   IDS software installation

If the IDS takes the form of a combination of specialized hardware and software (for example, Cisco IDS 4200 or RealSecure for Nokia), these steps are unnecessary. Since both the operating system and the IDS are pre-installed by the manufacturer or vendor, you can immediately move on to customizing.

Network-integrated systems (such as the Cisco Catalyst 6500 IDS Module, or Cisco Integrated Software) are somewhat different: With a hardware solution, it is necessary to customize the Catalyst 6500 module and its operating system, whereas, with a software solution, modification of the OS settings is unnecessary.

The following steps are required to configure the OS in Windows NT [ISS1-98]. Note that these steps are mainly required for network-level IDSs, since, for higher-level systems, the host's pre-existing configuration must be used. It should be emphasized that the steps described below are also applicable to other operating systems.

1. Windows NT installation according to the system requirements of the IDS
2. Installation of all required updates (service packs, hotfixes, or patches).
3. OS optimization (including the system registry, startup files, services, daemons, etc.).
4. Configuration of the network interfaces, such as unbinding all protocols (including IP) from the network adapter "listening" for network traffic. This enables the implementation of stealth mode (Fig. 11.5). The second adapter, responsible for communication with the management console, needs only to support the protocol used for this communication (usually TCP or UDP). However, some systems, such as Enterprise Security Manager, are capable of using IPX/SPX, or even DECnet. All "unnecessary" protocols (WINS, IPX, etc.) must be disabled. If the network sensor has only one network adapter, stealth mode can not be implemented since the sensor will be unable to maintain external communications. When installing a network-level security scanner, additional network adapter configuration is unnecessary.

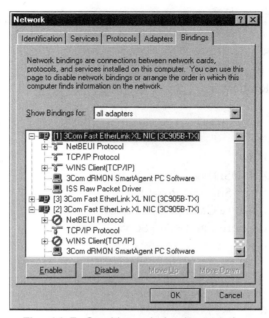

Fig. 11.5. Stealth mode implementation

5. To protect the host on which the network sensor is installed, only those network protocols, ports, and services used by the IDS need to be enabled. All the other network services on that host must be disabled by selecting **Control Panel** | **Network** | **TCP/IP** | **Properties** | **Advanced** | **TCP/IP Security** (Fig. 11.6). (These steps should be followed for each network adapter installed on the host.)

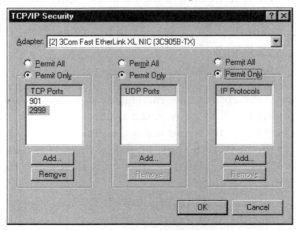

Fig. 11.6. Disabling unneeded ports and protocols (in RealSecure Network Sensor)

6. By default, Windows NT installation has the following active services:
    - Alerter
    - ClipBook Server
    - Computer Browser
    - Directory Replicator
    - Event Log
    - Messenger
    - Net Logon
    - Network DDE
    - Network DDE DSDM
    - NT LM Security Support Provider
    - Remote Procedure Call (RPC) Locator
    - Remote Procedure Call (RPC) Service
    - Schedule
    - Server
    - Spooler
    - UPS
    - Workstation

    In addition to the built-in components, the **Services** dialog might contain other services already installed on the host. As a rule, all these services can be disabled. The need for specific services depends on the method of remote control over the host on which the network sensor has been installed. The IDS might only require Event Log — needed for controlling system log files, and Schedule — responsible for scheduling processes, services, and other programs. (Schedule, for example, can be used to start the IDS automatically.) UPS service will be needed if the host is protected by an Uninteruptible Power Supply (UPS).

7. Windows NT security can be significantly strengthened by deleting unnecessary accounts and by the appropriate management of administrative accounts (for the local host and the IDS). Moreover, the system registry can be modified to protect logon and logoff procedures and control access from the network to the information stored on the host. If the host on which the IDS is located is managed by the IT department, and IDS-related permission is assigned to the IS department, their accounts must be separated.

8. Normally, users can shut down Windows NT without logging on to the operating system by selecting the **Shutdown** option from the **Logon** dialog. This option must be disabled by modifying the **ShutdownWithoutLogon** registry value, under

the following registry key: HKEY_LOCAL_MACHINE\SOFTWARE\Microsoft\ WindowsNT\CurrentVersion\Winlogon.

9. By default, Windows NT caches the logon information of users who logon to the system, which simplifies user access to other computers on the network and speeds up the authentication process. However, the host on which the network sensor is installed is usually a dedicated host. (It often has neither a keyboard nor a monitor.) In this case, the function is redundant and must be disabled by editing the CachedLogonsCount registry value, under HKEY_LOCAL_MACHINE\Software\ Microsoft\WindowsNT\CurrentVersion\Winlogon.

10. The next step limits the possibility of establishing anonymous connections to the host containing the network sensor by editing the RestrictAnonymous parameter under HKEY_LOCAL_MACHINE\SYSTEM\System\CurrentControlSet\Control\LSA.

11. The next step is to customize access to IDS files and directories, as well as to OS files and directories. In particular, resource sharing must be disabled.

12. Finally, to increase security, system auditing should be enabled.

13. If the IDS host uses special operating modes (RAID, backup network adapters, cluster configuration, etc.), all these components must be properly configured before IDS installation.

14. Other OS components (including network drivers, streamer drivers, etc.) should also be configured if necessary.

Before IDS software installation, it is advisable to make a backup copy of the software on the same media (for example, CD-ROM) to enable easy access to all distribution software (both OS and IDS), as well as to all updates. It is also advisable to document all the steps performed in installing the operating system. In addition, it is necessary to perform an integrity check on the OS files so that, should anything go wrong, it will be easy to understand what happened, and for what reason. These steps should be taken before beginning the IDS installation.

It is best to install the necessary software and hardware before beginning installation of the IDS on the chosen host, in order to enable a check of the presence of all the required components. Should a component be missing, it can be purchased before deploying the IDS. This step also allows identification of the difficulties and possible problems that may be encountered during installation and deployment. This is especially true for the so-called OEM versions of operating systems (usually Microsoft's) into which manufacturers — Compaq, Hewlett Packard, etc. — introduce modifications. These modifications can result in installation problems or even incompatibility.

Technical experts — from the vendor's technical-support service or from a consulting company — should be consulted if your personal experience with the particular hardware or software is limited. All activities in this direction and all advice received should be documented, increasing your relevant knowledge and making it easily accessible. Additionally, documenting any recommendations made by the consultant will provide proof in case those recommendations happen to be incorrect.

Some general recommendations should be made before describing an IDS installation. Although each IDS has specific features, there are some characteristics that are common to all of them. The time required for IDS installation and deployment — especially in large geographically distributed networks — should be noted and documented. If the IDS includes only one or two network sensors, this parameter is not of vital importance. However, if the system includes dozens or even hundreds of sensors, this parameter becomes crucial: If it takes one hour to install one sensor then — if deployment is done manually — it will take 100 hours to install 100 sensors. (Note that neither OS installation and configuration, nor the time needed to visit remote sites, are taken into account here.) Clearly, this approach is slow and inefficient.

Remote sites where an IDS is necessary very often lack qualified personnel capable of performing the IDS installation. In this case, it would be good to simplify and automate the installation process. Therefore, you will have to provide the list of default options, automatic installation procedures, and so on. (The RealSecure IDS, for example provides such capabilities via the AutoRecord mechanism. Using this, the administrator can create an installation script to record what is done during the installation of the first sensor. Then, using AutoInstall, it is possible to reproduce the same actions for other sensors in automatic mode [ISS1-00].)

If a security appliance — a specialized combination of software and hardware — has been chosen, then the whole installation process is straightforward: It need only be unpacked, connected to the system, and switched on. The operating system and sensor components must be pre-installed and preconfigured by the vendor. The administrator needs only to change some IDS settings from the central management console, according to the security policy and data processing technology adopted at the remote site.

After configuration, it is advisable to create a backup copy of the whole IDS, including the OS. Having a backup copy means that the system can quickly be restored to its original state if necessary. After creating the backup copy, the recovery process should be tested to make sure that the backup is usable and the restored IDS operates correctly. Symantec's Norton Ghost is one example of the wide variety of disk cloning utilities available.

Although the vendor's advertising slogans may suggest otherwise, IDS installation is not particularly straightforward (this is true for any security tool). On the contrary, each product is unique, and has its own specific installation and deployment features. Therefore, before beginning installation, reading all the supplied documentation — or at least the Readme file — is highly recommended, in order to avoid any problems.

For example, I once encountered just such an awkward situation. After deploying the RealSecure IDS, a customer noticed that no connection between the network sensors and the management console could be established, and wrote quite a long message requiring the vendor to correct this situation immediately. After investigation, it became clear that the customer's personnel had studied the installation instructions with insufficient care and, therefore, had performed the installation incorrectly, without exchanging authentication keys, without which communication between sensor and console is impossible. And another example: a client firm contacts the vendor by telephone, declaring that their IT personnel can not install the Internet Scanner system on a computer running Windows NT Server. This security scanner's system requirements, however, state that it requires Windows NT Workstation. The clients are surprised to be asked if they have consulted the Readme file: "Why should we? Everything was so obvious ..."

Specifying the Rules for Classical IDSs

As previously mentioned, network-level IDSs only operate with network traffic. When creating the rules for systems of this class, it is possible to use both internal and external information. Internal sources include the complete contents of the network packet, i.e.:

- ❏ Source and destination addresses
- ❏ Source and destination ports
- ❏ Packet length
- ❏ Connection state
- ❏ Data field
- ❏ Header flags (TCP protocol)

External sources use information, which is external in relation to network packets. A more detailed description of these information sources can be found in *Chapter 4*.

There are several ways to customize the templates of attacks to be detected. By making all signatures available — or nearly all, if there are some which it is certain will never be needed — and monitoring from the console, it is possible to determine which signatures are detected in the network, which events are important and which are not. After repeating this procedure within different segments of the network, it will be possible to create customized templates for sensors located at different points in the network. However, in practice, this approach ignores the possibility of missing some events when studying network traffic.

The second method comprises several steps:

1. A list of protocols, ports and addresses within the network segment should be created, based on the network map. (This is why the creation of a network map is so important.) If the IDS has to protect the network segment that is connected to public networks (such as the Internet), and the network is protected by a firewall, then the list used by the firewall can be used for the IDS. It is not advisable, however, to rely on that list completely; an additional check will be useful in any case.

2. A list of operating systems and software used within the protected network should be drawn up, again based on the network map. This list must include all installed updates (including service packs, hotfixes, and patches). Without this, the IDS will attempt to look for attacks that can not cause any damage. A typical example is the WinNuke attack, or Windows Out of Band, which can cause the failure of a host running Windows NT or Windows 95. However, this attack only presents a threat to hosts without the OOB-FIX installed on Microsoft Service Pack 2 or 3; in all other cases it is absolutely harmless. If this update is installed on hosts within the protected network segment, and the list that has been drawn up does not mention it, the IDS will waste resources searching for the appropriate signature within network traffic. If such attacks are numerous, the system performance may drop dramatically.

3. The collected information should be placed into a table, which later will be made into the rules for the IDS.

4. The IDS database must include only those signatures that correspond to the created table and to the list of signatures detected by the IDS.

5. If necessary, you can create custom signatures that are temporarily lacking in the database.

6. If necessary, each signature's properties (priority, threshold values) can be changed, and various types of responses can be enabled.

When customizing attack signatures, you should make sure that both the signatures and the rules that use them are based on a numeric representation of the sender's and the recipient's addresses, rather than on symbolic ones. Otherwise, if the DNS or WINS server is configured incorrectly or caused to fail by an intruder, the IDS will identify the attack source or target incorrectly. In this case, although a numeric representation of addresses is not user-friendly, it is more reliable and able to overcome most potential problems. An ideal approach is to use a symbolic representation when configuring the system — which also simplifies the configuration procedure — and then to translate this into numeric form. This principle is implemented in Check Point

Firewall-1, which provides the ability to create so-called network objects and assign them intuitive, user-friendly names. For example, it is easier to memorize a name such as Oracle_Finance_2Floor than 192.168.1.1. The RealSecure Network Sensor is based on the same principle (Fig. 11.7).

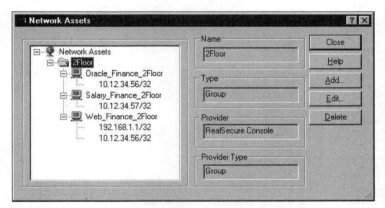

Fig. 11.7. Implementation of mapping numeric and symbolic names

The RealSecure SiteProtector system provides the broadest possibilities, allowing different methods of specifying network objects' names, from IP address and custom, user-defined names to NetBIOS and DNS names (Fig. 11.8).

All of the rules and signatures available to the IDS should not be enabled in alert mode, as this might have a negative impact on performance, as might the number of user-defined filters. Because of this, a preliminary stage — identifying all the protocols and operating systems in use in the protected segment — is necessary. In addition, a large number of rules complicates the IDS operation, and increases the probability of configuration errors.

From this point of view, the NetProwler system employs one of the most interesting mechanisms. This mechanism, intended to simplify the process of IDS configuration, carries out a preliminary scan of the hosts within the protected segment, in order to identify the operating systems running on those hosts (Fig. 11.9). After this, the IDS automatically initiates detection of those attacks that might be potentially dangerous for those operating systems. This approach is somewhat risky, however, because if the operating systems are incorrectly identified, the IDS will enable the wrong rules, and consequently, will detect the wrong attacks. Some potentially dangerous attacks may also be missed. Unfortunately, it is impossible to change the list of operating systems detected by the built-in scanner if some operating systems are identified incorrectly. If the developers eliminate this shortcoming, the mechanism may prove to be indispensable.

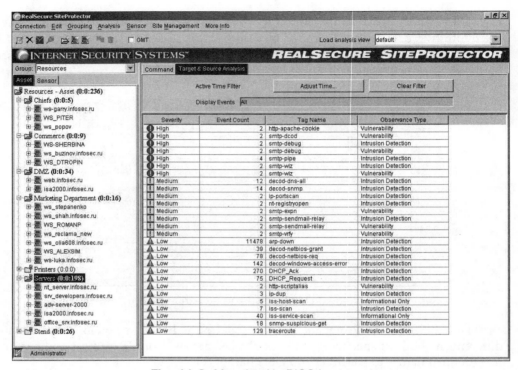

Fig. 11.8. Mapping NetBIOS host names

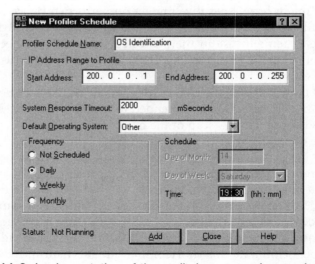

Fig. 11.9. Implementation of the preliminary scanning mechanism

The same principles that apply to network-level systems apply to host-level IDSs, with the exception of the information needed to determine the rules. Host-level systems operate with concepts such as "user," "application," etc. The rules should be documented after being determined, in order to be able to restore the operating settings as soon as possible when necessary.

The management console may need to be customized in the same way as the sensors. For example, custom filters may be required to prevent the console from displaying all events related to ARP activities. (There may be thousands of such events per day.) These filters differ from the sensor's filters in that they do not prevent the system from registering specific events but rather, simply do not display such events on the console. These filters are only applicable to the console on which they are created, providing flexible management capabilities that enable control over the IDS in a large distributed network.

Specifying the Rules for Security Scanners

Security scanners detect vulnerabilities rather than attacks, and operate at pre-defined times — this has a specific influence on their operation. For IDSs, it is possible to compose a list of operating systems used within the protected network segments (depending on the size of the segment); this is impossible for security scanners. This is especially true for scanning remote hosts that are far away from the scanning host and have dynamically assigned IP addresses (via DHCP).

In comparing various security scanners and the documentation supplied with them, I have noticed that not many vendors pay sufficient attention to strategies for the deployment, operation, and maintenance of their products. A pleasing exception to this rule is ISS, which pays significant attention to all of these aspects, both in its documentation [ISS7-00] and in its training course. In particular, ISS' documentation provides a useful table, which outlines the main steps to be performed by IS specialists when operating the Internet Scanner system, and which provides brief descriptions of the goals achieved by performing each step (Table. 11.3). The same approach can be easily extended to other security scanners.

Table 11.3. Measures to Be Taken by IS Personnel

Step	Goal
Notifying users	You should notify the owners of the scanned devices before starting this procedure, to reassure them that the scanning is not being performed by an intruder. Moreover, the scanning will enable them to adequately evaluate and eliminate the vulnerabilities detected.

continues

Table 11.3. Measures to be Taken by IS Personnel

Step	Goal
Changing scanning time and intervals	It is best to perform scanning at different times, and with different intervals, in order to compose a more detailed pattern and eliminate the time dependence.
Performing test scanning	After careful scanning of network devices and eliminating all critical vulnerabilities, it is recommended that you perform periodic test scans in order to make sure that these devices have not become more vulnerable.
Scanning new systems	New network devices should be scanned as soon as possible, in order to prevent the security level of the existing network configuration from decreasing.
Denial of scanning	In some cases, specific network devices might not be scanned (for example, if another organization is responsible for maintaining that device).
Testing for Denial of Service vulnerability	Tests of this type might cause malfunctions and/or failures of the devices being tested, and should only be performed if the device owners are notified beforehand. Besides this, it is necessary to perform certain steps — such as backup procedures — to prevent malfunctions and failures.

Scanning Strategy

The scanning strategy depends on the collected information stored in the network map. As mentioned earlier, when the network map is created, all hosts within the network are grouped by various distinguishing features (whether they belong to a physical or a logical segment, location, importance, vulnerability to specific attacks, etc.). These groups of hosts must be described in sufficient detail in order to avoid extra checks. On the other hand, a sufficient number of devices must be included in order to minimize the total number of required tests and the processing of the test results. In a specific organization, the devices included in these groups may vary, depending on the problems being solved and on the organization's field of activity. For example, in financial institutions, the group may consist of the servers of the accounting system, while, in a factory, these might be the components of the scheduling system. Following are some suggested grouping variants (note that some devices may be included in several groups simultaneously):

❏   All devices connected to the network (including the whole range of equipment used in the organization)

- ❏ Routers and other perimeter network equipment
- ❏ Switches, routers, concentrators, bridges and other internal network equipment
- ❏ DMZ devices (DNS, SMTP, FTP, web servers and so on)
- ❏ Firewalls and other perimeter protection tools (IDSs, authentication servers, certificate servers, etc.)
- ❏ Internal network protection tools (security servers, authentication servers, key-generation servers, LDAP servers)
- ❏ Workstations and servers involved in the organization's daily activities
- ❏ Workstations and servers involved in the organization's business-critical tasks (database servers, critical application servers, scheduling and management system components, accounting system servers, administrators' workstations)
- ❏ Internal web servers, intended to help in the organization's day-to-day tasks (for example, internal informational portals)

Fig. 11.10 shows an example of grouping the protected resources into six groups in the RealSecure SiteProtector system:

- ❏ Top management (Chiefs)
- ❏ Demilitarized zone (DMZ)
- ❏ Marketing department (Marketing Department)
- ❏ All servers (Servers)
- ❏ All printers (Printers)
- ❏ Demonstration facility (Stend)

Furthermore, you need to coordinate the scanning strategy with top management or other responsible people, and with the administrators of the scanned hosts. When implementing the scanning strategy, you will have to:

- ❏ Cooperate with the administrators of the scanned hosts or network segments and inform them of the scanning results, thereby allowing them to be on top of the security situation of the resources that they protect
- ❏ Coordinate all aspects of eliminating the detected vulnerabilities with top management

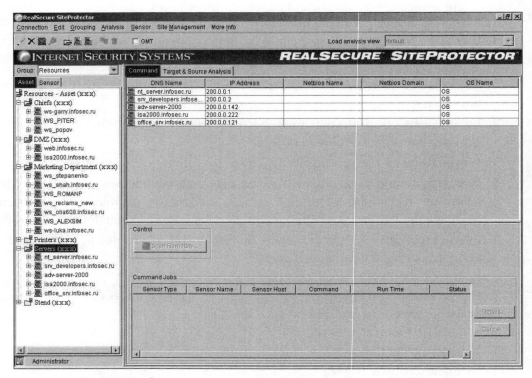

Fig. 11.10. Grouping protected devices in RealSecure SiteProtector

At the stage of performing initial scanning, and after developing and implementing a strategy for eliminating vulnerabilities, it is necessary to:

❏ Test specific groups of devices periodically, in order to detect new vulnerabilities and eliminate vulnerabilities detected during previous checks

❏ Detect new devices within the network, and apply to them all the above-listed operations for scanning

Scanning Tactics

Using security scanners, with the exception of tests for DoS vulnerability (and even this is not always true) has practically no influence on the performance of the devices within a corporate network. However, when performing a large number of tests, network traffic may intensify significantly, the workload of the tested devices may increase, and log files may grow in size. If the template used during scanning does not correspond to the type and/or configuration of the scanned devices, up to 80 percent of the test results will be practically useless. The efficiency of scanner usage increases significantly when performing so-called "selective scanning," which is geared toward specific devices within the corporate network.

From this point of view, after developing a scanning strategy — which implies classifying all the devices in the network into scanning groups and defining priorities for each group — it is recommended that you draw up a scheme for applying the strategy: in other words, tactics. The key tactical factor is the scanning goal for each group of devices. Recommended checks, including taking into account the probability of the presence of specific vulnerabilities, are configured according to the general principle adopted for typical corporate networks. If specific products or services — such as NCR Unix or Compaq Tru64 — are detected, the appropriate modifications must be introduced into the template.

Additionally, the same group of devices can be scanned with different goals in mind or, by way of contrast, different groups can be scanned for the same purpose, such as performing an equipment inventory, or detecting compromised hosts (e.g., hosts infected by Trojans).

Appropriate measures must be specified in the scanning plan. The scanning plan can be a table with columns listing the groups of "listening" devices and rows containing the scanning goals. The table's cells must contain information on the scanning goals and frequency (Table 11.4).

Table 11.4. An Example of a Scanning Plan

Goal	Device groups				
	All network devices	Account-ing system servers	Network equipment	Database servers	External Web servers
Inventory and classification	Weekly				
Network checks			Monthly		
Average number of checks		Monthly		Quarterly	Monthly
Maximum number of checks		Quarterly		When bring-ing into operation	
Web checks					Monthly
Denial of Service		Quarterly			
Port scanning (1-65535)	Monthly	Weekly		Weekly	Quarterly

The scanning frequency for specific device types depends on the importance of the devices included in the specific group, the frequency of configuration changes, the amount of free resources in the corporate network, etc. Recommended scanning goals and appropriate time intervals are outlined below.

- ❏ All devices within the corporate network or a specific segment (to perform inventory and classification): weekly. This process will detect new hosts within the network, as well as identify changes in the configuration of existing hosts.

- ❏ All hosts within the corporate network (to detect compromised hosts or traces of remote attacks): daily. Because of the significant time expenses and network traffic overload incurred, it is not recommended that you perform this check (including checking remote devices) from the central management console. Furthermore, this check becomes difficult to implement when the difference in time zones between the scanning and the scanned hosts reaches 8 to 9 hours.

- ❏ Important network devices (to detect traces of internal attacks or unauthorized configuration changes): weekly or monthly.

- ❏ Critical network hosts (in order to control availability): daily or hourly.

- ❏ Elements of active network equipment: quarterly, or when upgrading or replacing the equipment or software.

- ❏ DMZ devices: weekly, or when modifying the configuration.

- ❏ Perimeter protection tools: weekly or daily, as well as when introducing configuration changes.

- ❏ Most critical servers and workstations: selective testing, in order to detect vulnerabilities to Denial of Service attacks. Recommended when bringing the equipment into operation, reinstalling or upgrading the OS, introducing significant configuration changes, and when performing regular testing.

The same principles that apply to systems operating at a lower level apply to host-level security scanners, but with allowances made for the specific features of detected vulnerabilities.

Configuration of the Event Logging and Alerting Mechanisms

Upon registering security-related events, the IDS must do the following:

- ❏ Log the event and notify the administrator of the detected attacks, vulnerabilities, or other security policy violations.

❑ Log and issue notification of the events related to the IDS itself (e.g., when the log file is full, when the connection between the sensor and the console is interrupted, etc.)

Correct configuration of the event-logging and alerting mechanisms will decrease the interval between attack detection and the reaction to it. These mechanisms must be considered in such a way as to inform all responsible individuals only of the events that are actually important, such as:

❑ Attacks that really were implemented
❑ Potential attacks that could result in compromising the whole network
❑ Failed attempts to logon to the system
❑ Modifications or configuration changes introduced into the IDS or another installed security tool
❑ System messages (e.g., memory overflow, interruption of the connection between console and sensor, etc.).

The security policy — or the IDS operating plan — must describe all event-logging and alerting mechanisms, and list all events that will result in the activation of these mechanisms.

Log Files

There is no need to store log files for longer than 3 or 4 weeks. Since IDSs — with the exception of scanners and integrity control systems — are security tools operating in real-time mode, storing log files for longer periods has no practical purpose. Experience has shown that IDS administrators rarely investigate even events that took place during the previous week, to speak nothing about two or three-week-old records. This does not concern security scanners, which can access even three- or six-month-old records, in order to investigate the changes that have taken place within the scanned segment (Fig. 11.11). In any case, it is a good idea to archive log files after a specified time period, in order to store them for future use and access them as needed.

When configuring the logging subsystem, the following aspects should be taken into account:

❑ The location of the log files of each IDS component (local or remote). In some systems, these paths are specified by default. However, for some systems, the directory and filename for the log file must be specified explicitly.

❑ Expected size of the log file for each component. As a rule, for "classical" IDS sensors, it is possible to specify the maximum log-file size. For consoles or security scanners, on the other hand, this parameter is not specified, since it is impossible to know beforehand how rapidly the log file will fill up. There are two methods of specifying log-file size: by bytes or by records. Different IDSs combine both these methods. (It is actually quite difficult to choose between the two methods, as both of them have advantages.)

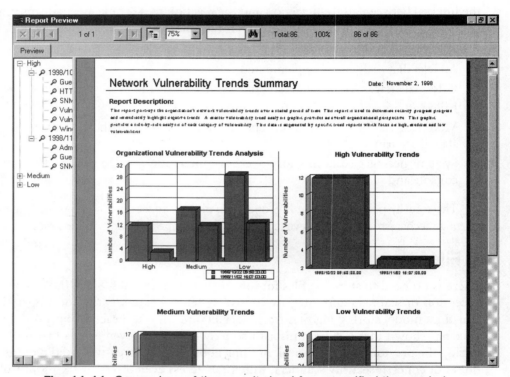

Fig. 11.11. Comparison of the security level for a specified time period

❑ Access rights to log files and their components. It is recommended that you make the list of users that have access to the logged data as short as possible. This is especially true for IDS systems that store critical information on system vulnerabilities, which can cause significant damage if misused. In some systems, such as RealSecure and Internet Scanner, access rights to log files and other components are set automatically during system installation. In other systems, this operation must be performed manually, using the mechanisms provided by the operating system.

❑ Using cryptographic transformations (integrity control and encryption) for additional protection of log files. As I already noted, it is not advisable to apply these operations to log files that are constantly having new records added relating to the attacks and vulnerabilities discovered, since this will have a negative impact on the system's overall performance. The continuous calculation and recalculation of checksums may take up all of the system's resources, which will reduce system performance, or even make the logging of some events impossible.

❑ **Log-file backup and recovery.** Since log files fill up quite rapidly, only those events that are really important should be logged; otherwise, log files will quickly grow in size and take up all the available disk space, and subsequent events will not be registered. This can sometimes serve as an opportunity to implement a Denial of Service attack (Log Flood) on the IDS. Since it is impossible to predict the rate at which log files will fill up with new records, it is recommended that you enable the automatic synchronization mechanism implemented in some IDSs (such as RealSecure). This makes it possible to copy the log file from the network sensor to the central console when specific criteria are satisfied (for example, when the number of records reaches a specified limit, or when the log-file size exceeds a certain value). If the criterion is satisfied, but synchronization can not occur — for example, if the connection between the sensor and the console has been interrupted — synchronization will be reattempted after the so-called "notification interval" elapses. Both the synchronization criterion and the notification interval must be specified by the administrator (Fig. 11.12).

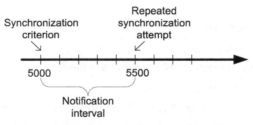

Fig. 11.12. Synchronization of log files

It should be specifically pointed out that currently, hard disks are inexpensive, and therefore, are not something on which users should economize. The amount of disk space for storing log files should not limit logging frequency or the number of registered events.

E-Mail Notifications and SNMP Traps

This is relatively simple, but, to be implemented properly, two important aspects must be taken into account. First, e-mail messages are unprotected, and any intruder can intercept, read, modify, or even replace them (especially if they are transmitted via public networks). Secondly, when using e-mail or SNMP notifications, you may encounter an "endless loop" situation (Fig. 11.13), although only in classical network-level IDSs. Although such cases are relatively rare, the possibility grows with cluster configurations made up of IDS sensors, or when there are two backup sensors from different manufacturers within the network segment.

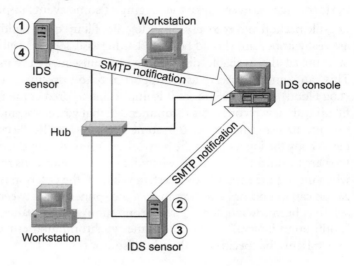

1 - generation of SMTP message to the console

2 - detection of SMTP traffic

3 - generation of SMTP message to the console

4 - detection of SMTP traffic

Fig. 11.13. The endless loop situation

Strengthening IDS Security

Despite the fact that an IDS is itself a security tool, it still needs protection against hacker attacks.

Backing up the IDS

The parallel use of two IDSs is quite often more efficient from a security point of view, but is significantly more expensive. (This is applicable only to network-level IDSs.) The advantages of such a solution are listed below.

❑   Controlling network traffic with two IDSs increases the probability of attack detection. Furthermore, combining two IDSs for parallel traffic processing increases the probability of detecting a vulnerability. Products from different manufacturers can use different approaches to detect the same vulnerability: It is quite possible that one will detect a vulnerability, while the other one will miss it. David Le Blanc, one of the leading developers of the Internet Scanner system, who has recently moved to Microsoft, provides the following illustrative analogy: "If you ask me if my friend is at home, I will try to call him. If he does not answer, I will call you and say that he is not at home. However, if you then go to visit him, knock on the door, and he opens it, do not call me a liar just because the plan that I suggested did not work. Perhaps I was not right, or it was necessary to use other methods, but I tried to do what I considered to be right." The same is also applicable to IDSs. For example, the differences between such systems as CyberCop Scanner and Internet Scanner lie in the fact that Network Associates' developers never add a check to their product if they are not sure that the check reliably detects a vulnerability. On the other hand, Internet Security Systems' developers add the check to their database even if it detects vulnerabilities with a certain probability of error. Later, after releasing a new version, they return to the added checks, improve them, add new mechanisms for detecting the same vulnerability, and so on. It is difficult to say for certain which approach is better: It is important to know definitively that a specific vulnerability is not present on the analyzed host, but on the other hand, if even the smallest chance of detecting a specific vulnerability exists, it would be wise to take that chance. Cisco has suggested a combined approach, implemented in its Secure Scanner, which works at the network level. This subdivides all vulnerabilities into the following two classes:

- *Potential vulnerabilities.* A potential vulnerability may exist in the system, but active probing checks (described in *Chapter 6*) will not confirm this. Checks for potential vulnerabilities are performed via header analysis, and by "nudging." Nudging is used for services that do not return headers, but react to simple commands, such as the HEAD command used to obtain the HTTP server version. After this information is obtained, Secure Scanner enables a special mechanism, known as a rules engine, which implements a set of rules that determine whether or not the potential vulnerability really exists, thus clarifying, which potential vulnerabilities actually exist in the system, and which ones require confirmation.

- *Confirmed vulnerabilities,* which have had their existence confirmed after being detected on the analyzed host by means of header analysis.

However, this product has not been supplied to clients since June 15, 2002. (http://www.cisco.com/warp/public/cc/pd/sqsw/nesn/prodlit/1736_pp.htm).

❏   If one of the systems is compromised, the second one will continue to operate.

❏ Combining IDSs from different vendors improves the overall reliability of the whole security infrastructure, and prevents an intruder who has exploited the vulnerabilities of the first IDS from compromising the other one.

Protecting against Unauthorized Access

To prevent intruders from getting unauthorized access to an IDS host and compromising it, the system's sensors and console must be placed in a physically secure location. For example, network sensors can be mounted in racks with other network equipment (routers, switches, etc.).

After installing a network sensor, it is best to disconnect unnecessary peripherals — monitor, keyboard, floppy-disk drive, CD-ROM drive, etc. — from it. In this case, even if intruders manage to penetrate the physically secure room where the IDS resides, they will not be able to introduce unauthorized modifications into its configuration. Authorized updates of the system software and signature database will have to be performed remotely (as in, for example, RealSecure SiteProtector and Cisco IDS 4200).

IDS Users

To ensure discretionary access control to the IDS, the operating system under which the IDS operates will have to be configured as described earlier in this chapter. First, the list of users granted access to the system must be limited, so that only specific individuals can access it. This will prevent unauthorized IDSs configuration, and reduce the risk of its failure. At least the following specialists must have access to the IDS:

❏ The IDS administrator, or operator, responsible for the configuration and monitoring of the controlled resources
❏ The OS administrator, responsible for its operation, software updates and so on

In most organizations, these employees work in different departments: the Information Security (IS) and Information Technology (IT) departments, respectively. In large companies with a hierarchical management system, the administration of the IDS can be delegated to more than two specialists. Consider, for example, a situation in which an administrator performs sensor configuration, an operator is responsible for network monitoring, while a third specialist manages attack response. (Usually, this specialist belongs to the incident-response team.) System operators have no right to change the IDS' configuration; should this be required, one employee must perform the functions included in both user categories.

If the IDS takes the form of a combination of software and hardware with built-in routing functions (e.g., Cisco's Secure Integrated Software or RealSecure for Nokia), then a network administrator from telecommunications department must manage the appliance.

A practice that is currently widely adopted is outsourcing, in which all security management is delegated to third-party firms. In this case, personnel from the third-party firm perform all functions related to controlling and managing the IDS and the operating system.

Access Rights to the IDS

If the IDS is controlled remotely and the reliability of communications between its components — for example, between a sensor and the console — needs improving, strict authentication mechanisms and cryptographic protection should be used. These methods are needed even if you access the IDS from internal network.

It is not a good idea to rely only on controlling access from specific addresses. First, control using dynamic address assignment (for example, DHCP) can not be guaranteed; second, address spoofing can allow an intruder to mimic an authorized user. A good way of getting around this problem is UAM (User to Address Mapping), developed and implemented by Check Point. Using Check Point's OPSEC SDK interface, it is possible to integrate UAM into an IDS. UAM is quite simple, and allows efficient user authentication in networks that use dynamic address assignment. Authentication includes the following steps:

1. When the computer starts up, it contacts the DHCP server, which assigns it an unused IP address. Simultaneously, the DHCP server contacts the UAM server and sends it information on the IP address that it has just assigned, along with the corresponding MAC address.
2. When the user logs on to the network, the user name and the host on which the user logged onto are sent to the UAM server.
3. The UAM server compares the data received at the first and the second steps and, as a result, gets accurate information about each user's address.

When providing access to various network resources, the security system operates with user names rather than with IP addresses.

Security Policy

The security policy — in particular, the policy on the intrusion detection infrastructure — must take the following aspects into account:

- ❏ The intrusion detection software's checksum (hash function)
- ❏ List of users with IDS access
- ❏ Security measures implemented to protect the IDS
- ❏ Schedule of backup operations for intrusion detection components

All IDS-related actions must be listed in appropriate documents, which taken together, comprise the organization's security policy. (This topic was covered in detail in *Chapter 7*.) When drawing up these documents, the following must be taken into account:

❑ Controlled resources (analyzed hosts)
❑ Most probable attacks
❑ Objects — protocols, addresses, ports, files, etc. — accessible from outside (for each protected resource)
❑ Subjects — users, applications, etc. — using the protected resources
❑ Who will manage the IDS, and how
❑ IDS rules and templates

Stealth Mode Implementation

Most IDSs can work with two network interfaces. The unprotected interface is used for traffic control, while the protected interface is used for response implementation and communication with the management console. This mode of IDS operation is known as stealth mode.

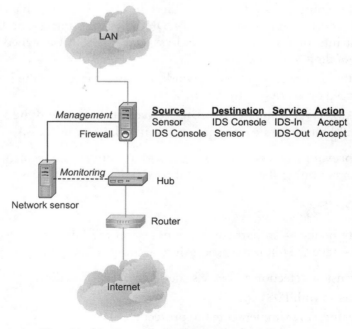

Fig. 11.14. Firewall configuration for IDS support

To avoid creating additional firewall rules for communication between the sensors and the console, the connection scheme in Fig. 8.4 is usually implemented. Sometimes, however, this is impossible, and in this case, additional firewall rules have to be created. To avoid introducing additional vulnerabilities into the network segment protected by the firewall, the firewall rules should be customized. There are usually two such rules (Fig. 11.14) — one for traffic transmitted from the IDS sensor to the console and one for traffic from the console to the sensor.

Automation

As mentioned in *Chapter 8*, automation is one of the important criteria that should be taken into account when selecting an IDS. As a rule, mechanisms built into the IDS provide an easy way of implementing scheduled system startups or report generation procedures. However, it is quite difficult to introduce intelligent automation functions using only GUI tools. The ideal solution for this situation is provided by the built-in scripting capabilities available both in Windows and Unix.

Below is a sample script that can be used for automating the process of security scanning of the specified hosts and generating a report after finishing the task (Listing 11.1). This example uses Internet Scanner 6.1, but such a script can be created for any other security scanner supporting command line mode [ISS9-00].

Listing 11.1. Automation of the Security Scanning Process and Report Creation (in Internet Scanner for Windows NT)

```
echo off
echo Scanning specified hosts and generating a report
echo
echo Changing to the Internet Scanner working directory
c:
cd c:\program files\iss\scanner6

echo Starting the scanning process from the command line
echo -k — system activation key preventing
echo unauthorized usage
echo -p — template describing the checks to be performed
echo -f — file containing the list of host to be scanned

Iss_WinNT.exe -k "iss.key" -p "L3 Finance Server on Unix.Policy" -f
Ä finance.hst

echo Starting the process of generating a report
echo based on the collected information
```

```
echo -X — generating report in HTML format
echo and saving it in N:\ForSendmail\Out\My
echo Reports\TechVuln\TechVulnSeverity
echo techvuln.sev — generating report for technical specialists
echo with sorting the detected vulnerabilities by the level of risk

Iss_WinNT.exe -X techvuln.sev="N:\ForSendmail\Out\
Ä My Reports\TechVuln\TechVulnSeverity"

echo End job
```

Practically all IDS operating tasks — except for analyzing the scanning results and editing the template used — can be combined with the capabilities provided by Windows NT Scheduler (AT). Scheduled starting of the batch file can easily be implemented using the AT (Windows NT) or CRON (Unix) utilities, as shown in Listing 11.2.

Listing 11.2. Using the AT Scheduler (Windows NT)

```
at 16:10 /every:M,T,W,Th,F "c:\nsb-finance.bat"
```

Combining Internet Scanner and RealSecure SiteProtector makes it possible to replace Listings 11.1 and 11.2 with a single window (Fig. 11.15).

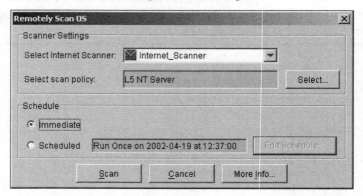

Fig. 11.15. Scheduled start of Internet Scanner with a predefined template

Possible Problems

Deploying and customizing an IDS in a corporate network is both very important and very difficult. The efficiency of the whole intrusion detection infrastructure depends on the correct solution. An administrator who notices no trace of hacker activity may either feel a false sense of security or accuse the vendor of selling a substandard product. An absence of any events on the IDS console may be due to the following:

❏ The sensor is configured incorrectly.

❏ The sensor's network interface responsible for network monitoring or the interface responsible for transmission of events to the management console is malfunctioning. (The console's network interface can also fail, but this is quite rare.)

❏ The network cable connecting the sensor or the console to the network equipment is damaged.

❏ The sensor or console is connected to a malfunctioning port of the switch, concentrator, splitter, or balancer.

❏ The sensor has been placed in an incorrect location and, consequently, can not detect any events.

❏ There is no suspicious activity. (This is purely hypothetical — I have never seen such a network.)

The second, third, and fourth causes are easily detected and eliminated. It is a good idea to use network equipment from well-known firms — such as 3Com, Intel, etc. — to avoid such problems. Network adapters and ports should be backed up, in order to provide continuity of the IDS' operation, even if a network component fails.

The first and fifth problems are the most common. To solve the first problem, the IDS will need to be reconfigured and customized. These topics were covered earlier in this chapter. Therefore, let's examine how to select locations for IDS components correctly. (Typical locations were covered in *Chapter 10.*) Practical experience shows that there are several typical errors that are made when deploying an IDS' network components.

The first error is the most common — incorrect selection of the sensor location. This is best illustrated by an analogy to traffic. For example, upon looking out of the window one morning, you see no cars on the road and decide that it will be possible to get to the office quickly and without problems. However, upon driving one block further down the road, you run into heavy traffic, and as a result, are late in getting to the office. Arriving late was a result of not anticipating the possibility of traffic jams, looking at the wrong location, and drawing the wrong conclusion. It is possible to make the same mistake with an IDS. Problems usually arise at the physical level rather than at the logical layer. (As previously noted, there are only seven logical variations.)

The second common error relates to data filtering, which is often recommended in order to improve the performance of the components responsible for detection of attacks and vulnerabilities, or to decrease the vast amount of data displayed on the management console. However, any mechanism must be used carefully. Sometimes, a seemingly insignificant event represents a missing link in the process of identifying unauthorized activity. If this event is neglected, the IDS filters it out, thus preventing the entire pattern from being analyzed.

The third important problem is a lack of understanding of network operations. When purchasing an IDS, most users erroneously think that it will solve all their problems. This is partially true, but in order to solve all the problems, the IDS must be "taught." This entails an understanding of network internal processes and a list of signatures of attacks and vulnerabilities based on the network map. Network map creation is especially important, since the IDS will only work efficiently — and justify its cost — provided that the map is properly created and maintained.

❗ *Practical example*

A client contacted me and accused us of selling him a substandard product. The client declared that the purchased IDS could not detect attacks on his web server, which had suffered damage as a result. After investigation, it became obvious that the client — who did not want to pay for technical support — had installed the IDS independently, and incorrectly, by enabling detection of HTTP attacks and deciding that this was enough: However, the web server was using port 8080, rather than the default port 80. Naturally, this was not taken into account when configuring the sensor. As a result, the sensor controlled HTTP traffic on port 80, and did not suspect that the web server was using port 8080. Fortunately, in this case, we persuaded the client to purchase a training course and implement an event-monitoring and incident response system.

It is worth mentioning once again that IDSs tend to be seen as being at fault for all network problems (such as reduction in performance, unexpected termination connection, loss of packets, failed identification, etc.). This becomes a particularly sore point when there are conflicts between the IT and IS departments. Sometimes, network administrators simply do not want to admit their errors, and therefore try to place the blame on some device that is outside their control, and whose operation they do not understand.

To resolve all possible conflicts in a businesslike manner, it is necessary to have a sound understanding of the working principles and specific features of the chosen IDS, and to know of all possible problems and how to solve them. This will help normalize relations with the IT department in case of conflicts.

Summary

In this chapter, I have tried to outline my point of view on basic aspects of IDS operation, based on my own practical experience. I hope that careful study of these problems will mean that you can smoothly deploy and operate IDSs from different manufacturers in your corporate networks, avoiding the most common problems.

CHAPTER **12**

Common IDS Problems

Despite all the advantages provided by intrusion detection systems, they are not a universal solution to all problems. Like any other security tool, intrusion detection systems have their own field of application and their own limitations. For example, the following problems are common for an IDS [Allen1-99]:

- ❏ Improvement of hackers' skills and qualifications, growth in the number of available automated hacking tools and their variety (see Fig. 2.12)
- ❏ Use of newer, more sophisticated penetration scenarios
- ❏ Use of encryption functions for transmission of malicious information (for example, TFN2K)
- ❏ Having to correlate data collected from the components of an IDS installed in a heterogeneous network combining Windows NT, Windows 2000, Linux, Solaris, HP UX, AIX, and other operating systems

❐ An increase in the amount of network traffic that needs to be analyzed

❐ Limited network visibility in networks with packet switching

❐ Performance problems in high-speed networks that do not always allow you to detect attacks in real-time mode (and, consequently, react to them in time)

❐ A lack of commonly adopted terminology in the field of intrusion detection

❐ The dependence of intrusion detection systems on their manufacturers, which introduces additional difficulties when purchasing such systems and working with them, thus making them inefficient

❐ The risk that is characteristic of manual response methods

❐ Attacks on intrusion detection systems

❐ A large number of false positives and false negatives

❐ An insufficient number of criteria for evaluating and testing such systems

General Problems

Let's consider the above problems in more detail, along with some others.

Updating the Signature Database

A lack of signatures for the most recently discovered vulnerabilities results in an increase in the risk of network penetration. The manufacturer (or vendor) must regularly update the signature database for attacks and vulnerabilities in order to ensure that its product is maintained in the most up-to-date state and meets all the requirements of a contemporary IDS. The less the period of time between the first report on a newly discovered attack or vulnerability and the appearance of a signature or check for it, the more efficient is the intrusion detection system (Fig. 12.1). The competitive potential of the manufacturer depends on the rate and quality of updates for the signatures that identify the newest attacker tools.

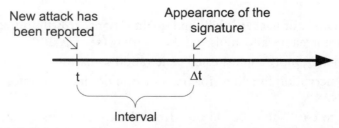

Fig. 12.1. The interval between a report of a new attack and the release of a signature for it

Heterogeneous Networks

The working environment that exists in contemporary heterogeneous networks complicates the normal operation of intrusion detection systems. This relates to the fact that in most operating systems, there are OS-specific data format standards or agreements. The IDS must collect, aggregate, summarize, and analyze this data. Furthermore, data on the attacks are quite often distributed to hundreds of hosts. One of the goals of intrusion detection systems is collecting data from different operating systems (Unix clones, Windows NT, Windows 2000 and Windows 9*x*, MacOS, OS/2, NetWare, etc.) in various network environments (Ethernet, FDDI, ATM, and so on). As of now, this task is still relatively difficult.

Unified Security Management

Unified security management is another problem of similar origin. It is possible to apply different policies to different IDS sensors. Furthermore, organizations can use different types of intrusion detection systems (for example, security scanners and classical intrusion detection systems), which significantly complicates the task of correlating their data. The incompatibility of the data collected from different intrusion detection systems from different vendors represents an even more serious problem.

Hopefully, the latter problem will be solved after the adoption of a data format standard for exchanging data between different intrusion detection systems. Such a standard is being developed in the IETF by the IDWG workgroup (which will be discussed later). Currently, however, each manufacturer uses proprietary methods to solve data compatibility problems. In *Chapter 9*, we mentioned such systems as Spitfire and SAFEsuite Decisions, which provide capabilities of analyzing data from different IDSs on a single console. For example, Spitfire supports such systems as RealSecure Network Sensor and Cisco IDS, while SAFEsuite Decisions, besides native support of RealSecure, ensures the integration of any other intrusion detection system using SDK.

The problem of joining heterogeneous security tools on a single console can also be solved only in certain cases. To do this, you can use SAFEsuite Decisions or net-Forensics. In addition, I should also mention the Dragon Server product, developed by the Network Security Wizards company and later purchased by Enterasys Networks. This system is very similar to the ISS solution, since it includes two components — the Dragon Sensor network intrusion detection system, and the Dragon Squire host-level

IDS (Fig. 12.2). The latter product can act as Syslog and SNMP servers, and is able to receive and analyze data from the following security tools:

- ☐ Firewalls:
  - Check Point Firewall-1
  - Cisco PIX Firewall
  - Raptor
  - NetScreen
  - Ipfilter
  - **IPCHAINS**
- ☐ Apache web servers
- ☐ Sendmail and Qmail
- ☐ Secure Shell
- ☐ Bind (DNS)

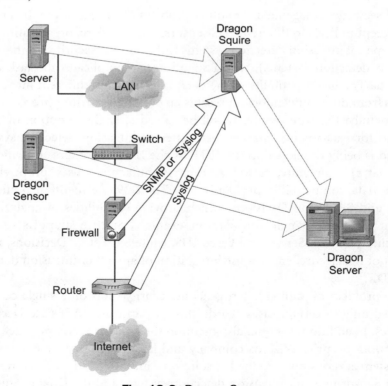

Fig. 12.2. Dragon Server

OS Vulnerability

Speaking about securing and trusting intrusion detection systems is a problematic area likely to cause conflict if you can not guarantee that the operating system under which the IDS will run is secure. Even if the intrusion detection system is implemented flawlessly (which in itself is hardly possible), a single security hole in the OS implementation can reduce all its advantages to zero.

▌ *Attack on NetProwler*

On June 21, 2000, hackers detected a new vulnerability in the NetProwler intrusion detection system from Symantec. Exploiting this vulnerability resulted in a system failure. The attack was implemented by means of sending fragmented packets to a host controlled by NetProwler. Since the operating system processed such packets incorrectly, the NetProwler IDS failed, since it was receiving these packets from the OS driver.

One possible method of eliminating this drawback is the development of reliable and bug-free operating systems. Currently, however, this goal is very difficult to achieve, since most organizations must use available software (which rarely includes reliable, bulletproof, and trusted operating systems). The second approach implies the use of specialized combinations of hardware and software. As a rule, the operating systems for such solutions are stripped of all unnecessary or redundant functions. However, this approach is only available for network-level intrusion detection systems for which the availability of a dedicated computer is one of the basic requirements.

Lack of a Mathematical Foundation

Since intrusion detection technologies still lack a solid mathematical foundation, there is no possibility of developing efficient methods of detecting attacks and efficiently counteracting them. For the moment, only the anomaly detection methods that are frequently used in commercial systems have a more or less solid theoretical basis. All the other existing intrusion detection methods are based either on the achievements of related fields of scientific knowledge or on the developer's personal opinion. The existing tools and mechanisms have no scientific basis, which keeps you from proving the efficiency of suggested solutions. The situation has recently begun to improve, but the results are still far from perfect.

False Positives

The problem of false negatives and false positives is a rather serious and important one. Most likely, it arises due to the lack of a mathematical foundation for intrusion detection technology. Quite a good example illustrating this situation was provided in *Chapter 4* — it was a case of locking the user account after three failed attempts of supplying the correct password. It is not too hard to figure out that the intruder can simply try to guess the password twice each time instead of three times. Proceeding in such a way, the limit of three failed attempts will never be reached, and thus the specified threshold value will never be exceeded. Because of this, the intrusion detection system will not notice this activity. Using the WIZ command in the Sendmail program is yet another example. Historically, this command was used for debugging purposes. However, using it incorrectly allows you to obtain unlimited access to the computer on which the Sendmail program is running. Now this command is used rather rarely when performing authorized actions, and therefore its usage is automatically considered an attack attempt.

False Negatives

Most intrusion detection systems tend to depend on the data sources of an attack. For example, some tools analyze the OS's log files (SysEvent.evt, SecEvent.evt, and AppEvent.evt for Windows 2000 or syslog for Unix). However, most attacks can be implemented in such a way as to generate no events that can be logged by the operating system. Some viruses work in exactly this way. To log as many events as possible, you must either enable the full set of the OS's auditing capabilities (which has a negative impact on system performance) or modify the OS itself.

Advances in the Field of Attack Tools

As was shown in Fig. 2.12, the tools used by attackers have become significantly more sophisticated during the last few years. Intruders use various scanners that can do hidden scanning, use decoy mode and Trojans, etc. This is confirmed by Pentagon experts, who have calculated that attack implementation tools are significantly improved approximately 1–2 times per year. There is quite a serious problem with tools that can be used both for malicious and authorized activities. The list of such tools includes remote administration tools such as NetBus or Remote Administrator, as well as instruments for detecting network adapters in promiscuous mode — for example, AntiSniff, IFStatus, or PromiScan. These tools can also be used both for detecting network adapters operating in promiscuous mode (in order to find unauthorized network sniffers) and for detecting intrusion detection systems (in order to develop a method of bypassing them).

Mobile Code

In this book, the term "mobile code" is used to designate the Java and ActiveX technologies, as well as scripting languages such as JavaScript, Jscript, and VBScript. Mobile code can be used as both an attack implementation tool and as an attack target.

In the first case, the danger originates from he fact that the code is downloaded to the user's workstation, where it runs as a normal program (which means that it can access system resources). In the second case, the main goal of an attacker is modification of the mobile code, which serves as a preliminary step before attacking the protected computer. Attacks on mobile code as a tool for performing specific functions are not currently widespread. Mainly, this relates to the fact that as of yet, such code is not used to perform any critical operations, such as financial transactions. However, there are already some examples of banking systems using Java technologies for communication with clients.

According to [Infosec1-01] data, 28% of companies have to face the problem of a lack of security in mobile code, and thus are exposed to a risk of attacks exploiting this feature. To accomplish an attack, mobile code can be implemented in the following forms:

❏   A virus that infects the operating system and destroys data stored on local disks. Usually, such a virus constantly modifies its code, thus complicating the procedures of detecting and eliminating it

❏   An agent intercepting passwords, credit card numbers, etc.

❏   A program that copies confidential files containing business and financial information

❏   A module causing Denial of Service.

Such programs can mimic animated banners, interactive games, sound files, etc. Although it is impossible to cover in detail all the aspects of mobile code protection in a single chapter, let's consider several examples that illustrate its influence on the operation of the host on which it is launched. This is the attack that is the simplest to perform. Therefore, any Internet user can be exposed to this risk. Such attacks are usually implemented using the following techniques:

❏   Creating high-priority processes performing unauthorized actions

❏   Generating a large number of windows

❏   "Capturing" a large amount of memory and important system classes

❏   Loading the CPU and causing it to enter an endless loop

In [McGraw1-97], there are several interesting examples illustrating the use of mobile code for malicious goals. Particularly interesting is the JavaScript example, which can cause the failure of the host on which it is launched. Notice that a few years have elapsed since this script was written!

Listing 12.1. An Example Illustrating the Malicious Usage of JavaScript

```
<HTML>
<HEAD>
<TITLE>Demonstration of Denial of Service attack</TITLE>
</HEAD>
<BODY>
<CENTER>
<H1>Demonstration of Denial of Service attack</H1>
<HR>Hi! How are you?<BR>
<HR>
</CENTER>
<SCRIPT>
while(1){  alert("All that glitters is not gold!")}
</SCRIPT>
</HTML>
```

As you can see, this script is very easy to implement — it has only one line of code (between the <SCRIPT> and </SCRIPT> tags) that starts an endless loop opening a window containing the following message: "All that glitters is not gold!," which can not be closed. To stop this loop, you have to kill the browser process using Task Manager (in Windows 2000).

The normal approach when detecting mobile code includes scanning all incoming traffic on ports 80 and 443, used by HTTP and HTTPS protocols, to detect suspicious elements (tags, for example). However, this is not sufficient to stop the mobile code, since ActiveX controls and Java applets can be obtained using other methods. For example, let's suppose that the applet (which usually has the CLASS extension) mimics an image file (and has the GIF or JPG filename extension). If the intrusion detection system interprets this file as an image file, it will be passed into the network, loaded into the browser cache, and cause the browser to fail, since the loaded file is not an image. This, however, is not what's important, since the mobile code is already on the computer. Later it can be activated, which will cause serious problems with system security. Another example is the use of a non-standard port for web server operation.

One possible way of protecting, for example, Java applets, is scanning all the traffic within the protected segment in order to detect the presence of specific code fragments. This detection is performed by means of searching for a number identifying byte-code, which in hexadecimal form might look like "CA FE BA BE." However, this approach is rarely used by manufacturers of security tools, since the traffic is usually too intense to filter it over each port to find specific text fragments.

Non-Traditional Channels of Attack Implementation

Strangely enough, most users, experts, and manufacturers believe that hackers use only traditional methods to implement attacks. However, hackers are always one step ahead of the developers of security tools. They are constantly inventing newer methods of attacks, such as Trojans and Internet worms that propagate via unusual channels rarely controlled by intrusion detection systems, such as ICQ, IRC, Flash, Napster, and so on. Besides this, experts do not deny the fact that attacks have been implemented that exploit security holes in various games, such as CounterStrike.

Insufficient Qualification of Personnel

This problem was already discussed in *Chapter 7*. However, I would like to cover it in more detail because of its importance. The qualification of the personnel operating and maintaining the intrusion detection system is one of the basic parameters that should be taken into account when evaluating the efficiency of the intrusion detection infrastructure. There are lots of examples in which the insufficient skill of an IDS operator resulted in extra time, productivity, and financial losses.

❗ *False Alert*

The IDS console displays a warning concerning the detection of an ICMP Flood attack. This attack implies the sending of a large number of ICMP queries to one of the most important hosts of the corporate network. The operator initiates the response procedure and alerts everyone. After an investigation, it becomes clear that a management system is installed on the attacked host, which periodically sends ECHO REQUEST messages in order to check the activity of managed hosts. In response, this system received a large number of ECHO REPLY packets during a limited time period. The IDS interpreted these reply packets as unauthorized activity (Fig. 12.3).

It should be noted, however, that a false sense of security is far worse than an actual lack of security. When you know that you have no protection, you are always alert, expecting your opponent to attack anytime and anywhere. On the other hand, if the company (especially a large one) has purchased some security tool (and this especially relates to a situation in which the security tool is expensive and actively promoted), the unskilled use of such a system and a lack of understanding of the danger represented by your virtual opponents can result in some rather sad consequences.

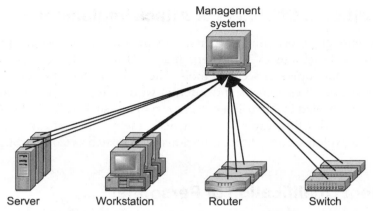

Fig. 12.3. Specific features of the management system operation

! Ford Does Not Know When It Was Hacked

In the spring of 2002, Ford Motors sent warnings to thirteen thousand of its clients, informing them that some information on credit towards purchasing a car had been stolen. The leakage of information took place as a result of cracking the web server of the Ford Credit department. The stolen information contained social security numbers and data on bank transactions of the users. Ford Credit employees could not determine the precise date of the theft — it was assumed that the intruders got access to the information somewhere during the period from April 2001 to February 2002. The fact was detected a year after the supposed attack. Employees of the company identified it by chance, when they noticed that intruders had used database software that differed from the software used in Ford Credit.

Problems with Intrusion Detection

As I already mentioned in *Chapter 2*, the following hierarchy exists in intrusion detection: security event, attack, and incident. Intrusion detection systems operate at the first and second levels of this hierarchy. The third (topmost) level lies beyond the consideration of intrusion detection systems. Although contemporary IDS products implement some mechanisms for identifying intruders (such as the Track Back mechanism in the ManHunt system from Recourse Technologies purchased by Symantec, or the prototype of the Attack Tracker from ISS), this problem has yet to be solved. Intrusion detection systems operate either with accounts within which the attack is implemented, or with addresses registered as the ones from which the attack originated. As I said before, the intruder can easily spoof these addresses, which complicates the detection of the actual address from which the unauthorized activity originated.

Attacks on the Intrusion Detection System

Intruders are constantly improving their skills, including skills in the field of attacking intrusion detection systems. For example, attackers implement more and more sophisticated methods for penetration and use improved attack methods, starting with automated tools for attack implementation and ending with the tools for hidden scanning.

The first thing that intruders usually attempt to do is identify the location of the intrusion detection system in the corporate network. This can be achieved by detecting a network adapter operating in promiscuous mode (for example, utilities like AntiSniff or IFStatus can be used for this purpose), or by analyzing the open ports used by the intrusion detection system for interacting with its components.

Attack on SessionWall-3

On June 7, 2000, a new document was published (**http://www.phate.net/docs /security/sw3paper.txt**) describing various ways of attacking the SessionWall-3 system (currently known as eTrust IDS). This system can be easily detected and identified using simple ICMP packets (a most serious vulnerability, which is not acceptable for any intrusion detection system). All other intrusion detection systems, such as RealSecure Network Sensor or Cisco IDS, can operate in so-called Stealth mode, which prevents intruders from detecting the IDS and, consequently, from attacking it.

Besides this example, there are other ones.

Attack on the Snort IDS

On June 17, 2000, a new vulnerability was detected in the Snort 1.6 intrusion detection system. This vulnerability resulted in a system failure after using the remote OS fingerprinting mechanism in the nmap scanner (`nmap - sO`) directed against a host with the installed Snort system.

Another Attack on SessionWall-3

On June 7, 2000, a new vulnerability in SessionWall-3 was revealed. The administrator's password in the SessionWall-3 intrusion detection system, allowing you to get access to the system, is stored in the system registry under the following key: `HKEY_LOCAL_MACHINE\ Software\ComputerAssociates\SessionWall\1.0\Security`. The password is stored as a text string to which the XOR operation is applied. Naturally, this allows the intruder to get the source password and change all its settings without much effort.

Attacks on BlackICE

On June, 21, 2000, several vulnerabilities were detected in the BlackICE intrusion detection system from NetworkICE. First, the vulnerability in NetworkICE ICEcap console allowed intruders that managed to get authenticated to enter fictious information into the system. ICEcap Manager is the HTTP service that listens to port 8081 and collects data from various BlackICE IDS sensors. Second, ICEcap Manager contains the built-in "iceman" user account, which by default uses a blank password. Thus, using this account, the intruder can access the BlackICE console and introduce unauthorized modifications into the configuration of the remote sensors.

Lack of Agreement between Manufacturers

The next problem relates to IDS manufacturers rather than to intrusion detection systems. IDS manufacturers still can not find a common language and agree to cooperate. For example, it would be wonderful if intrusion detection systems from different manufacturers could integrate with one another and coordinate their work. Right now, however, this is an unattainable dream. This is due to the fact that most manufacturers are reluctant to reveal their "know-how," and do not want to share their achievements and clients with other companies. This certainly does not bring any profit to end-users. This situation will not change until a common standard (such as IDWG) is developed and adopted. Currently, some steps have been taken towards standardization. They will be covered in *Chapter 14.*

Continuous Mergers and Acquisitions

The security tools market (and, particularly, the IDS market) is a very promising and dynamically evolving area of investment. In the near future, it should yield significant profit. For example, in contrast to 1998, when the total amount of the IDS market in U.S. was $136,000,000 (which exceeded the same parameter for the previous year by 137%), in 2004 this parameter is expected to reach a value of $1,227,000,000 [Kolodgy1-01]. Furthermore, in 1998, the proportion of security scanners to classical intrusion detection tools was given as 67% to 33%, while in 2004 this relationship is expected to become 54% to 46% (Table 12.1).

Table 12.1. Growth of IDS Sales

Security tools	1998	1999	2000	2001	2002	2003	2004
Security scanners (millions of dollars)	91	166.6	252.2	359.3	469.0	562.3	657.2

continues

Table 12.1 Continued

Security tools	1998	1999	2000	2001	2002	2003	2004
Growth (%)	141	83	51	42	31	20	17
Market (%)	67	59	52	51	51	52	54
Classical intrusion detection systems (millions of dollars)	45.3	115.7	234.2	350.8	443.5	519.1	570.1
Growth (%)	123	155	102	50	26	17	10
Market (%)	33	41	48	49	49	48	46
Total amount (millions of dollars)	136.3	282.3	486.4	710.1	912.5	1081.4	1227.3
Growth (%)	135	107	72	46	29	19	14

Because of this, several famous contracts were signed on the IDS market during the past few years, which are briefly outlined in Table 12.2.

Table 12.2. Mergers and Acquisitions on the IDS Market

Company	Intrusion detection systems	Comment
Cisco Systems	WheelGroup ($)	
Microsoft	ISS (A)	Microsoft has licensed from ISS the RealSecure technology for ISA Server
Nortel Networks (Bay Networks)	ISS (A)	
Lucent	ISS (A)	The Lucent company licensed from ISS its RealSecure intrusion detection system and now supplies it under the Lucent RealSecure trademark
Enterasys	Network Security Wizards ($)	
Hewlett Packard	Security Force ($)	
SAIC	Bellcore ($)	

continues

Table 12.2 Continued

Company	Intrusion detection systems	Comment
Intrusion.com (formerly ODS Networks)	ISS (A) SAIC ($) RSA Security ($) MimeStar ($)	The Intrusion.com company licensed from ISS the intrusion detection technology used in RealSecure Network Sensor and built it into its security appliances. Intrusion.com purchased its CMDS intrusion detection system (later renamed Kane Security Enterprise) from SAIC, and from RSA Security it licensed its Kane Security Monitor intrusion detection system and the Kane Security Analyst security scanner.
Nokia	ISS (A)	ISS incorporated Nokia security appliances.
Network Associates, Inc.	Secure Networks Inc. ($) TIS ($) ISS (A) Traxess ($)	As a result of an agreement reached by Network Associates and ISS, the latter has integrated its McAfee antiviral software into RealSecure Network Sensor, and NAI has integrated its network intrusion detection system into its Sniffer protocol analyzer.
Check Point Software	ISS (A)	The Check Point company has licensed from ISS its RealSecure IDS, and up until mid-2001, was releasing it under the Check Point RealSecure trademark.
Internet Security Systems	DBSecure ($) March Information Systems ($) Netrex ($) NetworkICE ($) vCIS ($)	
RSA Security (formerly Security Dynamics and RSA)	Intrusion Detection ($)	
BindView Corporation	Netect ($)	
Axent Technologies	Internet Tools ($)	
Symantec	Axent ($) L-3 ($) SecurityFocus ($) Recourse Technologies ($)	

continues

Table 12.2 Continued

Company	Intrusion detection systems	Comment
MEMCO Software	Abirnet ($)	
PLATINUM	MEMCO ($)	
Computer Associates	PLATINUM ($)	
	Security-7 ($)	
NFR	Anzen ($)	

Where:

$ — the company was purchased; A — an agreement to cooperate.

Let's consider the motives of these contracts. Provided that we ignore higher revenues (which, of course, is self-evident), the motives can be classified into two groups. Note that the agreements were bi-directional:

❑ Extending the range of supplied solutions
❑ Building the purchased technologies into the supplied proprietary solutions

Despite the above-mentioned benefits, the perspectives of the mergers and acquisitions above are not as promising as they might seem at first glance. First, not all products and solutions acquired as a result of mergers are really necessary to the purchasing company. As a result, redundant or unnecessary solutions are simply discarded, or the companies just cease to support them. Second, the quality of the technical support for purchased products is often very far from perfect. A third (unnecessary) layer often appears between the developer and end-user. The purchased product often has a low priority for the firm that purchased it. For example, the sales of the Cisco IDS and Cisco Secure Scanner in 1998 made up only 0.1% of the total sales amount for other Cisco solutions. At the same time, for ISS, this parameter nears 100%. By the way, as for Cisco Secure Scanner, this product completed its life cycle in the summer of 2002 — Cisco has ceased to sell it, and, starting in 2003, will not support it any longer. Third, customers must face a situation in which a single company supplies a wide range of solutions developed by other manufacturers, which are poorly integrated with one another. Although most companies take steps towards improving this situation, this work is still very far from being complete. Let us consider some typical examples.

Network Associates

Network Associates, Inc. (NAI) is an example of a company providing a whole range of information security tools to its customers. The corporation was founded as a result of the merging of two well-known companies — Network General and McAfee Associates. Starting in 1997, the newly founded corporation has purchased several other companies that previously held leading positions in the IS market, including:

❑ Pretty Good Privacy — developer of the popular PGP encryption tools family. By the way, beginning on March 1, 2002, development and sales of the PGP product family were stopped.

❑ Trusted Information Systems — developer of the TIS Gauntlet firewall and the Stalker IDS family: Stalker, Proxy Stalker, and WebStalker.

❑ Secure Networks — developer of the Ballista security scanner, which is now supplied under the CyberCop Scanner trademark.

❑ Dr. Solomon — a company specializing in the field of antiviral software.

The Network General company (whose best-known product is the Sniffer program) has licensed intrusion detection technology from the WheelGroup company, and on the basis of it, developed the CyberCop Network 1.0 network-level intrusion detection system. However, after Cisco Systems purchased WheelGroup, this license was suspended. Still, NAI has taken a fancy to the CyberCop product name, and it has become the trademark for all IDS solutions supplied by the company. Besides Cyber-Cop Scanner, Network Associates supplies the CyberCop Monitor host-level intrusion detection system and the CyberCop Sting deception toolkit. CyberCop Monitor also has quite an interesting background. Initially, NAI was selling the CyberCop Server system for log-file analysis, which was based on the Stalker product family (the technologies implemented in this product family were originally developed by the Haystack company and later purchased by Trusted Information Systems). At the same time, NAI supplied the CyberCop Monitor product. Later, both systems were combined within the framework of CyberCop Monitor.

What could possibly result from NAI's activity other than a wide range of IS solutions? First of all, some of the products developed by the purchased companies are now lost to end-users. For example, the PC Firewall product, announced by McAfee before merging with Network General, was quite a promising development project, to say nothing about such a popular encryption system as PGP (also purchased by NAI and also no longer released or supported). To summarize, end-users have not really gotten much benefit from NAI's purchase of all the above-mentioned companies, except for the fact that now all currently supported products can be purchased from the same vendor. What's even worse, the products supplied by NAI are not integrated with one another, which, from the end-user's point of view, significantly reduces or even brings to naught the efficiency of the plusses.

For example, such activity has caused Network Associates' stock to drop significantly, and much of the upper management to leave. In 2001, the General Manager, President, and Chief Financial Officer left the company, and the turnover for the 4th quarter of 2000 was three times lower than the previous year ($65 million in 2000 as compared to $218 million in 1999).

Furthermore, ISS and NAI have signed a cooperation agreement, within the framework of which, ISS gains the possibility of integrating RealSecure Network Sensor with the McAfee Antivirus, while NAI integrates RealSecure Network Sensor with Sniffer.

Hewlett Packard

Quite recently, Hewlett-Packard has also begun to pay significant attention to network security. As a rule, all of its efforts in this area relate either to extending the functionality of its HP OpenView network management system or to supplying combined solutions to corporate customers. Usually, all such solutions include information security tools from third-party companies.

One example illustrating the extension of HP OpenView's functionalities is the combined solution that integrates it with the Cisco PIX Firewall. As of now, this practice has proved to be rather fruitful and efficient. First, technical support for each product supplied by Hewlett Packard is delivered by the manufacturer of that product, and the range of solutions is practically as wide as the one provided by Network Associates.

However, Hewlett-Packard has also purchased several smaller manufacturers. For example, on August 2, 1999, it absorbed Security Force, Inc. — the developer of the SFProtect security scanner. Besides security analysis technology, Hewlett-Packard has also started to pay attention to intrusion detection (for example, IDS/9000) [Anderson1-99].

Internet Security Systems

Internet Security Systems has also widened the range of the solutions it offers by purchasing such companies as March Information Systems, DBSecure, and NetworkICE. Taking these events into account, ISS currently provides a whole range of security scanning tools, starting with network-level (Internet Scanner) and OS-level (System Scanner) tools and ending with DBMS-level scanners (Database Scanner). The intrusion detection tools supplied by this company also cover practically all levels — from RealSecure Network Sensor (network monitoring) and RealSecure Server Sensor (server monitoring) to RealSecure Desktop Protector (workstation monitoring) and RealSecure Web Protection for IIS (web server monitoring). In addition, ISS was the first company to begin to supply security scanners for wireless networks — the Wireless Scanner product. Finally, in contrast to all the other brands in the field of network intrusion detection, ISS also supplies a so-called inline IDS — the RealSecure Guard system — which, in contrast to other solutions, filters all network traffic rather than listening just to traffic within the network segment using the promiscuous mode of the network adapter. Thus, this system is similar to a firewall installed between protected and public networks.

Quite recently, ISS purchased another small company — vCIS — which has developed a behavior control technology that ISS plans to incorporate into its host-level intrusion detection systems.

Intrusion.com

The Intrusion.com company, previously known as ODS Networks, is also making large strides forward. For example, it has recently purchased such intrusion detection systems as:

❑ CMDS from the SAIC company, which in turn purchased it along with the Bellcore company.

❑ Kane Security Analyst and Kane Security Monitor from RSA Security. RSA Security (earlier known as Security Dynamics Technologies) in turn purchased these systems after purchasing the Intrusion Detection company.

❑ SecureNET PRO developed by MimeSTAR.

Symantec

Until recently, Symantec did not engage in purchasing other companies, its main field of activity being antiviral and system software. However, during the last two years, Symantec has also purchased several companies that specialize in aspects of information security. Axent, which in turn had purchased two smaller companies — Raptor and Internet Tools, known for their firewall and NetProwler intrusion detection system, respectively — was the first company on this list. Later, Symantec purchased the L-3 company, along with its two security scanners — Expert and Retriever. Unfortunately, neither of these systems was included into the range of tools offered by Symantec. One of the advantages of the Expert system was its capability of creating a graphic network map that specified all the detected vulnerabilities for all scanned hosts. The user interface provided by this system was very much like MS Visio's.

After purchasing L-3, there was a "calm," after which, in July of 2002, Symantec declared that it was purchasing three companies simultaneously — SecurityFocus, Riptech, and Recourse. The first company on this list is famous for its portal (http://www.securityfocus.com), as well as for its DeepSight analysis and correlation tools. The second and third are known for their intrusion detection and deception systems — ManHunt and ManTrap, respectively.

Some time earlier, Symantec purchased the MountainWave company, known for its CyberWolf technology that is used for collecting, analyzing, and correlating data received from heterogeneous security tools. Taking into account the purchasing MountainWave and SecurityFocus, as well as the efforts made by most manufacturers to develop event correlation tools, one can draw the conclusion that Symantec has decided to take one of the leading positions in this area of the market.

Hopefully, Symantec will not repeat the errors of Network Associates, and will not discard most of their purchased solutions (although such trends are already noticeable). For example, L-3's solutions are not offered any longer, and the MountainWave portal, which published late-breaking news in the field of information security and was used by most security specialists, has been closed.

What's Next...

Thus, the intrusion detection market is swiftly changing. But are these changes beneficial? Right now, it is rather hard to tell for sure, since the situation has not stabilized yet. On the one hand, progress is evident. Intrusion detection systems are being constantly extended and enhanced thanks to integration with other security tools. Furthermore, the integration of these tools into network management systems, such as HP OpenView, provides administrators with flexible capabilities of managing all security mechanisms from a single point.

On the other hand, there are also some negative trends, both objective and subjective. In contrast to the quality of technical support, which could improve with time, the situation with integration of the purchased products and technologies is somewhat different. In some cases, companies purchasing third-party tools manage to combine several technologies and efficiently integrate the purchased products, while in other cases such attempts fail. For example, at the time of writing, there is no central management for the NetProwler and Intruder Alert intrusion detection systems, both of which are supplied by Symantec.

As a result of these mergers, small businesses might be cut off from the information security market. As might be predicted, only those businesses that have developed either new and promising technologies (which are not currently widespread, and consequently have not been purchased by larger corporations) or high-quality products ensuring a high security level unattainable by the so-called "standard" solutions will retain their market positions. This, in turn, will result in a situation in which end-users will have to choose between large and poorly integrated products containing a set of dissimilar and often incompatible mechanisms, or a set of incompatible products. Mainly, this relates to companies that have purchased new technologies in order to widen the range of services supplied to customers (the most illustrative example is Network Associates).

Therefore, although large companies certainly benefit from such bargains, the advantages provided to the end-user are arguable. On the one hand, the consumer can now purchase security tools from a single vendor, but on the other hand, he or she is paying money for incompatible solutions and poor technical support.

Active Response

Despite new perspectives, the capabilities of automatically reconfiguring network equipment or security tools, as well as the possibility of automatically terminating network connections, must be handled with care. These mechanisms, besides serving the goals of company's employees and security personnel, can be exploited by intruders. For example, if the intruder implements an attack on one of the protected hosts, and, when doing so, spoofs his or her actual address with the address of an authorized host, the intrusion detection system can lock access from that host to protected resources (Fig. 12.4).

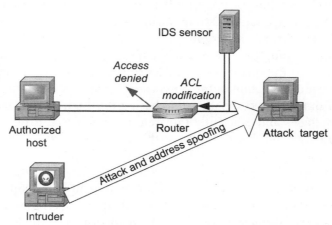

Fig. 12.4. The potential danger of reconfiguring network equipment

The second risk relates to the automatic termination of the connection with the attacking host. In this case, the intruder can also substitute the address of the host to or from which he or she wants to lock access for the actual address (Fig. 12.5).

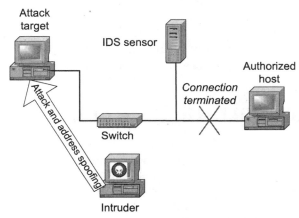

Fig. 12.5. The potential danger of automatically terminating network connections

All these specific features related to active responses are due to the fact that the current IP version does not provide the capability of unambiguously determining the source address of the attack. Therefore, intruders can easily change their actual addresses to any of the available 2^{32}. Because of this, these types of responses are recommended for use only within internal networks, or provided that the possibility of address spoofing is eliminated.

Recovery from Attack

Intrusion detection systems can help you detect an existing vulnerability before intruders can exploit it, and can help you identify an attack in the course of its implementation. They can also help you trace attacks that have already been implemented using the traces left by intruders in the attacked system. However, what can you do if the protected host has failed or was compromised as a result of an implemented attack? When dealing with vulnerabilities, the situation is more or less clear — this flaw can be automatically eliminated using the mechanisms implemented in a security scanner. Such mechanisms exist in most security scanners, including System Scanner, STAT, or SFProtect. The situation with attacks is much more complicated. For the moment, intrusion detection systems have no efficient mechanisms that allow you to restore attacked systems to their initial state. This problem is partially solved by integrity control systems, which, having detected unauthorized modifications introduced into a protected file, replace that file with its standard copy. This principle has been implemented in the AutoRestore mechanism of the CyberCop Monitor system, for example. Besides this, there are specialized tools intended only for restoring attacked systems. For example, the WebAgain system designed by LockStep Systems automatically detects all unauthorized changes introduced to web servers, and restores the entire contents of the server without user intervention. Another example is the ERD Commander 2002 system from Winternals Software, which restores a damaged Windows 2000 server after attacks or hardware failures. This system has even been licensed by Microsoft.

What You Should Do In Case of Attack

Earlier in this book, I provided an example in which an unskilled IDS operator was unable to distinguish an actual intrusion from normal network activity. Another example can be illustrated by a case in which the IDS registers the Email WIZ attack, which enables the intruder to get administrative privileges on the host where the Sendmail program is running. The operator initiates the procedure of incident investigation, activates all required tools, and notifies everyone who needs to know about the incident. However, if the operator knew that this attack causes damage only to outdated versions of Sendmail, there would have been no alarm raised. Another characteristic case is the Tribe Flood Network (TFN) attack. It can be implemented only against hosts running Unix. If your network is built exclusively on a Windows platform, then the arrival of the TFN event message indicates a false positive event. Consequently, an intrusion detection system must contain the appropriate manuals and guides describing the specific features of all specific attacks, including false positives. For each detected attack, it would be good to provide a list of characteristic features, descriptions, and answers to the following questions:

❏ Attack type
❏ Name displayed on the IDS console
❏ Technical description
❏ Variants of false positives
❏ Variants of false negatives
❏ Operating systems vulnerable to this attack
❏ Why this attack is important
❏ What should be done to eliminate the attack or the vulnerability resulting in its implementation
❏ References to CVE, X-Force, CERT, Bugtraq bulletins, Novell NetWare Knowledge Base, Microsoft Knowledge Base, etc.

Testing Intrusion Detection Systems

As I mentioned in *Chapter 9*, another problem relates to the lack of evaluation and testing criteria for intrusion detection systems. All existing methods are rather sparse and unsystematic. This situation is characteristic even for the test laboratories of various well-known magazines (PCWeek, Network Computing, etc.). Quite often, the testing is pre-paid by specific manufacturers. For example, I have seen the results of testing performed approximately at the same time and by the same testers whose results differed significantly. Besides this, a test lab performs experiments using test facilities that only model a real situation, but do not reproduce it completely. This, of course, does not give the testers the opportunity to forecast all situations that the customer might have to face. Quite often, a system that has shown ideal results during testing starts to malfunction in real-world conditions. Yet another shortcoming of such testing is the evaluation based on quantitative criteria. This means that all criteria are assigned weight coefficients, according to which the results are then summed to produce the total grade. The system that shows the best result according to this system of evaluation is then declared to be "the system of choice" or the "winner." This system does not take into account that fact that end-users might assign different weight coefficients to evaluation criteria according to their requirements. For example, some consumers give priority to the problem of centralized management of the IDS components, while for other companies this criterion is not a matter of primary importance. Because of this, I recommend that you critically evaluate various ratings and awards, even if they are assigned by well-known and popular magazines. Only the end-user can correctly evaluate a system. For this purpose, however, he or she must know the evaluation criteria and method. Currently, there is not much serious research work in this field, the best research being performed by the Los Alamos Test Lab [Jackson1-99] and NSS Network Testing Laboratories [NSS1-00]. The best result, however, was achieved by Lincoln Lab. This organization designed the first standard describing the testing method and requirements for the IDS testing process.

Semantic Compression

To ensure efficient intrusion detection, it is necessary to control and perform detailed logging of a large number of events taking place in the information system. This produces quite a large amount of data, most of which are not of any interest, but are stored for subsequent analysis in order to detect any suspicious events. Storing large amounts of data requires that you find a solution for the following two problems:

❑ Development of mechanisms for efficient usage of disk space designated for storing log files and network traffic data.

❑ Development of mechanisms for efficient representation of data that may be of any interest to the security administrator.

Both of these problems are interrelated. However, I will cover in detail only the second one. Most security specialists have encountered a situation in which the intrusion detection system generates thousands or even hundreds of thousands of records about various events taking place in large networks. No administrator is able to analyze these events manually. Although the intrusion detection systems available on the market provide tools for combining several events of the same type within a single record, the solutions they provide are far from perfect, and work on this must continue.

Currently, there are several manufacturers and research centers that develop efficient data representation methods. For example, at the end of June 1999, the ISS company announced the so-called Fusion Technology, which it implemented in the Fusion Security Module of its RealSecure SiteProtector product. The CERIAS research center also performs research work in this area. This center has even created a workgroup for developing an efficient log-file format and for convenient methods of representing log-file data to security administrators.

Lack of Mechanisms for Proving Attack Facts in Court

Collecting irrefutable proof for court or for an internal investigation is a logical accomplishment of an IDS. However, most of the problems that were already covered in this chapter prevent security specialists from collecting a sufficient amount of reliable data. These problems include the ambiguous identification of the intruder, or the probability of address spoofing. Besides this, representatives of legal organizations usually do not have the skills to allow them to make sense of the messages generated by intrusion detection systems. Because of this, contemporary intrusion detection systems must implement mechanisms that simplify the collection of proof and their representation in a form convenient for such individuals (police officers, lawyers, etc.). As of now there are not many intrusion detection mechanisms that provide this. RealSecure Network Sensor and SecureNet PRO are two of them. These systems implement event tracing mechanisms that allow you to record the whole sequence of the intruder's activities and then reproduce them (so-called replay or playback mechanisms). Notice that these events can be replayed in real-time, accelerated, or sloweddown modes, in order to analyze the intruder's methods, skills, the tools used for attack implementation, etc. This all should help to collect the proof required for a court.

Network-Level Intrusion Detection Systems

Now, after discussing the general problems common to all classes of intrusion detection systems, let's analyze network-level tools. This class of tools includes the most popular systems.

Networks with Switching

Networks with switching pose quite a lot of problems for network-level intrusion detection systems, as well as for network analysis in general. There are many possible ways to solve this problem. However, they all are not always satisfactory. More detailed information on this topic was provided in *Chapter 10*.

Networks with Channel Encryption

Obviously, if traffic is encrypted, it is impossible to detect any attack within it. A detailed illustration of this case was provided in Fig. 1.7. Thus, despite the fact that encryption strengthens security and prevents intruders from accessing the data being transmitted, if the encryption capabilities are incorrectly used, they become an obstacle to ensuring proper security. Do not forget that attacks can also be encrypted! The problem becomes especially important in distributed networks that have several offices communicating via public networks that are protected using VPN devices. If the intruder manages to penetrate one of the remote affiliates, he or she can use the VPN connection to penetrate another office, and the perimeter protection tools, including intrusion detection systems, will not notice anything.

Another problem relates to the fact that most hacker tools — especially the newer releases of Trojan horses and tools for implementing distributed attacks (such as TFN2K) — encrypt all commands and other traffic used for communication between their components. This also prevents security administrators from detecting and stopping unauthorized activity within a reasonable time.

Modems

Network-level intrusion detection systems can not always detect and identify attacks directed to network hosts in which modems are installed. If a modem is used as an entry point to the corporate network, it is relatively easy to detect attacks performed via that modem. On the other hand, host-level intrusion detection systems and security scanners (such as Internet Scanner or System Scanner) provide a more efficient way of solving this problem than network-level intrusion detection systems do.

Shortage of Resources

Network-level intrusion detection systems are installed in the most critical network segments. They must be capable of operating at the speeds provided by the network equipment, as well as of analyzing and storing information collected from hundreds of network hosts. Obviously, it is not easy to find an IDS that can satisfy these requirements.

The most common problems caused by resource shortages are briefly covered below.

High-Speed Networks

Currently, the network sensors of intrusion detection systems can not successfully handle attacks in heavily overloaded network segments (that operate at speeds above 100 Mbit/sec). Although there are solutions that are capable of handling such intense traffic, they are still quite rare and very expensive. The list of such systems includes RealSecure Gigabit Sensor and the Cisco Catalyst 6500 IDS Module. All these products allow you to detect an attack in Gigabit traffic, and some of them can operate in ATM networks.

Size and Number of Processed Packets

The number of packets processed per second and the average packet size are very important parameters of any network-level intrusion detection system. As was shown in *Chapter 10*, these parameters primarily influence the efficiency of the intrusion detection system.

Various Modifications of Attack Signatures

The number of signatures in the IDS database also influences the IDS throughput. Notice that when speaking about this parameter, we mean signatures rather than security events. For example, for the attack on the PHF CGI script mentioned in *Chapter 2*, there might be several interchangeable attack signatures:

- ❏ GET /CGI-bin/phf
- ❏ HEAD /CGI-bin/phf
- ❏ GET /%63%67%69%2d%62%69%6e/phf
- ❏ GET //CGI-bin/phf
- ❏ GET /CGI-bin/foobar/../phf

❑   GET /CGI-bin/./phf

❑   GET%00/CGI-bin/phf

Taking this into account, the formula provided in *Chapter 10* can be rewritten as follows:

```
Throughput = number of processed packets * average packet size * number
of signatures in the database * average size of the signature
```

For example, for the data provided above that has 4000 signatures (supposing that the average signature size is 20 bytes), the required throughput will be 3,600,000,000,000 (for 1500-byte packets) or 153,600,000,000 (for 64-byte packets) operations per second. Currently, such a performance can not be attained by general-purpose computers. Because of this, most existing intrusion detection systems miss some modifications of known signatures.

There is yet another problem related to the modification of attack templates. As I mentioned earlier, most intrusion detection systems operate on the principle of comparing fragments of network packets to a pattern (template). Using databases of well-known attacks enables you to identify the attacks that are highly probable. However, such systems can be easily deceived by simply introducing minor changes to the template. The list below provides several examples of this technique [Cohen1-99].

❑   Inserting additional characters with no particular meaning into the attack commands and data, which usually prevents the IDS from detecting such an attack.

❑   Replacing spaces with tab characters in commands that implement an attack.

❑   Changing the delimiter character in the system (for example, the space character can be replaced by %), which will cause specific problems in detecting the unauthorized activity. For example, a URL such as "/dir/examples attack/attack.asp" can be replaced by "/dir/examples%20attack/attack.asp."

❑   Redefining the standard sequence of actions taken when implementing an attack. For example, if the attack has the same effect when performing the commands "a;b;c" as when issuing the "b;a;c" sequence of commands, most intrusion detection systems will recognize the first attack, but will fail to identify the second variant.

❑   Defining a macro for a parameter used for attack implementation, such as "$P" instead of "/etc/passwd," or "%SystemRoot%" instead of "c:\winnt."

❑   Creating a script containing the commands issued when implementing an attack. If this operation is carefully planned, the intrusion detection system will fail to correlate the script name and the commands, which will result in a false negative.

Just as lazy as most people, hackers also try to automate routine processes. There have been a number of utilities released intended for automating attacks, such as Snot or Stick. For example, the Snot utility creates random packets based on the Snort IDS database. These random packets contain noise data that have no influence on the attack, but that are different from the attack signature contained in the Snort database. Other automated tools for deceiving intrusion detection systems include Stick, Whicker, etc.

Scanning Distributed in Time

Intrusion detection systems encounter difficulties when it is necessary to log a large amount of network traffic for a long time. Thus, they will have difficulties with detecting time-distributed scanning (implemented, for example, by using the -sI parameter with the Nmap v3 scanner) when the intruders address a specific port or address for several minutes or even hours. Such a scanning technique significantly complicates attack detection by an intrusion detection system.

Causing IDS Failures

Besides the problems that we have already covered, IDSs themselves can become the target of attacks. Causing an IDS to fail will enable the intruders to penetrate the corporate network without being noticed, and then to perform any unauthorized actions.

"Blinding" the Sensor

Most intrusion detection systems have problems when handling high-speed networks. As a result, if there is a heavy network workload, the sensor will start to miss some attacks, or may even fail. Thus, the intruder can neutralize the IDS by generating a large amount of traffic. This attack is possible in a few cases. First, it can be implemented by an intruder who is capable of generating a large amount of traffic within the same network segment in which the sensor is located. Secondly, this attack is viable when implementing a distributed attack on perimeter hosts. In this case, several dozens, hundreds, or even thousands of hosts can send packets at speeds ranging from 28.8 Kbit/sec to 64 Kbit/sec. With the large number of participants, the attack will have the effect of a flood, causing the attacked host to fail. Finally, there is a third, simpler and more dangerous approach. Using this technique, there is no need to generate a large amount of traffic or employ thousands of hosts to organize a distributed attack. Rather, it is sufficient to just imitate non-existent attacks to which the IDS is to react. In this case, the management console will be flooded with lots of false positive messages, making it impossible to detect the real attack among them. This attack is very dangerous in itself. What's even worse, there are special tools to automate this type of attack, such as Stick, which generates a false attacks with spoofed addresses based on Snort rules at a speed of 250 alarms per second.

Denial of Service

An intrusion detection system operating at the network level is a very complex system that is also vulnerable to DoS attacks. Some such problems are covered in [Paxson1-98]. All Denial of Service attacks on an intrusion detection system can be divided into the following two categories.

❐ Overload attacks
❐ Crash attacks

Overload attacks imply the creation of conditions under which the intrusion detection system will fail to (or simply will not) process or store the analyzed data. A Log Flood attack is a typical example of such an attack. If implemented successfully, it disrupts the operation of the event logging system or overwrites the recorded events (including the events that prove the presence of an attack in the network traffic). Fig. 12.6 shows the event log of an application vulnerable to such attacks (Event Viewer).

To eliminate the possibility of such an attack on the intrusion detection system, one can use various mechanisms. For example, RealSecure Network Sensor implements the Event Propagation mechanism, which allows you to reduce the number of events displayed on the console and stored in the database, thus protecting it from overflowing. Another advantage of this mechanism lies in the fact that it does not distract the administrator's attention with meaningless events.

The second class of attacks is similar to overloading. However, in contrast to the first class of attacks, which can be registered at least implicitly, the situation is more complicated with the second class. For example, the intruder can exploit bugs in the IDS code in order to cause it to fail. This is what happened with the outdated version of the RealSecure Network Sensor (v. 3.2.2), which failed when processing fragmented traffic. This type of attack is especially dangerous to systems that capture network traffic using an OS driver rather than a custom driver working directly with the network adapter. If this is the case, the intruder can exploit vulnerabilities of the network protocol stack of the operating system. As a result of such an attack, not only the OS will fail, but all applications as well.

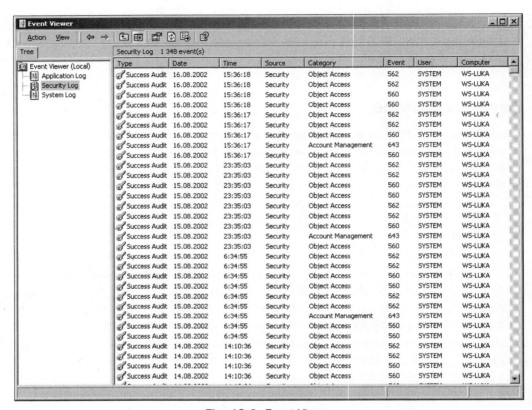

Fig. 12.6. Event Viewer

Simple Deception

This section describes easy ways of deceiving intrusion detection systems. More sophisticated methods of bypassing IDSs are covered in [Cohen2-99], [RFP1-99], and other sources.

Fragmentation

Fragmentation is a mechanism of dividing IP packets into a set of smaller fragments. When receiving such packets, the TCP/IP device reassembles them and passes them to the target device, or repeats the fragmentation and transmits them further. Most intrusion detection systems can not restore fragmented IP packets. This results in the possibility of them being bypassed, or even causing them to fail. This vulnerability is very dangerous, since currently there are specialized tools for fragmenting normal network traffic (such as FragRouter).

Changing Default Values

As I already mentioned, some intrusion detection systems presume that the source or destination ports unambiguously identify the protocol used for communication between several hosts. For example, port 80 corresponds to HTTP, port 23 to Telnet, port 31337 to the BackOrifice Trojan, etc. However, the intruder can use standard protocols on non-standard ports (for example, assign port 8081 to HTTP) or change the default ports, which will prevent some intrusion detection systems from processing such "non-standard" traffic.

Address Spoofing

Quite often, the attacker uses address spoofing — i.e., replaces his or her actual address with a false one, which complicates the detection of the attack source in a timely manner. For example, the Nmap scanner can generate packets containing decoy addresses, which will stuff the log file of the intrusion detection system. For an administrator, it is rather difficult to determine which addresses registered as the sources of attack are real and which have been spoofed by the intruder. Although the problem of detecting the real address of the attack source relates to the incident response problem that will be covered later, this problem is not the one to be neglected.

The Problem with UNICODE

There is yet another problem that could have been covered in the section dedicated to the modification of attack signatures. However, since this problem is rather important, I've decided to discuss it in a separate section. This problem comes about due to the fact that not all network-level intrusion detection systems can identify attacks using the UNICODE data format. Currently, UNICODE is supported by most software tools and standards, including Java, LDAP, XML, MS IIS, Apache, MS Office 2000, etc. The UNICODE standard uses the UTF-8 conversion scheme to convert UNICODE characters into sequences with a length from one to 4 bytes. Compatibility with ASCII is ensured using UTF-8. UNICODE allows you to have several representations for a single character. For example, the backslash "\" can be represented by the following hex values: 5C (single-byte sequence), C19C (two-byte sequence), and E0819C (three-byte sequence). For all applications supporting UTF-8, these three values are identical. Although quite recently the UNICODE Consortium abolished multiple representation for UTF-8 characters and released the "UTF-8 Corrigendum" document, applications developed before this document was published still support the outdated UTF-8 standard.

The next vulnerability related to UNICODE is caused by the fact that different applications or operating systems can interpret different UNICODE characters (also known as code points) similarly. For example, in [Hacker1-01], it was reported that MS IIS operating in Windows 2000 Advanced Server interprets the following UNICODE characters as "A": U+0041, U+0100, U+0102, U+0104, U+01CD, U+01DE, and U+8721. If we take into account the fact that IIS is case-insensitive (which means that it does not distinguish between uppercase and lowercase characters), we can easily draw the conclusion that the "A" character can be described by 30 different UNICODE combinations. Similarly, "E" has 34 representations, "I" 36, "O" 39, and "U" 58. By multiplying these values, we get 83,060,640 different combinations that can be used for the "AEIOU" string. Notice that all these representations will be interpreted absolutely equally.

One of the first UNICODE-related security problems described by [Xforce1-00] is related to MS IIS 4.0 and 5.0. For example, an attempt to access the following URL resulted in disk formatting:

```
http://www.domain.com/../../winnt/system32/cmd.exe?/c+format+c:
```

This was due to the fact that the " ../.. " fragment was capable of bypassing IIS 5.0 security and getting to the root directory of the web server. However, direct access to the specified address resulted in deletion of the " ../.. " and the display of an error message. Still, replacing this address with a URL containing a UNICODE fragment, such as:

```
"http://www.bank.ru/..%c1%9c../winnt/system32/cmd.exe?/c+format+c:"
```

allows you to execute an unauthorized command. Similar results can be obtained by using the following UNICODE fragments instead of "..%1c%9c..": "..%c1%1c..," "..%c0%9v..," "..%c0%af..," "..%c0%qf..," "..%c1%8s..," "..%c1%9c..," "..%c1%pc..," etc.

Sophisticated Deception

Skillful intruders can use more complicated methods of deceiving or bypassing intrusion detection systems. These methods of evasion are described in [Ptacek1-98]. The original version of this document is available at the following address: http://www.aciri.org/vern/Ptacek-Newsham-Evasion-98.ps (the HTML version can be viewed at the following address: http://www.robertgraham.com/mirror/Ptacek-Newsham-Evasion-98.HTML).

Let's consider one of the newer methods of bypassing an intrusion detection system. The RealSecure Network Sensor system provides the Event Propagation mechanism, which allows you to decrease the number of events displayed on the console and registered in the database. This mechanism, originally used to make intrusion detection systems less vulnerable to a DoS attack, can also be used for malicious purposes. For example, if the intruder knows that a network sensor stops registering `FTP_Put` events after detecting 100 such events logged in 2 minutes, it can imitate 100 normal `FTP_Put` events, and then perform the 101st — an `FTP_Put` operation containing an attack, which would not be displayed on the RealSecure console. RealSecure Network Sensor stops registering such events after the first 100 such events have been registered, and thus the hacker remains unnoticed. This example can serve as an additional illustration of the thesis that you should not inform all users of the specific features and individual settings of your security infrastructure in general, and the IDS in particular.

Host-Level Intrusion Detection Systems

Now we will discuss the drawbacks typical only for host-level intrusion detection systems.

Log-File Size

One of the main drawbacks of host-level intrusion detection systems is the necessity of storing large amounts of data. This problem is especially important for heavily loaded servers, since all events must be logged, which results in the uncontrollable growth of event logs.

Storage Interval

This problem is closely related to the log-file size problem, since the time interval during which the logged events must be stored depends directly on their accumulation. The longer you store log files, the more data they contain. On the one hand, since the data amount increases, the analysis becomes more efficient, and the probability of detecting sophisticated attacks or ones distributed in time also grows. On the other hand, it is problematic to store such amounts of data for a long time.

Performance Problems

Controlling all events that take place on a protected computer results in performance problems. This trend is especially obvious for systems that control the current activity of a specific user or any other network subject, since intrusion detection tools must control any chain of calls to the system resources and check if that specific action is authorized. For tools intended for log-file analysis, this problem is less critical, but it still retains its importance, since logging all activities significantly degrades the performance of the controlled host.

Protection of Log Files

The next problem specific to host-level intrusion detection systems is the protection of log files from unauthorized access. In network-level intrusion detection systems, all log files are stored only on the central console (for client/server architecture), while information from remote network sensors is transmitted to the console rather quickly. Thus, this information is not stored on the sensor for a long time. The situation is different for systems that analyze events on specific hosts. Such systems are approximately 10 or more times as numerous as network-level intrusion detection systems. Besides this, in contrast to network sensors that can be protected by strong security (since their only function is intrusion detection), host-level intrusion detection systems operate on hosts for which intrusion detection is not the primary function. As a rule, these hosts perform functions that are quite different, such as transaction processing, file storage, providing Web services, and so on. Furthermore, the list of users who have the right to access network sensors can be limited to one or two persons, which is clearly impossible for system sensors. By definition, such hosts must be accessed by hundreds or even thousands of users. This is why the problem of protecting the log-file data becomes so important for system sensors.

Types and Level of Detail of Logged Events

Besides the problems that were already mentioned, you must not forget yet another one, which is no less important. The available operating systems and applications do not log all the events that are possible in the analyzed software. Furthermore, even if some events are logged, the level of registered details is insufficient. This is especially true for Microsoft products.

Lack of a Universal Data Storage Format

There is also a problem with the development of a unified log-file format for intrusion detection systems. This aspect mainly relates to the limitations and specific features characteristic of different sources of information about attacks. For example, let's consider the most difficult case — two different operating systems such as Unix and DOS. The events registered in these two operating systems are very different. Some Unix operations are not applicable to DOS, such as usage of inter-processor links in multi-processor systems. Likewise, the loading and unloading of TSR programs in DOS has no adequate analog in Unix. Because of all this, it is rather problematic to develop a unified log-file format for both operating systems. Although research in this field has been going on for quite a long time (for example, consider the CERIAS project aimed at designing a universal data format for auditing systems, or the WELF extended log-file format for firewalls and VPN devices developed by WebTrends Corporations), more or less satisfactory results are not expected in the near future.

Summary

As was shown in this chapter, intrusion detection systems are not universal tools that can protect you against all disasters, and they can not serve as a single security tool used in a corporate network. Like all other security tools, they have their area of applicability and their limitations. To use IDSs efficiently, you must know these limitations. You also can not expect an intrusion detection system to solve unrealistic problems. Understanding these problems will help you to correctly plan your intrusion detection infrastructure.

CHAPTER 13

Standardization in the Field of Intrusion Detection

Currently, there are two strategies that have priority in standardization in the field of intrusion detection. The first line of research is the creation of protocols and interfaces that allow you to organize communications between intrusion detection systems from different manufacturers. The second is the development of requirements for testing and certifying intrusion detection systems.

The first step in this direction is development of the Common Intrusion Detection Framework standard (CIDF). The creation of the Intrusion Detection Working Group (IDWG), under IETF, served as an extension of this strategy. Currently, IDWG is very close to accomplishing its work on determining the requirements that will allow for the coordination and integration of the operation of intrusion detection systems from different manufacturers.

The second line of development is also very important. It includes the investigations performed by the Lincoln Laboratory and the Intrusion Detection Systems

Consortium (IDSC) under the International Computer Security Association (ICSA), as well as all research aimed at formalization of requirements for intrusion detection systems.

The Adaptive Network Security Alliance

On October 21, 1998, Internet Security Systems, in cooperation with other leading manufacturers, created the Adaptive Network Security Alliance (ANSA). This alliance is an initiative including a wide range of manufacturers, and is aimed at the development of an adaptive technology of network security management intended to significantly strengthen corporate security. The ANSA partners will be able to use the Adaptive Network Security (ANS) modules and SDK supplied by ISS, and integrate them with their products. The original ANS modules support a wide range of functional capabilities, including adaptive security for firewalls, VPN tools, antiviral software, intrusion detection systems, PKI, routers, switches, network and system monitoring, etc.

ANSA will provide modules intended for operation in the following key areas:

❑ *Active Response.* Thanks to ANSA, firewalls, routers, switches, and other devices will be provided with the capability of automatic self-configuration. This functionality will enable the network devices listed above to automatically reconfigure themselves to thwart attacks in real-time mode and prevent the intruder from repeating attempts to penetrate the network.

❑ *Lock Down.* An incorrect configuration can make any technology vulnerable to an attack or other malicious activity. ISS will work in cooperation with the ANSA partners in order to develop user templates aimed at significantly improving the reliability of the security configuration of network devices. This will allow customers to be sure that products purchased from ANSA partners will not be vulnerable to an intruder's attack and will function as intended by developers.

❑ *Decision Support.* Planning and decision-making processes in the field of information security require the analyst to process a vast amount of data from all security tools and network devices. ANSA will provide a mechanism for making quick and well-grounded decisions concerning the securing of large corporate networks by means of collecting, merging, and analyzing data received from various security tools and network devices developed by ANSA partners. The collected information will be transmitted to management consoles in order to be able to take immediate counteraction.

❑ *Adaptive Security Network Management.* ANSA will integrate Adaptive Network Security management with various network management platforms, such as HP

OpenView. This integration will ensure the strengthening of security, and at the same time will simplify the distribution of the security policy over the whole organization.

Currently, more than 70 leading manufacturers working in the field of information technologies participate in ANSA. This list includes the following companies: 3Com Corporation, Check Point Software, Compaq, Hewlett-Packard, Nortel Networks, Intrusion.com (formerly ODS Networks), Tivoli Systems Inc., VeriSign Inc., and V-ONE Corporation.

Unfortunately, things did not get much further than words. The alliance never implemented an actual project, and not long after its foundation, the alliance stopped its work altogether.

The Lincoln Laboratory Project

The IT group attached to Lincoln Laboratory (at MIT) under the aegis of DARPA and in cooperation with the Air Force Research Laboratory (AFRL) developed the first standard that described the requirements for intrusion detection systems and the methods for evaluating network-level intrusion detection systems. This project (http://ideval.ll.mit.edu) is confidential, and access to its materials is limited.

The OSEC Project

The OSEC (Open Security Evaluation Criteria) project solves problems similar to the ones solved by the Lincoln Laboratory project, and is also oriented towards testing network security tools. However, in contrast to the Lincoln Laboratory project, the OSEC standard is open. Its description can be found at the following site: http://osec.neohapsis.com/. At the time of writing, the developers have published criteria for testing network-level intrusion detection systems, and were in the process of preparing a similar standard for firewall testing. Besides the development of testing methods, the Neohapsis laboratory that developed these criteria is engaged in testing intrusion detection systems for their correspondence to these criteria. Currently, two systems have already undergone such tests — RealSecure Network Sensor from ISS, and IntruShield from IntruVert. As I am writing, the testing of Intrusion.com solutions is underway.

The Intrusion Detection Systems Consortium

The Intrusion Detection Systems Consortium (IDSC) was created on the basis of the International Computer Security Organization (ICSA), which was renamed the TruSecure company in October of 2000. The main goal of the IDSC was to combine developer efforts in the field of intrusion detection technologies. This consortium (http://www.icsalabs.com/HTML/communities/ids/index.sHTML) is open, and can be joined by any intrusion detection system manufacturer. IDSC is engaged in developing user training programs, IDS evaluation criteria, etc.

One of the first documents published by this consortium is the "IDS Buyers Guide" [ICSA1-00], released in December of 1999. Unfortunately, this document remains the only one that the consortium has produced. This guide is intended for training in the field of intrusion detection and security scanning. It also describes criteria to be taken into account when choosing intrusion detection systems and security scanners. The appendix to this document contains a list of 30 intrusion detection systems and security scanners, both commercial and freeware.

Currently, the following manufacturers are participants in IDSC:

❑ Computer Associates, Inc.

❑ Cisco Systems, Inc.

❑ IntruVert Networks

❑ NER Security

❑ SecureWorks

❑ Sourcefire, Inc.

❑ Tripwire, Inc.

Open Platform for Secure Enterprise Connectivity

The Check Point company has also not remained aloof from the development of standards in the field of information security in general, and intrusion detection in particular. In 1997, within the framework of the OPSEC technology (http://www.opsec.com) it developed the SAMP protocol (Suspicious Activity Monitoring Protocol), intended for integrating firewalls or VPN tools with intrusion detection systems. Implementation of this protocol provides the capability of issuing control commands transmitted from an intrusion detection system to the firewall in order to stop attacks or block suspicious traffic.

The Common Content Inspection Standard

The Common Content Inspection (CCI) standard, like SAM, is an API intended for additionally checking the traffic processed by the intrusion detection system sensor or by the firewall. Such checks might include detection of attack signatures, viruses, malicious mobile code, forbidden URLs, etc. The draft of the CCI interface (as well as all related documents that were not widely adopted, but still illustrate the direction of research and development) are available at the following address: http://www.stardust.com/cciapi/.

The Common Intrusion Detection Framework Project

The Common Intrusion Detection Framework (CIDF) project, sponsored by DARPA, was launched in January of 1997. Within the framework of this project, the developers aim to produce a universal protocol intended for information exchange between intrusion detection systems from different manufacturers. Note that CIDF (http://www.gidos.org/) is a research project that is not intended for the commercial market. It is used mainly by manufacturers of intrusion detection systems intended for use by governmental organizations (mainly in the USA). This project also integrates a special attack description language — Common Intrusion Specification Language (CISL) [Proctor1-01]. An example illustrating rules written using the CISL language is presented in Listing 13.1.

Listing 13.1. An Example Illustrating the Use of CISL for Describing Rules for Deleting the /etc/passwd File

```
(Delete
(When
    (Time '12:24 15 Mar 1999 UTC')
)
(Initiator
    (UserName 'joe')
    (UserID 1234)
    (HostName 'bank.ru')
)
(FileSource
    (FullPathName '/etc/passwd')
    (HostName 'bank.ru')
)
)
```

The Intrusion Detection Working Group

The Intrusion Detection Working Group (IDWG) was established by IETF. The goals of this group include the creation of unified data formats and standard procedures for exchanging information between intrusion detection systems and their components, including intrusion detection systems from different manufacturers. In contrast to the CIDF project, the standards developed by IDWG (http://www.ietf.org/html.charters/idwg-charter.HTML and http://www.semper.org/idwg-public) are oriented towards the commercial market. As of now, IDWG has released 6 documents, covering various aspects of IDS operation — starting with requirements to the IDS architecture, and ending with protocol specifications. The greatest interest has been aroused by the Intrusion Detection Message Exchange Format (IDMEF) and the Intrusion Detection Exchange Protocol (IDXP), which describe the mechanism and procedures of message exchange in intrusion detection systems. IDMEF messages are XML documents describing the attack, which are transmitted to the management console using the IDXP protocol (based on the BEEP protocol (Blocks Extensible Exchange Protocol)). Earlier, IDXP was known as IAP (Intrusion Alert Protocol), and was based on HTTP. The advantages of BEEP include the simplicity of developing custom communication protocols and support for confidentiality and authentication mechanisms using Transport Layer Security (TLS).

The Common Vulnerabilities and Exposures Database

As I mentioned in *Chapter 2*, there is no terminological unity among specialists in the field of intrusion detection. This results in confusion and misunderstanding. To improve this situation and eliminate the confusion when naming attacks and vulnerabilities, the MITRE Corporation in 1999 suggested a solution independent of manufacturers of intrusion detection systems, security scanners, etc, [Mann1-99]. This solution was implemented in the form of the CVE database (Common Vulnerabilities and Exposures). This enabled developers to specify a single name for a vulnerability, universally understandable to all professionals.

Besides MITRE experts, specialists from many other companies and organizations have participated in the development of the CVE database. The list of participants includes ISS, Cisco, BindView, Axent, NFR, L-3, CyberSafe, CERT, Carnegie Mellon University, SANS, UC Davis Computer Security Lab, CERIAS, etc. At the moment of this writing, the CVE database contained descriptions of more than 2220 vulnerabilities.

The ICAT Database

NIST also has made a contribution to research in the field of intrusion detection. The ICAT (Internet Categorization of Attacks Toolkit) database is one of the most important NIST achievements in this field. This database, available at http://icat.nist.gov/, merges and indexes attack and vulnerability databases developed by various organizations and centers, including CERIAS, FedCIRC, ISS X-Force, NIAP, SANS, SecurityFocus (formerly Bugtraq and NT Bugtraq), VulDa, etc. Besides the above-mentioned centers, ICAT complements its database with attacks obtained from hacker sites, such as http://www.rootshell.com, http://infilsec.com, and so on.

As a result, NIST has created one of the largest stores of attack and vulnerability descriptions, closely related to the CVE database. By September 9, 2002, this database contained more than 4800 records. Data registered in ICAT, after appropriate investigation, can also be included into the CVE database. In contrast to other databases — particularly the ones described in *Chapter* 2 — ICAT categorizes each vulnerability by 40 different characteristics, including:

❑ Manufacturers of vulnerable software or hardware (at the moment of this writing, the number of such manufacturers exceeded 500)
❑ Name and version of the software or hardware
❑ Risk level (high, medium, or low)
❑ The source from which the vulnerability description was obtained (CERT, X-Force, Microsoft, SecurityFocus, etc.)
❑ The source for exploiting this vulnerability (local or remote)
❑ The type of attack that can be implemented by exploiting this vulnerability (for example, Denial of Service)
❑ The result of exploiting this vulnerability (for example, interrupted availability)
❑ Vulnerability type (buffer overflow, condition out of range, etc.)
❑ Vulnerable operating system(s)
❑ Application type (application server, protocol, protocol stack, OS)
❑ Record type ("present in CVE," "candidate to CVE")
❑ Date when the record was included into the ICAT database

And this is not all. I should mention that, besides the development of the ICAT database, NIST released a document in 2001 outlining requirements to intrusion detection systems [Mell1-01].

The Intrusion Data Library Enterprise Database

Despite their significant contribution to information security research, both CVE and ICAT projects are oriented only towards supporting and maintaining a unified vulnerability database. Such databases are hardly suitable for attack descriptions. To eliminate this drawback, the Stanford Research Institute (http://www.sri.com/) has developed the IDLE database (Intrusion Data Library Enterprise). The IDLE database has an XML-based format, and is intended for aiding developers, researches, testers, and operators of various intrusion detection systems. This database can store various information on an attack, including:

- ❑ Records of OS log files
- ❑ Fragments of the network traffic
- ❑ Records from the log files created by application software
- ❑ File changes

The first trial version of the IDLE database is currently available. The same version is used in the SRI project. This project is coordinated by the UC Davis Computer Security Lab. Unfortunately, no information concerning the support of this product by developers of commercial products is available yet. Notice that the XML language is also used by the IDWG group.

DARPA Projects

DARPA sponsors quite a large number of perspective projects in the field of intrusion detection. In particular, besides the CIDF standard, the UC Davis Computer Security Lab, in cooperation with the Boeing Corporation, is developing the IDIP protocol (Intruder Detection and Isolation Protocol), intended for interaction between intrusion detection systems, firewalls, and routers. Like many other projects coordinated by DARPA, this project is unlikely to be used anywhere outside US governmental organizations. Also, there is very little information concerning this project.

CHAPTER 14

Incident Response

And so, you have now managed to customize your intrusion detection system, and the first message has appeared on its console. What now? How should you react to this message? Discard it as a meaningless one, or start the investigation of this incident? The decision-making process when detecting intrusions and for the subsequent implementation of these decisions is known as incident response.

Historically, it just so happened that intrusion detection and incident response developed as independent processes. However, the difference between them is gradually being eliminated, and it is currently impossible to imagine contemporary intrusion detection systems without incident response mechanisms. Notice that the response can be two-fold. The first type of response has been mentioned several times in this book. It assumes the implementation of specific actions in response to a registered event. For example, this can be reconfiguration of the firewall, or administrative notification of an active attack. One can conclude that this type of response operates only with the security events covered in *Chapter 2*. However, let's consider a situation when someone initiates a Denial of Service attack on your network and spoofs his or her actual address. We already looked at this example earlier in this book. In such a case, you must have at your disposal a special procedure or mechanism to identify the exact address of the intruder, in order to be sure that your system does not block an authorized user. The capability of identifying the incident source correctly is extremely important; otherwise, the response to that incident can become the cause of a new incident. A user account lockout after exceeding the predefined number of failed logons can serve as an example of such an incident. An intruder desiring to lock out an authorized user can undertake several attempts of logging on under that user's login name. As a result, the account of that user will be locked. By the way, you should bear this fact in mind when using security scanners that investigate the stability of password protection.

▌ *A Practical Example*

In my practice, I once encountered a case in which a customer used an Internet Scanner to check the host that played the role of domain controller. The user account management subsystem was set up in such a way that the user account was locked after the third failed logon attempt (see Fig. 4.1). The Internet Scanner, in the course of checking the domain controller, actually managed to lock all the accounts of domain users.

Consequently, the capability of differentiating an attack source is very important for selecting a specific type of response. The example provided above is rather simple, but it does not mean that the problem is not pertinent. To illustrate this statement, let's consider a more complicated situation. For example, practically everyone knows of the famous thriller *WarGames*, where a young hacker penetrates a military computer system and imitates an intrusion into US territory. The computer of the Department of Defense considered this imitation a real attack, and took counteractions — the US Army, Navy, and Air Force were brought to a state of Red Alert. Thus, only a few seconds separated the world from the beginning of a nuclear war. And this is not pure fiction. Such a situation could arise even now.

Note that most incidents create situations that make some types of responses worthless. For example, the Morris Worm that created such a mess in 1988 locked most of the Internet hosts used by security specialists from different countries all over the world for coordinating their activities. In this situation, e-mail was the only communication tool available to them. A similar situation arose in the US quite recently. Due to the emergency, a large number of pagers ceased to function, among which were many pagers used by Response Teams. Thus, a reliable type of response must be independent of the consequences of the attack. The Cyber Warning Intelligence

Network (CWIN), which is currently under construction, might become one such response variant. On December 4, 2001, this network was mentioned by Richard Clarke (the IS consultant to the US President) in his speech at the Global Tech Summit organized by the Business Software Alliance in Washington.

I hope I have assured you that the necessity of unambiguous identification of the attack source is beyond any doubt. However, if you return to *Chapter 2*, you will notice that that attack model does not work with the concept of an attack source. On the contrary, this concept is introduced only in the incident model. This is the main reason why contemporary intrusion detection systems can not unambiguously identify the source of unauthorized activity. The incident response process helps in solving this problem and allows you to quickly undertake the required counteractions.

As I mentioned in *Chapter 7*, the first steps that you must take before starting work with the IDS is to define the list of employees that will operate and control it. It does not make any sense to have a qualified expert sitting at the IDS console and waiting for an alert signal. In most cases, this function can be delegated to operators who might even lack much knowledge in the field of network security. Usually, such persons do not even know the meaning of such things as Ping of Death or Windows OOB. Most contemporary intrusion detection systems rate detected events by the level of risk, but practically none of them provides recommendations concerning the actions that should be taken when such attacks are detected.

Because of this, it is necessary to develop and approve documents that describe all actions that the operator must take when an attack is detected. Notice that the response to the same attack might be different depending on the concomitant factors. Consider, for example, a situation in which you have registered port scanning on your firewall. If the firewall is correctly configured, this is a minor threat that only requires you to identify the intruder's address. However, if your firewall supports VPN functions, and port scanning is performed from your partner with whom you have established a protected connection, this situation is much more dangerous than the previous one. This means that either your partner's network has been compromised or one of his or her employees is attempting to penetrate your network. Consequently, this incident requires a more detailed investigation, and is beyond the operator's competence. Note that since the operator usually lacks the required knowledge and experience, he or she might discard the second option without giving it any serious attention if there are no appropriate directives and documents.

Even for an experienced operator, most IDS messages look cryptic. For example, the management console might display messages on the detection of the "dot-dot" or "statd buffer overflow" vulnerabilities. The intrusion detection system should describe each of these detected events. Unfortunately, security tools that fully implement this function are not numerous. According to the results of numerous tests on this criterion, the system best explaining each of the detected attacks is RealSecure from ISS. Left-clicking a message corresponding to the detected attack displays a window containing a detailed interpretation of the attack, including a description of its working mechanism, a list of vulnerable operating systems, cases of false positives, and detailed directions for eliminating the possibility of this attack being implemented in the future. Cisco and ISS provide the capability of customizing IDS messages, which significantly simplifies the use of their systems for the customer.

Now let us suppose that the operator has correctly identified and registered an attack. He determined that this is not a false positive, and that the attack has a high level of risk. What should be done next? What actions must he perform when the detected event proves to be a real incident? Consider, for example, a case in which the intruder has exploited a web server vulnerability, gotten administrative privileges, and defaced the home page of the server. What should the operator do in this case? Disconnect the web server from the network and contact the Web master? Reinstall the operating system and web server software? Perhaps, add automatic locking of the connection from the identified IP address in order to prevent further attempts of attacks originating from that address? Or something else maybe?

Incident handling is a rather sophisticated mechanism, which intrusion detection systems can not implement without external assistance. In a best case scenario, depending on the attack target, type, and level of risk, an IDS can perform a predefined action, for example, close the connection with the attacking host, or reconfigure the router or firewall. Still, there remain quite a large number of questions. First, it is necessary to make the correct decision concerning the proper type of reaction to the detected event. A human must make this decision, while the intrusion detection system need only implement this decision. Secondly, an automatic response might also have negative consequences, as was demonstrated earlier.

All these facts allow us to draw the conclusion that incident response functions must be delegated to a special team, which must fulfill, coordinate, and support responses to incidents that affect information systems within the limits of a predefined area of responsibility. Such a group, known as a Computer Security Incident Response Team (CSIRT) must act within the framework of the procedures described in the security policy. The security policy adopted in the organization must strictly define the area of competence for the CSIRT group, in order to prevent a situation in which the CSIRT duplicates the functions of the IT department that users address for any occasion, both important and unimportant. In general, you must implement the following efficient security measures.

❑ When creating the CSIRT group, define the list of employees who must be contacted whenever an incident is reported. If your company is not a widely known one or an Internet portal, it is not necessary to free CSIRT members from other duties (although it is highly desirable). After all, your company does not become the target of an attack every day. For example, the incident response group might include employees from the telecommunications, IT, and IS departments, etc.

❏ Develop guidelines describing variants of response. For example, you must decide whether you will have the intruder accomplish his attack or stop it immediately. Sometimes, especially if you want to gather proof for court, it is best not to stop the attack and let the intruder to accomplish it, in order to gather additional information on the attacker and his actions. For this purpose, you can use deception systems ("honey pots").

❏ You need to develop and approve guidelines specifying variants of communication with other individuals in case of attack detection. Will you inform only the boss, managers, and upper managers of the company, or will you distribute information about the attack to other concerned parties? Do you participate in such organizations as FIRST? Will you inform someone outside the company, or will you consider this information as company confidential? Will you notify your partners that are connected to your network, and who are therefore also exposed to the risk? Will you inform the mass media? All these questions must be answered in this document.

❏ Inform all employees of the creation of the CSIRT group and its functions. First, you can do this by distributing a document within your company describing the aims and tasks of the CSIRT group. You can also create an internal web server containing information on registered incidents and special forms that the user must fill in when such a situation arises. An example of such a form was created by the CERT incident response group (ftp://info.cert.org/incident_reporting_form).

Besides incident response functions, the CSIRT group might be engaged in the following activities [Brown1-98].

❏ Publishing information on detected vulnerabilities (such as the X-Force group does)

❏ Creating technical reports on specific attacks and vulnerabilities

❏ Training users

❏ Analyzing security and evaluating risk

❏ Providing consulting services in the field of information security

❏ Developing incident response tools and tools for tracing the intruder

Such groups can work within the framework of the whole Internet community (for example, CERT), within the limits of specific country, and within the framework of specific department, manufacturer, or company [Brown1-99]. Let's concentrate on the latter variant.

The incident response process is made up of 6 steps [SANS1-98].

1. *Preparation.* This step includes the development of the security policy and several other guidelines that were already covered in this chapter.
2. *Identification.* At this stage, it is necessary to determine if the incident really took place. If the incident is confirmed, you need to determine its parameters (including the intruder's address, attack route, proof, etc.).
3. *Moderation.* Here you must localize the incident as soon as possible, and prevent it from propagating further.
4. *Elimination.* This step aims to eliminate the problem (such as vulnerability) that has resulted in the incident.
5. *Recovery.* The result of the action performed at this step is the complete recovery of the system after the incident.
6. *Feedback.* At this final step, it is necessary to investigate and explore the registered incident in as much detail as possible, in order to develop adequate measures for preventing such incidents from happening in the future.

Investigation of Unexpected Changes

If the integrity control system detects any modifications that can not be classified as authorized changes (for example, missing files or newly created files), it is necessary to immediately start incident response procedures. The security policy adopted in the organization must contain strict definitions of the duties and authorities of security administrators for the integrity control of the file structure of your system. Ordinary users must be informed of these authorities. When informing users of the basic principles of the organization's security policy, instruct them to immediately inform the security administrator about any changes in the file structure that they might notice.

Do not forget that after any authorized modification introduced into the protected files, it is necessary to update the attributes of each file or directory (date, time, size, checksum, etc.). A similar requirement is also applicable to the hardware. If any device appears unexpectedly, this must be investigated. After any such incident, it is necessary to update the network map according to the actions performed as a result of the investigation.

As I already mentioned, some files change frequently, sometimes several times per second. Besides log files, the list of such files includes transaction logs of databases or user applications. Temporary files (such as paging files) are a special case. It is certainly rather difficult to trace such changes and react to them. In this case, methods of the content analysis of such files (transactions, log-file records, etc.) prove to be more efficient.

Documenting all Failed Attempts

All detected violations must be registered in special logs. You can initiate various response procedures based on the registered data. However, practical experience has shown that you can not always be sure that there has been an attack on specific resources of your corporate network. Sometimes specific events might seem suspicious, and these suspicions must not be neglected. You should document any suspicious events so that when additional information is collected, you can return to them and perform a more detailed investigation.

The same log that contains registered attacks and attack attempts must contain the actions taken during the incident investigation and response, and should carefully document the result of these actions. If attacks continue, this will help you to quickly reproduce the most efficient counteraction measures.

Summary

Detailed coverage of the incident response procedures goes beyond the framework of this book, which is dedicated to intrusion detection technologies and systems that implement such technologies. More detailed information on this topic is provided in [Navy1-96], [Northcutt1-96], [NRL1-95], [Wack1-91], [Smith1-94], [Chen1-00], [Chen1-95], [Longstaff1-93], and [Brownlee1-96].

APPENDIX A

List of Ports Frequently Used by Trojans

№	Port	Name
1	2	Death
2	20	Senna Spy FTP Server
3	21	Back Construction, Blade Runner, Doly Trojan, Fore, Invisible FTP, Juggernaut 42, Larva, Motlv FTP, Net Administrator, Senna Spy FTP Server, Traitor 21, WebEx, WinCrash
4	22	Shaft
5	23	Fire Hacker, Tiny Telnet Server — TTS, Truva Atl
6	25	Ajan, Antigen, Email Password Sender — EPS, EPS II, Gip, Gris, Happy99, Hpteam mail, I love you, Kuang2, Magic Horse, MBT (Mail Bombing Trojan), Moscow Email trojan, Naebi, NewApt worm, ProMail trojan, Shtirlitz, Stealth, Tapiras, Terminator, WinPC, WinSpy
7	31	Agent 31, Hackers Paradise, Masters Paradise

continues

Continued

№	Port	Name
8	41	Deep Throat, Foreplay or Reduced Foreplay
9	48	DRAT
10	50	DRAT
11	59	DMSetup
12	79	CDK, Firehotcker
13	80	AckCmd, Back End, CGI Backdoor, Executor, Hooker, RingZero
14	81	RemoConChubo
15	99	Hidden Port
16	110	ProMail trojan
17	113	Invisible Identd Deamon, Kazimas
18	119	Happy99
19	121	JammerKillah
20	123	Net Controller
21	133	Farnaz
22	142	NetTaxi
23	146 (TCP/UDP)	Infector
24	170	A-trojan
25	334	Backage
26	420	Breach
27	421	TCP Wrapper trojan
28	456	Hackers Paradise
29	513	Grlogin
30	514	RPC Backdoor
31	531	Rasmin
32	555	Ini-Killer, Net Administrator, Phase Zero, Phase-0, Stealth Spy
33	605	Secret Service
34	666	Attack FTP, Back Construction, Cain & Abel, NokNok, Satans Back Door — SBD, ServU, Shadow Phyre
35	667	SniperNet

continues

Continued

№	Port	Name
36	669	DP trojan
37	692	GayOL
38	777	AimSpy, Undetected
39	808	WinHole
40	911	Dark Shadow
41	999	Deep Throat, Foreplay or Reduced Foreplay, WinSatan
42	1000	Der Spaher / Der Spaeher
43	1001	Der Spaher / Der Spaeher, Le Guardien, Silencer, WebEx
44	1010	Doly Trojan
45	1011	Doly Trojan
46	1012	Doly Trojan
47	1015	Doly Trojan
48	1016	Doly Trojan
49	1020	Vampire
50	1024	NetSpy
51	1042	BLA trojan
52	1045	Rasmin
53	1049	/sbin/initd
54	1050	MiniCommand
55	1054	AckCmd
56	1080	WinHole
57	1081	WinHole
58	1082	WinHole
59	1082	WinHole
60	1090	Xtreme
61	1095	Remote Administration Tool — RAT
62	1097	Remote Administration Tool — RAT
63	1098	Remote Administration Tool — RAT

continues

Continued

№	Port	Name
64	1099	Blood Fest Evolution, Remote Administration Tool — RAT
65	1170	Psyber Stream Server — PSS, Streaming Audio Server, Voice
66	1200 (UDP)	NoBackO
67	1201 (UDP)	NoBackO
68	1207	SoftWAR
69	1212	Kaos
70	1234	Ultors Trojan
71	1243	BackDoor-G, SubSeven , SubSeven Apocalypse, Tiles
72	1245	Voodoo Doll
73	1255	Scarab
74	1256	Project NEXT
75	1269	Matrix
76	1313	NETrojan
77	1338	Millenium Worm
78	1349	Bo dll
79	1492	FTP99CMP
80	1524	Trinoo
81	1600	Shivka-Burka
82	1777	Scarab
83	1807	SpySender
84	1966	Fake FTP
85	1969	OpC BO
86	1981	Bowl, Shockrave
87	1999	Back Door, TransScout
88	2000	Der Spaher / Der Spaeher, Insane Network
89	2001	Der Spaher / Der Spaeher, Trojan Cow
90	2023	Ripper Pro
91	2080	WinHole

continues

Continued

№	Port	Name
92	2115	Bugs
93	2140 (UDP)	Deep Throat, Foreplay or Reduced Foreplay
94	2155	Illusion Mailer
95	2255	Nirvana
96	2283	Hvl RAT
97	2300	Xplorer
98	2339 (TCP/UDP)	Voice Spy — OBS!!! namnen har bytt plats
99	2345	Doly Trojan
100	2565	Striker trojan
101	2583	WinCrash
102	2600	Digital RootBeer
103	2716	The Prayer
104	2773	SubSeven , SubSeven 2.1 Gold
105	2801	Phineas Phucker
106	2989 (UDP)	Remote Administration Tool — RAT
107	3000	Remote Shut
108	3024	WinCrash
109	3128	RingZero
110	3129	Masters Paradise
111	3150	The Invasor
112	3150 (UDP)	Deep Throat, Foreplay or Reduced Foreplay
113	3456	Terror trojan
114	3459	Eclipse 2000, Sanctuary
115	3700	Portal of Doom — POD
116	3791	Total Solar Eclypse
117	3801	Total Solar Eclypse
118	4000	Skydance
119	4092	WinCrash
120	4242	Virtual Hacking Machine — VHM
121	4321	BoBo
122	4444	Prosiak, Swift Remote

continues

Continued

№	Port	Name
123	4567	File Nail
124	4590	ICQ Trojan
125	4950	ICQ Trogen (Lm)
126	5000	Back Door Setup, Blazer5, Bubbel, ICKiller, Sockets des Troie
127	5001	Back Door Setup, Sockets des Troie
128	5002	Shaft, cd00r
129	5010	Solo
130	5011	One of the Last Trojans — OOTLT
131	5025	WM Remote KeyLogger
132	5031	Net Metropolitan
133	5032	Net Metropolitan
134	5321	FileHotcker
135	5343	WCrat — WC Remote Administration Tool
136	5400	Back Construction, Blade Runner
137	5401	Back Construction, Blade Runner
138	5402	Back Construction, Blade Runner
139	5512	Illusion Mailer
140	5550	Xtcp
141	5555	ServeMe
142	5556	BO Facil
143	5557	BO Facil
144	5569	Robo-Hack
145	5637	PC Crasher
146	5638	PC Crasher
147	5742	WinCrash
148	5760	Portmap Remote Root Linux Exploit
149	5882 (UDP)	Y3K RAT
150	5888	Y3K RAT
151	6000	The Thing
152	6006	Bad Blood

continues

Continued

№	Port	Name
153	6272	Secret Service
154	6400	The Thing
155	6666	Dark Connection Inside, NetBus worm
156	6667	ScheduleAgent, Trinity, WinSatan
157	6669	Host Control, Vampire
158	6670	BackWeb Server, Deep Throat, Foreplay or Reduced Foreplay, WinNuke eXtreame
159	6711	BackDoor-G, SubSeven , VP Killer
160	6712	Funny trojan, SubSeven
161	6713	SubSeven
162	6723	Mstream
163	6771	Deep Throat, Foreplay or Reduced Foreplay
164	6776	2000 Cracks, BackDoor-G, SubSeven , VP Killer
165	6838 (UDP)	Mstream
166	6883	Delta Source Dark Star
167	6912	Shit Heep
168	6939	Indoctrination
169	6969	GateCrasher, IRC 3, Net Controller, Priority
170	6970	GateCrasher
171	7000	Exploit Translation Server, Kazimas, Remote Grab, SubSeven 2.1 Gold
172	7001	Freak8
173	7215	SubSeven, SubSeven 2.1 Gold
174	7300	NetMonitor
175	7301	NetMonitor
176	7306	NetMonitor
177	7307	NetMonitor
178	7308	NetMonitor
179	7424 (TCP/UDP)	Host Control
180	7597	Qaz
181	7777	Tini

continues

Continued

№	Port	Name
182	7789	Back Door Setup, ICKiller
183	7983	Mstream
184	8080	Brown Orifice, RemoConChubo, RingZero
185	8787	Back Orifice 2000
186	8988	BacHack
187	8989	Rcon, Recon, Xcon
188	9000	Netministrator
189	9325 (UDP)	Mstream
190	9400	InCommand
191	9872	Portal of Doom — POD
192	9873	Portal of Doom — POD
193	9874	Portal of Doom — POD
194	9875	Portal of Doom — POD
195	9876	Cyber Attacker, Rux
196	9878	TransScout
197	9989	Ini-Killer
198	9999	The Prayer
199	10067 (UDP)	Portal of Doom — POD
200	10085	Syphillis
201	10086	Syphillis
202	10101	BrainSpy
203	10167 (UDP)	Portal of Doom — POD
204	10520	Acid Shivers
205	10528	Host Control
206	10607	Coma
207	10666 (UDP)	Ambush
208	11000	Senna Spy Trojan Generator
209	11050	Host Control
210	11051	Host Control
211	11223	Progenic trojan, Secret Agent

continues

Continued

№	Port	Name
212	12076	Gjamer
213	12223	Hack?99 KeyLogger
214	12345	cron / crontab, Fat Bitch trojan, GabanBus, icmp_pipe.c, Mypic, Net-Bus, NetBus Toy, NetBus worm, Pie Bill Gates, Whack Job, X-bill
215	12346	Fat Bitch trojan, GabanBus, NetBus, X-bill
216	12349	BioNet
217	12361	Whack-a-mole
218	12362	Whack-a-mole
219	12623 (UDP)	DUN Control
220	12626	ButtMan
221	12631	Whack Job
222	12754	Mstream
223	13000	Senna Spy Trojan Generator
224	13010	Hacker Brasil — HBR
225	14500	PC Invader
226	15092	Host Control
227	15104	Mstream
228	15858	CDK
229	16484	Mosucker
230	16660	Stacheldraht
231	16772	ICQ Revenge
232	16969	Priority
233	17166	Mosaic
234	17300	Kuang2
235	17449	CrazzyNet
236	17777	Nephron
237	18753 (UDP)	Shaft
238	19864	ICQ Revenge
239	2000	Millenium
240	2001	Millenium, Millenium (Lm)
241	20001	AcidkoR

continues

Continued

№	Port	Name
242	20023	VP Killer
243	20034	NetBus 2.0 Pro, NetRex, Whack Job
244	20203	Chupacabra
245	20331	BLA trojan
246	20432	Shaft
247	20433 (UDP)	Shaft
248	21544	GirlFriend, Kid Terror
249	21554	Exploiter, Kid Terror, Schwindler, Winsp00fer
250	22222	Donald Dick, Prosiak
251	23005	NetTrash
252	23023	Logged
253	23032	Amanda
254	23432	Asylum
255	23456	Evil FTP, Ugly FTP, Whack Job
256	23476 (TCP/UDP)	Donald Dick
257	23477	Donald Dick
258	26274 (UDP)	Delta Source
259	26681	Voice Spy — OBS!!! namnen har bytt plats
260	27374	Bad Blood, SubSeven , SubSeven 2.1 Gold, Subseven 2.1.4 DefCon 8
261	27444 (UDP)	Trinoo
262	27573	SubSeven
263	27665	Trinoo
264	29104	NetTrojan
265	29891	The Unexplained
266	30001	ErrOr32
267	30003	Lamers Death
268	30029	AOL trojan
269	30100	NetSphere
270	30102	NetSphere
271	30103 (TCP/UDP)	NetSphere

continues

Continued

№	Port	Name
272	30133	NetSphere
273	30303	Sockets des Troie
274	30947	Intruse
275	30999	Kuang2
276	31335	Trinoo
277	31336	Bo Whack, Butt Funnel
278	31337	Back Fire, Back Orifice (Lm), Back Orifice russian, Baron Night, Beeone, BO client, BO Facil, BO spy, BO2, cron / crontab, Freak88, icmp_pipe.c, Sockdmini
279	31337 (UDP)	Back Orifice, Deep BO
280	31338	Back Orifice, Butt Funnel, NetSpy (DK)
281	31338 (UDP)	Deep BO
282	31339	NetSpy (DK)
283	31666	BOWhack
284	31785	Hack'a'Tack
285	31788	Hack'a'Tack
286	31789 (UDP)	Hack'a'Tack
287	31790	Hack'a'Tack
288	31791 (UDP)	Hack'a'Tack
289	32001	Donald Dick
290	32100	Peanut Brittle, Project nEXT
291	32418	Acid Battery
292	33270	Trinity
293	33333	Blakharaz, Prosiak
294	33577	PsychWard
295	33777	PsychWard
296	33911	Spirit 2000, Spirit 2001
297	34324	Big Gluck, TN
298	34444	Donald Dick
299	34555 (UDP)	WinTrinoo
300	35555 (UDP)	WinTrinoo

continues

Continued

№	Port	Name
301	37651	Yet Another Trojan — YAT
302	40412	The Spy
303	40421	Agent 40421, Masters Paradise
304	40422	Masters Paradise
305	40423	Masters Paradise
306	40426	Masters Paradise
307	41666	Remote Boot Tool — RBT
308	44444	Prosiak
309	47262 (UDP)	Delta Source
310	50505	Sockets des Troie
311	50766	Fore, Schwindler
312	51966	Cafeini
313	52317	Acid Battery 2000
314	53001	Remote Windows Shutdown — RWS
315	54283	SubSeven , SubSeven 2.1 Gold
316	54320	Back Orifice
317	54321	Back Orifice, School Bus
318	57341	NetRaider
319	58339	Butt Funnel
320	60000	Deep Throat, Foreplay or Reduced Foreplay, Sockets des Troie
321	60068	Xzip 60068
322	60411	Connection
323	61438	Bunker-Hill
324	61466	TeleCommando
325	61603	Bunker-Hill
326	63485	Bunker-Hill
327	64101	Taskman / Task Manager
328	65000	Devil, Sockets des Troie, Stacheldraht
329	65432 (TCP/UDP)	The Traitor (= th3tr41t0r)
330	65534	/sbin/initd
331	65535	RC1 trojan

List of Most Frequently Scanned Ports

Service	Port	Protocol	Attack probability	Description
Reserved	0	TCP/UDP	High	This port can't be present — neither as a source nor as a destination port
	0–5	TCP	High	Sscan scanner
Echo	7	TCP/UDP	High	UDP attack
Systat	11	TCP	High	Information about user processes
Netstat	15	TCP	High	Network state
chargen	19	TCP/UDP	High	UDP attack
ftp	20, 21	TCP	Medium	FTP server
ssh	22	TCP	Medium-High	SSH server

continues

Continued

Service	Port	Protocol	Attack probability	Description
ssh	22	UDP	Low	Outdated pcAnywhere version
telnet	23	TCP	High	Telnet server
smtp	25	TCP	High	Attempt of relaying e-mail or scanning the security system for vulnerabilities
domain	53	TCP	High	DNS falsification
tftpd	69	UDP	Medium-High	Alternative FTP server, lacking security mechanisms
finger	79	TCP	Low	Information about the user
pop-3	109, 110	TCP	High	Frequently used for penetration
sunrpc	111	TCP/UDP	High	Frequently used for penetration
nntp	119	TCP	Medium-High	News server used for spam
ntp	123	UDP	Low	Network time synchronization
netbios-sn	137	TCP/UDP	Medium	Windows systems
netbios-dgm	138	TCP/UDP	Medium	Windows systems
netbios-ssn	139	TCP	Medium	Windows systems
imap	143	TCP	High	Frequently used for penetration
snmp	161, 162	UDP	Medium	Remote network administration
exec	512	TCP	High	Intranet only
biff	512	UDP	High	Intranet only
login	513	TCP	High	Intranet only
who	513	UDP	High	Intranet only
shell	514	TCP	High	Intranet only
syslog	514	UDP	High	Intranet only
printer	515	TCP	High	Intranet only

continues

Continued

Service	Port	Protocol	Attack probability	Description
talk	517	UDP	Medium	Intranet only
ntalk	518	UDP	Medium	Intranet only
route	520	UDP	High	Routing
uucp	540	TCP	Medium	UUCP
mount	635	UDP	High	Daemon has vulnerabilities in security system
socks	1080	TCP	High	Used for spam
SQL	1114	TCP	High	Sscan
openwin	2000	TCP	High	Open Windows
NFS	2049	TCP/UDP	High	Remote access to files
pcanywhere	5632	UDP	Low	PcAnywhere
X11	6000+n	TCP	High	X Window
NetBus	12345, 12346, 20034	TCP	High	Trojan for Windows system
BackOrifice	31337	UDP	High	Trojan for Windows system
Traceroute	33434– 33523	UDP	Low	Incoming traceroute request (for Unix)
Ping	8	ICMP	Medium	Incoming ping request
Redirect	5	ICMP	High	Redirection
Traceroute	11	ICMP	Low	Outgoing traceroute request

APPENDIX C

List of Internet Address Ranges

№	Starting address	Ending address	Belongs to
1	0.0.0.0	2.255.255.255	Reserved by IANA
2	3.0.0.0	4.255.255.255	ARIN
3	5.0.0.0	5.255.255.255	Reserved by IANA
4	6.0.0.0	6.255.255.255	ARIN
5	7.0.0.0	7.255.255.255	Reserved by IANA
6	8.0.0.0	9.255.255.255	ARIN
7	10.0.0.0	10.255.255.255	Reserved by IANA
8	11.0.0.0	13.255.255.255	ARIN
9	14.0.0.0	14.255.255.255	Reserved by IANA

continues

Continued

№	Starting address	Ending address	Belongs to
10	15.0.0.0	22.255.255.255	ARIN
11	23.0.0.0	23.255.255.255	Reserved by IANA
12	24.0.0.0	24.131.255.255	ARIN
13	24.132.0.0	24.135.255.255	RIPE
14	24.136.0.0	26.255.255.255	ARIN
15	27.0.0.0	27.255.255.255	Reserved by IANA
16	28.0.0.0	30.255.255.255	ARIN
17	31.0.0.0	31.255.255.255	Reserved by IANA
18	32.0.0.0	36.255.255.255	ARIN
19	37.0.0.0	37.255.255.255	Reserved by IANA
20	38.0.0.0	38.255.255.255	ARIN
21	39.0.0.0	39.255.255.255	Reserved by IANA
22	40.0.0.0	40.255.255.255	ARIN
23	41.0.0.0	42.255.255.255	Reserved by IANA
24	43.0.0.0	57.255.255.255	ARIN
25	58.0.0.0	60.255.255.255	Reserved by IANA
26	61.0.0.0	61.255.255.255	APNIC
27	62.0.0.0	62.255.255.255	RIPE
28	63.0.0.0	63.255.255.255	ARIN
29	64.0.0.0	64.255.255.255	ARIN
30	65.0.0.0	127.255.255.255	Reserved by IANA
31	128.0.0.0	139.19.255.255	ARIN
32	139.20.0.0	139.29.255.255	RIPE
33	139.30.0.0	140.255.255.255	ARIN
34	141.0.0.0	141.85.255.255	RIPE
35	141.86.0.0	145.223.255.255	ARIN
36	145.224.0.0	145.254.255.255	RIPE
37	145.255.0.0	149.131.255.255	ARIN

continues

Continued

№	Starting address	Ending address	Belongs to
38	149.132.0.0	149.134.255.255	RIPE
39	149.135.0.0	149.201.255.255	ARIN
40	149.202.0.0	149.204.255.255	RIPE
41	149.205.0.0	149.205.255.255	ARIN
42	149.206.0.0	149.251.255.255	RIPE
43	149.252.0.0	150.253.255.255	ARIN
44	150.254.0.0	150.254.255.255	RIPE
45	151.0.0.0	151.2.255.255	ARIN
46	151.3.0.0	151.5.255.255	RIPE
47	151.6.0.0	151.12.255.255	ARIN
48	151.13.0.0	151.82.255.255	RIPE
49	151.83.0.0	151.90.255.255	ARIN
50	151.91.0.0	151.93.255.255	RIPE
51	151.94.0.0	151.94.255.255	ARIN
52	151.95.0.0	151.95.255.255	RIPE
53	151.96.0.0	160.43.255.255	ARIN
54	160.44.0.0	160.63.255.255	RIPE
55	160.64.0.0	160.215.255.255	ARIN
56	160.216.0.0	160.220.255.255	RIPE
57	160.221.0.0	163.155.255.255	ARIN
58	163.156.0.0	163.175.255.255	RIPE
59	163.176.0.0	163.255.255.255	ARIN
60	164.0.0.0	164.40.255.255	RIPE
61	164.41.0.0	164.127.255.255	ARIN
62	164.128.0.0	164.143.255.255	RIPE
63	164.144.0.0	169.207.255.255	ARIN
64	169.208.0.0	169.223.255.255	APNIC
65	169.224.0.0	171.15.255.255	ARIN

continues

Continued

№	Starting address	Ending address	Belongs to
66	171.16.0.0	171.33.255.255	RIPE
67	171.34.0.0	192.70.255.255	ARIN
68	192.71.0.0	192.71.255.255	RIPE
69	192.72.0.0	192.106.143.255	ARIN
70	192.106.144.0	192.106.147.255	RIPE
71	192.106.148.0	192.106.195.255	ARIN
72	192.106.196.0	192.106.197.255	RIPE
73	192.106.198.0	192.161.255.255	ARIN
74	192.162.0.0	192.162.255.255	RIPE
75	192.163.0.0	192.163.255.255	ARIN
76	192.164.0.0	192.167.255.255	RIPE
77	192.168.0.0	192.255.255.255	ARIN
78	193.0.0.0	195.255.255.255	RIPE
79	196.0.0.0	196.255.255.255	ARIN
80	197.0.0.0	197.255.255.255	Reserved by IANA
81	198.0.0.0	198.17.116.255	ARIN
82	198.17.117.0	198.17.117.255	RIPE
83	198.17.118.0	200.255.255.255	ARIN
84	201.0.0.0	201.255.255.255	Reserved by IANA
85	202.0.0.0	203.255.255.255	APNIC
86	204.0.0.0	209.255.255.255	ARIN
87	210.0.0.0	211.255.255.255	APNIC
88	212.0.0.0	213.255.255.255	RIPE
89	214.0.0.0	216.255.255.255	ARIN
90	217.0.0.0	223.255.255.255	ARIN
91	224.0.0.0	239.255.255.255	ARIN
92	240.0.0.0	255.255.255.255	Reserved by IANA

APPENDIX D

List of First-Level Domains

№	Name of the First-Level Domain	Description
1	ac	Ascension Island
2	ad	Andorra
3	ae	United Arab Emirates
4	af	Afghanistan
5	ag	Antigua and Barbuda
6	ai	Anguilla
7	al	Albania
8	am	Armenia
9	an	Antilles

continues

Continued

№	Name of the First-Level Domain	Description
10	ao	Angola
11	aq	Antarctic
12	ar	Argentina
13	as	Samoa Islands
14	at	Austria
15	au	Australia
16	aw	Aruba
17	az	Azerbaijan
18	ba	Bosnia and Herzegovina
19	bb	Barbados
20	bd	Bangladesh
21	be	Belgium
22	bf	Burkina Faso
23	bg	Bulgaria
24	bh	Bahrain
25	bi	Burundi
26	bj	Benin
27	bm	Bermuda Islands
28	bn	Brunei
29	bo	Bolivia
30	br	Brazil
31	bs	Bahama Islands
32	bt	Bhutan
33	bv	Bouvet Island
34	bw	Botswana
35	by	Belarus
36	bz	Belize

continues

Continued

№	Name of the First-Level Domain	Description
37	ca	Canada
38	cc	Cocos (Keeling) Islands
39	cd	Democratic Republic of Congo
40	cf	Central African Republic
41	cg	Congo Republic
42	ch	Switzerland
43	ci	Cote d'Ivoire
44	ck	Cook Islands
45	cl	Chile
46	cm	Cameroon
47	cn	China
48	co	Colombia
49	com	Commercial companies (mainly in USA)
50	cr	Costa Rica
51	cu	Cuba
52	cv	Cape Verde
53	cx	Christmas Islands
54	cy	Cyprus
55	cz	Czech Republic
56	de	Germany
57	dj	Djibouti
58	dk	Denmark
59	dm	Dominica
60	do	Dominican Republic
61	dz	Algeria
62	ec	Ecuador
63	edu	Educational institutions

continues

Continued

№	Name of the First-Level Domain	Description
64	ee	Estonia
65	eg	Egypt
66	eh	Western Sahara
67	er	Eritrea
68	es	Spain
69	et	Ethiopia
70	fi	Finland
71	fj	Fiji
72	fk	Falkland Islands
73	fm	Federated States of Micronesia
74	fo	Faroe Islands
75	fr	France
76	ga	Gabon
77	gb	Great Britain
78	gd	Grenada
79	ge	Georgia
80	gf	French Guiana
81	gg	Guernsey
82	gh	Ghana
83	gi	Gibraltar
84	gl	Greenland
85	gm	Gambia
86	gn	Guinea
87	gov	Governmental organizations (mainly in USA)
88	gp	Guadeloupe
89	gq	Equatorial Guinea
90	gr	Greece

continues

Continued

№	Name of the First-Level Domain	Description
91	gs	South Georgia
92	gt	Guatemala
93	gu	Guam
94	gw	Guinea-Bissau
95	gy	Guyana
96	hk	Hong Kong
97	hm	Heard and McDonald Islands
98	hn	Honduras
99	hr	Croatia
100	ht	Haiti
101	hu	Hungary
102	id	Indonesia
103	ie	Ireland
104	il	Israel
105	im	Isle of Man
106	in	India
107	int	International organizations
108	io	British Indian Ocean Territory
109	iq	Iraq
110	ir	Iran
111	is	Iceland
112	it	Italy
113	je	Jersey
114	jm	Jamaica
115	jo	Jordan
116	jp	Japan
117	ke	Kenya

continues

Continued

№	Name of the First-Level Domain	Description
118	kg	Kyrgyzstan
119	kh	Cambodia
120	ki	Kiribati
121	km	Comoros
122	kn	Saint Kitts and Nevis
123	kp	Korean People's Democratic Republic
124	kr	South Korea
125	kw	Kuwait
126	ky	Cayman Islands
127	kz	Kazakhstan
128	la	Laos
129	lb	Lebanon
130	lc	Saint Lucia
131	li	Liechtenstein
132	lk	Sri Lanka
133	lr	Liberia
134	ls	Lesotho
135	lt	Lithuania
136	lu	Luxemburg
137	lv	Latvia
138	ly	Libya
139	ma	Morocco
140	mc	Monaco
141	md	Moldova
142	mg	Madagascar
143	mh	Marshall Islands
144	mil	Military organizations (in USA)

continues

Continued

№	Name of the First-Level Domain	Description
145	mk	Macedonia
146	ml	Mali
147	mm	Myanmar
148	mn	Mongolia
149	mo	Macao
150	mp	Mariana Islands
151	mq	Martinique
152	mr	Mauritania
153	ms	Montserrat
154	mt	Malta
155	mu	Mauritius
156	mv	Maldives
157	mw	Malawi
158	mx	Mexico
159	my	Malaysia
160	mz	Mozambique
161	na	Namibia
162	nc	New Caledonia
163	ne	Niger
164	net	Networking and communications companies
165	nf	Norfolk Islands
166	ng	Nigeria
167	ni	Nicaragua
168	nl	The Netherlands
169	no	Norway
170	np	Nepal
171	nr	Nauru

continues

Continued

№	Name of the First-Level Domain	Description
172	nu	Erotic servers
173	nz	New Zealand
174	om	Oman
175	org	Non-commercial organizations
176	pa	Panama
177	pe	Peru
178	pf	French Polynesia
179	pg	Papua New Guinea
180	ph	Philippines
181	pk	Pakistan
182	pl	Poland
183	pm	Saint Pierre and Miquelon
184	pn	Pitcairn Island
185	pr	Puerto Rico
186	pt	Portugal
187	pw	Palau
188	py	Paraguay
189	qa	Qatar
190	re	Reunion
191	ro	Romania
192	ru	Russia
193	rw	Rwanda
194	sa	Saudi Arabia
195	sb	Solomon Islands
196	sc	Seychelles
197	sd	Sudan
198	se	Sweden

continues

Continued

№	Name of the First-Level Domain	Description
199	sg	Singapore
200	sh	Saint Helena
201	si	Singapore
202	sj	Svalbard and Jan Mayen Islands
203	sk	Slovakia
204	sl	Sierra Leone
205	sm	San Marino
206	sn	Senegal
207	so	Somalia
208	sr	Surinam
209	st	Sao Tome e Principe
210	su	USSR
211	sv	El Salvador
212	sy	Syria
213	sz	Swaziland
214	tc	Turks and Caicos Islands
215	td	Chad
216	tf	French Southern Territories
217	tg	Togo
218	th	Thailand
219	tj	Tajikistan
220	tk	Tokelau
221	tm	Turkmenistan
222	tn	Tunis
223	to	Tonga
224	tp	East Timor
225	tr	Turkey

continues

Continued

№	Name of the First-Level Domain	Description
226	tt	Trinidad and Tobago
227	tv	Tuvalu
228	tw	Taiwan
229	tz	Tanzania
230	ua	Ukraine
231	ug	Uganda
232	uk	Great Britain
233	um	U.S. Minor Outlying Islands
234	us	USA
235	uy	Uruguay
236	uz	Uzbekistan
237	va	Vatican
238	vc	Saint Vincent and Grenadines
239	ve	Venezuela
240	vg	British Virgin Islands
241	vi	Virgin Islands (USA)
242	vn	Vietnam
243	vu	Vanuatu
244	wf	Wallis and Futuna Islands
245	ws	Samoa
246	ye	Yemen
247	yt	Mayotte
248	yu	Yugoslavia
249	za	South Africa
250	zm	Zambia
251	zr	Zaire
252	zw	Zimbabwe

List of Protocol Identifiers for IPv4

Number	Keyword	Protocol
0	HOPOPT	IPv6 Hop-by-Hop Option
1	ICMP	Internet Control Message
2	IGMP	Internet Group Management
3	GGP	Gateway-to-Gateway
4	IP	IP in IP (encapsulation)
5	ST	Stream
6	TCP	Transmission Control
7	CBT	CBT
8	EGP	Exterior Gateway Protocol
9	IGP	Any private interior gateway (used by Cisco for their IGRP)

continues

Continued

Number	Keyword	Protocol
10	BBN-RCC-MON	BBN RCC Monitoring
11	NVP-II	Network Voice Protocol
12	PUP	PUP
13	ARGUS	ARGUS
14	EMCON	EMCON
15	XNET	Cross Net Debugger
16	CHAOS	Chaos
17	UDP	User Datagram
18	MUX	Multiplexing
19	DCN-MEAS	DCN Measurement Subsystems
20	HMP	Host Monitoring
21	PRM	Packet Radio Measurement
22	XNS-IDP	XEROX NS IDP
23	TRUNK-1	Trunk-1
24	TRUNK-2	Trunk-2
25	LEAF-1	Leaf-1
26	LEAF-2	Leaf-2
27	RDP	Reliable Data Protocol
28	IRTP	Internet Reliable Transaction
29	ISO-TP4	ISO Transport Protocol Class 4
30	NETBLT	Bulk Data Transfer Protocol
31	MFE-NSP	MFE Network Services Protocol
32	MERIT-INP	MERIT Internodal Protocol
33	SEP	Sequential Exchange Protocol
34	3PC	Third Party Connect Protocol
35	IDPR	Inter-Domain Policy Routing Protocol
36	XTP	XTP
37	DDP	Datagram Delivery Protocol

continues

Continued

Number	Keyword	Protocol
38	IDPR-CMTP	IDPR Control Message Transport Proto
39	TP++	TP++ Transport Protocol
40	IL	IL Transport Protocol
41	IPv6	IPv6
42	SDRP	Source Demand Routing Protocol
43	IPv6-Route	Routing Header for IPv6
44	IPv6-Frag	Fragment Header for IPv6
45	IDRP	Inter-Domain Routing Protocol
46	RSVP	Reservation Protocol
47	GRE	General Routing Encapsulation
48	MHRP	Mobile Host Routing Protocol
49	BNA	BNA
50	ESP	Encap Security Payload for IPv6
51	AH	Authentication Header for IPv6
52	I-NLSP	Integrated Net Layer Security TUBA
53	SWIPE	IP with Encryption
54	NARP	NBMA Address Resolution Protocol
55	MOBILE	IP Mobility
56	TLSP	Transport Layer Security Protocol using Kryptonet key management
57	SKIP	SKIP
58	IPv6-ICMP	ICMP for IPv6
59	IPv6-NoNxt	No Next Header for IPv6
60	IPv6-Opts	Destination Options for IPv6
61	Any host internal protocol	
62	CFTP	CFTP
63	any local network	
64	SAT-EXPAK	SATNET and Backroom EXPAK

continues

Continued

Number	Keyword	Protocol
65	KRYPTOLAN	Kryptolan
66	RVD	MIT Remote Virtual Disk Protocol
67	IPPC	Internet Pluribus Packet Core
68	Any distributed file system	
69	SAT-MON	SATNET Monitoring
70	VISA	VISA Protocol
71	IPCV	Internet Packet Core Utility
72	CPNX	Computer Protocol Network Executive
73	CPHB	Computer Protocol Heart Beat
74	WSN	Wang Span Network
75	PVP	Packet Video Protocol
76	BR-SAT-MON	Backroom SATNET Monitoring
77	SUN-ND	SUN ND PROTOCOL-Temporary
78	WB-MON	WIDEBAND Monitoring
79	WB-EXPAK	WIDEBAND EXPAK
80	ISO-IP	ISO Internet Protocol
81	VMTP	VMTP
82	SECURE-VMTP	SECURE-VMTP
83	VINES	VINES
84	TTP	TTP
85	NSFNET-IGP	NSFNET-IGP
86	DGP	Dissimilar Gateway Protocol
87	TCF	TCF
88	EIGRP	EIGRP
89	OSPFIGP	OSPFIGP
90	Sprite-RPC	Sprite RPC Protocol
91	LARP	Locus Address Resolution Protocol
92	MTP	Multicast Transport Protocol

continues

Continued

Number	Keyword	Protocol
93	AX.25	AX.25 Frames
94	IPIP	IP-within-IP Encapsulation Protocol
95	MICP	Mobile Internetworking Control Pro
96	SCC-SP	Semaphore Communications Sec. Pro
97	ETHERIP	Ethernet-within-IP Encapsulation
98	ENCAP	Encapsulation Header
99	Any private encryption scheme	
100	GMTP	GMTP
101	IFMP	Ipsilon Flow Management Protocol
102	PNNI	PNNI over IP
103	PIM	Protocol Independent Multicast
104	ARIS	ARIS
105	SCPS	SCPS
106	QNX	QNX
107	A/N	Active Networks
108	IPComp	IP Payload Compression Protocol
109	SNP	Sitara Networks Protocol
110	Compaq-Peer	Compaq Peer Protocol
111	IPX-in-IP	IPX in IP
112	VRRP	Virtual Router Redundancy Protocol
113	PGM	PGM Reliable Transport Protocol
114	Any 0-hop protocol	
115	L2TP	Layer Two Tunneling Protocol
116	DDX	D-II Data Exchange (DDX)
117	IATP	Interactive Agent Transfer Protocol
118	STP	Schedule Transfer Protocol
119	SRP	SpectraLink Radio Protocol
120	UTI	UTI

continues

Continued

Number	Keyword	Protocol
121	SMP	Simple Message Protocol
122	SM	SM
123	PTP	Performance Transparency Protocol
124	ISIS	ISIS over IPv4
125	FIRE	FIRE
126	CRTP	Combat Radio Transport Protocol
127	CRUDP	Combat Radio User Datagram
128	SSCOPMCE	SSCOPMCE
129	IPLT	IPLT
130	SPS	Secure Packet Shield
131	PIPE	Private IP Encapsulation within IP
132	SCTP	Stream Control Transmission Protocol
133	FC	Fibre Channel
134–254	Unassigned	
255	Reserved	

Bibliography

[Allen1-99] Allen, Julia, Alan Christie, William Fithen, John McHugh, Jed Pickel, and Ed Stoner. State of the Practice of Intrusion Detection Technologies. Technical Report, CMU/SEI-99-TR-028, ESC-99-028, January 2000.

[Allen2-99] Allen, Julia, William Fithen, and Ed Stoner. Deploying Firewalls. Security Improvement Module, CMU/SEI-SIM-008, May 1999.

[Anderson1-99] Anderson, Craig, and Dennis Hardman. Hewlett-Packard on Enterprise Network Security. Hewlett Packard, 1999.

[Aslam1-96] — Aslam, Taimur, Ivan Krsul, and Eugene H. Spafford. Use of a Taxonomy of Security Faults. The COAST Laboratory, 1996.

[Astithas1-99] — Astithas, Panagiotis. Intrusion Detection Systems. 1999.

[Bace1-00] — Bace, Rebecca Gurley. Intrusion Detection. Macmillan Technical Publishing, 2000.

[Banks1-98] Banks, Michael A. Web Psychos, Stalkers, and Pranksters: How to Protect Yourself in Cyberspace. The Coriolis Group, ASIN: 1576101371; issue 10 (May 9, 1997).

[Bejtlich1-00] Bejtlich, Richard. Interpreting Network Traffic: A Network Intrusion Detectors Look at Suspicious Events. v2.6. March 27, 2000.

[Bellovin1-94] Bellovin, Steven M., and William R. Cheswick. Firewalls and Internet Security, Repelling the Wily Hacker, 1994, Addison-Wesley Publishing Company, p. 76.

[Brown1-98] West-Brown, Moira J., Don Stikvoort, and Klaus-Peter Kossakowski. Handbook for Computer Security Incident Response Teams (CSIRTs). CMU/SEI-98-HB-001. December 1998.

[Brown1-99] West-Brown, Moira J., and Klaus-Peter Kossakowski. International Infrastructure for Global Security Incident Response. CERT Coordination Center. Carnegie Mellon University. June 4, 1999.

[Brownlee1-96] Brownlee, Nevil, and John White. Framework for Security Incident Response. The University of Auckland. 1996.

[Cannady1-98] Cannady, James. Artificial Neural Networks for Misuse Detection. 1998. http://secinf.net/info/ids/nn-idse/.

[Capell1-98] Capell, Peter. Analysis of Courses in Information Management and Network System Security & Survivability. December 1998. SPECIAL REPORT, CMU/SEI-99-SR-006.

[CERT1-00] Identify data that characterize systems and aid in detecting signs of suspicious behavior. CERT Coordination Center. Carnegie Mellon University. October 18, 2000.

[CERT1-99] Choosing an Operating System. CERT Coordination Center. Carnegie Mellon University. February 12, 1999.

[CERT2-00] Manage logging and other data collection mechanisms. CERT Coordination Center. Carnegie Mellon University. October 18, 2000.

[Chen1-00] Staniford-Chan, Stuart Gresley. Internet Trap and Trace. Silicon Defense. July 20, 2000.

[Chen1-95] Staniford-Chan, Stuart Gresley. Distributed Tracing of Intruders. University of California, Davis.

[Cheung1-99] Cheung, Steven, Rick Crawford, Mark Dilger, Jeremy Frank, Jim Hoagland, Karl Levitt, Jeff Rowe, Stuart Stanford-Chen, Raymond Yip, and Dan Zerkle. The Design of GrIDS: A Graph-Based Intrusion Detection Systems. 26 January 1999.

[CIAC1-94] Pichnarczyk, Karyn, Steve Weeber, and Richard Feingold. Unix Incident Guide: How to Detect an Intrusion. CIAC-2305 R.1. Lawrence Livermore National Laboratory. December, 1994.

[Cisco1-00] System Error Messages for 12.0 T. Cisco Systems. 2000.

[Cisco1-99] Cisco NetSonar Security Scanner. User Guide. Cisco Systems. 1999.

[Cisco2-00] Cisco IOS Firewall Intrusion Detection System. Cisco Systems. 2000.

[Cisco1-02] The Science of Intrusion Detection System Attack Identification. Cisco Systems. 2002.

[Cohen1-98] Cohen, Fred. A Note on the Role of Deception in Information Protection. 1998.

[Cohen2-99] Cohen, Fred. 50 Ways to Defeat your Intrusion Detection System. http://all.net/journal/netsec/9712.html.

[Compaq1-98] Planning, Deploying, and Operating Internet Security Systems' RealSecure on Compaq Servers. First Edition. December 1998. Compaq Computer Corporation.

[Cooper1-01] Cooper, Mark, Stephen Northcutt, Matt Fearnow, and Karen Frederick. Intrusion Signatures and Analysis. New Riders Publishing, 2001.

[Crosbie1-95] Crosbie, Mark. Defending a Computer System using Autonomous Agents. In Proceedings of the 18th NISSC, October 1995.

[Crosbie1-98] Crosbie, Mark, and Gene Spafford. Applying Genetic Programming to Intrusion Detection. 1998.

[CSI1-02] 2002 CSI/FBI Computer Crime and Security Survey. Vol. VIII, No 1. Spring 2002. Computer Security Institute. Federal Bureau Investigation's Computer Intrusion Squad.

[CyberCop1-00] CyberCop Scanner for Windows NT and Windows 2000. Getting Started Guide. Version 5.5. Network Associates. 2000.

[Daymont1-00] Daymont, Josh. How Hackers Hide: A look at intruder behavior within compromised targets. ISS Connect 2000. 19-24, March, 2000.

[Denmac1-99] Network Based Intrusion Detection. A review of technologies. Denmac Systems, Inc. November 1999.

[Edward1-99] Amoroso, Edward G. Intrusion Detection: An Introduction to Internet Surveillance, Correlation, Traps, Trace Back, and Response. Intrusion.Net Books, 1999.

[Edwards1-02] Edwards, Simon. Vulnerabilities of Network Intrusion Detection Systems: Realizing and Overcoming the Risks. The Case for Flow Mirroring. TopLayer Networks, 2002.

[Edwards1-97] Edwards, Mark Joseph. Internet Security with Windows NT. 29th Street Pr; Bk&CD-Rom Edition, November 1997.

[Eckmann1-00] Eckmann, Steven, Giovanni Vigna, and Richard Kemmerer. Attack Languages. University of California, 2000.

[EY1-02] Global Information Security Survey 2002. Ernst & Young LLP. 2002.

[Firth1-97] Firth, Robert, Gary Ford, et al. Detecting Sign Intrusion. Security Improvement Module. CMU/SEI-SIM-001. Software Engineering Institute. Carnegie Mellon University. August 1997.

[Frederick1-00] Frederick, Karen. Abnormal IP Packets. www.securityfocus.com. October 13, 2000.

[Freiss1-98] Freiss, Martin. Protecting Networks with SATAN. O'Reilly & Associates, Inc. 1998.

[Germanow1-99] Germanow, Albert. Plugging the Holes in eCommerce: The Market for Intrusion Detection and Vulnerability Assessment Software, 1999–2003. IDC, July, 1999.

[Gong1-02] Gong, Fengmin. Next Generation Intrusion Detection Systems. IntruVert Networks, Inc. March 2002.

[Graham1-00] Graham, Robert. Frequently Asked Questions (FAQ): Network Intrusion Setection Systems. Version 0.8.3. March 21, 2000. http://www.robertgraham.com/pubs/network-intrusion-detection.html.

[Habra1-92] Habra, Naji, and Isabelle Mathieu. ASAX: Software Architecture and Rule-Based Language for Universal Audit Trail Analysis. Proceedings of ESORICS'92, European Symposium on Resarch in Computer Security, November 23-25 Toulouse, Springer-Verlag 1992.

[Hacker1-01] Hacker, Eric. IDS Evasion with Unicode. January 3, 2001.

[Howard1-97] Howard, John D. An Analysis Of Security Incidents On The Internet. 1989–1995. April, 1977. www.cert.org.

[Howard1-98] Howard, John D., and Thomas A. Longstaff. A Common Language for Computer Security Incidents. Sandia National Laboratories. October, 1998.

[Hurwicz1-98] Hurwicz, Michael. Cracker Tracking: Tighter Security with Intrusion Detection. BYTE, May 1998.

[ICSA1-00] Intrusion Detection Systems. Buyer's Guide. ICSA Labs. 2000.

[Infosec1-01] The 2001 Information Security Industry Survey. Information Security Magazine. October, 2001.

[Intrusion1-00] SecureNet Pro Software's SNP-L Scripting System. Intrusion.com. Release 1.0. July 2000.

[ISS1-00] RealSecure Getting Started. Version 5.5. Internet Security Systems, 2000.

[ISS10-00] Gigabit Ethernet Intrusion Detection Solutions Top Layer Networks & Internet Security Systems. Internet Security Systems RealSecure Network Sensors & Top Layer Networks AS3502 Gigabit AppSwitch Performance Test Results and Configuration Notes. Internet Security Systems, Top Layer Networks, July 25, 2000.

[ISS1-02] Internet Risk Impact Summary for December 22, 2001 through March 21, 2002. X-Force Global Threat Operations Center. Internet Security Systems, 2002.

[ISS2-02] Internet Risk Impact Summary for March 26, 2002 through June 24, 2002. X-Force Global Threat Operations Center. Internet Security Systems, 2002.

[ISS1-98] Locking down a Windows NT Host for Intrusion Detection. Internet Security Systems. March 26, 1998.

[ISS1-99] Network- vs. Host-based Intrusion Detection: A Guide to Intrusion Detection Technology. Internet Security Systems, 1999. .

[ISS2-00] Klaus, Chris. Top Threats Facing Internet Security Today. ISS Connect 2000. 19-24, March, 2000.

[ISS2-99] Intrusion Detection for the Millennium. Internet Security Systems, 1999. .

[ISS3-00] Kennis, Pim. SmIDS - Smarter Intrusion Detection System. ISS Connect 2000. 19-24, March, 2000.

[ISS3-99] Network- vs. Host-based Intrusion Detection: A Guide to Intrusion Detection Technology. Internet Security Systems, 1999.

[ISS4-00] RealSecure Signatures. Version 5.5. Internet Security Systems, 2000.

[ISS4-99] Adaptive Network Security Manager Module Programmer's Reference Manual. Internet Security Systems, February 1999.

[ISS5-00] RealSecure Console User Guide. Version 5.5. Internet Security Systems, 2000.

[ISS6-00] RealSecure Server Sensor User Guide. Version 5.5. Internet Security Systems, 2000.

[ISS7-00] Internet Scanner Getting Started. Version 6.1. Internet Security Systems, 2000.

[ISS8-00] Doty, Ted. The "Right" Amount of Security. Auditors helping Operations Improve Security. ISS Connect 2000. 19-24, March, 2000.

[ISS9-00] Internet Scanner User Guide. Version 6.1. Internet Security Systems, 2000.

[Jackson1-99] Jackson, Kathleen. Intrusion Detection System (IDS). Product Survey. Version 2.1. Los Alamos National Laboratory. June 25, 1999.

[Kochmar1-98] Kochmar, John, Julia Allen, et al. Preparing To Detect Signs of Intrusion. Security Improvement Module. CMU/SEI-SIM-005. Software Engineering Institute. Carnegie Mellon University. June 1998.

[Kolodgy1-01] Kolodgy, Charles, Chris Christiansen, and Brian Burke. Gaining Control over Infrastructure: Intrusion Detection and Vulnerability Assessment. IDC. March 2001.

[KPMG1-02] 2002 Global Information Security Survey. KPMG. 2002.

[Laswell1-99] Laswell, Barbara S., Derek Simmel, and Sandra G. Behrens. Information Assurance Curriculum and Certification: State of the Practice. September 1999. Technical Report, CMU/SEI-99-TR-021, ESC-TR-99-021.

[Lindqvist1-99] Lindqvist, Ulf, and Phillip A. Porras. Detecting Computer and Network Misuse Through the Production-Based Expert System Toolset (P-BEST). In Proceedings of the 1999 IEEE Symposium on Security and Privacy, Oakland, California, May 9–12, 1999.

[Longstaff1-93] Longstaff, Thomas A. Results of a Workshop on Research in Incident Handling. Special Report CMU/SEI-93-SR-20. September, 1993.

[Mann1-99] Mann, David E., and Steven M. Christey. Towards a Common Enumeration of Vulnerabilities. January 8, 1999.

[Markoff1-95] Markoff, John, and Katie Hafner. Cyberpunk: Outlaws and Hackers on the Computer Frontier. Simon & Schuster; ISBN: 0684818620 November 1995.

[McClure1-01] McClure, Stuart, Joel Scambray, and George Kurtz. Hacking Exposed: Network Security Secrets and Solutions. Osborne McGraw-Hill; 3-rd edition, September, 2001.

[McGraw1-97] McGraw, Gary, and Edward W. Felten. Java Security: hostile applets, holes & antidotes. John Wiley & Sons. 1997.

[Me1-98] Me, Ludovic. GASSATA, a Genetic Algorithm as an Alternative Tool for Security Audit Trail Analysis. 1998.

[Mell1-01] Mell, Peter, and Rebecca Bace. Intrusion Detection Systems. NIST Special Publications 800-31. 2001.

[Mell1-99] Mell, Peter. Computer Attacks: What They Are and How to Defend Against Them. NIST, Computer Security Division. 1999.

[Mell2-99] Mell, Peter. Understanding the World of your Enemy with I-CAT (Internet-Categorization of Attacks Toolkit). NIST, Computer Security Division. May 26, 1999.

[Microsoft1-00] Security Event Descriptions. Microsoft Corporation, June 21, 2000. http://support.microsoft.com/support/kb/articles/q174/0/74.asp.

[Microsoft2-00] Auditing User Authentication. Microsoft Corporation, February 18, 2000. http://support.microsoft.com/support/kb/articles/q174/0/73.asp.

[Miller1-00] Miller, Toby. ECN and Its Impact on Intrusion Detection. Global Information Assurance Certification. 2000.

[NASL1-00] Deraison, Renaud. The Nessus Attack Scripting Language Reference Guide. Version 1.0.0pre2. 16 April 2000.

[Navy1-96] computer incident response guidebook. Module 19. Information systems security (INFOSEC). Program guidelines. Department of the Navy Navso P-5239-19 AUGUST 1996 .

[NetProwler1-00] NetProwler User Guide. Version 3.5. Getting Started. Axent Technologies. 2000.

[NetScout1-02] Miller, Leslie. A Network Under Attack: Leverage Your Existing Instrumentation to Recognize and Respond to Hacker Attacks.

[NetRanger1-99] NetRanger User Guide. Version 2.2.1. Cisco Systems. 1999.

[NetworkICE1-00] Protocol Analysis vs Pattern Matching in Network and Host Intrusion Detection Systems. November, 2000.

[Newman1-98] Newman, David, Tadesse Giorgis, and Farhad Yavari-Issalou. Intrusion Detection Systems: Suspicious Finds. Data Communications, August 1998.

[NFR1-99] NFR Intrusion Detection Appliance. User's Guide. Version 4.1.1. Network Flight Recorder, Inc. 1999.

[NFR2-99] NFR Intrusion Detection Appliance. Advanced User's Guide. Version 4.1.1. Network Flight Recorder, Inc. 1999.

[NIST1-91] Description of Automated Risk Management Packages that Nist/Ncsc Risk Management Research Laboratory Have Examined. Updated March 1991.

[Northcutt1-96] Northcutt, Stephen. NSWC Dahlgren Computer Security Incident Handling Procedure. October, 1996.

[Northcutt1-99] Northcutt, Stephen. Network Intrusion Detection. An Analyst's Handbook. New Riders Publishing. 1999.

[Northcutt1-00] Northcutt, Stephen. Network Intrusion Detection. An Analyst's Handbook (2nd Edition). New Riders Publishing. 2000.

[NRL1-95] NRL IS Security Incident Response Plan. Naval Research Laboratory. IS Security Group - Code 1220.2. May 15, 1995.

[NSS1-00] Intrusion Detection & Vulnerability Assessment. Test Results (Edition 1). An NSS Group Report. NSS Group. December 2000.

[NSS1-01] Intrusion Detection Systems. Group Test (Edition 2). An NSS Group Report. NSS Group. December 2001.

[NSS1-02] Intrusion Detection Systems. Group Test (Edition 3). An NSS Group Report. NSS Group. July 2002.

[Paxson1-98] Paxson, Vern. Bro: A system for Detecting Network Intruders in Real-Time. Lawrence Berkeley National Laboratory. 14, January, 1998.

[Phrack1-00] Phrack 51. LOKI2 (the implementation).

[Phrack2-00] Phrack 49. Project Loki: ICMP Tunneling.

[Polk1-92] Polk, Timothy. Automated Tools for Testing Computer System-Vulnerability. December 3, 1992.

[Power1-95] Power, Richard. Current and Future Danger: A CSI Primer on Computer Crime and Information Warfare. Computer Security Institute. 1995.

[Proctor1-01] Proctor, Paul E. Practical Intrusion Detection Handbook. Prentice Hall, 2001.

[Ptacek1-98] Ptacek, Thomas H, and Timothy N. Newsham. Insertion, Evasion, and Denial of Service: Eluding Network Intrusion Detection. January, 1998.

[Ranum1-98] Ranum, Marcus J. Intrusion Detection: Challenges and Myths. http://secinf.net/info/ids/ids_mythe.html.

[Ryan1-99] Ryan, J., M. Lin, and Miikkulainen, R. (1997). Intrusion Detection with Neural Networks. AI Approaches to Fraud Detection and Risk Management: Papers from the 1997 AAAIWorkshop (Providence, Rhode Island), pp. 72–79. Menlo Park, CA: AAAI.

[RFC1-90] RFC 1191. Path MTU Discovery.

[RFC1-99] RFC 2481. A Proposal to add Explicit Congestion Notification (ECN) to IP.

[RFC1-00] RFC 2884. Performance Evaluation of Explicit Congestion Notification (ECN) in IP Networks.

[RFP1-99] Rain Forest Puppy. A look at whisker's anti-IDS tactics.

[Riptech1-02] Riptech Internet Security Threat Report. Attack Trends for Q1 and Q2 2002. Volume II. Riptech, Inc. July 2002.

[Ruiu1-01] Ruiu, Dragos. IDS Review. www.securityportal.com, February 26, 2001.

[SANS1-00] Reading Perimeter Logs FAQ. Global Incident Analysis Center. SANS Institute. 2000.

[SANS2-00] SANS Salary Survey 2000. Version 2. SANS. December, 2000.

[SANS1-01] How To Eliminate The Ten Most Critical Internet Security Threats. Version 1.32. SANS. January 18, 2001.

[SANS1-02] The Twenty Most Critical Internet Security Vulnerabilities. Version 2.504. SANS. May 2, 2002.

[SANS1-98] Computer Security Incident Handling, Step by Step. SANS Institute. 2000.

[SC1-00] Intrusion Detection. Test Center. SC InfoSecurity Magazine. June 2000. http://www.scmagazine.com/scmagazine/2000_06/testc/testc.html.

[Schaer1-00] Schaer, David, Russel Lusignan, Oliver Steudler, and Jacques Allison. Managing Cisco Network Security: Building Rock-Solid Networks. Syngress Publishing, 2000.

[Schneier1-00] Schneier, Bruce. Semantic Attacks: The Third Wave of Network Attacks. Crypto-Gram. October 15, 2000.

[Schneier1-01] Schneier, Bruce. Natural Advantages of Defense: What Military History Can Teach Network Security, Part 1. Crypto-Gram. April 15, 2001.

[Schneier2-01] Schneier, Bruce. Defense Option: What Military History Can Teach Network Security, Part 2. Crypto-Gram. May 15, 2001.

[SecurityFocus1-02] ARIS Top Ten 2001 Threats. SecurityFocus. January 31, 2002.

[SecurityTracker1-02] SecurityTracker Statistics. April 2001 – March 2002. www.securitytracker.com.

[Seifried1-00] Seifried, Kurt. Attack Detection.

[Shipley1-99] Shipley, Greg. ISS RealSecure Pushes Past Newer IDS Players. Network Computing, 17 May 1999.

[Shipley2-99] Shipley, Greg. Intrusion Detection, Take Two. Network Computing, 15 November 1999.

[Shipley1-00] Shipley, Greg. Watching the Watchers: Intrusion Detection. Network Computing, 13 November 2000.

[Smith1-94] Smith, Danny. Forming an Incident Response Team. Australian Computer Emergency Response Team.

[Smith1-00] Smith, Randy Franklin. Interpreting the NT Security Log. Windows 2000 Magazine/RE, 3, 2000.

[Smith2-00] Smith, Randy Franklin. Monitoring Privileges and Administrators in the NT Security Log. Windows 2000 Magazine/RE, 4, 2000.

[Spitfire1-99] Spitfire User Guide. Version 4.0. MITRE Corporation. 1999.

[Spitzner1-00] Spitzner, Lance. Watching Your Logs. How to automate your log filtering? 19 July, 2000.

[Stang1-93] Stang, David, and Sylvia Moon. Network Security Secrets. Hungry Minds, Inc; ASIN: 1568840217; Bk&2 disks edition, August 1993.

[Stewart1-99] Stewart, Andrew J. Distributed Metastasis: A Computer Network Penetration Methodology. The Packet Factory. August 12, 1999.

[Sting1-99] CyberCop Sting. Getting Started Guide. Version 1.0. Network Associates. 1999.

[Stoll1-00] Stoll, Clifford. Cuckoo's Egg: Tracking a Spy Through the Maze of Computer Espionage. Pocket Books, October 2000.

[Strebe1-99] Strebe, Matthew, and Charles Perkins. Firewalls 24seven. Network Press. 1999.

[Sundaram1-96] Sundaram, Aurobindo. An Introduction to Intrusion Detection. 1996.

[Tasker1-99] Tasker, Pete, Margie Zuk, Steve Christey, Dave Mann, Bill Hill, and Dave Baker. Common Vulnerabilities and Exposures (CVE). MITRE. September 29, 1999.

[TCP1-97] TCPDUMP. Reference Manual Page. 30 June 1997.

[TechRepublic1-01] Network Security Survey. TechRepublic. September 13, 2001.

[Vacca1-96] Vacca, John R. Internet Security Secrets. Hungry Minds, Inc; ASIN: 1568844573; Bk&Cd edition (January 1996).

[Wack1-91] Wack, John P. Establishing a Computer Security Incident Response Capability (CSIRC). NIST Special Publications 800-3. November, 1991.

[WebTrends1-00] WebTrends Security Analyzer. Platform for Open Security Testing. Security Developer's Kit. March 2000 Edition. WebTrends Corporation.

[WebTrends1-98] WebTrends Security Analyzer. Security Developer's Kit. December 1998 Beta II Edition. WebTrends Corporation.

[Xforce1-00] Serious flaw in Microsoft IIS UNICODE translation. Internet Security Systems Security Alert. October 26, 2000.

[Yocom1-00] Yocom, Betsy, Kevin Brown, and Dan Van Derveer. Cisco offers wire-speed intrusion detection. Network World, December 18, 2000.

Index